Advanced Level Media

Angela Bell, Mark Joyce and Danny Rivers

LAUNCESTON COLLEGE
MEDIA STUDIES
DEPT.

Hodder & Stoughton

A MEMBER OF THE HODDER HEADLINE GROUP

Order queries: please contact Bookpoint Ltd, 39 Milton Park, Abingdon, Oxon OX14 4TD. Telephone: (44) 01235 400414, Fax: (44) 01235 400454. Lines are open from 9.00–6.00, Monday to Saturday, with a 24 hour message answering service. Email address: orders@bookpoint.co.uk.

A catalogue record for this title is available from The British Library

ISBN 0340 674024

First published 1999

Impression number	10	9	8	7	6	5	4	3	2	1		
Year		2004	2003	2002	2001	2000		1999		1998		

Cover illustration from Jon. H. Hamilton
Typeset by Wearset, Boldon, Tyne and Wear.
Printed in Great Britain for Hodder & Stoughton Educational, a division of Hodder Headline Plc, 338 Euston Road, London NW1 3BH by Scotprint, Musselburgh, Scotland.

Contents

The Media

January 1 2001

Price: 20 ECU

INSIDE...
...global moguls exposed
...swots make vids
...radio turned me on

EXCLUSIVE: THE FULL MEDIA MONTY

TEACHERS REVEAL ALL

This issue...

- *concepts*
- *industries*
- *audiences*
- *genres*
- *cinema*
- *TV*
- *radio*
- *newspapers*
- *films*
- *practical work*
- *and more...*

Media Studies is a subject that is attracting students in increasing numbers but what's in it for them? Our education correspondent has been trying to find out.

Students coming to Media Studies may think it's all Spice Girls and *EastEnders* but teachers are quick to point out that there is more to it than that.

To find out the real lowdown, *The Media* went to talk to teachers Angela Bell, Mark Joyce and Danny Rivers, who have just published a new media text book, *Advanced Level Media*, which claims to give students the 'full media monty'. The contents look comprehensive with chapters on media concepts and genres as well as case studies.

Institutions

Danny Rivers says: 'We have tried to provide a detailed guide to the key media industries such as Broadcasting, The Press, Advertising, Film, News and Music and we have looked at the way that they operate on a global scale.' These institutions need audiences for their products and Rivers says the book will also alert students to the way people 'absorb or react to the media'.

This book isn't just about theory though, and Angela Bell is quick to point out that there is great importance placed on putting theory into practice.

Practical Work

'Practical work has been worked through step by step using actual examples of student work where possible. We hope it will be helpful to students and teachers alike.'

Case Studies

Students also tend to forget about using examples when answering exam questions and '... a feature of this book is the use of case studies throughout', said Mark Joyce. 'We hope that this will encourage students to watch the films and TV programmes and use examples when writing essays.'

Book Style

All three say the book has additional benefits such as pictures, margin notes, clear bullet-pointed text and a glossary but, ultimately, the real judge must be the discerning media reader.

So read on...

Dog snapped in reservoir howler, page 3.

ALSO... Agony aunties, Clare Smith & Sarah Dobson probe your problems & deal with your dilemmas

ACKNOWLEDGEMENTS

We would like to thank our partners and families who have given us essential support despite the many `lost weekends'. We would also like to thank the many colleagues who have been generous with their time and thoughts on a number of issues. Thanks to Melanie Hall at Hodder & Stoughton, to Carolyn Rivers for her artwork, and to the following former students and the University of Cambridge Local Examination Syndicate who have allowed us to use media coursework: Kate Procter, Sarah Milbourn, Jennifer Pilbeam, Fiona Adams, Richard Smith, Deryn Kempson-Grey, Terry Worthington, Michelle Alger, Rachel Baddley.

The authors and publisher would also like to thank the following for permission to reproduce copyright illustrative material:

Extract from The BBC's Nine O'Clock News reproduced by permission of the BBC, pages 124, 126, 127.

Heinz and Steve Marinker at Bates Dorland for reproduction of *Toast to Life* advertising campaign, pages 169 - 177.

KFM - Hits and Memories, particularly Andrew Deans and Dominic King for permission to reproduce KFM Transmission Area Map and for their co-operation in the broadcasting case study, page 83.

News International for reproduction of the front pages of *The Sun* and *Today* newspapers, pages 118, 119.

The Voice newspaper for reproductions in the case study on the press, pages 106, 107, 108.

The BFI (photographs), pages 32, 33, 136, 211, 213, 214, 216, 223, 227, 229, 231, 233, 234, 241, 243, 244, 254, 257, 259, 261, 264, 272, 274, 277, 278, 281, 282, 291, 294, 295, 310, 312, 314, 315.

The Kobal Collection (photographs), pages 25, 37.

The Ronald Grant Collection (photographs), page 308; Carlton UK Television / Ronald Grant Collection (photographs), page 215.

1

CHAPTER **1** Realism

This chapter examines the concept of realism in relation to three texts.

▤ A Labour Party election broadcast, 21 April 1997

▤ A drama documentary, *Hillsborough*, broadcast on ITV, 5 December 1996

▤ A feature-length documentary film, *The Thin Blue Line*, Errol Morris, 1987, USA

This chapter also explores the idea that realism is not an inherent feature of a text but is always constructed by the text.

AN ELECTION BROADCAST

In one of the Labour Party's election broadcasts in 1997 a relatively unusual approach was adopted. As in many such broadcasts the centre of attention was the leader but in this case Tony Blair was not only presented as a person operating in the political sphere but as a person with an existence outside of politics. As a party leader he was shown speaking on a platform, listening attentively on the street and moving from place to place by car, train and plane. The broadcast, however, wanted to stress that Blair was a private individual as much as a public figure. The director of the broadcast, Molly Dineen, offered her services to make the broadcast. As a documentary film-maker she aims to achieve 'a familiarity, an intimacy with people, in the hope that audiences will respond to them as human beings rather than dismiss them as stereotypes.'[1] She presents Tony Blair as a human being by the following means:

▤ The content of the broadcast

▤ The style of the broadcast

Content

Tony Blair talks (to the camera) about his parents, his childhood ambition to play football for Newcastle United, and his scepticism of politicians as a youth.

He is seen playing football and tennis and joking with his children in the kitchen about the homework load likely to be imposed on them by future education minister, David Blunkett.

Style

Although Molly Dineen was able to film over a number of weeks the style communicates spontaneity and a lack of contrivance. In the kitchen of his home Tony Blair is shot from a low angle as if from the point of view of a seated visitor. The lighting is natural. He has a shadow on the side of his face and a shadow is cast on the wall. He is wearing a casual dark blue shirt and talks in an unrehearsed way about the possibility of change in Britain. In the footage of a car journey the camera initially makes several adjustments in position before settling on a close-up of Tony Blair in which he addresses the camera directly as if to a fellow passenger. The style is conversational but determined. The shots in the kitchen and car are contrasted with shots of a speech. Here again Blair, now wearing a suit and tie, is alone in the frame and shot from below but the frame is static, he is evenly lit and speaks decisively.

The artifice of realism

The broadcast presents Tony Blair as a private individual as well as a public figure and asserts that he is prepared to be a politician despite some of the irksome tasks associated with the role such as having to pose for photographers. The nature of the film was duly celebrated by the Labour Party campaign manager, Peter Mandelson, who stated that, 'It is about Blair the man. It is not gimmicky or flashy and it has no artifice, it has no varnish. It is almost raw in its treatment of Tony Blair.'[2]

The rawness or realism of the film can, however, be considered to be its artifice. The film wishes to communicate a portrait of Tony Blair and it wishes to substantiate its claim to be realistic by drawing on techniques of film-making pioneered by **Direct Cinema** and **Cinéma Vérité**. The resultant election broadcast is therefore no less a construction than the earlier election broadcast which supported Neil Kinnock's campaign in 1987 which used a much more extravagant style. The fact that the camera goes out of focus momentarily when Tony Blair is playing football underlines the deliberate exploitation of this effect as the film has obviously been carefully edited and is based on a lot of footage.

The broadcast establishes its realism, then, by structuring its visual and verbal material around the plausible division between the private individual Tony Blair and the public figure of the leader of the Labour Party and secondly by its stylistic choices that complement the public/private division. The aim was to convince the audience that they were watching a realistic portrayal of Tony Blair. This may not have been a vain hope because although the election broadcast broke with the conventions of the form it did employ recognisable documentary techniques. The fact that the film was stated to be 'raw' and without 'artifice' suggests that it was successful in disguising its own construction. The film was able therefore to communicate its message within an accepted mode of realism and as an example it serves to illustrate and confirm the idea that realism is constructed and also that any 'realism' must be subject to a consensus.

DIRECT CINEMA AND CINÉMA VÉRITÉ

Direct Cinema was an approach to documentary film-making envisaged by Robert Drew, a *Time-Life* journalist, in the 1950s. His dream was a 'theatre without actors' in which events were captured as they happened. This ambition became more possible as improvements in 16mm filmstock meant that 16mm cameras could be used instead of the heavier 35mm cameras and film-makers could use natural light rather than have to set up lights in a location.

The development of portable sound recording equipment and then the ability to record images and sounds in synchronisation without the visual and sound recording equipment being connected finally liberated the documentary film-maker. The use of zoom lenses and directional microphones furthered the goal of capturing reality unobtrusively. *Primary* (1960) was the first direct cinema film and was an account of a primary election contest between John F. Kennedy and Hubert Humphrey. This film fulfilled the requirements of Richard Leacock, who worked on *Primary* and remains one of the main advocates of direct cinema; he endorsed the fact that the film contained no interviews, no re-enactments, no staged scenes and very little use of narration. D. A. Pennebaker who also worked on *Primary* continued the tradition with films like *Don't Look Back* (1967) which documented Bob Dylan's 1965 British tour. In his introduction to the book of this film Pennebaker communicates the flavour of direct cinema:

'The cameraman (myself) can only film what happens. There are no retakes. I never attempted to direct or control the action. People said whatever they wanted and did whatever. The choice of action lay always with the person being filmed. Naturally, I edited the material as I believed it should appear, but with the absolute conviction that any attempt to distort events or remarks would somehow reveal itself and subject the whole to suspicion. The order of the film is almost chronological and nothing was staged or arranged for the purpose of the film. It is not my intention to extol or denounce or even explain Dylan, or any of the characters therein. This is only a kind of record of what happened.'[3]

Cinéma Vérité (cinema truth) developed at the same time in France, stemmed from the same impulse and took advantage of the same technology as direct cinema. A key aspect which differentiates it from direct cinema is that the practitioners of Cinéma Vérité advocated the intrusion of the film-maker into the process of film-making. The technique was to provoke answers to questions posed by the film-makers rather than assume the detachment described above by Pennebaker. The film-maker Jean Rouch expresses the virtue of cinéma vérité in the following way.

'At first, of course, there is a self-conscious "hamminess". They say to themselves, "people are looking at me I must give a nice impression of myself." But this lasts only a very short time. And then, very rapidly, they begin to try to think – perhaps for the first time sincerely – about their own problems, about who they are and then they begin to express what they have within themselves. These moments are very short, and one must know how to take advantage of them'[4]

The term cinéma vérité is often used as a blanket term, which includes direct cinema. The style however is no longer restricted to documentaries. Police series like *NYPD Blue* and *Homicide* communicate a sense of immediacy by using constant mobile framing in conjunction with a rapid and sometimes disorienting editing style.

Realism as a consensual concept

Essentially realism is a consensual concept: it is a matter of agreement over what constitutes realism in a media text. All media texts have to convince their audiences. They can only do so however if there are understandings that are shared by the producers and consumers about what constitutes realism. The shared understandings will involve both the content of a text and its form. As a result a factual programme such as a news programme or a documentary will have to convince its audience that there is a relationship between the text and a reality beyond the text. It will also have to conform to the rules and conventions of a news programme or a documentary. These rules and conventions change over time but are not erratic or unstable as they are secured and validated by media institutions and by the community of programme and film-makers.

A fictional text does not have the same connection to a reality beyond the text but it has to convince its audience in relation to the genre or form within which it is operating. A science fiction film, for example, will draw on previous science fiction texts. It will have to persuade its audience that the action is taking place in another time, usually in the future. The characters tend to behave, however, in a way that is recognisable from everyday life and the film will work if the audience is convinced by the protagonists and their relationships even if the setting and the events are unlike anything the audience has experienced.

Mediation and drama documentary

A key fact to bear in mind is that all media texts are representations of events and not the events themselves. The credence an audience gives to any particular text will depend on the extent to which it is aware that the text is constructed. For example, a Conservative Party supporter might see the Labour Party broadcast discussed above as a mediated product rather than one that provides privileged access to Tony Blair. In this case the political allegiance of a viewer might establish a mood of scepticism. It is also easier to see a text as constructed if the viewer has first hand experience of events or can draw on a range of alternative sources of information.

Drama documentary and documentary drama

Both draw on actual events and tend to use a visual style with an improvisatory feel. They will tend to use real locations and employ natural lighting and sound. Drama documentaries however tend to be reconstructions based on a single set of events whereas documentary dramas tend to put many different cases together to produce a single story.

A DRAMA DOCUMENTARY

A media form which raises questions about the relationship of texts to reality is the **drama documentary**. Many drama documentaries or documentaries that incorporate dramatic reconstructions do not create controversy: their realism is accepted and it is given the consent of the audience. If the text, however, poses a challenge to the way events have been represented then it might fail to achieve a consensus about its realism. *Hillsborough*, written by Jimmy McGovern, for example, recreated events surrounding the FA Cup semi-final between Liverpool and Nottingham Forest at the Sheffield Wednesday football ground in April 1989 when 96 people died and 400 were injured.

The programme used many techniques to convince the audience of its reality.

- A statement on the screen that opens the film says that it is a dramatised reconstruction of events between 1989 and 1991 and that the drama is based entirely on fact using court transcripts and eye witness reports. The film thus invites the trust of the audience
- The semi-direct address by witnesses who are presented alone in the frame in head and shoulder shots as if they are being interviewed
- The use of actual BBC television footage as well as constructed television footage
- The use of hand-held cameras and tightly-framed shots from within the confusion of events with people often passing in front of the camera
- The choice of actors and actresses who regularly appear in dramas that emphasise realism

Jimmy McGovern wanted to demolish the myth that the disaster was a product of drunken Liverpool football fans and to establish that the disaster was a product of the police's failure to activate proper crowd control. *Hillsborough* is harrowing, compelling and presents the emotional truth of the events for all those connected to the dead and injured fans as well as a convincing argument for the criminal culpability of the police in the disaster. The techniques it uses, however, do not overcome the feeling that it is selective in its representation of the events. McGovern takes the point of view of the families who suffered great loss and treats them with sympathy while the police are represented in a way which rules out the same kind of identification. As a result Jimmy McGovern's scrupulous use of the known facts is undermined by the dramatic construction and visual style of the film.

A FEATURE-LENGTH DOCUMENTARY FILM

Is documentary truth, stranger than fiction? If *Hillsborough* raises doubts about the relationship between media texts and reality then *The Thin Blue Line* asserts the necessity to be sceptical. This film by Errol Morris is an investigation of the murder of a policeman in Dallas in 1976. The film uses familiar documentary techniques to tackle its subject.

- Interviews with Randall Adams who was convicted of the offence; with a younger man, David Harris whom Adams met in Dallas; with policemen, lawyers and witnesses
- The use of maps, diagrams, drawings and close-up shots of stories about the crime in newspapers

The film combines this approach with reconstructions of the killing. In itself this is not unusual but the reconstructions in this case are highly stylised and what is more they offer eight different versions of the events that happened that night. In addition the film uses excerpts from feature films which is very unusual and the score by Philip Glass is more noticeable than is usually the case in a documentary, because it is based on repetitive arpeggios that support the dream-like quality of the images.

In proceeding in this way the film might seem to make light of the killing but the serious point that the film wants to make is that knowledge of the event is severely limited as there are so many contradictory accounts by interviewees who have different interests. The film therefore cannot, and refuses to, offer the definitive visual version of the murder. The film is, however, concerned with the truth of the matter even if this is in a tentative and qualified way. As Bill Nichols argues:

> [by] 'making the process by which truth is constructed more evident, by showing how multiple truths based on different assumptions and motivations contend with one another, he may be inviting us to draw our own conclusions on the basis of facts and stories that do not readily admit of unequivocal resolution into a single truth. Randall Adams may indeed be innocent, but the film invites us to experience the uncertainty that licenses divergent narratives of explanation for anyone without firsthand knowledge of the original event. Morris refrains from using the power of the photographic image to appear to certify (through "authentic" re-enactments) a degree of certainty that remains unavailable outside the cinema.'[5]

Morris gives us access to differing perspectives on the events that might have left the audience adrift with no chance of arriving at a safe and secure haven of truth. The film, however, does have an implicit argument. It delivers its information slowly and deliberately in the best thriller tradition. For example, David Harris, who is shown in interview throughout the film is revealed towards the end of the film to be wearing handcuffs when he lifts up his hands for the first time. This small detail makes him seem much more threatening than he seemed at first. Also, throughout the film the audience is expected to work on the knowledge that is offered and to enjoy the many ironic juxtapositions created through editing. For example, after Adams, accompanied by a re-enactment, tells of a threatening interrogation in police custody the film cuts to one of the interrogating officers who talks of having a 'casual, friendly conversation'. The conclusion that the film works towards is that it is more likely that David Harris killed the policeman than Randall Adams and remarkably for a film that had such an experimental method it actually played a role in Adam's release from prison in 1989. But as Morris himself has said, 'There is no reason why documentaries can't be as personal as fiction film-making and bear the imprint of those who made them. Truth isn't guaranteed by style or expression. It isn't guaranteed by anything.'[6]

 **FURTHER WORK**

'Non-fictional texts are as much works of the imagination as fictional ones.' Discuss this statement in relation to a film or television documentary.

'Drama documentaries and films like Oliver Stone's *JFK* tend to manipulate their audience rather than inform it.' Discuss.

FURTHER READING

Fiske, John, *Television Culture*, Routledge, 1987 (Chapters 2 and 3)

Branston, Gill and Stafford, Roy, *The Media Student's Book*, Routledge, 1996 (Chapters 15 and 16).

Macdonald, Kevin and Cousins, Mark, (eds), *Imagining Reality*, Faber & Faber, 1996.

O'Sullivan, Tim, Dutton, Brian and Rayner, Philip, *Studying the Media*, Edward Arnold, 1994.

Williams, Christopher, (ed.), *Realism and the Cinema*, Routledge and Kegan Paul/BFI, 1980.

Goodwin, Andrew and Whannel, Gary, (eds), *Understanding Television*, Routledge, 1990 (Chapter 5).

FURTHER VIEWING

Hoop Dreams (Steve James, Frederick Marx, and Peter Gilbert, USA, 1994)

This is Spinal Tap (Rob Reiner, USA, 1984)

Shoah (Claude Lanzmann, Poland/France, 1985)

JFK (Oliver Stone, USA, 1991)

999 (BBC Television)

Crimewatch (BBC Television)

Videonation (BBC Television)

Homicide (USA series broadcast on Channel 4)

Notes

1 In *Imagining Reality: The Faber Book of Documentary*, Kevin Macdonald and Mark Cousins (Eds), p365.

2 Quoted in *Independent*, 21 April 1997.

3 *Don't Look Back*, Ballantine Books, 1968.

4 Kevin Macdonald and Mark Cousins (eds), *ibid*, p269.

5 *Representing Reality*, Indiana University Press, 1991, p101.

6 Quoted by Linda Williams in *Mirrors without Memories: Truth, History and the New Documentary*, Film Quarterly, Vol. 46, Number 3, Spring 1993, p13.

CHAPTER **2** # Ideology and Representation

THE CONCEPT OF IDEOLOGY

The media represent the world to us and therefore it is important to study the ideas driving these representations. The view that these ideas serve the interests of dominant groups within society is basic to the concept of ideology. John B. Thompson argues that 'the concept of ideology can be used to refer to the ways in which meaning serves, in particular circumstances, to establish and sustain relations of power which are systematically asymmetrical – what I shall call "relations of domination". Ideology, broadly speaking, is *meaning in the service of power*.'[1] This approach to the concept is based then on the idea that social groups do not have the same amount of power in society because they do not have the same command over resources, and therefore do not receive the same level of rewards either in material terms (such as income) or in symbolic terms (such as respect).

In trying to unravel this concept, it is useful to begin by examining a recent issue where there are distinct ideological responses. In the case of the girl boxers outlined below, individuals responded to an event. These individual responses however reflect different assumptions about gender that many people share. The responses therefore exemplify an ideological debate. Such debates involve a clash of ideas and assumptions about the world and the importance of the media is that they play a role in disseminating these debates.

 GIRL BOXERS

In October 1997, the Amateur Boxing Association's rules permitted female boxers to fight in competitions for the first time. This change of rules provoked different reactions that encapsulate opposing ideological views about women.[2]

A conservative response was expressed by Henry Cooper (a former heavyweight champion) who said, 'Women are made differently from men. Their entire body structure is not like a man's. Women are made for loving and not hitting'[3]; and Brendan Ingle (Prince Naseem's trainer) who said 'more and more girls are taking up sports like kick boxing and it's not ladylike. The concept is not right.'

A response in favour of the ABA's decision was expressed by George Burton (a boxing promoter) who said, 'In a couple of years time people will say, what was all the fuss about? Women can stand more pain than men – just look at childbirth'; and Barry McGuigan (a former featherweight boxing champion) who said, 'We cannot be chauvinistic about this. If we are going to defend boxing as a sport, we must allow women to take part too.'

A further response from the British Medical Association (BMA) stressed the dangers of boxing irrespective of sex. It also commented that this was an area where the idea of equal opportunities for men and women led in an insane direction.

The comments given above draw upon different assessments of female biology and also different assessments of the social role of girls and women. The immediate news issue was an impending match, following the rule-change, between two teenage girls, but the comments offered did reveal the continuing concern with what is acceptable in terms of gender in the field of sport. The issue of female boxing is therefore a part of the larger ideological debate about gender and gender roles which has been carried on in earnest since the 1960s.

However, these comments also revealed, in microcosm, the essential features of ideological debates in general:

- They centre on social categories rather than individuals – in this case, men and women
- They highlight inequalities of power – in this case, between men and women
- Members of the social categories involved, and others, have to be persuaded to see the world around them in a new way – in this case Barry McGuigan employs the concept of chauvinism which is applied to men who show no acknowledgement of the abilities of women
- The status quo is defended by reference to what has always been the case and what is therefore regarded as natural – in this case the concept of being 'ladylike'
- They often involve the participation of those who might be a source of authoritative knowledge: scientific bodies like the BMA or social scientists and other experts
- They involve value judgements about how things have been and how they ought to be in the future. As a result factual knowledge may not be decisive in ideological debates as those involved in them may judge a body of facts to be distorted or discoloured by accepted ways of thinking
- There may not be an easy answer to any particular issue that arises within an area of ideological debate in that individuals may have conflicting thoughts on the issue. For example, in the case of boxing an individual might be anti-boxing but at the same time against institutions that exclude women

In addition, ideological struggles often involve the formation of organisations or some kind of collective response to remedy the current inequalities. In the case of gender the **women's movement** that developed in the 1960s has played a role in changing the law as well as changing ideas and behaviour in everyday life. For example, it is common for people to use the term 'sexism' or use the expression 'male chauvinist'. In this way ideology is embedded in language and everyday life.

WOMEN'S MOVEMENT

The women's movement is not a fixed set of ideas and institutions. It is composed of many different interpretations of feminism and different ways of achieving feminist goals.

Some seek to change the situation of women within the current institutions. They are concerned with equality of opportunity. They seek to expand employment opportunities or increase the representation of women in political institutions for example. Equality of opportunity as a value is widely accepted in Western society so this kind of feminism finds wide support amongst women as well as many men.

Socialist feminists are more concerned with social class inequalities and the way that these are linked with gender inequalities and also racial inequalities.

Radical feminists see the domination of men over women as the most important division in society and so are wary of working within the system or focussing on other issues of inequality. These feminists are more likely to use the concept of patriarchy, which is used as a summary term for the domination of men over women, which runs throughout societies' institutions and ideas.

The origins of the concept of ideology

**Karl Marx
(1818–83)**

Marx established the idea that how a society produces its livelihood shapes everything else in society and is also the key factor in social change. He analysed capitalism as an economic system that produced two major social classes: the bourgeoisie who owns the means of production and live off profits and the proletariat who sell their labour to survive. Eventually the proletariat (working class) would seek to overthrow capitalism as it became subject to greater economic crises and as they began to see through the ideas that served to justify the economic, social and political dominance of the bourgeoisie.

The concept of ideology is used currently to analyse a range of representations including gender, sexuality, race and ethnicity. **Karl Marx** used it initially however in his analysis of social class and capitalism. Marx argued that ideas in society are used to maintain social relationships based on inequalities of power. He asserted that the ruling ideas are the ideas of the ruling class. He stated very strongly therefore that ideas sustained and masked social inequality and exploitation. Later writers, including those who are Marxists, have wanted to retain the idea that the economy is the most important institution in society but they have placed more importance on the independence of ideas from the economy. As a result it is necessary to examine representations in society without assuming that they all serve the interests of a dominant class or dominant classes.

The mass media and ideology

The media contribute to the ways in which people make sense of the world but media texts are not usually constructed to develop a coherent view of the world. They contain therefore many different elements, some of which are taken from the world outside the media and some of which relate closely to other media texts. In both fictional as well as non-fictional texts, however, the media can be seen as creating and sustaining meanings and working on the currently available meanings by producing re-combinations of them and variations on them.[4] As a result the elements in any particular text might be contradictory: some of the elements might imply that change in society is required whereas others might suggest satisfaction with the status quo. The important point however is that so long as social inequalities that are a source of political contention exist there is a role for ideological criticism. Ideological analyses of media products will therefore by required to analyse representations of, for example, social class, gender, race, ethnicity or sexuality.

THE TERMINATOR

The Terminator (James Cameron, 1984) is a science fiction film that contains interesting representations of gender, especially that of the main female protagonist Sarah Connor. Initially it appears to be a film with a 'masculine' profile: it stars Arnold Schwarzenegger, contains violent scenes and chases and involves a struggle between two men, or rather between a cyborg and a man. The cyborg has travelled through time from a future in which machines are bent on exterminating mankind. It has the task of killing Sarah Connor, the mother of John Connor, who is leading the resistance to the machines. Kyle Reese has been sent back through time by John Connor to prevent the murder of his mother. Kyle is eventually killed but not before he has informed Sarah of her historic role.

As the film progresses the development of Sarah Connor becomes a major focus of the narrative. At first she is a put-upon waitress who has to be rescued from the terminator by Kyle Reese. He then describes her role in the future in the following way, 'The legend Sarah Connor taught her son to fight, organise, prepare from when he was a kid, when you were hiding before the war.' Sarah responds, 'I'm not tough or organised now!' but in the film we see her dress Reese's wound; help him to make bombs; eventually destroy the terminator and, in the final sequence of the film, prepare for the birth of her child, fathered by Kyle Reese.

In conclusion, there is some tension in the representation of Sarah Connor in this film. Kyle Reese describes the women of the future as 'good fighters' and Sarah emerges as this kind of woman. On the other hand, Sarah's role is traditional in that she is destined to be the mother and nurturer of the saviour of mankind who, inevitably, is a man. The representation of Sarah Connor is unusual because she combines two views of women – a dominant view that a woman's place is in the home as mother and nurturer and an opposing view that the lives of women should not be restricted in this way. Henry Cooper would probably find it difficult to accept that Sarah Connor is made for fighting and 'loving'.

FURTHER WORK

Gender
Take a sport and analyse the representations of gender in that sport across a range of texts.

Undertake the 'alternative sports' radio production (Exercise 2) in Part Five, Chapter 22.

Ideological approaches in film
'Importantly, ideological approaches reject the view of the film text as "unitary" in meaning; that is, as making only one kind of sense, without contradictions, exceptions, or variations in the interpretations made by different members of the audience. Rather, the text is a kind of battleground for competing and often contradictory positions. Of course, this competition usually results in a victory for the culture's dominant posi-

tions, but not without leaving cracks or divisions through which we can see the consensualising work of ideology exposed.'[5]

Discuss this quotation with reference to a contemporary film or contrast a contemporary film with a film from the same genre, for example, from an earlier period.

FURTHER READING

Cormack, Mike, *Ideology*, B. T. Batsford, 1992.
Turner, Graeme, *Film as Social Practice*, (2nd edition), Routledge, 1993, Chapter 6.

FURTHER VIEWING

Rosie the Riveter (Connie Field, US, 1980)
Hollywood Shuffle (Robert Townsend, US, 1987)
Brassed Off (Mark Herman, UK/US, 1996)
The Full Monty (Peter Cattaneo, US/UK, 1997)

Notes

[1] John B. Thompson, *Ideology and Modern Culture*, Polity, 1990, pp6–7.

[2] The *Guardian*, 2 October 1997.

[3] Quoted in *Ibid*.

[4] John Ellis, *Visible Fictions*, Routledge, 1982, pp14–15.

[5] Graeme Turner, *Film as Social Practice*, (2nd edition), Routledge, 1993, p147.

CHAPTER 3 Audiences

'Texts don't make meanings; audiences make meanings.'

Anon

APPROACHES TO THE CONCEPT OF 'AUDIENCE'

No media product is put together without some idea of the audience that is going to see, read or hear it; hence, the concept of 'audience' is at the heart of all media study and it would be a truism to say that the whole of this book is, in essence, discussing the interaction between media and audience. As media audiences can be defined and approached in a number of ways, this introduction to the concept of 'audience' will seek to indicate particular areas for discussion, some of which will be discussed in detail and some of which will be discussed in greater detail in other chapters.

The audience as segments of a consumer market

For the purposes of advertising, the target audience is viewed as a segment of a consumer market by advertisers who use the following two criteria:

■ Demographics – the consumer is categorised in terms of concrete variables such as age, class, gender, geographical area, etc.

■ Psychographics – the consumer is categorised in terms of their needs and desires such as those who aspire to a richer lifestyle or those who want to make the world a better place

(See Chapter 10, Advertising, 'Audience Segmentation'.)

The audience as a market for media products

This audience might also be subdivided in a number of ways.

Genres, product and station

By far the easiest way to define a target audience is by describing it in terms of a suitable genre or product. In other words, a new product may be described as appealing to soap watchers or *Guardian* readers or Channel 4 viewers and immediately it is possible to imagine the type of audience being targeted.

Niche and mass audiences

These audiences are categorised in terms of size. For instance, *American Football Big Match* can be seen as niche programming whereas *EastEnders* has a mass audience. It used to be thought that, for commercial stations, only mass audiences were worth targeting but channels such as Channel 4 have proved that targeting small but high earning groups can be very profitable for advertisers.

Narrowcasting

Initially, channels such as BBC2 and Channel 4 were seen as narrowcast channels because they appealed to smaller sections of audience than BBC1 and ITV but with the advent of satellite, cable and digital dissemination it is now possible to dedicate whole channels or stations to a specific interest such as the Sci-Fi Channel, Sky Sports 1/2/3 or MTV; this is referred to as narrowcasting. These dedicated channels allow for interest-specific advertising.

Infotainment

These programmes mix the giving of information with light entertainment.

Scheduling

In the broadcast media, there is a great deal of attention paid to targeting certain groups of people throughout the day which is important because different groups will watch at different times. For instance, housewives and the unemployed are considered to be the daytime audience and they are offered **infotainment** such as *Richard and Judy* and *Oprah* or daytime soaps such as *Young Doctors* and *A Country Practice*. Whereas, young people coming home late at weekends are targeted by programmes such as *The Word*, *The Girlie Show* and *Eurotrash*. Schedulers also aim to keep audiences watching throughout the evening by constantly previewing later programmes and by presenting a continuity of broadcast flow. 'Hammocking', 'inheritance' and 'pre-echo' are all ploys used by schedulers to gain audiences for new or flagging programmes by enlisting the audiences of successful programmes. New programmes are 'hammocked' when they are placed between two successful programmes. If the new programme is placed after the successful programme it is hoped that it will 'inherit' some of the audience. 'Pre-echo' refers to the practice of placing a new programme before an established programme so that people switching on early are exposed to it.

BROADCAST FLOW

This describes the way that schedulers try and create a seamless flow of programmes throughout the day's broadcasting in an attempt to keep the audience from switching off or switching stations. In many ways the schedulers try and fool the audience into the belief that they are watching one continuous narrative so that they will not turn off at programme junction points. How is this seamlessness conveyed?

- Advertisements – on commercial stations these often reflect the programme being broadcast and so it will seem that they are part of the narrative

- Trails – programmes that are going to be broadcast later in the day's viewing or later in the week's viewing are constantly trailed so that the audience will keep watching

- Presenters and **idents** – these are used to link the narratives to give people a feeling of either being addressed personally or the feeling of some sort of loyalty to a particular station. The stunning BBC2 idents have become a reason in their own right for watching the station!

- Juxtaposition – programmes have to be fitted together with some care as a sudden switch from a light entertainment programme to a heavy documentary would be too jarring. Imagine juxtaposing *The Wheel of Fortune* with a documentary on poverty and starvation in Africa

Broadcast flow has been affected in some degree by new technology. Video and tape recorders have allowed broadcast programmes to be recorded and consumed out of the sequence of flow and this can disrupt the schedulers' cleverly constructed flow of narrative. It is also possible to switch channels now without moving from the sofa by utilising the 'zapper' and this again allows the audience to move from channel to channel and disrupt the flow with relative ease.

Idents

Visual or aural logos which identify either a broadcast programme or a station.

The audience as a commodity

In this approach the audience themselves become a commodity which is sold to the advertisers. For instance, the advertising break within *Coronation Street* is viewed by an audience of *circa* 16 million. This huge audience means that the networks can charge more for advertising in that peak viewing slot. Thus, the size of the audience becomes a commodity that can be marketed to advertisers. (See Chapter 13, Soap Opera.)

The audience response to the media

This area is the source of the biggest debate surrounding media audiences because so little has really been discovered about the way that audiences receive and make sense of media texts. The outline areas for debate are as follows:

- The effect the media have on the audience
- The way audiences use the media
- The ways audiences read media texts

These debates are discussed in greater detail below.

Hypodermic syringe model – a short term effect theory

It has been a popular belief since the 19th century that 'violent images' in media texts could influence the actions of vulnerable sections of society. Effects of media texts on audiences have been the subject of study for nearly as long and the initial research centred on the hypodermic model; in this theory it is suggested that the audience receive an 'intravenous injection' of a media text – which could be negative (eg violent murder) or positive (eg heroic act) and are stimulated into a response. David Glover suggests that the roots of this theory are 'deeply ingrained in modern societies' and suggests two reasons why. First of all he says the theory drew on the assumption 'that the social upheavals associated with industrialisation had made people extremely vulnerable so that they were easily swayed by any attempt to grab their attention or provide them with novel experiences. Thus they were prey to political demagogues and readily duped by the new mass media.' Secondly, he says that the hypodermic theory also came from behaviourist school of thought in psychology which saw '... all human action as modelled on the conditioned reflex so that one's personality consisted of nothing more than responses to stimuli in the individual's environment which formed stable and recognisable patterns of behaviour.'[1]

A number of examples have been used to add weight to the hypodermic theory. One often quoted example is the 1938, radio dramatisation of the H. G. Wells play *War of the Worlds* which caused a panic reaction across America because people genuinely believed aliens had landed. Another is the Hungerford massacre in August 1987, when it was suggested that Michael Ryan had been influenced by scenes in the film *Rambo* before committing the shootings. In 1993, it was also suggested that scenes from the film *Child's Play 3* had influenced Robert Thompson and John Venables, the two boys accused of killing James Bulger. The public outcry spurred by comments from the judge at the trial, Mr Justice Morland, who said he suspected '... exposure to violent video films may be in part an explanation for this terrible crime' resulted in more regulations surrounding the sale of videos the following year. However, all of these examples are subject to argument. Research conducted by Hadley Cantril, published in 1940, revealed that among other things the reaction to the Wells' play had a great deal to do with people tuning in late to the broadcast and failing to realise it was fiction; he also found that, at that particular historical moment, there was a prewar world-wide political and economic nervousness which made people 'expect' bad news. In the case of *Rambo* and *Child's Play 3*, there is no proof that viewing these videos prompted the violent acts. In fact, in the latter case, there is no proof at all that the two boys had ever viewed that particular video.

Intervening variables

These are various influencing factors, which intervene between the sender and receiver of a message and consequently affect the way that a message is received. Intervening variables could include aspects such as peer group influences, the time of day or personal motivation.

The weakness of this model is that audiences are seen as passive and malleable with no thought of their own. Watson and Hill point out that it assumes that the mass media have a 'direct, immediate, and influential effect upon audiences' and also '... it overlooks the possible effects of **intervening variables** in the communication process and presents the masses as being unquestioning receptacles of media messages.'[2]

Inoculation model – a long term effect theory

Inoculation theory suggests that long term exposure to repeated media messages makes audiences 'immune' to them. Thus, for example, prolonged exposure to media violence would desensitise the audience so that they would no longer be shocked by it; it follows that someone thus desensitised might be more likely to commit a violent act as it is not seen as an extraordinary action. One argument put forward during the Bulger murder trial, and possibly also implied in the judge's words quoted above, was that the two accused boys had been subject to long term exposure to so-called video nasties and therefore they felt that violent acts were normal behaviour. At the time, Mary Whitehouse, President of the National Viewers and Listeners Association, said: 'The crudity of violence, showing people skinned alive for example, for that type of film to be received as entertainment says an awful lot about the way society is being corrupted.'[5]

NARCOTISING DYSFUNCTION

This concept of audience reception suggests that the mass media render the audience incapable of action. The term describes the way that prolonged media exposure can act like a narcotic drug on the brain causing apathy. Another way of describing those afflicted with this disease might be the term 'couch potato'.

Two-step flow model – a long term effect theory

Hypodermic theory suggests that there is a direct one-step effect of the media on the audience but a study conducted in 1940 by Paul Lazarsfeld on the US presidential election came up with some important findings that led to the formulation of the two-step model of communication flow. Lazarsfeld discovered that 50% of the voters in the presidential election had decided their voting preference six months prior to the election and despite media debates and coverage, coupled with persuasive presidential campaigns, they had not changed their minds. The study also discovered that individual views were most affected by opinion leaders who played a key role in the communication process. Opinion leaders both filtered and disseminated media messages; thus Lazarsfeld discovered a two-step communication flow from the medium through the opinion leader to the individual.

PASSIVE, SEMI-ACTIVE AND ACTIVE AUDIENCES

Hypodermic and inoculation models of communication view the audience as passive receivers of media output. The audience is perceived as a sponge absorbing everything contained within media texts without selection or rejection. Two-step flow is a semi-active model of audience reception because it implies some action on the part of the audience. Watson and Hill speak of the 'process of the interpretation' of media messages in this model that makes it different from earlier ones by presenting the audience as 'interacting and responsive individuals' as opposed to 'socially isolated, passive atoms.'[4] The following uses and gratifications model views the audience as active users of media texts who are capable of selecting and rejecting media messages and making use of media texts to gratify a complex set of needs.

Uses and gratifications model

This relatively new model radically changed research surrounding audience reception. Commenting on this fresh approach in 1970, James Halloran said that it let study move away from 'thinking in terms of what media do to people' and substituted the idea of 'what people do with the media'.[5] The thinking went even further than this because the model suggested that what people do with the media was governed by what they need from the media. These needs have been most usefully categorised by McQuail, Blumler and Brown[6] who identified four major types. These are as follows:

- The need to reinforce a view of personal identity by comparing our own roles and values with similar roles and values represented in the media – for example teenagers might use certain soap operas to reference how other teenagers behave in relationships; buying *Loaded* magazine might reinforce the buyer's self-perception that he is 'one of the lads'

- The need to have companionship and interaction with others. In this case the media might be used in a number of ways; it could become a companion – for instance, an elderly person living by her/him self might have the radio on all day for companionship – or it could be that specific characters within the media become so well-known by the audience they take on the role of a 'real' friend or acquaintance. The media also offer common ground that can be referenced in conversation with others; thus, the media is used to aid social contact

- The need to be informed. The media can offer information on many levels. For instance, this process might be as broad as the press and broadcast news offering us information on day to day happenings or it might be as narrow as an individual going to an Open University programme for specific information for a specific OU course

- The need for entertainment and diversion. This identifies both the need for fantasy as an escape from the constraints of reality and the need to recharge or purge emotions. In practice, this could mean imagining yourself into the role of the superhero/heroine or it could mean going to a comedy film to have a good laugh

The assumption within this model is that individuals are active participants in the mass communication process. People are seen to be able to select and reject aspects of media output according to individual needs. The problem with this assumption is that the audience is always seen to be seeking gratification of specific needs when in fact this is not necessarily always the case. Watching TV, as we all know, can often be a result of being too lazy to get up and switch it off and, frequently, advertising media intrude into our lives because it is simply not possible to ignore them. Another problem is that this model doesn't attribute the media with any direct short or long term effect on the audience at all. Media watchers who witnessed the birth of New Labour in 1996 and have followed Gazza being turned variously from hero to villain to hero *ad nauseam* in the tabloids will realise that the mass media is influential in forming opinions and changing beliefs.

PRIMARY, SECONDARY AND TERTIARY MEDIA INVOLVEMENT

The intensity of audience involvement with a specific medium at a specific time will also vary and this will contribute to the way that the particular media text is being received. Often this is most easily highlighted by logging our media involvement throughout the day and describing the reasons why and consequently how we consume the media during that time. The three categories of involvement are as follows:

■ Primary involvement – which implies that someone is completely consumed by watching a specific TV programme or reading a specific publication

■ Secondary involvement – which implies that someone may be occupied in another task but half listening at the same time. For instance, someone may be ironing while also watching *EastEnders*

■ Tertiary involvement – which implies that at the most the medium is just a background to what we are doing. This could apply to people who keep the radio on all day but are moving from room to room – in essence a tangential involvement.

Cultural effects – a long term effect theory

The thinking behind this theory centres on the long-term effects of particular ideological representations on our beliefs and values. Media representations of beautiful women, for instance, have been influential in giving both males and females a view of an 'ideal' woman. This ideal woman is, essentially, quite unnatural and while mothers have tried to be serene as the OXO mum, young girls have been conditioned to believe they should be as thin as the catwalk supermodels. It is interesting that the media now stand accused of subjecting men to similar ideological representations of 'male perfection' which require men to be a 'new man' who is 'behaving badly' while striving for the rugged good looks and rippling torso of a participant in *Gladiators*.

The encoding/decoding model – the giving and taking of a media message

The **encoding/decoding** model put forward by Stuart Hall[7] and David Morley[8] centred on the idea that audiences vary in their response to media messages. This is because they are influenced by their social position, gender, age, ethnicity, occupation, experience and beliefs as well as where they are and what they are doing when they receive a message (see primary, secondary tertiary reception above). In this model, media texts are seen to be encoded in such a way as to present a **preferred reading** to the audience but the audience does not necessarily accept that preferred reading. Hall categorised three kinds of audience response.

■ Dominant – the audience agree with the dominant values expressed within the preferred reading of the text

■ Negotiated – the audience generally agree with the dominant values expressed within the preferred reading but they may disagree with certain aspects according to their social background

■ Oppositional – the audience disagree with dominant values expressed within the preferred reading of the text

David Morley's study of audience responses to the news magazine programme *Nationwide* largely fitted with Hall's categorisations listed above. But

Encoding/ decoding

Any communication, and a mass media text is no exception, consists of a series of signs organised by certain rules or codes into a meaningful message. Codes can be visual or aural. In a newspaper, for instance, the type of language used and the way that the language is presented in a certain typeface within a certain lay out on the page are all codes that form the message that is being conveyed.

Preferred reading/meaning

This term describes the way that a media message is specifically encoded so that the audience will make sense of it in a certain way.

Morley also discovered that certain groups, for example one group of young black further education students, found the programme simply had to relevance to their world whereas a group of shop stewards approved of the populist style[9]. This highlighted the importance of the knowledge, tastes and values or **cultural competence** that individuals/groups brings to texts which subsequently affects the way those texts are enjoyed.

The individual and the text

The idea that media texts contain a preferred reading carries with it the implication that a number of readings are possible. Some texts are more open to different readings than others and are consequently referred to as polysemic. Another possible rejection of the preferred reading might occur if individuals or groups counter it on the basis of their own ideas or experience and produce what is referred to as an **aberrant decoding**.

VIOLENCE AND THE MEDIA

'On November 25, 1995, unidentified thugs perpetrated an especially pointless and sadistic act of violence against an innocent employee of the New York City subway system.

Squirting a huge quantity of flammable liquid into a Brooklyn token booth, they then lit a match and blew it to pieces, burning toll-taker Harry Kaufman, aged 50, over most of his body. After remaining for two weeks in critical condition, Kaufman died of his injuries, leaving behind the two children he had been working overtime to support through college.

This horrible incident might have been ignored as just another example of random urban cruelty except for the eerie resemblance between the attack and scenes in a movie that had been released just four days earlier. In *Money Train*, a mindlessly violent 'action film' in which Wesley Snipes and Woody Harrelson play New York City transit cops, a vicious pyromaniac executes two fiery assaults on toll booths that are identical in virtually every detail to the episode that killed Harry Kaufman.'

Michael Medved in *Screen Violence*[10]

'The hunt for witches to explain society's ills is ancient in our blood, but unholy for that none the less. The difference is that now we do not blame the village hag and her black cat but the writer, photographer and film-maker. Increasingly indicted by art and fearful of technology, our society scours them for scapegoats, in the process ignoring Shakespeare, who reminds us that artists do not invent nature but merely hold it up to a mirror. That the mirror now is electronic, widescreen or cyberspace is all the more intimidating to the unschooled and the more tempting to the lawyers.'

Oliver Stone in *Screen Violence*[11]

'On May 5 1964, at Birmingham Town Hall, I warned: "If you constantly portray violence as normal you will help to create a violent society." People learn from watching others. I think we're being extraordinarily childish if we don't accept that. For intelligent people to say violent films do not have an effect is nonsense. They are running away from the implications. We are *all* responsible for this state of affairs. It's because we have accepted violent material on our screens, and actually enjoy it and laugh at it. We wonder, then, why violence occurs.'

Mary Whitehouse in the *Guardian*[12]

'The violence in *Reservoir Dogs* was acceptable because it was shown to hurt. It was not something to laugh at.'

Barry Norman in *The Sunday Times*[13]

'We see the terrible murders in Liverpool and Cardiff . . . I don't think film or TV has anything to do with those things at all.'

Michael Winner in *The Sunday Times*[14]

'Movie violence is like eating salt. The more you eat, the more you need to eat to taste it at all.'

Alan Pakula[15]

In the 1990s a number of violent films such as *Reservoir Dogs* (Quentin Tarantino, 1991), *Child Play 3* (Jack Bender, 1991), *Pulp Fiction* (Quentin Tarantino, 1994) and *Natural Born Killers* (Oliver Stone, 1994), have become the focus for the one vital question of the media violence debate: does exposure to screen violence have an 'effect' on audiences?

The debate is divided into two camps. On the one hand there are those who believe that exposure to screen violence has a negative 'effect' on audiences and can result in:

▓ Individuals imitating violent events on screen, for example, copy-cat killings (see Medved quotation)

▓ Audiences becoming desensitised to violence – accepting higher levels of violence in society

On the other hand there are those who believe that exposure to media violence has a limited effect. They claim that there is no firm evidence to link screen violence to real life violence, and that other factors such as social background are more significant.

The proponents of the 'effects' debate draw upon the large body of American research that claims to prove scientifically that the media has an 'effect' on audiences. The study most frequently cited is Albert Bandura's 1963 'Bobo' doll experiment.[16] A 'Bobo' doll is a large inflatable doll with sand in its base which when knocked down stands back up again. In laboratory conditions Bandura proved that children who had previously seen adults hitting the doll (whether live or on film) were more likely to hit the doll than a control group who had not. Critics of the experiment claim that laboratory conditions do not mirror real life and in any case hitting a doll is not the same as 'real' violence.

Other studies have adopted a different approach. Drabman and Thomas (1974),[17] for example, attempted to prove that children exposed to violent material became desensitised. Hans Eysenck and D. K. B. Nias describe the experiment in their article 'Desensitisation, Violence and the Media'.[18]

'Children who had watched a violent scene from *Hopalong Cassidy* were compared with a control group, who had not seen a film, for tolerance of violent acts. This was done by asking each subject to keep an eye on a couple of children who were playing in another room, and to summon the experimenter if there was any trouble. They were able to watch the children by way of a videotape monitor; by this technique it was possible to arrange for both groups of subjects to see exactly the same sequence of events. After playing peacefully the two children started to abuse each other verbally and then to fight during the course of which the TV camera was knocked over and contact was eventually lost. The measure of attitude to aggression was the time taken before the subject sought help from the experimenter . . . Just over half the control subjects notified the experimenter of the argument before physical fighting began, whereas only 17 per cent of the film group did.'

Both these studies are based on short-term effects within controlled conditions. There are a number of studies, however, that have attempted to find out the long-term effects of exposure to screen violence. For example, Eron *et al.* (1972)[19] concluded that it was possible to prove that 8 to 9-year-old boy's exposure to violent television resulted in an increased level of aggression aged 18 to 19. A later study observed that the best predictor of whether someone will commit a violent crime aged 30 was the amount of violent television that they watched aged eight.

William Belson in his book *Television Violence and the Adolescent Boy* (1978)[20] also attempted to prove that boys' exposure to violent television led to aggression. His research involved 1,565 boys in London aged between 12 and 17: it was designed to be as rigorous as possible and to eliminate some of the problems associated with earlier studies. Guy Cumberbatch in 'Violence and the Mass Media: Research Evidence'[21] describes the research.

'It attempted to measure children's exposure to television violence in their earlier years and to link this to self-reported violent behaviour through a sophisticated system of matching heavy and light viewers of television violence. This matching was done according to over 200 different measures and thus attempts – reasonably well in fact – to overcome the serious problem that any correlation between delinquency and exposure to television violence could be due to a third variable like social class causing both... Belson concludes that boys with high levels of exposure to television violence commit 49% more acts of serious violence than those who see little.'

Despite Belson's attempts to monitor the integrity of the data, some commentators pointed out some surprising contradictions. Dennis Howitt, for example, has pointed out the fact that 'heavy and light viewers of television violence are less aggressive than middle range viewers'.[22] In other words if the levels of violent television were increased violence in society as a whole would decrease. Howitt's interpretation of Belson's research serves to demonstrate how all violence 'effects' studies should be treated with caution as data can often give conflicting results and flaws in methodology can invalidate conclusions.

Child's Play 3 and Natural Born Killers

'The music is heavy and pounding. The camera scans over a mass of decapitated dolls' heads and severed limbs, all shrouded in cobwebs. A pulverised body, spattered in blue paint is hoisted overhead. Blood, thick and gooey, drips into a bubbling cauldron of molten plastic below. Phoenix-like, the moulded outline of a doll's face emerges, its cheeks blood-stained, its eye sockets empty. It screams.'

Description of scene from *Child's Play 3* by Sally Weale[23]

'Oliver Stone's film, *Natural Born Killers*, is linked to ten deaths, six of them in the US, where it opened two months ago. Most recently, a 14-year-old from Dallas, Texas, accused of decapitating a girl of 13, tells friends he wanted to kill someone and become "famous, like the natural born killers." '

Mike Ellison[24]

A number of films in the 1990s have been accused of directly influencing the behaviour of audiences. Both *Child's Play 3* and *Natural Born Killers*, for example, are said to have stimulated individuals to commit murder.

What is interesting about the controversy surrounding *Child's Play 3* and the murder of Jamie Bulger is that it seems unlikely, as noted previously, that John Venables and Robert Thompson ever saw the film. In any case *Child's Play 3* could not be described as ultra-violent – it is a typical 'horror' film and certainly includes no scenes in which a toddler is murdered by children. For want of any other plausible explanation, however, Mr Justice Morland, the trial judge, suggested that the children may have been influenced by the violent videos rented by their father 'including possibly *Child's Play 3*, which has some striking similarities to the manner of the attack on James Bulger.'[25] The remarks stirred up a moral panic about screen violence in the tabloid press, which resulted in tightening up of the legislation governing the rental and sale of videos in 1994.

Natural Born Killers was, according to its director Oliver Stone, intended to be a direct criticism of the media, but entered the debate on the effects of the portrayal of violence because of several well-documented cases of individuals who had seen the film and subsequently committed murder. The most often cited American case is that of Nathan Martinez who became obsessed with *Natural Born Killers*, seeing the film ten times, before shooting dead his step-mother and step-sister. A Panorama

Figure 3.1 Scene from *Natural Born Killers*   © Kobal Collection

Special: *The Killing Screens*[26] reconstructed the days before and after the murders, concentrating on Martinez's identification with the central character in the film. The programme seemed in no doubt that this 'copy-cat' killing provided direct evidence that the film had caused the murders.

Martin Barker in his article 'Violence'[27] argued strongly against the case put forward by *The Killing Screens*. He claims that it is too easy to take the 'common sense' view that if an individual watches a violent film and then commits a violent crime there must be a connection. Instead he claims that it is not the film itself that has an 'effect' on audiences but the discourses built around it. He states: 'I am therefore quite prepared to believe that Martinez *was* influenced by his seeing of the film – because he had been endlessly told that this was a film which might authorise violence. In just the same sad way, it is not hard to find, in the reports of witch trials, young and old women *claiming* to be witches, because that is the lens through which *their* culture invited them to see themselves.'

What is screen 'violence'?

Much of the research into screen violence takes little account of the context of the violence, preferring to classify films and programmes by simply counting the acts of 'violence' on screen. A film could therefore be classed as 'very violent' because of its high body count, ignoring whether or not the film provided a moral framework to the killings.

A major problem, however, is defining what is meant by 'violence'. It could mean, for example, any of the following situations:

- Tom hitting Jerry over the head with a hammer
- Phil and Grant having a fist fight in Italy with the locals in *EastEnders*
- Will Munny (Clint Eastwood) killing Little Bill at the end of *Unforgiven*
- A news report from the war zone in Bosnia during the fighting
- Mr Blonde (Michael Madsen) cutting off a policeman's ear in *Reservoir Dogs*

In each case the 'violence' is very different. There is clearly a distinction to be drawn between fictional violence and violence from the real world. However, whether the violence is fictional or non-fictional it is received in a cultural context, which affects how the violence is understood. The cartoon format of *Tom & Jerry*, for example, allows violent actions to take place (Tom's teeth being knocked out for instance), but the violence is meant to be humorous (the characters do not appear to experience any suffering) and the audience know that its effects will be short-lived. The fistfight in *EastEnders* is coded in a similar manner although it does have the consequence of Phil and Grant temporarily ending up in prison. The scene also, however, fulfils the audience's expectation of the Mitchell brothers as characters – it would be out of character for them not to get involved in a fight with the locals.

Unforgiven contains some disturbingly violent scenes including the killing of Little Bill. The film belongs, however, to the western genre, which typically involves violent conflict between different groups. As in many other westerns it is clear in *Unforgiven* that violence is necessary to achieve justice. The 'violence' of the film also has a very real effect, for example characters that are shot don't just silently fall down, and they suffer a great deal. It is clear, therefore, that the violence of *Unforgiven* must be examined with reference to both the western genre as well as the film as a whole.

News reports often contain disturbing images of violence or the effects of violence. Research studies have shown that this 'real' violence is more disturbing to children than fictional violence. Guy Cumberbatch, for example, interviewed a group of 305 children aged between 13 and 18 and claimed that 82% of the children found violence in the news more upsetting than in videos or computer games. The research makes it clear that children can distinguish between real and fictional violence and it has been pointed out that 'Children don't find fiction frightening; or if they do, they often enjoy it . . .'.[28] It is, however, also the case that despite 'real' violence being more disturbing it is, like fictional violence, set in the context of the news programme genre in which news reports attempt to set the violent scenes in context.

The unrelenting violence of the ear-slicing sequence in *Reservoir Dogs* is perhaps nearing the boundary of what is 'acceptable' on film. Like most other films, however, the violent actions result in the perpetrator's downfall. It is also significant that the other characters regard Mr Blonde as an out of control psychopath who does not act like a 'professional'.

 MORAL PANIC

The mass media, in particular the tabloid press, play a key role in creating moral panics by responding to the concerns of public figures. The concern might be about the behaviour of certain individuals or groups or certain events which are perceived as threatening to social order. It is, however, the 'hysterical, stylised and stereotypical'[29] manner in which the situation is reported that blows its true significance out of all proportion. Moral panics can result in government legislation to deal with the perceived problem. It could be argued, for example, that the 'moral panic' about video nasties was responsible for the Video Recording Act 1984. Moral panics in the 1990s have centred on the ownership of knives and guns and have also resulted in legislation to control their use.

CENSORSHIP

Debates over media violence usually culminate in calls for ever tougher measures to control the content of films but especially videos and TV programmes which are viewed in the home.

Film

The current system of classification for films: U, PG, 12, 15, 18, R18 restricts some age groups from viewing material that is regarded as unsuitable. For example the BBFC (British Board of Film Classification) guidelines for a 15 film offer the following: 'Themes requiring a more mature understanding. Full frontal nudity in a non-sexual context; impressionist sex; more extensive use of expletives; mildly graphic violence and horror with some gore. Soft drugs may be seen in use, but not so as to condone or normalise ... no details of harmful or criminal techniques, eg how to break into cars, pick locks etc.'

Video

Initially videos were not subject to censorship, but concern grew in the early 1980s about violence in videos given the following facts:

▪ Children can obtain easier access to films on video than in cinemas

▪ Scenes can be replayed on a VCR

▪ The VCR has the capacity to 'freeze' images

This moral panic led to the Video Recording Act 1984, which ensured that all videos were subject to classification. In consequence as James Ferman, the director of the BBFC acknowledges, a film released on video is subject to closer scrutiny and more likely to receive a more restrictive certificate than one released in cinemas.

Television

Television programmes including those from cable and satellite channels are also subject to strict rules about the portrayal of violence. The ITC acknowledges that the real world contains violence in many forms and that television has a duty to reflect this fact. Television has to acknowledge however that 'the portrayal of violence, whether physical, verbal or psychological, is an area of public concern...' With this public concern in mind broadcasters must according to ITC guidelines.

▪ Avoid concentrations of violence in their schedules and be mindful of the time of screening of programmes containing violence

▪ Note the lack of evidence that violence used to achieve good or legitimate goals or violence that places the audience at a distance whether through time, space or ritual is therefore harmless

▪ Be aware that explicit violence especially if sudden or unexpected is most likely to offend and that gratuitous violence cannot be defended

▪ Take care to consider the impact of violence on young or socially or emotionally insecure viewers

▪ Avoid depictions of violence that use ingenious or unfamiliar methods that can be easily imitated[30]

The ITC does not seek to suppress imagination, creativity or realism because of the vulnerability of a minority of the population but it does emphasise that in the sensitive area of violence 'risks require special justification' and states decisively, 'If in doubt, cut.'[31] All of the five terrestrial channels also follow guidelines concerning the 9.00 pm 'watershed' that discourages the broadcasting of 'adult' material until after 9.00 pm. Even encrypted and subscription channels must conform to certain scheduling guidelines. For example '18' rated films can only be shown after 10.00 pm and 'R18' films cannot be shown at all.

In America the Government has passed legislation to ensure that all new TV sets will be fitted with a 'V' chip. The 'V' chip ('V' stands for violence) is an electronic device that allows the operator to block out programmes defined as violent or sexually explicit. It is possible that a similar system will be adopted in the UK, which will raise a number of questions.

- Who will be responsible for classifying the many thousands of programmes?
- Will the context of the violence in each programme be taken into account?
- Will the device discourage film- and programme-makers from tackling serious issues for fear of losing ratings?

Internet

The ability to download violent or sexually explicit images from the Internet, which remains largely free from any sort of control, has also caused concern. The Internet is at present limited in its ability to transmit films and programmes because of its reliance on the telephone network, which is not designed to process large amounts of data. Optical cable, capable of transmitting high quality moving images, however, has already been developed in America. The widespread introduction of optical cable will probably result in the merger of Internet and cable television technology. This will render classification and censorship obsolete as the task will be too great.

 **FURTHER WORK**

Scheduling

During one evening's viewing on one particular channel, make a note of how many times other programmes are trailed or advertised by a presenter. Make a note of the trails and see if any of them are for new programmes. If the trails are for new programmes look at the schedules and see where they are going to be placed. Then ask yourself why they are being placed in that particular timeslot.

Make a one day diary of your media consumption and then make a note of (a) your involvement (primary, secondary, tertiary) with those media during the day and (b) your use of the media during the day. For instance, are you using it for relaxation, information, company? Is there any correlation between the two?

Media/violence debate

Rarely does a week go by without the public being confronted with a moral panic in the media: for example excessive violence in television and film. Consider in detail a recent example of a moral panic in the media.

'...there simply isn't a "thing" called "violence in the media" that either could or couldn't "cause" social violence. There is nothing to be researched. That being so, it means that 70 years of research have poured hundreds of millions of dollars and pounds down the drain of meaningless questions – as much a waste of effort and resources as all the commissions and researches into witches.' [Martin Barker 'Violence', *Sight and Sound*, June 1995]

Discuss the above quotation with reference to the media/violence debate.

FURTHER READING

Barker, Martin and Petley, Julian, (eds), *Ill Effects: The Media/Violence Debate*, Routledge, 1997.

Barker, Martin, 'Violence' in *Sight and Sound*, June 1995

Burton, Graeme, *More Than Meets the Eye*, Edward Arnold, 1990

Cumberbatch, Guy and Howitt, Dennis, *A Measure of Uncertainty: The Effects of the Mass Media*, John Libbey, 1989.

Donnellan, Craig, (ed.), *Television and Censorship*, Independence, 1996.

French, Karl, (ed.), *Screen Violence*, Bloomsbury, 1996.

Glover, David, 'The Sociology of the Mass Media: Media Effects' in Michael Haralambos, (ed.), *Sociology: New Directions*, Causeway, 1985.

Halloran, James D., (ed.), *The Effects of Television*, Panther, 1970.

Lewis, Justin, *The Ideological Octopus*, Routledge, 1991.

Marris, Paul, and Thornham, Sue, (eds), *Media Studies: A Reader*, Edinburgh University Press, 1996 (Section on: Reception: 'Effects' to 'Uses').

Morley, David, *Television, Audiences and Cultural Studies*, Routledge, 1992.

Miller, David and Philo, Greg, 'Against Orthodoxy: the Media Do Influence Us' in *Sight and Sound*, December 1996.

Philo, Greg, *Seeing and Believing: The Influence of Television*, Routledge, 1990.

Watson, James and Hill, Anne, *A Dictionary of Communication and Media Studies*, 4th Edition, Edward Arnold, 1997.

Notes

[1] David Glover 'The Sociology of the Mass Media' in Michael Haralambos, (ed.), *Sociology: New Directions*, Causeway, 1985, p373.

[2] James Watson and Anne Hill, *A Dictionary of Communication and Media Studies* Fourth Edition, 1997, Edward Arnold, p162.

[3] The *Guardian*, 26 November 1993.

[4] James Watson and Anne Hill, *ibid*, p162.

[5] James D. Halloran, (ed.), *The Effects of Television*, Panther, 1970, quoted in Len Masterman, *Teaching the Media*, Comedia, 1985, p216

[6] Denis McQuail, (ed.), *Sociology of the Mass Media*, Penguin, 1972.

[7] Stuart Hall *et al.*, *Culture, Media, Language*, Hutchinson, 1980.

[8] David Morley, *The Nationwide Audience*, BFI, 1980.

[9] See Morley's study discussed in *Sociology: New Directions*: 'The Sociology of the Mass Media', p388.

[10] In 'Hollywood's Four Big Lies' in Karl French (ed.), *Screen Violence*, Bloomsbury, 1996, p20.

[11] In 'Don't Sue the Messenger' in *ibid*, 1996, p237.

[12] Quoted in the *Guardian*, 26 November 1993 in the context of the Jamie Bulger murder.

[13] Quoted in *The Sunday Times*, 14 March 1993.

[14] Ibid

[15] Extract from Michael Medved's *Hollywood vs America* in *The Sunday Times*, 14 February 1993.

[16] A. Bandura, D. Ross and S. A. Ross, 'Imitation of film-mediated aggressive models', *Journal of Abnormal and Social Psychology*, 66.

[17] R. S. Drabman, and M. H. Thomas (1974), 'Does media violence increase children's tolerance of real-life aggression?' *Developmental Psychology*, 10, 418–21.

[18] In Paul Marris and Sue Thornham (eds), *Media Studies: A Reader*, Edinburgh University Press /Maurice Temple Smith Publishers, 1996, p263.

[19] L. D. Eron, M. M. Leftkowitz, L. R. Huesmann and L. O. Walter, 'Does Television violence cause aggression?', American Psychologist 27.

[20] Farnborough, Teakfield.

[21] In Guy Cumberbatch and Dennis Howitt, *A Measure of Uncertainty: The Effects of the Mass Media*, John Libbey, 1989, p43–44.

[22] Quoted in David Glover, 'The Sociology of the Mass Media' in Michael Haralambos, (ed.), *Sociology: New Directions*, Causeway, 1985, p393.

[23] The *Guardian*, 26 November 1993.

[24] The *Guardian*, 25 October 1994.

[25] Quoted in the *Guardian*, 27 November 1993.

[26] First broadcast 27 February 1995.

[27] *Sight and Sound*, June 1995.

[28] Quoted by Charles Arthur 'Children more upset by "real" TV violence,' *Daily Telegraph*, 1995 in *Television Censorship*, Independence, 1996.

[29] Stanley Cohen in *Folk Devils and Moral Panics*, MacGibbon and Kee, 1972 quoted in Watson and Hill *ibid*, p145.

[30] Adapted from ITC Programme Code (January 1998), pp4–5.

[31] 'Violence on Television', *ITC Guidelines* (section on violence).

CHAPTER **4** **Tools of Analysis**

READING TEXTS: FILM

The idea of being taught to 'read' a film may sound laughable to many, as even young children are familiar with the formal conventions of films. The ability to understand them is acquired, like language, unconsciously through experience. Films, however, like language, follow rules of which audiences tend to remain unaware. Most films are designed to disguise their artificial nature. This means that the audience becomes involved in the plot, but does not think about how the film has been constructed. The aim of this section is to uncover the elements involved in the construction of a film and to examine how they are used to create meaning. There are five key elements involved.

■ *Mise-en-scène*

■ Cinematography

■ Editing

■ Sound

■ Narrative

Mise-en-scène

The term *mise-en-scène* translated literally from the French means 'placed in the scene'. It was first used in the theatre and referred to the way in which a director arranged theatrical elements and events on stage. In film studies it is used to describe everything that can be seen in a single shot, such as the following:

■ Setting

■ Props and costumes

■ Performance

The term also includes the way in which these elements are placed and lit. A number of film theorists have extended *mise-en-scène* to include how a scene is recorded by the camera. For example, the way in which the characters are framed, the position of the camera and whether it is mobile or static. The term must therefore be treated with caution, as it possesses more than one meaning.

Mise-en-scène was developed as a critical tool in film studies to allow the contribution of directors working within the **Hollywood studio system** to be recognised. Prior to this directors were thought to have little or no creative control over a film, simply following the shooting script supplied by the studio. In most cases the director would only be involved in a project for two or three weeks during shooting, and would not be involved in any post-production work such as editing.

Setting

Where a director chooses a set a film is vital to its success, as settings immediately communicate a sense of time and place to an audience. The opening shots of *Heat* (Michael Mann, 1996), for example, establish that the film is set in 1990s Los Angeles. The city is not depicted as a neutral environment, however, but an alienating one which dwarfs its inhabitants. The setting of *Heat* is thus used to introduce a key theme of the film.

Settings must ultimately convince audiences of their reality and allow the narrative to flow unimpeded in a believable space. To achieve this directors take great pains to ensure that sets are authentic in every detail. Audiences would not question, for example, the realism of the heroin addicts' flat featured in the opening sequences of *Trainspotting* (Danny Boyle, 1996).

Hollywood studio system

Refers to the way in which the five major and three minor Hollywood studios in the period approximately 1930–50 operated as factories, making films on an assembly line basis, as well as being involved in their distribution and exhibition.

Figure 4.1 *Mary Shelley's Frankenstein*: The importance of setting   © BFI

Figure 4.2 *Once Upon a Time in the West*: The importance of costume   ©BFI

In some films, however, the settings are stylised to reinforce the themes of the film. For example in *Edward Scissorhands* (Tim Burton, 1990) the houses are all painted in pastel colours and are unnaturally neat and tidy. It subsequently becomes clear from the narrative that the inhabitants are unable to accept individuals who don't share their values. Tim Burton is, of course, also making a comment on the nature of small town America.

In *Mary Shelley's Frankenstein* (Kenneth Branagh, 1994) the sets also contribute significantly to the meaning of the film. In the scene where Victor Frankenstein learns about the death of his mother, his father stands halfway up a vast flight of stairs covered in blood. He is starkly emphasised by the pale coloured marble walls and floor of the set, as well as its sheer size and sparseness. The set powerfully captures the characters' sense of isolation and despair after their loss and makes the audience understand why Frankenstein subsequently swears to conquer death.

Props and costumes

Try to imagine a gangster without a gun, a private eye without a hat and trenchcoat, or a sheriff without a badge. The difficulty of the task demonstrates the importance of iconography to the creation of meaning in genre films. It certainly supports the argument that a genre is defined by its iconography.

The majority of props are placed in a set to fulfil the audience's demand for realism. A police station, for example, must contain a large number of objects to make it appear authentic. In some instances, however, objects acquire additional symbolic meanings that are important to the plot of the film. In *Sleeping with the Enemy* (Joseph Ruben, 1991) for example, the Julia Roberts character knows that her husband is close by because of the straightened towels in the bathroom and neatly lined up tins in the kitchen. In *For a Few Dollars More* (Sergio Leone, 1966) the pair of watches carried by El Indio and Colonel Mortimer are clearly vital to the plot, but Leone builds up narrative tension by waiting until the end of the film to reveal their full significance to the audience.

Costumes are also used to give extra meanings to characters. In *Scarface* (Brian de Palma, 1983), for example, Al Pacino's swiftly acquired wealth is partly signified by his flashy designer clothes. In many films such as *Shane* (George Stevens, 1953) costumes are used symbolically. Wilson the 'bad' gun-fighter, for example, wears black, while Shane wears buckskins, associated with the natural world. This is taken to extremes in films such as *Star Wars* (George Lucas, 1977) in which the forces of good and evil are clearly delineated by their costume.

Performance

Much of the meaning created in a scene arguably originates from the performance of the actors and actresses. It is difficult, however, to weigh up the relative contributions of the performers and other elements such as setting, props, editing and sound. The Commutation Test, devised by John O. Thompson,[1] is a method of assessing the contribution of the performer. The idea is to mentally substitute one performer for another and to see if the swop would change the meaning of a film. What would happen, for example, if Bruce Willis in *Pulp Fiction* was replaced by Kevin Costner? What the test really highlights is the fact that many established stars carry with them additional meanings that are often vital to the success of a film. In *Unforgiven*, for example, the director (Clint Eastwood) relies on the audience's knowledge of Eastwood's previous roles in order to first thwart but finally fulfil their expectations. A similar example is that of Al Pacino in *Heat* (Michael Mann, 1996).[2] The audience will be familiar with his previous roles in *Scarface* (Brian de Palma, 1983) and *Carlito's Way* (Brian de Palma, 1993) and his presence on screen is enhanced by the audience's prior knowledge of what Richard Dyer terms **performance signs**.

Lighting

Audiences are often not aware of the artifice involved in shooting a film and this especially applies to the use of lighting. Lighting is used to allow the audience to follow the action clearly, but also to make a film look realistic. Its codes and conventions are therefore deliberately concealed from the audience. Most films are lit using a three point lighting system which combined with **high key, low contrast lighting** is designed to eliminate shadows and create an even and natural appearance.

Performance signs

Dyer claims that the repetition of performance signs will contribute to the development of a star image over a number of films. They are concerned with how the performer carries out the necessary actions and speaks the necessary lines. They include:

- Voice
- Gestures
- Body posture
- Body movement

High key, low contrast lighting

Refers to a style of lighting which allows a full range of tones to be seen in each shot. These scenes tend to be brightly lit, but a similar effect can be achieved with less overall light.

THREE POINT LIGHTING

Three point lighting is the term used to describe a system of lighting which uses three separate light sources for each shot involving central characters.

- Key light (the main source of light, placed in front of the characters)

- Fill light (less intense, placed near to the camera to soften and remove shadows)

- Backlight (makes the characters stand out against the background as well as balancing the overall lighting effect)

Film directors can use lighting, however, in a more expressive manner. In *Seven* (David Fincher, 1995), for example, **low key lighting** contributes to the mood of foreboding that pervades the film.[3] In *The Usual Suspects* (Bryan Singer, 1996), it conveys mystery.

Low key lighting

Refers to a system of lighting in which shadows are not eliminated by fill lighting, but used to add to the overall visual effect of the *mise-en-scène*.

Cinematography

The aspects of *mise-en-scène*, outlined earlier, are not unique to film and could all be achieved on a theatre stage. The addition of the camera, however, brings possibilities that are unique to cinema.

Point of view

In theatre the audience remains distant from the performers, and can only experience the action from their own point of view. The film camera, however, allows the audience to experience both **objective and subjective** views of the action. In the boxing ring sequences of *Raging Bull* (Martin Scorsese, 1980), for example, the audience are shown objective shots of Jake La Motta and his various opponents in the ring, but are also privileged with subjective shots from the point of view of both boxers. The audience thus 'experience' the fight for themselves, which encourages close identification with the characters.

Objective and subjective

Most shots in mainstream cinema are objective. In a scene in which two characters are present, for example, the audience would be able to see both clearly. In a subjective shot of the same scene, however, the audience would see one of the characters from the point of view of the other.

Filmstock

The choice of filmstock is vital to the overall look of a film. *Schindler's List* (Steven Spielberg, 1993), for example, is shot using a fast black and white filmstock, which adds to the documentary feel of the film, but also gives great clarity and depth to the images. In *JFK* (Oliver Stone, 1991) a number of different filmstocks are used to allow Stone to reconstruct recent history effectively. The present is shot in colour, but events remembered by key characters are shot in sharp black and white. In the final scenes of the film the 'true' story of Kennedy's assassination is pieced together using reconstructed footage, interspersed with the original footage taken at the time of the incident. The overall effect is convincing, despite the blurring of fact and fiction.

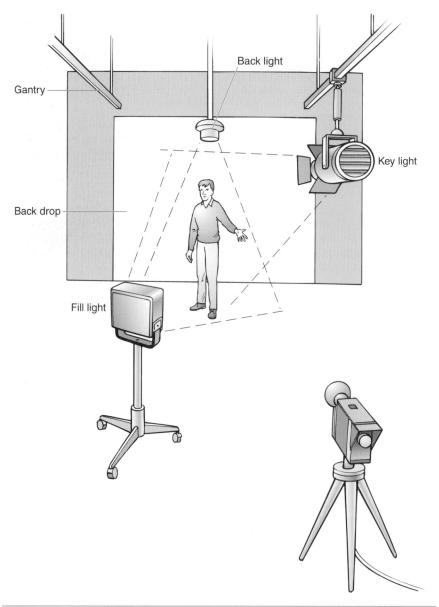

Figure 4.3 An illustration of the three point lighting system

Zoom lens

A shot employing a zoom lens is often confused with a tracking shot. Whereas a tracking shot involves physically moving the camera towards the subject, the camera in a zoom shot remains stationary. These two methods of getting closer to an object or character, however, produce very different results on screen.

Lenses and filters

The look of individual shots can be altered by the selection of different lenses. The lens most commonly used is the standard lens, which is designed to give a similar perspective on the world as the human eye. The other lenses, including wide-angle, telephoto and **zoom**, have distorting properties which can be used creatively by the film-maker. Filters placed over the lens can be further used to control the look of the film.

Figure 4.4 *Seven*: The use of low key lighting   © Kobal Collection

Focus and depth of field

Focus can be used creatively to highlight different objects or characters in a scene. A director could, for example, focus on a character in the foreground and then refocus on one in the background, rather than using editing. The term depth of field refers to the depth of focus in a shot. In a scene that had a shallow depth of field, for example, only the objects in the foreground would be in focus.

Camera positions

The position of the camera can be varied to allow the audience closer or more distant views of characters or objects. In most films each scene follows an established pattern in which longer shots are used at the start, followed by closer shots as the scene reaches its climax.

CAMERA POSITIONS RELATING TO PERFORMERS

■ Extreme long shot (ELS)

Also called the 'establishing shot' as it is often the first shot of a scene. Performers are distant in the setting.

■ Long shot (LS)

The setting still takes up most of the frame, but performers are closer to the camera.

■ Medium long shot (MLS)

The performer is framed from the knees up.

■ Medium shot (MS)

The performer is framed from the waist up.

■ Medium close shot (MCS)

The performer is framed from the chest up.

■ Close up (CU)

Frames parts of the body, such as head or hands.

■ Extreme close up (ECU)

Frames part of the face, such as eyes or mouth.

Extreme long shot

 Medium close shot

Long shot

 Close up

Medium long shot

 Extreme close up

Medium shot

Figure 4.5 An illustration of various camera positions relating to performers

High angle

Low angle

Figure 4.6 An illustration of the use of camera angles

Camera angles

The angle at which a camera is placed can produce surprisingly different meanings. If a character is filmed from a low angle, for example, the effect is to make him or her look powerful. The opposite is true if the character were to be filmed from a high angle. The camera can, more unusually, also be tilted on its horizontal axis so that the whole scene appears to be tipping over to the left or right. In *The Third Man* (Carol Reed, 1949), for example, the confusion and moral ambiguity of post-war Vienna is partly suggested by the use of such canted shots of the city streets and sewers.

Camera movement

The movement of the camera can vary from tracking shots on dollies to jerky hand-held shots. The development of **steadicam** in the 1970s enabled a number of film-makers to make extensive use of smooth travelling shots. In *Goodfellas* (Martin Scorsese, 1990), for example, a travelling shot is used to chart Henry Hill and Karen's progress from the side entrance of the Copacabana restaurant, passing a queue of people waiting at the main entrance, through doors, corridors and kitchens, greeting and passing a variety of characters, before finally entering the main dining area where a table at the front of the action is immediately set up. The smoothness of the steadicam shot mirrors the effortless way in which Henry sails past all the potential obstacles. The scene leaves the audience in no doubt about Henry's position in gangster circles. Brian De Palma achieves a similar effect in the opening sequence of

Steadicam

A damped suspension camera harness, worn by the operator. The device allows adjustment to be made to remove the jerkiness associated with hand-held filming. This can also give the impression that the camera is floating in mid-air. Its use was celebrated in *The Shining* (Stanley Kubrick, 1980).

The Bonfire of the Vanities (1990) when Peter Fallow's progress from underground car park to press conference is tracked by a steadicam for nearly five minutes.

In *Born on the Fourth of July* (Oliver Stone, 1989) mobile camera shots are used in a very different way. In one scene, in which the US soldiers accidentally fire upon a village, the camera moves so quickly that it is difficult for the audience to follow the action. When the soldiers discover a hut full of dead and wounded villagers, the disorienting camera movements and camera positions reflect the shock and confusion of the soldiers as they come to terms with the consequence of their actions. The scene is further enhanced by the mobile camera's ability to place the audience directly amongst the action, rather than remaining distant.

Speed of motion

The speed that the film passes through the camera can be increased from the standard 24 frames per second to produce slow motion when projected back at normal speed. This can be effective for emphasising significant actions. Key sections of the fight sequences in *Raging Bull*, for example, are frequently in slow motion. In *When Saturday Comes* (Maria Giese, 1995) slow motion is further used to build suspense when Jimmy Muir (Sean Bean) takes the match-deciding penalty.

Editing

Most films are constructed out of several thousand separate pieces of film that are painstakingly joined together by an editor. Many directors and critics have argued that editing is the essence of cinema. They claim that meaning is produced *between* shots rather than from the content of individual shots. Other critics, such as André Bazin, have argued that editing is disruptive and artificial, as it distorts the space and time of a scene. They argue that editing forces the audience to remain passive and to accept a fixed interpretation of a scene.

Editing serves a variety of purposes in a film and allows the director to achieve a number of effects.

- To **cut** to different locations or to intercut between events happening at two places at once

  In the opening of *Four Weddings and a Funeral* (Mike Newell, 1994), for example, shots of Charles (Hugh Grant) and Scarlett (Charlotte Coleman) asleep in bed are intercut with shots of other guests getting ready and travelling to the wedding

- To leave out unnecessary parts of the action and compress time

  In *Field of Dreams* (Phil Robinson, 1989), for example, the 1,500 mile journey that Ray (Kevin Costner) makes to Boston, in search of Terence Mann, is compressed into a sequence of shots lasting under one minute. The ultimate extension of this technique is achieved using Hollywood montage in which a quick succession of events over a period of time is shown. In *Raging Bull* (Martin Scorsese, 1980) the successful career of the boxer Jake La Motta is shown by combining shots (mostly still photographs) taken from a number of different fights interspersed with home movie footage of La Motta's home life

---

André Bazin (1919–58)

A French film critic and theorist (and editor of the influential film journal *Cahiers Du Cinéma*) Bazin was concerned with the cinema's ability to record reality. He saw in cinema a means of capturing a record of events before the camera with minimum mediation.

Cut

The majority of shots are simply cut together directly. More unusual methods of joining shots include dissolves, fades and wipes which are sometimes used to indicate the end of a scene or to signal the start of a flashback sequence.

- To vary the point of view

  In *The Wrong Trousers* (Nick Park, 1993), for example when Gromit is spying on the Penguin, the audience is shown shots from both their points of view

- To build suspense and tension

  In the gunfight at the climax of *The Good, the Bad and the Ugly* (1966) Sergio Leone creates a dramatic effect by using a combination of music, tighter and tighter close-ups of the three characters and a shortening of shot length. In the Chicago station shoot-out in *The Untouchables* (Brian De Palma, 1987) a similar effect is also achieved

- Create places that do not exist in real life (creative geography) and imply emotions

  For example, many of the scenes in *Dead Men Don't Wear Plaid* (Carl Reiner, 1982), are constructed by intercutting new footage with shots from old films (see also: **the Kuleshov effect and creative geography**)

A FILM WITHOUT EDITING: *ROPE* (ALFRED HITCHCOCK, 1948)

Rope is shot in ten-minute takes, which are carefully joined to give the impression of continuous action.

- The film is set in one location

- It contains a limited number of characters (two, for much of the time)

- It has a plot time (1 hour and 30 minutes) that closely matches its screen time (1 hour and 20 minutes)

- It rarely allows the audience subjective shots of the characters

The above points illustrate that although it is possible to make a film without editing, it does put a limit on how the film extends into space and time. The lack of editing in *Rope* (which is about committing a 'perfect' murder) is, however, highly successful in building up tension over the entire length of the film as the audience wait for the two murderers to be uncovered.

THE KULESHOV EFFECT AND CREATIVE GEOGRAPHY[4]

In the early 1920s a young Soviet film-maker, Lev Kuleshov (1899–1970), carried out a number of experiments involving editing. He attempted to demonstrate that when two pieces of film are placed side by side the audience immediately draws the conclusion that the two shots must be directly related in some way. The

'Kuleshov effect' as it became known is outlined here by Vesvolod Pudovkin, another famous Soviet director:[5]

'Kuleshov and I made an interesting experiment. We took from some film or other several close-ups of the well known Russian actor Mosjukhin. We chose close-ups which were static and which did not express any feeling at all – quiet close-ups. We joined these close-ups, which were all similar, with other bits of film in three different combinations. In the first combination the close-up of Mosjukhin was immediately followed by a shot of a plate of soup standing on a table. It was obvious and certain that Mosjukhin was looking at this soup. In the second combination the face of Mosjukhin was joined to shots showing a coffin in which lay a dead woman. In the third the close-up was followed by a shot of a little girl playing with a funny toy bear. When we showed the three combinations to an audience which had not been let into the secret the result was terrific. The public raved about the acting of the artist. They pointed out the heavy pensiveness of his mood over the forgotten soup, were touched and moved by the deep sorrow with which he looked on the dead woman, and admired the light, happy smile with which he surveyed the girl at play. But we knew that in all three cases the face was exactly the same.'

Kuleshov carried out further experiments using editing in which he cut together separate shots of a walking man, a waiting woman, a gate, a staircase and a mansion. When the shots were combined the audience assumed that the different elements were present at the same location. Kuleshov had discovered the cinema's ability to link entirely unrelated material into coherent sequences. He termed the technique 'creative geography'.

Continuity: classical Hollywood editing

The act of breaking a film up into thousands of separate pieces should in principle disrupt the flow of the narrative. In practice, however, each individual edit is disguised using a variety of different methods and remains almost invisible to the audience. This system of editing was developed in Hollywood in the 1910s and 1920s and subsequently became the international standard of film-making. Classical Hollywood editing, as it became known, is based on a number of rules that ensure continuity between shots. It is centred on the idea that all cuts must be motivated in some way. When a character, for example, looks off screen left and the next shot is of what she or he was looking at, the motivation of the shot is established. The two key rules are given below.

- The 180 degree line rule
- The 30 degree line rule

The 180 degree line rule involves the drawing of an imaginary line between two characters in a scene (see Figures 4.7, (a) to (c)). Usually the characters are introduced using an establishing shot followed by a number of alternating shots that are closer to the characters. The rule dictates that the area of space behind the two characters cannot be entered by the camera, as it would reverse their position on screen – a character on the left in one shot, would suddenly appear on the right in the next. It might also introduce new background details that would confuse the audience.

The 30 degree line rules states that a change of angle within a scene should be more than 30 degrees, as changes of less tend to disconcert the audience.

These rules are supported by a number of conventions that help to disguise the edits and guide the audience's understanding of space. The conventions are as follows:

- Match on action

  This involves the practice of disguising edits by cutting on action. A closer shot of a character, for example, could be achieved by cutting half way

(a)

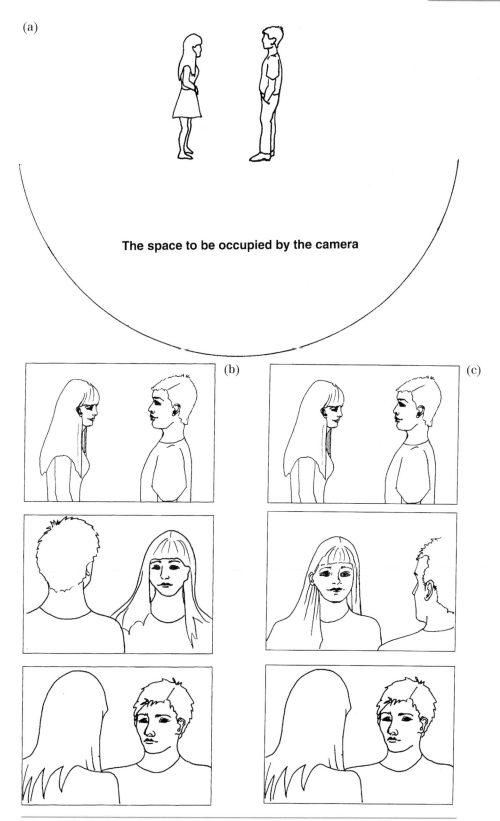

The space to be occupied by the camera

(b)

(c)

Figure 4.7 Breaks the 180 degree angle rule   Conforms to the 180 degree angle rule

through the action of picking up a drink. The next shot could then finish the action, thus making the edit less noticeable

- Eyeline match

  Shots of characters looking at something that cannot be seen by the audience, are usually followed by a cut to the object. The disruption caused by the cut is minimised, because the audience are already expecting to see the object in question

- Matching image cut

  Cuts between different locations, or different parts of the same location, are disguised by matching elements of the previous shot to the new one. For example, characters could be placed in similar positions or certain colours and shapes could be present in both scenes

Sound

The importance of sound to a film will vary like all the other elements involved in the construction of a film. Also the relative value of the voices, the sound effects and the music – the components of the soundtrack – will vary from film to film. Bill Varney, the sound re-recordist said of two of his films:

'... the soundtrack of *Out of Africa* was – I'd hate to use the word *ordinary*, but it was. It was a fairly simple soundtrack: Good dialogue, good sound effects, and beautiful music, all craftily interwoven into a marvellous soundtrack. But ... *Raiders [of the Lost Ark]* leaned heavily – very heavily – on its powerful and dynamic soundtrack to make it into the truly successful adventure film that it was'.[6]

Both *Raiders of the Lost Ark* and *Out of Africa* won Academy Awards for their soundtracks which demonstrates that a successful soundtrack must serve the purposes of the particular film in question.

Analysing a scene

There are endless possibilities in the creation of a soundtrack and different films create very different aural environments, even if the physical setting is very similar. *Raiders of the Lost Ark* (Steven Spielberg, 1981), for example, opens with a sequence in a South American jungle in which Indiana Jones and his band move through the forest. They are accompanied by the following effects:

- An orchestral score which features brass instruments
- A cacophony of sounds produced by unidentified birds, animals and insects
- The sound of their feet crossing the forest floor

These sounds are exaggerated and slightly comic and thereby create a feeling of apprehension about what is lurking in the undergrowth. The jungle in his film, however, is not the focus of interest but provides a setting for the action. In *The Emerald Forest* (John Boorman, 1985), on the other hand, the forest and its inhabitants are a central concern. This film features the Amazon rain forest and when Tommy, whose father is working on a dam being constructed nearby, enters the forest he finds himself in a magical world. The harsh, low pitched sounds of the construction work are replaced by the following sounds:

- The tinkling of bells which is supplemented by a long sustained note from a bass flute
- The soft, high-pitched cries of birds and the gentle animation of insect activity
- The feathery impact of Tommy's feet on the forest floor

This forest is the natural habitat of the ants carrying leaves and the Indians, the Invisible People, who are barely distinguishable from the undergrowth. The sounds suggest an unknown enchanted and self-contained world, which is under threat from outside.

By manipulating the soundtrack, the two films offer their own interpretation of the forest and successfully create the atmosphere, emotional orientation and expectations required by the narrative.

Diegetic and non-diegetic sound

Most films contain what are termed diegetic and non-diegetic sounds. Diegetic sounds belong to the world of the film and include, therefore, voices, sounds and any music that comes from a source within the setting, for example, from a radio or a juke box. It also includes a voice over commentary from one of the film's protagonists, for example, Sarah Connor in *Terminator 2* (James Cameron, 1991). Non-diegetic sound is sound not produced by anyone or anything within the world of the film – for example the explanatory voice-over (by Martin Scorsese) at the beginning of *The Grifters* (Stephen Frears, 1990). The most primary component of non-diegetic sound, however, is music that fulfils an important function in most films and audio-visual texts. As Bruce Kawin in *How Movies Work*[7] says, music has its 'its own history and power, and its use can constitute a leap into another language.' The importance of this other language for film-makers is illustrated by the music for the film *Paris, Texas* (1984). **Wim Wenders**, the director, had the music of Ry Cooder in mind all through the shooting of the film and he commented that 'when we finally recorded the music Ry was playing directly to the images. So it felt like he was re-shooting the whole picture and like his guitar was really strangely related to our camera, like it was a second time this whole film was shot.'[8] It is clear from this description that the music complemented and amplified the effect of the images.

Music can increase the power of a flow of images in three main ways.

- It can supply/add to the emotional dimensions of a film

  For example, The Doors' song *The End* which opens *Apocalypse Now* establishes a sombre and pensive mood in conjunction with images of conflagration and the whirring sound of helicopters. Music can also reveal, clarify or foretell emotions that are not openly expressed in the images. In *Someone to Watch Over Me* (Ridley Scott, 1987), for example, policeman Mike Keegan, has the job of protecting Claire Gregory who has witnessed a murder. When they make two excursions from her apartment, early on in the film, the use of sentimental ballads like *What More can I Ask* and *Someone to Watch Over Me* establish the possibility of a romantic attachment

Wim Wenders (1945–)

Born in Dusseldorf, West Germany, he made a number of short films as a film student, before making his first feature films in the early 1970s. His films reveal his love of rock music and Hollywood films, but also anxiety about the dominance of American culture.

■ It can supply/add to the factual dimension of a film

Young Soul Rebels (Isaac Julien, 1991), for example, hints at the time and place with its use of *Parliament* and *X-Ray Spex* before providing a more precise time in the sub-title: London, June 1977 – the Queen's Silver Jubilee. The use of the **tabla** in the credit sequence of *Bhaji on the Beach* (Gurinder Chada, 1994) suggests that the film will centre on Asian characters and not the white youth spray painting the wall next to a swastika

■ It can supply/add to the aesthetic dimensions of a film

Generally it can help to structure the film, because music will help the film to flow over the edits. If a lot of narrative information is being compressed into a sequence then music can prevent it from becoming too fragmented as in, for example the first phase of the barn raising sequence in *Witness* (Peter Weir, 1985) or the minibus journey to Blackpool in *Bhaji on the Beach*. Characters may also have their own musical motif or style of music such as in *The Good, the Bad and the Ugly* (Sergio Leone, 1966). Music may also forewarn the audience of events to come. For example, the expectation that something is about to happen in a suspense film is often cued by the build up of the music.

In conclusion an emotional, a factual and an aesthetic dimension can be identified, but in practice one piece of music may make a contribution to all three dimensions. For example, in *Paris, Texas* the use of Ry Cooder's slide guitar evokes loneliness, the openness of the desert landscape and it supplies a unifying element to the soundtrack.

Overall, film analysis probably underestimates the importance of the soundtrack. In the cinema or elsewhere an audience *looks at* the images, but actually *inhabits* the sound-world of the film especially in the contemporary cinema auditorium with its sophisticated multi-speaker sound system. The soundtrack establishes acoustically the contours of the film's world. It establishes the dimensions and depths of this world. It also **anchors** the meaning of the images in a scene and clarifies their narrative direction, which is why even silent cinema used music and sound effects.

Although the soundtrack usually supports the images, some films exploit a disparity between soundtrack and image. This possibility gives film-makers scope to create humour, irony and emotional discomfort. All three are created in *Reservoir Dogs* (Quentin Tarantino, 1994), for example, when Mr Blonde (Michael Madsen) tortures a policeman to the accompaniment of *Stuck in the Middle With You* by Stealers Wheel, although individual members of the audience might only experience the emotional discomfort.

Narrative

The primary function of most films is to tell a story. The *mise-en-scène*, cinematography, editing and sound are entirely subservient to the narrative, creating a seamless flow that centres the viewer within the story, which is narrated in an **unrestricted** way. Film narratives also share a number of other features that audiences have come to expect, including: the role of the **protagonist**, the problems faced by the protagonist and the resolution of these problems.

Tabla

The tabla, from north India, is a set of two drums. They are played with the fingertips and the palms of the seated drummer.

Anchors

Roland Barthes (1915–80) asserted that all images are open to interpretation and have many possible meanings. He called this phenomenon polysemy. If images are accompanied by a written text or sound, however, this makes the images less open to differing interpretations. He called this process anchorage.

The narratives of most films are centred on one or two main protagonists, whose lives are disrupted by an outside event, or the presence of an unfulfilled desire. The plot is then about removing the disruption, or fulfilling the desire. The rest of the events in the plot are usually initiated by the protagonists and have a clear **cause and effect** relationship to other events.

The role of the protagonist, however, is not an easy one. Films would be very short if disruptions were easily removed and desires achieved without effort. The overcoming of obstacles by the protagonists takes up the majority of **screen time**. It also allows the protagonist to prove him or herself worthy of the role to the audience. The protagonist usually encounters 'bad' characters, who work against his or her interests and who must be defeated (the western genre provides the clearest cut examples of good characters versus bad characters). Protagonists also frequently become involved in a romantic sub-plot that runs parallel to the main narrative. Finally, at the end of the film the protagonist will have resolved all the obstacles encountered and their lives will once again be stable and happy.

SCREEN TIME

Bordwell and Thompson[9] have drawn a distinction between the story time, the plot time and the screen time of films.

- Story time: the earliest event referred to in the film to the latest event

- Plot time: the earliest event that the audience see in the film to the latest event

- Screen time: the actual playing time of the film

In *Field of Dreams* (Phil Robinson, 1989) for example, the total story time stretches from 1896 to the film's present (1986). The plot of the film, however, only stretches back to 1972 (if the jump in time is included). Finally, the screen time is only 1 hour and 46 minutes.

There are other devices used in films that make the audience sympathise with and relate to the protagonist. One of these is varying the depth of knowledge that the audience is given about each character. The more important a character is to the narrative the more information the audience will be given. The use of stars in the key roles further helps the audience to (a) immediately identify the protagonist and (b) make use of their knowledge of the star to predict how the protagonist will act. In *Dances With Wolves* (Kevin Costner, 1990), for example, Costner's character (Lt John Dunbar) has similarities with his previous roles, such as Elliot Ness in *The Untouchables* or Ray Kinsella in *Field of Dreams*.

FIELD OF DREAMS (1989)

Director:	Phil Robinson
Producers:	Lawrence Gordon, Charles Gordon
Screenplay:	Phil Robinson
Length:	106 mins

Cast

Ray Kinsella:	Kevin Costner
Annie Kinsella:	Amy Madigan
Shoeless Joe Jackson:	Ray Liotta
Mark:	Timothy Busfield
Terence Mann:	James Earl Jones
Dr 'Moonlight' Graham:	Burt Lancaster
Archie Graham:	Frank Whaley
John Kinsella:	Dwier Brown

'... The one constant through all the years ... has been baseball. America has rolled by like an army of steamrollers, its been erased like a blackboard, rebuilt and erased again, but baseball has marked the time. This field, this game, is part of our past ... It reminds us of all that was once good, and it could be again.'

Extract from Terence Mann's speech from near the end of the film

Field of Dreams is about Ray Kinsella, an Iowa farmer, who, guided by a mysterious voice, ploughs up his corn and builds a baseball field. The field has supernatural properties and is soon populated by long dead baseball stars. Some of these players (including the famous Shoeless Joe Jackson) had been banned from professional baseball for life after throwing the 1919 World Series. The field has the power to fulfil the desires of all the characters in the film as well as offering solutions to the problems faced by society in general. These solutions involve drawing upon the values of the past, symbolised by baseball, to influence the present. *Field of Dreams* also provides a near perfect example of a mainstream narrative. The film is tightly structured around a number of enigmas which are only resolved at the end.

The film starts with a montage sequence of photographs and film footage, which establish Ray and Annie Kinsella as protagonists and give the audience information about their background. The sequence is held together by Ray's voice-over, that gives the impression that he is confiding in the audience. The scene establishes the family as stable and happy, but also hints at Ray's need for self-fulfilment when he states 'Before I heard the voice I'd never done a crazy thing in my life.' The statement immediately raises the interest of the audience, who wants to know: what voice? And what crazy thing? The film begins to provide answers by starting the flashback sequence that comprises the rest of the film.

The flashback begins with both Ray and the audience hearing the voice in the corn saying: 'Build it, and he will come.' It is significant that the audience can hear the voice, but Annie and her daughter can not. This creates a bond between Ray and the audience, allowing them to understand his motivation to build the baseball field. The audience now have three further questions.

■ What is the voice asking Ray to build?

■ To whom does the voice belong?

■ Who is *he*?

It is quickly revealed to Ray and the audience that 'it' is a baseball field and 'he' refers to Shoeless Joe Jackson. After some deliberation and much to the amusement of his neighbours, Ray starts ploughing up his corn (note the way that time is compressed in this scene). The opening sequences establish that Ray, as protagonist, is responsible for making events happen. The audience is provided with clear motivation for his actions, which are logically connected to his previous actions. Ray, for example, does not just build the baseball pitch because of the voice, but because he feels the need to do something impulsive and illogical.

The film, however, raises further questions through a second message: 'Ease his pain' which initiates Ray's journey to Boston in search of the writer Terence Mann. The audience is led to believe that it is Mann's pain that is being referred to, but it is only at the end of the film that this is shown not to be the case. The withholding of information throughout the film in this way keeps the audience interested in the plot. The audience is also, however, given information not possessed by the other characters. When Ray phones Annie from Minnesota, for example, the audience sees Mark and his partners discussing buying the farm, because the mortgage payments have not been paid. Ray, meanwhile, remains unaware of the situation. This has the effect of making the audience side with Ray, as well as starting a countdown towards an inevitable showdown between Ray and Mark. The audience, however, are sometimes given vital plot information without fully realising its significance. On the journey back to Iowa, for example, Ray tells Terence Mann how his father died before they could reconcile their differences or meet his wife and grand-daughter. It is only at the end of the film when Ray meets his father again that its importance is understood.

The ending of the film offers almost perfect resolution in which all questions are answered and the desires of the characters have been fulfilled.

- Ray Kinsella is reconciled with his father (and gets the chance to play catch with him) and is also fulfilled through the activities associated with building the field and the search for Terence Mann and Doc. Graham. The financial future of the farm is also guaranteed

- Terence Mann is reinvigorated and his disillusionment with life evaporates. He now feels the need to write once again

- Shoeless Joe Jackson is able to play baseball again with professional players

- John Kinsella is reconciled with his son and gets to meet his son's wife and granddaughter

- Mark is finally able to see that the field has value beyond its land value. Ironically, the field now has a commercial value beyond his wildest expectations

- Dr 'Moonlight' Graham has his chance to bat in a big league game, but also the opportunity of using his skills as a doctor

The film also offers a solution to the problems of America, as well as helping to overcome the fear of death by proving the existence of an after-life.

Models of narrative

A number of models have been proposed that attempt to explain how narratives work. Most of these models were devised with reference to folk tales and myths and have been subsequently applied to films. Despite each model taking a different analytical approach, they all suggest that narratives are structurally similar.

TRISTAN TODOROV (1939–   ) AND VLADIMIR PROPP (1895–1970)

Todorov, a Bulgarian literary theorist, suggests that most narratives start with a state of equilibrium in which life is 'normal' and protagonists happy.[10] This state of normality is disrupted by an outside force, which has to be fought against in order to return to a state of equilibrium. The model can easily be applied to a wide range of films.

Propp, a Russian critic and literary theorist, analysed 100 Russian fairy tales in the 1920s. He proposed in *The Morphology of the Folk Tale*[11] that it was possible to classify the characters and their actions into clearly defined roles and functions (8 character roles and 31 narrative functions). In other words Darth Vader and The Joker would not be seen as having individual characteristics, but both having the role of 'villain'. Films such as *Star Wars* (George Lucas, 1977) fit Propp's model precisely, but a significant number of more recent films such as *Pulp Fiction* (Quentin Tarantino, 1994) and *The Usual Suspects* (Bryan Singer, 1996) do not. The model is useful, however, as it highlights the similarities between seemingly quite different stories.

The Morphology of the Folk Tale

Published in 1928 in Russia, was not translated into English until 1958.

Vladimir Propp's character roles

- The hero (seeks something)
- The villain (opposes the hero)
- The donor (helps the hero by providing a magic object)
- The dispatcher (sends the hero on his way)
- The false hero (falsely assuming the role of hero)
- The helper (gives support to the hero)
- The princess (the reward for the hero, but also needs to be protected from the villain)
- Her father

Propp's narrative functions[12]

Narratives do not have to include all the functions, but they should be in the order listed.

Preparation

- A member of a family leaves home
- A prohibition or rule is imposed on the hero
- This prohibition or rule is broken
- The villain makes an attempt at reconnaissance
- The villain learns something about his victim
- The villain tries to deceive the victim to get possession of him or his belongings
- The victim unknowingly helps the villain by being deceived or influenced by the villain

Complication

- The villain harms a member of the family
- A member of the family lacks or desires something
- This lack or misfortune is made known; the hero is given a request or command, and he goes or is sent on a mission or quest
- The seeker (often the hero) plans action against the villain

Transference

- The hero leaves home
- The hero is tested, attacked, interrogated, and, as a result, receives either a magical agent or a helper
- The hero reacts to the actions of the future donor
- The hero uses the magical agent
- The hero is transferred to the general location of the object of his mission or quest

Struggle

- The hero and villain join in direct combat
- The hero is branded
- The villain is defeated

▩ The initial misfortune or lack is set right

Return

▩ The hero returns

▩ The hero is pursued

▩ The hero is rescued from pursuit

▩ The hero arrives home or elsewhere and is not recognised

▩ A false hero makes false claims

▩ A difficult task is set for the hero

▩ The task is accomplished

Recognition

▩ The hero is recognised

▩ The false hero/villain is exposed

▩ The false hero is transformed

▩ The villain is punished

▩ The hero is married and crowned.

CLAUDE LEVI-STRAUSS (1908–   )

Whereas Propp was interested in the chronological flow of the story, another approach influenced by Levi-Strauss (a French anthropologist) was to examine how stories unconsciously reflect the values, beliefs and myths of a culture. These are usually expressed in the form of oppositions in the text. Umberto Eco,[13] for example, uncovered 14 oppositions from a group of Bond novels (including *Goldfinger*):

Bond ↔ M
Bond ↔ Villain
Villain ↔ Woman
Woman ↔ Bond
Free World ↔ Soviet Union
Great Britain ↔ Non-Anglo-Saxon Countries
Duty ↔ Sacrifice
Cupidity ↔ Ideals
Love ↔ Death
Chance ↔ Planning
Luxury ↔ Discomfort
Excess ↔ Moderation
Perversion ↔ Innocence
Loyalty ↔ Disloyalty

The oppositions are clearly apparent in the film *Goldfinger*; for example the plot clearly places western capitalism against communism and Bond against Goldfinger.

Alternative Narrative: Art Cinema

Not all films have the same approach to film form and narrative as described above. Many films from around the world and especially from Europe are said to belong to **art cinema** rather than mainstream cinema.

ART CINEMA AS AN INSTITUTION

Art cinema attracts an international, educated audience. The films are screened in special art-house cinemas and many productions are financed by government subsidy and/or television involvement. This cinema is further supported by film festivals, film critics, journals and publishing ventures such as the British Film Institute's Film Classics series. An all-embracing definition would include the following:

- Films by directors with a global reputation for contributing to cinema as an art (*The Seventh Seal*, Ingmar Bergman, Sweden 1956)

- Films from around the world that have a distinctive national character (*Blood Wedding*, Carlos Saura, Spain, 1981)

- Films that explore social and/or political issues (*A Short Film about Killing*, Krzysztof Kieslowski, Poland, 1988)

- Films that attract public interest, controversy and debate (*Last Tango in Paris* Bernardo Bertolucci, France/Italy/USA, 1973)

- Films that are recognised as landmarks in cinema history (*Citizen Kane,* Orson Welles, USA, 1941)

- Experimental or avant-garde films (*Un Chien Andalou,* Luis Buñuel and Salvador Dali, France, 1928)

David Bordwell has identified a distinctive form of narration in art cinema. He emphasises the ways in which art cinema diverges from classical Hollywood narrative and narration to achieve much more ambiguity than is normally found in mainstream cinema.

- The main protagonist does not have clear-cut goals or discernible motives.
- There is not always a clear cause and effect relationship between events
- The operation of chance is often important
- Screen time is often used without driving the narrative forward
- There is no guarantee that all the loose ends of the narrative will be tied up

Films such as *Blow Up* (Michelangelo Antonioni, UK, 1966), *Alice in the Cities* Wim Wenders, Germany, 1973), and *Vagabond* (Agnès Varda, France, 1985) exemplify some or all of these features.

These characteristics, along with the frequent use of real locations and non-professional performers have led to the claim that art cinema is more true to life. This is offset, however, by the emphasis on the artistry of the director. As a result the realism of art cinema has to be weighed against the importance of the individual director's interpretation of reality.

Since the late 1960's, however, the differences between art cinema and mainstream cinema have become less distinct. North American film-makers, for example, have drawn on world cinema and film movements while independent film-makers like Hal Hartley, produce films that are closer to art cinema than mainstream cinema in terms of their editing, cinematography and narrative pace.

READING TEXTS: TELEVISION

It can be useful to use the ideas about *mise-en-scène* and how the camera, editing and sound to analyse the output of television. Films themselves form an important part of television schedules and the BBC, Channel Four and, to a lesser extent, ITV stations produce films; some of which receive theatrical screenings. Also much contemporary television drama tends to be more like cinema than theatre.

It is also possible, to an extent, to recreate the viewing conditions of the cinema in a domestic setting especially when viewing an individual item like a feature film. This has been made more possible by the introduction of the video cassette recorder and the increasing numbers of video cassettes to play on them, as well as the development of nicam digital stereo sound and wide-screen television. Also, improvements in sound and image are set to continue with the introduction of digital television transmissions and high-definition television sets that will give enhanced picture resolution.

Some significant differences between film and television remain, however, even given the fact that the majority of households do not possess the more advanced technology.

- The sets of television programmes are sparser and lack the detail of a film set

  As a result there is less reliance on *mise-en-scène* and more reliance on the soundtrack even though it is less complex than in the cinema. What people say in television is generally more important and this concentration on dialogue rather than action means that many programmes can be easily followed just by listening to the soundtrack. This makes it possible to release a TV series such as *Blackadder* on *audio* tape. This emphasis on sound is complemented by the greater use of close shots in the range of television productions

- There are a range of **formats** in television

  For example, there are situation comedies in which the characters do not develop, but in each episode they confront a different situation. By contrast, serials and soap operas have characters and plots which develop over a number of episodes, but like situation comedies have no conclusion. Other programmes like mini-series or serialised novels do have closed endings, like films, but are not typically viewed in one sitting like a film.

- Television contains a wide range of genres

  Some of these genres like crime dramas, medical dramas and documentaries are related to film genres. But others, like music programmes, talk shows, game shows, news and sports programmes, have no equivalent in the contemporary cinema.

- Narrative is important in many television genres (including news and documentaries), but television is more likely to address its audience directly than cinema. Television is therefore able to achieve a greater feeling of psychological intimacy than cinema in which the narration is impersonal and does not usually seek to create a community of viewers.

Format

Refers to the way a programme or series is organised. For example, in one series each episode will be complete whereas in another there will be developments in the plot.[14]

The range of material on broadcast television makes generalisation very difficult except to say that the form of any particular programme becomes regularised in terms of its style and content. As John Ellis puts it:

'Broadcast TV's formidable output of material contains many different forms of:

- **Organisation of voice and image**
- **Gesture and writing**
- **Editing and visual effects**
- **Image superimposition and compositing**
- **On-screen time and space**
- **Music and sound effect**
- **Emotional effect and physical presence**
- **Frame edge and image detail**
- **The accidental and the calculated**
- **Broadcast time and duration'**[15]

Yet as Ellis points out, audiences can instantly recognise types of programmes on encountering them. Television programmes do not pose the same problems of interpretation that some films do. Audiences are adept at identifying and enjoying the way any particular programme conforms to or departs from the established form. For example, *This Life* had many of the features of a soap but departed from a soap in terms of its explicit sexual content; its series structure and its visual style of mobile camerawork, tight framing and fast editing which contributed to the egotistical intensity of the characters.

READING TEXTS: MUSIC VIDEO

One of the forms that contribute to the variety of contemporary television is the music video. They can be seen and heard in a number of formats.

- As items in a programme which is not dedicated to music, for example *The Big Breakfast* on Channel Four
- As items in a music programme which also features performers in the studio, for example *Top of the Pops* on BBC1
- As items in a programme given over to videos on a channel with a mixed service, for example *The Chart Show* on ITV
- As items in a programme on a channel specialising in music, for example **MTV**

Music videos are also available for hire or purchase with one, some, or all of the following features:

- A compilation of videos by one or a number of artists. Typically these would have been broadcast when the recordings were originally released
- Concert footage
- Documentary footage
- Interview material

MUSIC TELEVISION (MTV)

MTV began as a 24 hour cable television channel on 1 August 1981, targeting an audience of 12- to 34-year-olds. It boosted the production of music videos especially when their potential selling power became apparent. This realisation tends to favour the well-established stars that are more attractive to advertisers who provide most of MTV's income. Other income comes from sponsorship and since 1984 the broadcast of the videos themselves.

At first MTV lost money, but it quickly became a global phenomenon: MTV Europe and MTV Australia were launched in 1987; MTV Brazil in 1990; MTV Asia in 1991. By 1991 MTV was according to Corinna Sturmer available in 201 million households across 77 countries in five continents.[16] It was initially a joint venture by Warner Brothers and American Express, but was subsequently acquired by Viacom in 1985.

A music video's reason for being is the release of a record. Its main function is to act as an advertisement for this record. It also serves to contribute to the image of an artist or band and to maintain the visibility of performers in the absence of personal appearances. As an advertisement, however, it is unusual in that it not only promises certain satisfactions on the purchase of a commodity but also makes it possible to enjoy that commodity without buying it and with the added bonus of the accompanying images. It may be, however, that the images are not so much a bonus as a sign of a return to the importance of vision in the enjoyment of music.

Analysing music video

The music video exists to sell a recording and it usually involves some kind of appearance or performance by the recording artist(s). Often the performers directly address the camera (and the absent audience) or are seen in concert with a live audience, even if this is an event set up for the video. These features underline the point that the music is more important than the images and therefore it could be argued that the rules of feature film making are irrelevant to the analysis of music video. On the other hand it is useful to ask how the music is related to the images and to examine the style of a music video in terms of its *mise-en-scène*, editing and use of the camera. Ideas from **semiology** can also provide a useful tool for analysis.

SEMIOLOGY

The starting point for semiology is that we communicate using a wide range of signs including spoken and written language, photographs, television programmes and films. It is clear that any language is a highly organised form of communication. There are rules or codes which may be absorbed in daily activity and/or learned in an educational setting. In the case of a film or television programme words and images are also organised to communicate meanings and therefore operate according to codes even though they may not be as fixed as the rules of grammar.

Ferdinand de Saussure (1857–1913), a Swiss academic, is seen as the founder of modern linguistics. He envisaged a science of signs, semiology, based on his analysis of language. Saussure saw a sign as being composed of two inseparable elements, the signifier and the signified. The signifier is the physical form of the sign, for example, words either spoken or on a page. The signified is what is expressed by the sounds or image. He stressed that the relationship between the signifier and the signified is arbitrary. For example, the word aeroplane bears no relationship to a machine which flies but it is accepted that the group of letters refers to that object. Saussure's ideas can be applied to audio-visual texts. In such texts a number of signifiers are in play simultaneously. A music video, for example, will make use of the following:

- Visual signifiers such as camera movement and editing – these signifiers not only reveal to the audience what has been assembled before the camera but also create meanings themselves

- Musical signifiers such as the type of instrumentation, the rhythm and the nature of the lyrics

- Cultural signifiers such as hairstyles, gestures, demeanour and dress

A group of signifiers may add up to the signified of a 'heavy metal' video or 'rap' video. The audience will recognise the codes that are employed and respond according to taste.

C.S. Peirce (1839–1934), a North American philosopher, used the term semiotics to define his study of signs. He distinguished between the three following signs.

- An iconic sign in which there is a visual connection between the sign and what it represents – there is a physical resemblance between a photograph of Blackpool Tower and the tower itself, for example

- An indexical sign in which there is a causal connection between the sign and what it represents – for example sweat on a person's brow indicates heat or perhaps fever while echoey sounds indicate the physical dimensions of a place

- A symbolic sign in which there is a conventional connection between the sign and what it represents – for example words, objects and gestures have meanings in a culture although the connection is arbitrary (see Saussure).

In a particular image these three types of sign or ways of making meaning can be seen as three aspects of the same image. For example, in a video for a song about loss of love a person sitting on the floor hunched up against the wall will look to be in a state of despair (iconic sign); be assuming a posture that the audience works out to be a result of despair (indexical sign); be interpreted to be assuming a posture that conventionally expresses despair (symbolic sign).

Mise-en-scène and meaning

Meanings are created in music videos, as in films, by the people, objects and settings that are recorded by the camera. The French semiologist **Roland Barthes** used the terms denotation and connotation to analyse images and these can be applied to music videos as well as other audio-visual texts. When the elements in the *mise-en-scène* are filmed an act of denotation takes place. This means that a number of elements are assembled, recorded and can be explored by the audience visually. The act of denotation is, however, accompanied inevitably by an act of connotation. This is because all images and constituents of images carry associations which 'impregnate the whole of the image.'[17] Barthes also referred to the way in which denotations draw on myths, which are sets of ideas and images current in a society, that seem to be unquestionable and natural. For example, in the video for *Heal the World* by Michael Jackson shots of children are assembled (denotation); children are represented as innocent (connotation) and children are the bearers of a conflict free future (myth). The mythical aspect of the video is made clearer when it is placed alongside news footage of Albanian children armed with rifles in 1997, for example.

Roland Barthes (1915–80)

A French writer who continues to have a great influence on the study of the ways meanings are produced in a wide range of texts and the relationship between the texts and power in society. Two of his key books are *Mythologies* published in 1972 and *Image Music Text* published in 1977.

Cinematography and editing

An important aspect of music videos is their use of the camera: its positions, movements, framing of the images and use of filmstock and lenses. Generally it is subject to much more manipulation than would be found in a feature film and the same applies to the linking and ordering of images. Generally the editing style is characterised by rapid cutting and a constant breaking of continuity in terms of space and time.

Visual style and the soundtrack

The whole emphasis in the visual style of a music video is on movement. A music video is therefore potentially very fragmented for the following reasons.

- The cinematography and editing do not tend to have a predominantly narrative purpose as in a feature film
- The images are often not related to the lyrical content of the song
- Some videos also contain film clips – for example the video of *Big Gun* by AC/DC incorporates clips from *The Last Action Hero* but in this case the band are even joined on stage in the video by Arnold Schwarzenegger, the star of the film in which the song is featured

A number of features of music videos, however, give them cohesion.

- The music is short and has a structure involving repetition and the use of familiar musical elements
- The presence of the artists and a concentration on their performance
- The repeated plays of a current recording facilitate the familiarity of the audience
- The cultural knowledge of the audience will ensure knowledge of the form

of music videos and also a wide range of well-known and even esoteric references

■ The enjoyment of movement which is a visual complement to the energy of the music

READING TEXTS: RADIO

On the face of it, examining the way we analyse radio should be easy. After all what is there to analyse? There are no images[18] and there is no written text; there is only sound to create images. Students often make the mistake of thinking that this makes radio a boring medium in which to work because they imagine the creative possibilities must be limited but, when students begin recording and mixing radio programmes, they are usually pleasantly surprised at the medium's versatility. After all, with one note from a steel drum and the chirrup of a cicada the listener can be conveyed to a Caribbean island; it is difficult for students to create similarly exotic backdrops quite so easily on video. In fact, there is no place as exotic or fantastic as the imagination and the function of good radio is to stimulate that imagination aurally.

Formats

In the following list, some attempt has been made to identify the main formats used on the radio in Britain today. The formats below are divided between music and talk based radio – and indeed some stations do have dedicated talk or music output – but many stations move between these formats at different times of the day. Nevertheless, for the most part, radio stations predominantly broadcast music: This is for two reasons; one is that talk based radio is expensive and the other is that music is ideally suited to the medium.

Music based radio

■ DJ plus music
For a long time, radio has been dominated by this format but gradually over the years the disc jockeys have turned into presenters who are constantly endeavouring to involve the listener by using audience participation aspects such as quizzes, phone ins, requests, etc.

■ Posse plus music
Banter between DJs at programme junction points and between DJs and newsreaders or traffic reporters was soon identified as adding to radio's appeal. Posse or group presentation became a format in itself and the listener's position began to swing between being directly addressed by a presenter to listening in on an overheard 'posse' conversation

Talk based radio

- Magazine format

  This is usually a presenter/presenters plus features, interviews, discussions, etc. An easily identifiable example of this is the drive time slot on most local radio stations. Mornings and evenings tend to be the times when people are listening in the car on the way home from work and so the items within slots such as these tend to be short and easily dropped into or out of.

No discussion of talk based radio can avoid some mention of:

- BBC Radio Four

  The only station to use fiction and documentary genres in much the same way as TV. It moves between light entertainment, information and high culture with relative ease. Among other things, Radio Four offers plays, soap opera, news, documentaries, arts programmes and quizzes

No matter whether the radio format is talk based or music based, the medium is still delivering messages to the audience and these messages have to be put together using certain codes and conventions.

The construction of an aural narrative

The radio narrative is constructed using four key components.

- Words
- Sounds
- Music
- Technical/generic convention

In both radio fiction and factual programmes, these key components are the only tools that can be used to tell the story, create character, paint the backdrop and build emotion.

Words

Radio drama has a great deal in common with Shakespearean drama in the respect that the scene often has to be set by words alone. The time of day, fog, cold, description of location, people's clothing, whom someone is looking at – if these things are important they must either be set up by a narrator or they must be presented naturally within the dialogue. Even in a factual piece, it might also be necessary to 'set the scene' a little. For instance, a reporter may begin a news item with: 'As I look down on the city, I can see the scene of the accident . . .' Words create meaning in two ways: *what* is said say and *how* it is said.

What is said – language

- Register and address

  People adopt different speech registers in different situations. Some are more formal than others. Newsreaders used to use a very formal address and register. On Radio One, the news now feels like a message passed on

Two way
A discussion between the bulletin reader and a reporter on the spot.

Voice piece
An item from a reporter unpunctuated by actuality.

by your mate next door. The bulletin reader and the reporters are on first name terms and much is made of **two way** reports which amount to conversations between the bulletin reader and the reporter instead of just the direct address of the **voice piece**

- Jargon

  Everyone has heard those nightmare interviews where someone starts talking in incomprehensible jargon. Scientists, doctors, the legal profession and media studies lecturers are particularly prone to this. This could exclude some sections of the population from understanding the message

- Idiom and dialect

  Dialect should not be confused with accent as it refers to those words which belong to groups from a particular region, social group, etc. Obviously, dialect words are not necessarily understood by all; together with accent, dialect can be a strong tool in the representation of character.

How it is said – paralanguage

Paralanguage or non-verbal vocal communication is hugely important within the radio narrative. Paralanguage encompasses all those aspects of speech that surround language; it excludes the actual meaning but it might include some of the following:

- Speed and pace

  How quickly someone speaks or the feeling of immediacy that is conveyed will affect the way the message is mediated. Reading speed varies according to the programme and the target listener; 160 to 180 words per minute is normal for a newscast. It takes about 3 to 4 seconds to speak 10 to 12 words. One side of double spaced A4 (about 300 words) takes about one and a half minutes to deliver

- Pauses and hesitation

  Long pauses, no pauses, stutters, 'ums' and 'ahs' will change the nature of the address

- Volume, pitch and cadence

  Imagine the difference between a loud deep voice and a quiet high pitched voice and the emotions they convey. Cadence is the way that a voice moves up and down; this can make someone sound cynical or quizzical

- Accent

  This immediately tells us something about the cultural background of the speaker and may well suggest a stereotype, eg the country yokel or the upper class twit

Sound effects and music

Sounds are enormously important in setting the scene but they work on the audience's imagination in a different fashion than in the visual media; in those media, sounds usually accompany images as part of a whole representation. For instance, a dog will be seen and heard barking on TV but on radio the dog's presence will be *indicated* purely by the sound of the bark. Branston and Stafford point out this difference in function: '. . . the sound image is more indexical than iconic, an index being a sign that works by establishing a relationship between itself and reality rather than simply offering a resemblance.'[19] Obviously, the indicative function of sound on radio allows more scope for the imagination. The dog indicated by the bark on radio can be as placid or as ferocious as fantasy allows.

However, sound and music on radio do share two functions with the visual media.

- They are often used metaphorically either to reveal a character's emotions or to replace action in the storyline. For instance, the sound of a storm might be used to reveal a character's inner turmoil or a compelling love song might be used as 'shorthand' to present a burgeoning relationship and in doing so will replace pages of dialogue
- Sounds and music are also used to create emotions. A creaky door and eerie music produce suspense in a radio thriller and in a news bulletin galvanising music creates the idea of immediacy and authority

Music is also used purely as a link between programmes and as an entertainment in itself.

Generic conventions

The generic conventions will also effect the radio narrative although the fiction genres are not used on most radio stations. The factual and fiction generic conventions of radio and TV are very similar. The news conventions certainly have a great deal in common and items within a radio news bulletin such as a two-way, **wrap, clip,** voice piece are identical to those on TV.

Technical conventions

Technical conventions are immensely important in the production of meaning and these are dominated by the following processes:

- Recording can either be undertaken in a studio, on a portable MD, DAT, cassette or reel-to-reel recorder. The distance from the microphone will indicate whether a person is close to, or far away from, the action. The location of the recording will also make the sound vary. For instance, a room could have an echo or it could be acoustically dead
- The way the sounds are mixed together can also affect meaning
- Editing can be executed on reel-to-reel or it can now be undertaken digitally using MD, DAT or computer editing. Radio editing can be almost unnoticeable and consequently enables greater unseen manipulation – particularly manipulation of 'actuality'

Clip
An item which moves straight from the bulletin reader to a clip of actuality. The actuality (see Chapter 7) could be a soundbite from a famous person or a vox pop, etc.

Wrap
A news item that moves from the bulletin reader to the reporter to a clip of actuality and then back to the reporter.

FURTHER WORK

Mise-en-scène

Show how the concept of *mise-en-scène* can be used in the process of analysing the meaning of a film. Make reference to at least one film or scene in some detail.

Cinematography

Practical work in groups of four or five.

Produce two short films (at least 12 to 14 shots each) centred on either:

- A romantic encounter
- A threatening encounter

that are identical in content, but shot in completely different ways. You may wish to use sound/dialogue, but a silent film can be equally effective. You must produce a full storyboard of your sequence before you start.

Areas to consider: Camera placement, high/low angles, camera movement.

Editing

Practical work in groups of four or five.

In no more than 16 shots, shoot a simple action that obeys the rules of classical Hollywood continuity editing. For example:

- Meeting a friend
- Following a suspect (private-eye style)
- Stealing a car (only pretend)

You must fully storyboard your short film before starting shooting.

Use the tripod at all times as Hollywood films rarely contain hand-held camera shots.

Do television genres employ the same sort of editing techniques as feature films?

Sound

Study the use of sound in a film and comment on how it contributes to meaning.

Compare and contrast a film with a specially composed score with one that uses pre-existing recordings.

Narrative

Questions that could be asked of any narrative film:

- Examine the relationship between plot and story
- How does the film allow the audience to build up story information?
- Identify the key event which sets the plot in motion
- To what extent does the film withhold causes and/or effects?
- How are the events ordered in the film in relation to their occurrence in the story?
- How important is time in the film?
- To what extent is the space of the story greater than the plot?
- How closed or open is the ending of the film?

- To what extent is the narration of the film restricted or unrestricted?
- To what extent is the narration of the film objective or subjective?

What are the principal expectations about story telling which audiences bring to mainstream narrative films?

To what extent would you agree that all narrative films conform to the same basic narrative patterns?

FURTHER READING

Bordwell, David, *Narration in the Fiction Film*, Routledge, 1988.
Bordwell, David and Thompson, Kristen, *Film Art: An Introduction* (4th edition), McGraw Hill, 1993.
Crisell, Andrew, *Understanding Radio*, Methuen, 1986
Giannetti, Louis, *Understanding Movies* (7th edition), Prentice Hall, 1996.
Izod, John, *Reading the Screen*, York Press, 1989.
Kawin, Bruce F., *How Movies Work*, Macmillan Publishing Company, 1987.
Monaco, James, *How to Read a Film*, New York: Oxford University Press, 1981.
Nelmes, Jill, (ed.), *An Introduction to Film Studies*, Routledge, 1996.
Turner, Graeme, *Film as Social Practice* (2nd edition), Routledge, 1993.

FURTHER VIEWING

Mise-en-scène
The Cook, the Thief, his Wife and her Lover (Peter Greenaway, 1989)
Orlando (Sally Potter, 1993)
Seven (David Fincher, 1995)
Trainspotting (Danny Boyle, 1996)

Cinematography
Apocalypse Now (Francis Coppola, 1979)
Born on the Fourth of July (Oliver Stone, 1989)
JFK (Oliver Stone, 1991)
The Double Life of Veronique (Krzysztof Kieslowski, 1991)

Editing
A Hard Day's Night (Richard Lester, 1964)
Raging Bull (Martin Scorsese, 1980)
The Hand that Rocks the Cradle (Curtis Hanson, 1992)
La Haine (Mathieu Kassovitz, 1995)

Sound
The Conversation (Francis Coppola, 1974)
Blow Out (Brian De Palma, 1981)
The Sacrifice (Andrei Tarkovsky, 1986)
Jurassic Park (Steven Spielberg, 1993)

Narrative
Rebel Without a Cause (Nicholas Ray, 1955)
Die Hard 2 (Renny Harlin, 1990)
Unforgiven (Clint Eastwood, 1992)
Reservoir Dogs (Quentin Tarantino, 1992)

Alternatives

Slacker (Richard Linklater, 1991)
Until the End of the World (Wim Wenders, 1991)
The Double Life of Veronique (Krzystof Kieslowski, 1991)
Gas, Food, Lodging (Alison Anders, 1992)
Mystery Train (Jim Jarmusch, 1993)

Notes

[1] 'Screen Acting and the Commutation Test', in Christine Gledhill, *Stardom: Industry of Desire*, Routledge, 1991.

[2] A useful comparison can be made between *Heat* and Michael Mann's earlier television film, *LA Takedown*, based on the same script. The actors playing the key roles in *LA Takedown* don't have the presence of Pacino and De Niro and consequently the audience is not convinced of the motivation for their actions. It would also be easy to argue, however, that the power of *Heat* derives from its powerful *mise-en-scène*, cinematography and editing which enables Mann to communicate to the audience the character and influence of the city.

[3] An interview with Darius Khondji, the cinematographer of *Seven* in *Sight and Sound* April 1996 (Vol. 6, Issue 4) provides insight into the 'colour noir' approach.

[4] Adapted from Mark Joyce, 'The Soviet montage cinema of the 1920s' in Jill Nelmes, (ed.), *An Introduction to Film Studies*, Routledge, 1996, p335.

[5] In a lecture given at the London Film Society in February 1929. From Vsevolod Pudovkin, 'Types Instead of Actors', in his *Film Technique and Film Acting*, London, Gollancz, 1929.

[6] *Movie Makers at Work: Interviews by David Chell*, Redmond: Microsoft Press, 1987, p109.

[7] New York: MacMillan, 1987, p449.

[8] *Motion and Emotion*, Paul Joyce, 1989, a television documentary for Channel Four about Wim Wenders.

[9] *Film Art: An Introduction* (Fourth Edition), McGraw-Hill, 1993.

[10] *The Poetics of Prose*, Blackwell, 1977

[11] University of Texas Press, 1975.

[12] As summarised by John Fiske in *TV Culture*, Methuen, 1987.

[13] *The Role of the Reader: Explorations in the Semiotics of Texts*, Hutchinson, 1981.

[14] James Monaco, *How to Read a Film*, Oxford University Press, 1981, p398.

[15] Adapted from *Visible Fictions*, Routledge, 1992, p273.

[16] 'MTV's Europe: An Imaginary Continent?' in Tony Dowmunt, (ed.), *Channels of Resistance: Global Television and Local Empowerment*, BFI, 1993, p51.

[17] *Image, Music, Text*, Fontana Press, 1987, p42.

[18] At the moment of writing, new technology has been developed which will allow images to be broadcast with digital radio. This will not be an alternative to TV with moving pictures but pictures and supporting text, which will require a special receiver.

[19] Gill Branston and Roy Stafford, *The Media Student's Book*, Routledge, 1996, p160

2

INTRODUCTION

Part Two examines the mass media as industries. The following trends can be identified.

- A small number of large companies tend to dominate the market for any particular type of media product such as a film or a musical recording
- These companies tend to be a part of larger groupings involved in the production of a wide range of different goods
- These larger groupings or conglomerates have increasingly come to specialise in media and entertainment products
- The media conglomerates operate on a world-wide scale
- The media groups are always subject to political and legal regulation in the countries in which they operate
- The media operate in a context of continual technological change

CHAPTER **5** # British Broadcasting

(**CONTENTS OF THIS CHAPTER**)

- **Radio broadcasting in Britain**

- **Television broadcasting in Britain**

- **British broadcasting in the 1990s**

- **Case study: Local media organisation: KFM Hits and Memories (96.2 MHz, 101.6 MHz)**

'Broadcasting is the transmission of radio and television programmes intended for general public reception, as distinguished from private signals directed to specific receivers. In its most common form broadcasting may be described as the systematic dissemination of entertainment, information, education programming, and other features for simultaneous reception by a scattered audience, individually or in groups, with appropriate receiving apparatus.[1]

From: *The New Encyclopaedia Britannica*

RADIO BROADCASTING IN BRITAIN

The history of British broadcasting can be traced back to 14 November 1922 when the British Broadcasting Company, licensed by the Post Office, first began broadcasting in London (on 15 November broadcasting also began in Manchester and Birmingham). The privately owned company was set up and controlled by manufacturers of broadcasting equipment with the intention of increasing sales of radio receivers. The service was funded not through advertising but by radio set owners who paid a licence fee of ten shillings to the Post Office (half the amount was kept by the Post Office, the other half passed on to the company). The popularity of the new medium was such (by 1925 reception covered 85 per cent of the population) that the government proposed changes to the practice of allowing a private company to act as a monopoly broadcaster to the nation. Instead of assuming state control, however, the company was given the status of an independent public corporation by Royal charter on 1 January 1927 and awarded a ten-year licence.

The first director general of the BBC, John Reith (1899–1971), later Lord Reith, was a crucial figure in shaping the newly formed corporation. Reith, a high-minded, upper middle class, Presbyterian Scot, believed that broadcasting should offer a public service to the nation, claiming that it should educate and inform as well as entertain. Paddy Scannell summarises a statement given by Reith about the role of broadcasting written in 1925:

'The service must not be used for entertainment purposes alone. Broadcasting had a responsibility to bring into the greatest possible number of homes in the fullest degree all that was best in every department of human knowledge, endeavour, and achievement. The preservation of a high moral tone – the avoidance of the vulgar and the hurtful – was of paramount importance. Broadcasting should give a lead to public taste rather than pander to it.'[2]

As general manager of the British Broadcasting Company Reith had already established the principle of political neutrality during the 1926 general strike. In practice however, 'neutrality' meant following the government line or losing autonomy. The general strike was perceived as bringing Britain close to revolution and key figures in the Conservative government including the home secretary, Winston Churchill, argued that the BBC should be taken over by the government and used for propaganda purposes. Reith disagreed, stating that the government should trust the BBC to remain impartial. He argued that if the BBC was taken over by the government, listeners would lose confidence and in any case the strikers would quickly close the service down. Reith stated: 'It was no time for dope, even if the people could have been doped.'[3] During the strike, however, the government was allowed to broadcast its point of view but the leaders of the trade unions were denied access to the airwaves. Left wing critics subsequently blamed the BBC for the collapse of the strike (Reith also received a knighthood in the same year). The episode underlined the power of the new medium but also exposed the uneasy relationship between broadcasters and government that still persists today.

PUBLIC SERVICE BROADCASTING

The concept is associated with John Reith, but is still relevant today as all five British terrestrial channels retain public service obligations. They must, as Reith first stated about the newly formed BBC, inform and educate as well as entertain. The concept of public service broadcasting also acknowledges the vital role played by broadcasting in allowing the public to make informed decisions about key events in a democratic society. Paddy Scannell states that for Reith '. . . broadcasting had an immense potential for helping in the creation of an informed and enlightened democracy. It enabled men and women to take an interest in many things from which they had previously been excluded. On any great public issue of the day radio could provide both the facts of the matter and the arguments for and against.'[4]

In the 1990s a number of influential critics have argued that the increasing number of cable and satellite channels have rendered the concept of public service broadcasting obsolete, claiming that the market will provide what the public want. Others use the American model to illustrate that quantity does not always mean quality.

The service offered by the BBC up until the outbreak of the Second World War offered a diverse range of programmes including: news, poetry and prose readings, talks, discussions, drama, sport, religion, classical and light music, variety and light entertainment and children's programmes. Critics of the BBC in this period claimed that its output did not appeal to a wide enough audience, primarily targeting middle class families. This view was reinforced by a number of practices at the BBC, for example:

- BBC announcers were required to wear dinner jackets when broadcasting
- Regional accents were outlawed
- BBC staff were subject to Reith's code of morality – infidelity could result in dismissal

James Curran and Jean Seaton in *Power without Responsibility: the Press and Broadcasting in Britain* comment on the period: 'In a decade of hunger marches and "red united fighting fronts", the BBC regarded a succession of royal broadcasts as the triumph of outside broadcasting and actuality reporting. Broadcasting in the 1930s was dominated by state openings, royal anniversaries, visits, deaths and births, and by the Coronation.'[5]

The Ullswater Report on Broadcasting of 1936 was set up to consider the future of the BBC when its charter expired on 31 December of the same year. Its general conclusions were positive, including praise for the BBC's impartiality, and the charter was renewed for a further ten years. A number of areas, however, were criticised including the heaviness of the Sunday programming. Andrew Crisell in *Understanding Radio* describes the service: '. . . [transmission] . . . did not begin until 12.30 pm and consisted only of religious services, talks and classical music.'[6] The report also recommended that the number of governors be increased from five to seven and that the service should continue to be funded by licence fee rather than through advertising.

There was no doubt however that, despite the criticisms levelled at the BBC, it had been an astonishing success. Asa Briggs in *The Golden Age of Wireless: The History of Broadcasting in the United Kingdom Volume II* comments on the rate of growth of both listeners and the BBC staff in the period: 'On 1 September 1927 the BBC employed 773 people. There were then 2,178,259 wireless licence holders. On 1 September 1939 the BBC employed nearly 5,000 people and there were 9,082,666 wireless-licence holders.'[7] Reith resigned from the BBC in 1937 leaving behind an independent, stable and well structured, organisation that was to provide a key role in the Second World War.

Broadcasting and the Second World War (1939–45)

The BBC escaped direct government control during the Second World War, despite the efforts of Winston Churchill to make it part of the Ministry of Information. The corporation was, however, rigorously controlled by government through indirect means and once again only retained autonomy because it followed the government line.

The BBC had the vital role during the war of unifying the people of Britain as well as bolstering morale (a role that is celebrated in Humphrey Jennings' film *Listen to Britain*). The need to appeal to a wider, more diverse audience during the war forced the BBC to re-examine its approach to the style and content of programmes (the price of radio sets by 1944 had also fallen to a level that could be afforded by the majority of the population). Curran and Seaton note observe that Clement Attlee, the Deputy Prime Minister (and the leader of the Labour Party), complained that the monopoly of upper class voices was likely to offend workers.[8] The existing service was therefore split into the Home Service and the Forces Programme. The Home Service continued the traditional BBC approach aimed at predominantly middle class audiences, but the Forces Programme was targeted at a new audience: the working class. Tim O'Sullivan *et al* describe how the new programmes attempted to appeal to their audience.

'The style and content of the language [of the programmes] became more popular and down to earth, with slang, humour, innuendo and occasionally some irreverence or vulgarity. Shows were often broadcast from factory canteens or barracks, and the "live" audience was heard either through their laughter and applause or when "ordinary" members of the public spoke directly into the microphone to make requests or to send messages. New programmes like *We speak for Ourselves* allowed working class people to be heard for the first time on the radio, and fictional drama series like *The Plums* were based on a supposedly "typical" working class family and tried to reflect the realities of urban war-time life: bombings, rationing, shift work and members of the family fighting away from home.'[9]

News reporting during the war

Although entertainment was a vital aspect of the BBC's output there was also an overwhelming need for news. Early news reports were dull, heavily censored, and often underplayed the extent of allied defeats. As the war progressed, however, news reports increasingly valued topicality and realism, attracting large audiences. For example, *War Report* first broadcast on D-Day 6 June 1944 regularly attracted audiences of between 10 and 15 million.[10] These changes were in part a natural consequence of recent Allied successes but also due to the use of portable recording equipment that allowed reporters at the front line to send back vivid descriptions of the fighting accompanied by the real sounds of battle.

When Germany surrendered in 1945 the BBC had firmly established its authority as a monopoly broadcaster that could appeal to all the classes.

Post-war

After the war the BBC retained the principle of targeting different audiences using more than one channel. The Home Service continued unchanged and the Forces Programme was renamed the Light Programme with its emphasis on entertainment and popular music. A third channel named the Third Programme was also introduced in 1946 which was 'an unashamedly "highbrow" network devoted to the arts, serious discussion and experiment.'[11] These three channels continued unchanged until 1967 when pressure from the pirate radio stations forced the BBC to embark on a radical shake-up.

 PIRATE RADIO

Pirate radio stations such as Radio Caroline (first broadcast 28 March 1964) took advantage of the gap in the British market for pop music programmes targeted at the young. Pirate stations, located in ships and forts in British coastal waters, were initially exempt from British laws governing broadcasting. They were phenomenally successful (by 1967, nine pirate stations were broadcasting) attracting 15 million listeners by the end of 1965. Andrew Crisell states that: 'Caroline and a nearby ship broadcasting as Radio London were the slickest and most professional and reached the largest population and their impact was sensational. A Gallup poll found that in its first three weeks Caroline gained seven million listeners from a potential audience of only 20 million.'[12] Profits from the stations were high as they were funded by advertising and did not pay royalties on the records they played. The pirate stations were eventually outlawed in 1967 when the Marine Broadcasting Offences Bill was passed by the Labour government.

The 1967 line-up listed below survives to the present day with the addition of Radio Five in 1990 (later Radio Five Live).

- Radio One – set up as a pop music station targeting the audiences that had previously tuned in to the pirate stations
- Radio Two – took over the role of the Light Programme
- Radio Three – took over the role of the Third Programme
- Radio Four – took over the role of the Home Service

The other key development in terms of radio broadcasting was the development of BBC local radio services. The BBC believed that local radio services should consist of:

- **'Community service, representing all the local interests of each area: social, industrial, business, and every form of public activity;**
- **Education, in co-operation with local schools, as well as working with universities, colleges, and similar bodies, correspondence courses of study for adult education;**
- **Light entertainment, local as well as nation.'[13]**

The first of these, Radio Leicester, opened in 1967 and numbers of BBC local stations grew rapidly. In 1997 there were 42 local stations.

Radio sets had also become much smaller and cheaper in the post-war era with the introduction of transistors that replaced the large and costly wireless valves. Frank Gillard of the BBC commented, 'The transistor has made the radio into the truly ubiquitous mass medium. Radio is no longer something which you necessarily have to go. Radio goes with you'.[14] By 1978, 68 per cent of Britain's radio sets were either portable or mobile and by 1990 85 per cent of British cars were fitted with radios.[15]

Commercial radio

The BBC radio monopoly was broken in 1973 when franchises were awarded to new local commercial radio stations after the publication by the Conservative government of a White Paper entitled *An Alternative Service of Broadcasting*. The commercial stations were placed under the control of the ITA (Independent Television Authority) which was subsequently renamed the Independent Broadcasting Authority). By 1979, 19 local stations were operating and in 1997 there were nearly 200.

The 1990 Broadcast Act loosened the regulatory controls on commercial stations, lightening public service obligations as well as relaxing rules relating to ownership of radio stations. More local radio licences were granted and for the first time in 1992 franchises were offered for national commercial stations. The current national commercials include Classic FM, Virgin 1215 and

Figure 5.1 Listening figures 6 January–30 March 1997[16]

	Weekly reach* (millions)	Total hours** (millions)	Share of listening
All radio	**40.46**	**830**	**100%**
All BBC	**27.25**	**402**	**48.4%**
BBC Radio One	10.28	91	11%
BBC Radio Two	8.79	104	12.6%
BBC Radio Three	2.38	10	1.2%
BBC Radio Four	7.99	84	10.2%
BBC Radio Five Live	5.53	29	3.5%
BBC Local/Regional	9.33	82	10%
All commercial	**28.36**	**410**	**49.4%**
Local commercial	23.66	329	39.7%
Classic FM	4.68	27	3.3%
Virgin 1215	2.87	21	2.6%
Talk Radio UK	1.79	12	1.5%
Atlantic 252	3.50	20	2.4%

*weekly reach counts adults over 15 listening for at least five minutes in average week

**total hours is the overall number of hours of adult listening in an average week

Talk Radio UK. Classic FM is currently the commercial station with the largest audience. In addition there are five regional stations including: Century Radio, Galaxy Radio, Heart FM, Jazz FM and Scot FM whose licence stipulates that they should 'broaden the range of audience choice.' In the future it is likely that the number of local, regional and national radio channels will proliferate resulting in increased competition for listeners and advertising revenue. This will be technically possible because of the development of digital broadcasting, which uses less band width than analogue broadcasting thus freeing space for additional stations. The BBC has already invested substantially in digital broadcasting equipment; it turned on its first digital audio transmitter on 27 September 1995.

THE RADIO AUTHORITY

The Radio Authority has licensed and regulated commercial radio since January 1991 as it is one of three bodies which took over the work of the Independent Broadcasting Authority (IBA) after the changes brought about by the 1990 Broadcasting Act. This body has a number of functions.

■ To plan frequencies

■ To appoint licensees with a view to broadening listener choice and to enforce ownership rules

■ To regulate programming and advertising

It is also required to consult with its licensees and agree codes covering engineering, advertising and sponsorship. If licensees do not adhere to these codes they can be sanctioned by the Authority. For instance, if a station is licensed to play Country Music then it must play an agreed amount of Country Music or it can be sanctioned

In 1996, there were 261 complaints made about local independent radio programmes and 48 of these complaints were upheld by the Authority; there were also 363 complaints made about advertisements of which 87 were upheld. The Authority can sanction licensees in a number of ways: it can revoke the licence, shorten the licence or impose fines. In 1996, nine fines were imposed for breaches to agreed codes including one £3,000 fine (Scot FM) for 'offensive broadcast' and one £2,000 fine (Leicester Sound) for broadcasting 'insufficient speech and 60s/70s music' (*The Radio Authority Annual Report and Financial Statements*, 1996).

TELEVISION BROADCASTING IN BRITAIN

Television broadcasting began as an experimental service in the London area on 26 August 1936, serving approximately 300 viewers. By 1938, however, there were 11,000 receivers in regular use. As most programmes were live resources were stretched as 'Every hour of screen time needed six or seven hours of rehearsal. . .'[17] Early programmes included: *Picture Page* (1936), 'A hugely popular magazine programme of topical and general interest', *Theatre Parade* (1936) which 'presented scenes from popular London theatre productions of the time', *For the Children* (1937), 'the first television programme specially designed for children of school age', the England versus Scotland *FA Cup Final* (1938) as well as numerous comedies and plays such as *Gaslight* by Patrick Hamilton (1939).[18]

The sets had ten inch screens and were very expensive (prices ranged up to £100), while the programmes on offer were targeted at middle class audiences. The initial broadcasts used John Logie Baird's mechanical system but this was replaced on 2 November 1936 by Isaac Shoenberg's more sophisticated 405 line electronic scanning system that was retained until 1962 when the 625 line system was adopted.

Pre-war television broadcasting was not perceived as a threat to radio and many critics did not think that the idea would catch on (a similar situation took place in America after the war when Hollywood studio executives proclaimed that television was just a fad and would not present a threat to the film industry). Television broadcasting ceased on 1 September 1939 (during a Mickey Mouse cartoon) at the outbreak of the war, but resumed on 7 June 1946. The early service had small audiences and most of the BBC's resources continued to be ploughed into radio. A key event that increased the popularity of television (by 1952 only 1 in 20 households owned a TV set) was the coronation of Elizabeth II in 1953. The live broadcast that included footage from inside Westminster Abbey was seen on television by over 20 million people (double that of the radio audience) despite there only being 350,000 television sets in the country.

The BBC television service remained a monopoly until 1956, following the passing of the 1954 Television Act by the Conservative government, ITV first began broadcasting. Independent Television had similar public service obligations to the BBC but it was regulated by a new body, the Independent Television Authority (ITA), which laid down strict rules about how it should operate. For example, 'A proper balance was required in subject matter and a high general standard of quality. Due "accuracy and impartiality" were required for the presentation of any news given in programmes, in whatever form.

Figure 5.2 Growth of television audience[19]

Year	Number of new licence holders
1946–47	14,560
1947–48	57,000
1948–49	112,000
1950–51	420,000
1951–52	685,319
1952–53	693,192
1953–54	1,110,439
1954–55	1,254,879
1955–56	1,235,827
1956–57	1,226,663
1957–58	1,123,747
1958–59	1,165,419

There were also to be "proper proportions" in terms of British productions and performance in order to safeguard against dumping of American material.[20] A key difference between the BBC and ITV was that the ITV companies would be funded by advertising and not by the licence fee.

The ITV companies attracted large audiences with light entertainment programmes such as *Take Your Pick* (first shown in 1955), the first quiz show on British TV 'to use the studio audience as part of the show, helping to create and at the same time to emphasise the tensions of the game'[21] and *Sunday Night at the London Palladium*. Imported American programmes such as *Dragnet* (1955), a police series about the routine work of the Los Angeles city policy department were also popular.

In March 1956 a Gallup poll in London and Birmingham revealed that audiences had a strong preference for ITV (see Figure 5.3).[22]

In 1957 '. . . out of 539 programmes listed by TAM [Television Audience Measurement] in the top ten ratings, 536 were from ITV and only three produced by the BBC.'[23] The declining audiences for BBC programmes made a number of commentators at the time question whether paying the licence fee could still be justified – an argument that has persisted into the 1990s. The ITV companies were also financially successful – so successful that they were described as 'just like having a licence to print your own money'.[24] The BBC responded to the threat from ITV with a range of new programmes in the late 1950s and early 1960s that had wide appeal, such as *Tonight* (1957), *The Ken Dodd Show* (1959), *Juke Box Jury* (1959), *Steptoe and Son* (1962) and *Z Cars* (1962) eventually winning back a larger audience share.

In the 1960s and 1970s two influential reports on broadcasting brought further changes to British broadcasting.

Figure 5.3 Viewing preferences for London and Birmingham in 1956

	London	Birmingham
Prefer ITV	60	58
Prefer BBC	16	16
No choice	19	20
Don't know	5	7

The Pilkington Committee Report on Broadcasting (1962)

The Pilkington committee concluded that commercial television 'operates to lower standards of enjoyment and understanding' and expressed concern about ITV's 'comprehensive carelessness about moral standards generally.' The committee's negative comments about the ITV companies helped the BBC, rather than commercial television, to secure its second channel in 1964. BBC2 was set up to provide alternative programmes to BBC1 that did not necessarily appeal to mainstream tastes. In 1967 the BBC gained a further advantage with the introduction of colour broadcasting to BBC2.

The Annan Commission Report on Broadcasting (1977)

Amongst the Annan report's recommendations was the provision of a fourth channel catering for minority interests, which was supplied with programmes from outside agents rather than by in-house production. James Watson and Anne Hill in *A Dictionary of Communication and Media Studies* claim that 'What Annan wanted above all was a shift from **duopoly** to a more diverse system of broadcasting in Britain: "We want the broadcasting industry to grow. But we do not want more of the same ... What is needed now are programmes for the different minorities which add up to make the majority." '[25]

Following the Annan report Channel Four was launched in 1982. Channel Four's remit is to 'provide programmes with a distinctive character and to appeal to tastes and interests not generally catered for by Channel Three'[26] and has proved that it is possible to make money (in terms of advertising revenue) from minority audiences. Previously Channel Four was funded by the ITV companies (via a 13.6 per cent levy on their advertising revenue) who in return sold Channel Four's advertising space – keeping the proceeds. Since the 1990 Broadcasting Act, however, Channel Four is allowed to sell its own advertising space.

Channel Four does not make its own programmes; instead it operates as a 'publisher broadcaster' by commissioning material from independent producers. A unique feature of the station is that it is not required to provide a 'balance' of views within individual programmes as long as a balance is achieved in other programmes over time. The station has courted controversy from the start with 'bad' language in *Brookside* and films that attracted complaints about representations of sex and violence.

Duopoly

In broadcasting duopoly refers to the equal split in the market between the BBC and the commercial terrestrial channels. In the age of cable and satellite broadcasting and the proliferation of channels the term has less relevance.

VIDEO

The video recorder (VCR) was introduced commercially to the British public in the late 1970s and was an instant success. Three incompatible formats were initially launched: Sony's Betamax, JVC's VHS and Philips' V2000. VHS won the contest (despite Betamax being technically superior) due to the availability of rental titles on VHS and currently approx. eighty per cent of households own VCRs. The VCR allows the viewer to construct his/her own schedule from recorded programmes prompting ITV companies and advertisers to express concern about the ability of video recorders to fast forward through advertising breaks. In the 1990s the nicam stereo VCR forms the heart of Dolby pro-logic home cinema systems capable of delivering high quality images and multi-channel sound. The format is soon, however, to be replaced by digital video.

Satellite and cable broadcasting

In the late 1980s terrestrial television's monopoly was challenged by the arrival of satellite television which promised viewers more choice through a wide selection of channels that appealed to different tastes and interests. Rupert Murdoch's SKY satellite service first began broadcasting in March 1989 closely followed by BSB (British Satellite Broadcasting) which used a 'squarial' to receive programmes rather than a satellite dish. Whereas BSB aimed its programmes upmarket, SKY aimed down market (C2DE market). The cost of buying SKY's receiving equipment was also lower than BSB's. The competition between the two companies combined with a slower than expected take-up of the service by the public and the substantial investment required to set the services up, resulted in both companies having enormous financial losses. In 1991 BSB and SKY merged to become BSkyB. The new company decided to continue the service using SKY's technology resulting in the obsolescence of thousands of 'squarials'.

Critics of the new service claimed that it appealed to the lowest common denominator (BSkyB does not have public service obligations) and pointed out that 12 channels did not necessarily mean 'choice' but just more of the same. Rupert Murdoch, however, firmly believes that satellite broadcasting offers a service not available through the existing terrestrial channels, which have been dominated by the tastes and assessments of quality of a narrow elite.

Concern was also expressed about the impact satellite broadcasting would have on ITV and Channel Four. If satellite proved popular advertisers would start moving away from ITV and Channel Four, resulting in a decrease in revenue and subsequent decrease in the amount of money for programmes (BSkyB has over six million paying subscribers). Finally a number of commentators argued that satellite broadcasting which involved a monthly fee and initial set up costs could only be received by the financially well off – thus breaking the tradition of broadcasting being available to everyone. More recently this debate has re-emerged when events of 'national importance' such as football matches have been only available on pay satellite services. Recent advances in technology have allowed satellite broadcasts the option of offering 'pay to view' services, in which viewers must pay a one-off fee to watch an individual programme.

The further proliferation of new channels in the 1990s has resulted in a partial fragmentation of audiences. The traditional notion of broadcasters 'binding the nation together' with popular programmes watched by a large proportion of the population is being replaced by 'narrowcasting' in which programmes and channels are targeted at specific groups rather than a broad mix of viewers. Satellite channels such as *Sci-Fi Channel*, *Paramount Comedy*, *Family Christian Network* and *Eurosport* are good examples of 'narrowcasting'. It has become clear, however, that 'unprofitable' minority interests are unlikely to be catered for by cable and satellite services. Steve Peak and Paul Fisher comment that the '... cable TV future is in "channels tightly targeted to significantly niche groups and high price, high quality mainstream movie, entertainment, music and sports channels." '[27]

Despite the perceived separation of cable and satellite channels from terrestrial television there is a degree of crossover. For example a number of cable and satellite channels use material generated by the BBC/ITV companies in the past. Terrestrial TV stations have also bought popular satellite programmes such as *The Simpsons*, *Beavis and Butthead* and *The X-Files*. There are additionally companies with stakes in terrestrial channels as well as in satellite and cable ones. For example, Granada owns Granada TV and LWT but also has shares in BSkyB.

NEWS INTERNATIONAL

Rupert Murdoch's News International has recently been at the centre of debates about ownership and control of the British media. A number of commentators fear that Murdoch's ambitions to gain further stakes in the British television market will have a negative impact on the industry. In 1997 News International owned 40 per cent of BSkyB as well as the *Sun*, *The Times*, the *News of the World*, and *The Sunday Times*. In America, News Corporation (News International is the British arm of the larger company) owns amongst others: Fox TV network, Fox Film Studio, Fox Video and New World Communications Group. News Corporation also has substantial media interests in Asia and Australia.

BRITISH BROADCASTING IN THE 1990S

The 1990 Broadcasting Act formalised the government White Paper *Broadcasting in the 1990s: Competition, Choice and Quality* (published in 1988). Its guiding principles are:

- 'Broadcasting services must remain independent of Government editorially and, as far as possible, in economic and regulatory terms
- Because of broadcasting's power, immediacy and influence, there remains the need for regulation to guarantee standards, particularly regarding taste and decency and to protect viewers and listeners against exploitation and poor quality programming
- New services, programmes and methods of transmission and payment should not be artificially restricted. Direct payment for television through subscription should be encouraged and advertising and sponsorship should be more flexible
- Restrictive practices should be discouraged and it must be made as easy as possible for new services to be launched
- Independent producers should be given more scope
- Broadcasting companies and organisations should be run efficiently to enable them to offer audiences good value for money and compete effectively with one another and with overseas broadcasters
- Through greater competition, pressures should be exerted to hold down television advertising rates'[28]

The Act proposed a fifth new terrestrial channel as well as further satellite services. Changes were also made to the way in which broadcasting was regulated. The IBA, for example, was split into the new Radio Authority and the ITC (Independent Television Commission) which was instructed to regulate with a 'light touch'.

ITC (INDEPENDENT TELEVISION COMMISSION)

The ITC regulates all commercial television services in Britain including cable and satellite. It has a statutory duty to 'draw up and enforce a code governing due impartiality and a general code governing portrayal of violence, appeals for donations and such other matters concerning standards and practice for programmers as the Commission considers appropriate.'[29]

The Code is not designed to cover every eventuality and can be modified where circumstances demand it. It focuses on aspects of broadcasting that have attracted debate or controversy. For example, the Code has a family viewing policy which states that 'Material unsuitable for children must not be broadcast at times when large numbers of children may be expected to be watching.' It assumes that fewer children will be watching as the evening progresses and that '9.00 pm is normally fixed as the time up to which licensees will regard themselves as responsible for ensuring that nothing is shown that is unsuitable for children.'[30] This policy has had an impact on the screening of feature films. The following basic rules apply:

■ No '12' rated version should normally start before 8.00 pm on any service.

■ No '15' rated version should normally start before 9.00 pm (8.00 pm on premium rate subscription services, contents permitting).

■ No '18' rated version should start before 10.00 pm on any service (Note that this rule may be relaxed in the case of films classified 15 or more years ago which are clearly suitable for earlier transmission).

■ No 'R18' rated version should be transmitted at any time.

■ No version which has been refused a BBFC video classification should be transmitted at any time.

In applying these rules, the BBFC video classification should always be preferred, where available, to the cinema classification.[31]

Other key elements of the Code are concerned with the following:

■ Privacy and gathering information – 'the broadcasters freedom of access to information and their freedom to publish'[32]. This is limited by '...considerations of national security, [from] the requirements of the Broadcasting Act and from the individual citizen's right to privacy.'[33]

■ Impartiality – 'The Broadcasting Act requires the ITC to do all it can to secure that due impartiality is preserved on the part of the person providing the service as respects matters of political or industrial controversy or relating to current public policy,'[34] The term 'due' is used to stress that '...judgement will always be called for'[35] especially with regard to the range of factual programmes.

In addition the Code has sections on: Party Political and Parliamentary Broadcasting; Terrorism, crime, anti-social behaviour; Other legal matters; Images of very brief duration; Charitable appeals and publicity for charities; Religion; Other programme matters; Communication with the public.

The ITC also sets minimum requirements for certain types of programmes. Examples of these include the following:

■ 'News: three programmes each weekday with 20 minutes at lunchtime, 15 minutes early evening and half an hour in peak times. This requirement is met by ITN.

■ Current affairs: an average of one and a half hours a week.

■ Children: ten hours weekly average.

■ Religion: two hours weekly average.

■ Regional programmes: minimum amounts vary from one region to another.'[36]

The 'free market' approach adopted by the Act suggested that competition would bring increased quality as well as giving audiences further choice of channels and programmes. A test of the 'market' principle came in October 1991 when the new ITV franchises were announced. Previous franchises had been awarded on the basis of programming quality but the new system was based on the highest cash bid (with the addition of a 'quality threshold' that most bidders passed with ease). James Watson and Anne Hill comment that, 'Prior to the announcement of the franchises by the ITC, existing franchise-holders had tightened their financial belts – cutting back on programme invest-ment, laying off staff – in order to have enough cash to place a winning bid. Thus, it was argued by critics, "quality" was already being sacrificed even before the quality threshold had been crossed.'[37] Many companies had to submit very high bids in order to win the franchises inevitably leading to less money being available for programmes. For example, Carlton TV won the London weekday franchise with a bid of £43.17 million a year. Others that faced no competition, however, such as Central TV, only submitted a bid of £2,000 a year.

CHANNEL FIVE

The franchise for Channel Five was awarded in October 1995 to Channel Five Broadcasting led by two millionaire socialists, Greg Dyke and Lord Hollick with a bid of £22 million. Surprisingly Channel Five Broadcasting was chosen in preference to two competitors who offered higher bids because on paper it offered greater diversity of programming. Mr Dyke claimed that 'We will produce some innovative stuff, which we hope will be offensive. I believe that part of the broadcaster's role is to push back boundaries.'[38] Channel Five had to spend nearly £150 million retuning the nations' video recorders that are tuned into the same frequency as Channel Five. Channel Five started broadcasting on 30 March 1997 (with the help of the Spice Girls) and can potentially reach approximately 45 million viewers, although it still cannot be received in a number of key areas such as the South East. The channel has yet to make a substantial impact in terms of programming and could be much more innovative in its approach. Its budget of £110 million for programming is, however, tiny compared to the £600 million available to ITV's network programme-makers.

Figure 5.4 TV statistics for 1996–97

> **Ownership and viewing habits**
> - 97% of households have a TV set
> - 64% have two sets and 28% three or more
> - 40% of leisure time is spent watching TV
> - 37% of households with children under 16 have TVs in the children's bedroom[39]
>
> **Share of total audience for 12 months ending March 1997**
>
> | | |
> |---|---|
> | BBC1 | 32.2% |
> | BBC2 | 11.7% |
> | ITV | 33.1% |
> | C4/S4C | 10.7% |
> | Cable | 8% |
> | Satellite | 4.3%[40] |
>
> Currently there are over six million paying subscribers to BSkyB. Cable television, however, has only attracted 2.6 million subscribers even though over nine million homes have been wired.[41]

The BBC in the 1990s

The Green paper on the future of the BBC (1992) came to the following conclusions:

- The BBC remain a public service broadcaster
- The licence fee should remain the central method of funding
- The Governors of the Corporation should not oversee management of programmes
- The BBC should become more efficient[42]

On 1 May 1996 the BBC's charter was renewed for a further ten years until 2006. This followed the government White Paper: *The Future of the BBC: Serving the Nation, Competing Worldwide* (1994). The Paper reinforced the importance of public service broadcasting but significantly stressed the importance of developing commercial services as well as cable and satellite opportunities. Subsequently in November 1997 the BBC started a 24 hour news service available on cable channels (paid for by the licence fee) as well as an Internet news service. Some critics in the 1990s have questioned whether the BBC is still fulfilling its obligations as a public service provider, claiming that it panders to popular taste with an increased output of light entertainment in an attempt to win audiences.

AUDIENCE RESEARCH: BARB[43]

Measurement of television audiences is carried out by BARB (the Broadcasters' Audience Research Board) which is jointly owned by the BBC and ITV Network Centre. For the ITV companies it is vital to know the size of the audience for each programme so they can tell advertisers the likely reach of their adverts. It is equally important for the BBC to know how many viewers are watching its programmes in order to justify the continued existence of the licence fee.

The data is collected electronically by meters attached to TV sets. Four thousand seven hundred homes participate in the survey and these are carefully chose to be representative of the whole country. The electronic meter registers when the set is switched on and off and which channel it is tuned to. In addition the meter can register which member of the family is watching the set via a remote control unit (each member of a household is assigned a different number). The data is then transmitted to BARB's central computer automatically. BARB also measure audience appreciation of programmes via a national panel of 3,000 viewers. Members of the panel complete a viewing booklet each week giving programmes a score of 1 to 6. This data is compiled into a weekly Audience Appreciation Report.

The future of broadcasting

'Everything is going to be digital'

Michael Green, Chairman of Carlton Communications[44]

'The who, the how and the when of the digital age remain crucial questions for Britain. Our prosperity, jobs – even our cultural identity – depend on getting the answers right.'

John Birt, the director-general of the BBC[45]

Figure 5.5 BARB viewing figures week ending 2 November 1997[46]

BBC1		ITV	
Programme	**Millions**	**Programme**	**Millions**
EastEnders (Thu/Sun)	18.96	*Coronation Street* (Fri)	15.79
EastEnders (Tues/Sun)	18.44	*Emmerdale* (Tues/Wed)	13.36
EastEnders (Mon/Sun)	15.48	*London's Burning*	12.63
Casualty	12.86		
National Lottery Live (Sat)	10.65	**Channel Four**	
Animal Hospital	10.59	**Programme**	**Millions**
Neighbours (Tues)	10.24	*Brookside* (Fri/Sat)	6.03
		Brookside (Tues/Sat)	5.76
BBC2		*Friends*	5.49
Programme	**Millions**	*Brookside* (Wed/Sat)	5.44
Have I Got News for You	7.46	*Countdown* (Fri)	4.36
Ground Force	5.39	*Cutting Edge*	4.20
Top Gear	5.18	*Countdown* (Tues)	4.15
Shooting Stars	5.00		
Simpsons (Mon/Sun)	4.62	**Channel Five**	
The Natural World	4.59	**Programme**	**Millions**
Two Fat Ladies	3.96	*Baby's Day Out*	2.23
		World Cup Football	1.98
ITV		*Vanishing*	1.70
Programme	**Millions**	*Family Affairs* (Fri/Sun)	1.14
Coronation Street (Mon)	18.22	*The Sweeney*	1.13
Coronation Street (Wed)	17.38	*Family Affairs* (Thur/Fri)	1.12
Heartbeat	16.53	*Family Affairs* (Wed/Thur)	1.12
Coronation Street (Sun)	15.83		

'With more channels there will be more TV, from more points of view. We can then come to see TV as no more sinister than books. My guess is that in 20 years time people will look back on the impartiality requirements on broadcasting as quaint history, like censorship of the theatre and newspapers in the 18th century. The present rules will wither away.'

Kelvin MacKenzie, managing director of Live TV and ex-*Sun* editor[47]

Broadcasting is likely to undergo radical change in the near future with Digital Terrestrial Television (DTT) due for launch in July 1998. DTT will enable 36 channels to be broadcast, simply requiring the addition of a decoder box that can be plugged into existing television sets to receive them (expected cost approximately £250). Digital satellite services have also been developed that, potentially, will offer up to 200 channels. Digital TV has the further advantage of offering CD quality sound and over twice the picture resolution of conventional broadcasting (it will be complemented by digital video).

The BBC has embraced the idea of digital television and has joined with Flexitech Plc to produce programmes for commercial subscription channels. In order to pay for digital TV the BBC has made a number of tough financial decisions. 'The first drive for efficiency was Producer Choice which reduced costs by a claimed 30 per cent. Now the new ten year strategy, Extending Choice in the Digital Age, contains the promise of cuts of £1.8 billion from conventional BBC budgets. The justification is a BBC prediction that by 2005 up to ten per cent of households will have digital TV services.'[48]

It seems likely that in the more distant future (at least in Britain) there will be the possibility of programmes on demand. In other words viewers will be able

Figure 5.6 Digital television: the main players

- BBC Digital TV
- British Digital Broadcasting (jointly owned by Carlton and Granada)
- Digital 3 and 4 Ltd

The digital channels are grouped into six 'multiplexes' (blocks of transmissions). The channels are likely to be allocated as follows.

Multiplex A
Probably S4C in Wales, Gaelic programmes in Scotland

Multiplex B
BDB multiplex
   Granada Plus, Sky Movies, Carlton Select, BBC Horizon, Sky Sports

Multiplex C
BDB multiplex
   BBC Style/Showcase, Sky 1, The Movie Channel, Carlton Films, Granada Good Life

Multiplex D
BDB multiplex
   Carlton Entertainment, Public Eye (including Sky News), Granada TV Shopping, Granada Sports Club, BBC One-TV.

BBC Multiplex
BBC1/2, 24 hour news, BBC Choice, BBC Inform

Channel Three/Four Multiplex
Digital 3 and 4 Ltd
   Channel Three, Channel Four, Teletext Ltd, ITV2, Channel Four Film Club[49]

to access programmes stored centrally at any time they choose. They will additionally be able to pause, replay and fast forward the programmes as required. Ultimately television services will be combined with the Internet which at present is limited by its capacity to process images. This could result in individuals being able to 'publish' their own programmes on the Net as well as 'interacting' with existing ones.

LOCAL MEDIA ORGANISATION: KFM *HITS AND MEMORIES* (96.2 MHz, 101.6 MHz)

'We are looking forward to having a full and truly local service.'
Andrew Dean, KFM Managing Director, speaking in June 1995, a month before the launch of this new local radio station.[50]

The franchise

KFM, which started broadcasting in July 1995, was one of six local independent radio stations which were awarded licences by the Radio Authority in that year. The race for the licence had begun in October 1994 when KFM was one of five consortia who put in bids for the eight-year franchise for a new commercial radio station to cover the West Kent and North East Sussex region (see Figure 5.7). This area is the heart of London's commuter belt. It has a high density population with a large proportion of high income professionals with considerable spending power; consequently, although it covers a small area, it was a potentially lucrative radio licence for the eventual winner. KFM based its bid on a promise to provide the business community and the local population with a music-led station – playing music from the 60s through to the 90s – together with regular local, national and international news plus local traffic and travel features. The bids for the franchise were judged on three criteria.

- The strength of the financial plan
- The quality of the programme research conducted
- The sales and marketing expertise of the consortium

KFM finance and organisational structure

The initial investment pledges of over half a million pounds came from local businesses as well as private individuals and it was projected that a loss in the first year would be turned into a small profit by the second year of trading; Andrew Dean, KFM's Managing Director, says they were, in fact, trading profitably 'six months ahead of schedule'. Apart from the normal business costs of staffing, premises and so on, eight per cent of the total income is levied by the PRS (Performing Rights Society) and the MCPS (Mechanical Copyright Protection Society). The station also has to pay annual fees to the Radio Authority.

Local independent radio stations are run by surprisingly few staff – this enables them to keep advertising rates as low as possible – and KFM is no exception. It has 15 full time staff and ten freelances but many of the full time staff have more than one job. For instance, the Managing Director is also Head of Sales and the Programme Controller and his Deputy double as presenters.

Target audience and advertising

The potential listening audience for this franchise was 160,000 and KFM initially aimed to get at least a third of this number listening for a few hours a week. Its format is described as Adult Contemporary as it targets 25 to 54-year-olds.

In August 1995, a RAJAR (Radio Joint Audience Research) survey revealed that commercial radio had, for the first time, seized more than half of British radio listeners while regional BBC stations had lost nearly ten per cent of their listeners. A survey undertaken in March 1997 by First Survey Research showed that although the combined BBC stations still reached a larger percentage of potential listeners than did the combined independent stations in the local area, KFM's weekly reach at one in five (see Figure 5.9) was equal to the reach of BBC Radio Four.

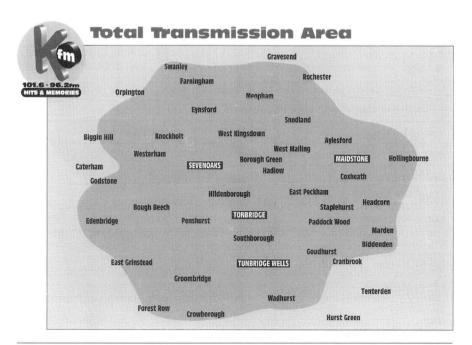

Figure 5.7 KFM's total transmission area   ©KFM

In terms of social classification, KFM's target segment is ABC1s – the top three social groups in terms of earnings. The station also presumes to have a higher number of female than male listeners.

Figure 5.8 Job roles at KFM

Managing Director/Head of Sales				
Receptionist/ Secretary	Finance Manager	Programme Controller/Presenter	Advertising Sales Team	Head of News
	Traffic Manager	Deputy Programme Controller/Presenter		Senior Journalist
	Traffic Assistant	Presenters		Journalist

SOCIAL CLASSIFICATION

Audience segmentation by social class is based on earning power.

A	Upper middle class	Higher managerial, administrative or professional
B	Middle class	Intermediate managerial, administrative or professional
C1	Lower middle class	Supervisory or clerical and junior managerial, administrative or professional
C2	Skilled working class	Skilled manual workers
D	Working class	Unskilled manual workers
E	Lowest subsistence levels	State pensioners, casual workers, people on social security

Commercial radio is the fastest growing advertising sector in Britain. In 1995, radio advertising revenue increased by over 200 per cent. About £300 million was spent on radio advertising in 1996 which accounted for four per cent of the advertising market share. The Advertising Association say that this figure could eventually rise to a seven per cent share of the total British advertising market.

On average, KFM has six to seven minutes of advertising per hour. Although

Figure 5.9 The weekly reach of radio stations, 1997

Radio station	% of potential local market reached
KFM	20%
Southern FM	3.3%
Invitee FM	13%
BBC Radio Kent	13%
BBC Radio Five Live	10%
BBC Radio Four	20%
BBC Radio Three	10%
BBC Radio Two	6.7%
BBC Radio One	13%

Source: First Survey Research

advertisements can be 15 or 45 seconds in length most radio advertisements are 29 seconds (cost circa £20); this means that there is capacity for about 12 advertisements to be broadcast in an hour. Fifteen per cent of KFM's advertising comes from national companies such as Habitat, British Gas and Carphone Warehouse but, predominantly, the station offers a service to local businesses and 85 per cent of the advertising is from that sector. Local advertisers include: a shopping mall, car dealers and car accessory dealers, double glazing companies and small local retailers. Health clubs, as well as local accountants and solicitors also promote their services over the local airwaves. Andrew Dean, KFM's Managing Director, says that local companies find radio advertising more successful than newspaper advertising for three reasons.

- The radio listener cannot skip over/escape the advertisements as they can with those in print
- Constant repetition makes radio advertisements more memorable than those in local newspapers
- Radio advertisements give the overall impression that a company is 'dynamic and exciting' and that it is 'financially secure'

Commercial radio offers more scope for promotion than just standard advertising slots; there is also the opportunity for programmes or competitions to be sponsored by organisations and businesses. On KFM, a number of shows are sponsored by local businesses. Traffic and travel news is sponsored by a carphone company and the breakfast show by a laser game. There are also numerous phone-in competitions with local sponsorship; these offer the opportunity to win anything from a set of luggage, to a ticket to a local show or a free meal at a local restaurant.

Scheduling

KFM broadcasts for 24 hours a day. It is a 'music led' station and, consequently, it is music rather than talk that predominates. The 1997 programme schedule shows that the day is divided into fairly large programme blocks inviting audience participation in numerous competitions, contests and challenges. As well as this entertainment

Figure 5.10 KFM programme schedule 1997

Monday–Friday	
6 am–10 am	*Ansell's Breakfast Club* with Nigel Ansell – music, news, travel showbiz, 'Krazy' competitions, fun and topicality
10 am–3 pm	Gavin McCoy's *Bit In The Middle* – with *Heaven at Eleven* (3 love songs), the KFM challenge and *KFM Today* at 1 pm
3 pm–6.30 pm	*Drive Time* with Clark Kent – including *KFM Konnection Kontest* and *KFM Tonight* at 6.30 pm
7 pm–8 pm	The *KFM Hit Wave* – non stop hits
8 pm–10 pm	*The Evening Show* with Gary Neal – featuring *Triple Track* and *Triple Play*, *Chart Check* and lots of fun
10 pm–6 am	*Into The Night* with Jerry Wright – with *Midnight Love* between 12 pm and 1 am, non-stop love songs
8 pm Friday–12 pm Sunday	*The Best of the Best More Music Weekend* – the maximum music allowed by law with loads of chances to win a prize

and 'fun' participation plus its musical *Hits and Memories*, the station also offers listeners a range of information including:

- National and local news
- National and local sports news
- National and local entertainment news
- Local traffic and travel information
- Local job vacancies

Most news on British commercial radio is provided by IRN (Independent Radio News). IRN supplies soundbites and other actuality and then the bulletin editor at the radio station will create a bulletin using this material and material from the station's own local reporters. This is a two way process, as national news frequently breaks locally, and a local radio report will be fed back to IRN and become part of the national news.

KFM does not offer the open access programming – programmes made by local organisations – which was the hallmark of community radio. Dominic King, KFM's Head of News, says that this type of programming is often designed so that radio stations can 'pat themselves on the back' for offering a public service when really they are only offering 'obscure time slots' such as Sunday afternoons when few people are listening. King believes that the community's voice is best heard within the news and stresses the importance of 'a strong news team within a local radio station' who can go out into the community to cover local stories and glean local views on national and local events. KFM newsroom employs three full time journalists and believes this offers both the potential for 'truly local' reporting on local issues and for a local slant to be presented on national issues. An example of the latter occurred during the week after Princess Diana's death when KFM broadcast a special service from her old school, West Heath in Sevenoaks. KFM also extends news bulletins and offers interpretation and comment from local 'experts' during special news events such as the budget. In summary then, KFM news offers the community a voice as follows:

- A KFM news phone line where the public can leave messages about stories in their area or they can leave their views on the news
- The capacity for in-depth local news coverage by the news team
- Local **vox pops** within news bulletins on current news issues

Vox pop

Literally translated from the Latin 'vox populi' means 'voice of the people'. A vox pop is gained by asking one question on a news issue to members of the public who then offer an opinion. The anonymous answers are then edited into a fast moving sequence that can be included within a news bulletin or a news feature.

FURTHER WORK

Standards in broadcasting

How successful is contemporary British broadcasting (TV and/or radio) in upholding the standards of PSB?

Discuss the contention that public service broadcasting as envisaged by Lord Reith is in terminal decline.[47]

Scheduling

What are 'classic notions of broadcast flow and scheduling'? How have they been influenced by satellite and cable TV technologies such as VCRs?

Funding

Should the BBC be funded by advertising or subscription rather than the licence fee?

Local radio

Some advantages of local radio advertising have been itemised in the case study. By making a close study of local radio and newspaper advertising within your area see if you can create a more comprehensive list of the advantages and disadvantages of advertising within these media. You might also like to think about the advantages/disadvantages of different classifications of advertising as well as the service these media provide to different types of advertiser.

How far can KFM or any local media organisation you have studied be said to offer 'a full and truly local' media service to the community?

 FURTHER READING

Briggs, Asa, *The Birth of Broadcasting, The History of Broadcasting in the United Kingdom Volume I*, OUP, 1961.

Briggs, Asa, *The Golden Age of Wireless, The History of Broadcasting in the United Kingdom Volume II*, OUP, 1965.

Briggs, Asa, *The War of Words, The History of Broadcasting in the United Kingdom Volume III*, OUP, 1970.

Briggs, Asa, *Sound and Vision, The History of Broadcasting in the United Kingdom Volume IV*, OUP, 1979.

Chapman, Robert, *Selling the Sixties: the Pirates and Pop Music Radio*, Routledge, 1992.

Crisell, Andrew, *An Introductory History of British Broadcasting*, Routledge, 1997.

Crisell, Andrew, *Understanding Radio*, 2nd edition, Routledge, 1994.

Curran, James and Seaton, Jean, *Power Without Responsibility: the Press and Broadcasting in Britain* (5th edition), Routledge, 1997.

Geddes, Keith, *Setmakers: A History of the Radio and Television Industry*, BREMA, 1991.

Hayward, Philip and Wollen, Tana, (eds), *Future Visions: New Technologies of the Screen*, BFI, 1993.

HMSO, *Broadcasting*, 1993.

MacCabe, Colin and Stewart, Olivia, (eds), *The BBC and Public Service Broadcasting*, Manchester University Press, 1986.

Madge, Tim, *Beyond the BBC: Broadcasters in the Public in the 1980s*, Macmillan, 1989.

O'Malley, Tom, *Closedown? The BBC and Government Broadcasting Policy, 1979–1992*, Pluto Press, 1994.

Peak, Steve and Fisher, Paul, (eds), *The Media Guide 1997*, Fourth Estate, 1996.

Peak, Steve and Fisher, Paul, (eds), *The Media Guide 1998*, Fourth Estate, 1997.

Scannell, Paddy and Cardiff, David, *A Social History of British Broadcasting Volume One 1922–1939*, Basil Blackwell, 1991.

Sendall, Bernard, *Independent Television in Britain: Volume I: Origin and Foundation 1946–62*, MacMillan, 1982.

Vahimagi, Tise, (compiler), *British Television: An Illustrated Guide*, Oxford University Press, 1994.

Watson, James and Hill, Anne, *A Dictionary of Communication and Media Studies*, 4th edition, Edward Arnold, 1997.

Winston, Brian, *Technology of Seeing: Photography, Cinematography and Television*, BFI, 1996.

Notes

1 From 'Broadcasting' in *The New Encyclopaedia Britannica*, Macropaedia Vol. 3, 15th edition (1974), Encyclopaedia Britannica Inc., 3:309.

2 Paddy Scannell, 'Public Service Broadcasting: The History of a Concept', in Andrew Goodwin and Gary Whannel, (eds), *Understanding Television*, Routledge, 1990, p13.

3 James Curran and Jean Seaton, *Power Without Responsibility: The Press and Broadcasting in Britain*, 2nd edition, Methuen, 1985, p137.

4 Paddy Scannell, *ibid*, p14.

5 Second edition, Methuen, 1985, p141.

6 Methuen, 1986, p24.

7 OUP, 1965, p6.

8 James Curran and Jean Seaton, *ibid*, p171.

9 Tim O'Sullivan, Brian Dutton and Philip Rayner, *Studying the Media: An Introduction*, Edward Arnold, 1994, pp55–57.

10 Andrew Crisell, *Understanding Radio*, Methuen, 1986, p26.

11 *ibid*, p27.

12 *Understanding Radio*, Methuen, 1986, pp33–34.

13 *The Sunday Times*, 21 May 1964 quoted in Chapman, Robert, *Selling the Sixties: the Pirates and Pop Music Radio*, Routledge, 1992, p44.

14 Quoted in Andrew Crisell, *Understanding Radio* (2nd edition), Routledge, 1994, p29.

15 *ibid*.

16 Steve Peak and Paul Fisher, (eds), *The Media Guide 1998*, Fourth Estate, 1997, p214. Original source: Rajar.

17 Tise Vahimagi, (compiler), *British Television: An Illustrated Guide*, Oxford University Press, 1994, p3.

18 *ibid*, pp5–13.

19 James Curran and Jean Seaton, *ibid*, p201. Original source: BBC Handbooks (1946–59).

20 James Watson and Anne Hill, *A Dictionary of Communications and Media Studies* (4th edition), Arnold, 1997, p230.

21 Bernard Sendall, *Independent Television in Britain, Volume 1: Origin and Foundation 1946–62*, Macmillan, p321.

22 Quoted in Bernard Sendall, *ibid*, p135.

23 James Curran and Jean Seaton, *ibid*, p199.

24 Roy Thomson, (later Lord Thomson of Fleet) quoted in Bernard Sendall, *ibid*, p150.

25 Arnold, 1997, p7.

26 Steve Peak and Paul Fisher, (eds), *The Media Guide 1997*, Fourth Estate, 1996, p166.

27 *ibid*, p171.

28 Adapted from HMSO, *Broadcasting*, 1993, pp7–8. Crown copyright is reproduced with the permission of the Controller of Her Majesty's Stationery Office.

29 The ITC Programme Code, January 1998, Foreword, p1.

30 *ibid*, p1.

31 *ibid*, p2.

32 *ibid*, p9.

33 *ibid*.

34 *ibid*, p14.

35 *ibid*, p15.

36 Steve Peak and Paul Fisher, *ibid*, p152.

[37] *A Dictionary of Communication and Media Studies* (4th edition), Arnold, 1997, p22.

[38] Quoted in *The Times*, 28 October 1995.

[39] Steve Peak and Paul Fisher, (eds), *The Media Guide 1998*, Fourth Estate, 1997, p164.

[40] Steve Peak and Paul Fisher, *ibid*, pp147 & 164. Original source: BARB.

[41] Statistical information from Steve Peak and Paul Fisher, *ibid*.

[42] Stuart Price, *The Complete A–Z Media and Communication Handbook*, Hodder & Stoughton, 1997, p30.

[43] Information below adapted from BARB publication: *BARB A General Guide*.

[44] Quoted in the *Guardian*, 1 February 1997.

[45] Quoted in Steve Peak and Paul Fisher, (eds), *The Media Guide 1997*, Fourth Estate, 1996, p180.

[46] *Media Week*, 14 November 1997, p30.

[47] Quoted in Steve Peak and Paul Fisher, *ibid*, p180.

[48] Quoted in Steve Peak and Paul Fisher, *ibid*, pp180–181.

[49] Steve Peak and Paul Fisher, (eds), *The Media Guide 1998*, Fourth Estate, 1997, p187.

[50] *Tonbridge Courier*, 9 June 1995.

CHAPTER **6** The Press

'This is not a time for recriminations, but for sadness. However, I would say that I always believed the press would kill her in the end. But not even I could imagine that they would take such a direct hand in her death as seems to be the case. It would appear that every proprietor and editor of every publication that has paid for intrusive and exploitative photographs of her, encouraging greedy ruthless individuals to risk everything in pursuit of Diana's image, has blood on their hands.'[1]

Earl Spencer speaking on the day after his sister, Diana, Princess of Wales, died in a car accident in Paris while being followed by paparazzi

Paparazzi

These are freelance photographers who are prepared to go to unscrupulous lengths to take candid shots of celebrities and royalty. The word was coined by Frederico Fellini, who named a character in *La Dolce Vita* (1960), Paparazzo. According to Emily Moore the word paparazzi comes from two Italian words, paptacci meaning mosquito and razzi meaning the popping of light bulbs.[2]

The Press and its **paparazzi** came in for heavy criticism following the death of Diana, Princess of Wales – not least from her brother Earl Spencer quoted above. This backlash has affected self-regulation and it might eventually result in an increase in legislation surrounding privacy of the individual but nevertheless it is the time for all media students to be 'watching this space' with interest. Important issues are under discussion here because Diana's death affected the press in a number of ways; it prompted the discussion of tighter curbs on press reporting but it also affected newspaper buying and, of course, it highlighted the power that the press has in giving importance to, and representing, people and issues in a particular way. The simple fact that Diana's death had hundreds, if not thousands, of times more column inches devoted to it than that of Mother Teresa in the same week speaks volumes.

LANDMARKS IN PRESS HISTORY

- 1476   First English Book is printed by William Caxton
- 1702   First English daily newspaper, the *Daily Courant*, is published.
- 1785   First issue of the *Daily Universal Register* (eventually *The Times*)
- 1800   The lawbreaking radical 'unstamped' press increasing
- 1819   'Gagging' laws increase legal restraints on the radical press
- 1853   The abolition of advertisement duty makes it cheaper to advertise
- 1855   The removal of stamp duty makes it cheaper to produce newspapers legally
- 1861   The removal of paper duty makes newsprint cheaper
- 1870   Education Act increases literacy and gives newspapers a wider readership
- 1920s   This period until the Second World War became known as the era of the press barons. Within this era, the circulation of national dailies goes from 5.4 to 10.6 million.
- 1921   Lord Northcliffe owns *The Times*, the *Daily Mail*, the *Weekly Despatch* and the *London Evening News*
- 1921   Lord Rothermere, Lord Northcliffe's brother, owns the *Daily Mirror*, the *Sunday Pictorial*, the *Daily Record*, the *Glasgow Evening News* and the *Sunday Mail*
- 1937   Lords Kemsley, Beaverbrook and Camrose control 59 per cent of national Sunday newspaper sales
- 1941   The *Communist Daily Worker* and the *Week* are closed down by the government for 'impeding the war effort by setting people against the war'.[3]
- 1947   The press becomes fully independent of political party control
- 1970s   Marks the return of partisan papers
- 1974   The *Sun* switches from Labour to Conservative Party support
- 1977   Lord Matthews is head of the Express Group
- 1981   Murdoch takes over *The Times*
- 1984   Robert Maxwell takes over the Mirror Group
- 1985   Conrad Black takes control of the Telegraph Group
- 1985   Lord Stevens takes over the Express Group
- 1985   Eddy Shah launches *Today* using new cold composition print technology
- 1986   Rupert Murdoch breaks the print unions with a stand-off at his new Wapping printing plant. This paves the way for fundamental changes in publishing.
- 1988   Murdoch, Maxwell and Stevens control 57 per cent of total daily and Sunday circulation
- 1991   Maxwell dies in a drowning accident and revelations of fraud and misdealings follow

PRESS OWNERSHIP TODAY

Ownership has moved on from the era of the press barons where strong pro-prietors with strong views directly influenced decisions concerning editorial content. Today, the popularity of those papers owned by media mogul, Rupert Murdoch, makes him an enormously powerful and influential figure but not in the same day-to-day way. The Monopolies and Mergers Commission (MMC) has in the past attempted to prevent too many media outlets ending up in the same hands but it is now fighting a losing battle because of the global diversity of conglomerate interests. Media moguls own terrestrial/satellite TV stations, film companies, news organisations and so on across the world.

Who owns what – national newspapers

Of course, this situation is constantly changing but at the time of writing the following is the case:[4]

- **News International** (Rupert Murdoch) – It controls 35 per cent of national circulation with the *Sun*, *The Times*, the *News of the World*, *The Sunday Times*
- **Mirror Group Newspapers** – It controls 26 per cent of national circulation with the *Daily Mirror*, the *Sunday Mirror*, the *Daily Record*, the *People* Mirror Group also own 43 per cent of Newspaper Publishing which owns the *Independent*, the *Independent on Sunday*
- **United News and Media** – It controls 13 per cent of national circulation with the *Daily Express*, the *Sunday Express*, the *Daily Star*
- **Daily Mail and General Trust** – It controls 12 per cent of national circulation with the *Daily Mail*, the *Sunday Mail*
- **The Telegraph** – (Conrad Black) – It controls 7 per cent of national circulation with the *Daily Telegraph*, the *Sunday Telegraph*
- **Guardian Media Group** – It controls 3 per cent of national circulation with the *Guardian*, the *Observer*
- **Pearson** – It controls 1 per cent of national circulation with the *Financial Times*
- **The European** – This company owned by the Barclay brothers runs the *European*, newspaper. The Barclays also own the *Scotsman*

READERSHIP AND THE 'POST-DIANA' FACTOR

Newspaper readership is more buoyant in Britain than anywhere else in the world; 60 per cent of people over 15 read a national daily newspaper and 70 per cent read a Sunday newspaper. The reason for this buoyancy is the success of the popular daily and Sunday tabloids who have fed their readers a palatable dish of soundbite news and popular entertainment. The tabloids have always had much larger circulation figures than the broadsheet newspapers but the broadsheets have high income readers which is attractive to advertisers. British broadsheets have also learnt from the tabloid experience; they had to. The immediacy of broadcast news has meant that in order to survive all newspapers have had to rethink their function. Newspapers are no longer 'first with the news'; consequently, the emphasis has shifted towards human-interest features and news analysis, and away from the hard news of the past. Peak and Fisher say, 'The response to these changes has been variously (and snobbishly) interpreted as yoofing up or dumbing down. The tabloids have grown tackier and the broadsheets have turned themselves into broadloids with bigger pics and more soft features pegged to predetermined headlines.'[5] This form of reporting inevitably means that there is more editorial comment and of course it also means a greater reliance on soft news stories about celebrities and entertainment.

Figure 6.1 Circulation figures for newspapers in October 1997 compared with figures for January to June 1997

	January–June 1997	October 1997	% change
Popular daily tabloids			
The *Sun*	3,894,007	3,749,138	−3.7
The *Mirror*	2,366,434	2,300,504	−2.8
Mid-market daily tabloids			
The *Daily Mail*	2,152,874	2,208,144	+2.6
The *Daily Express*	1,227,300	1,209,920	−1.4
Broadsheets			
The *Daily Telegraph*	1,124,640	1,099,953	−2.2
The *Times*	747,710	814,899	+9
The *Guardian*	408,790	408,374	−0.1
The *Financial Times*	312,723	333,309	+6.6
The *Independent*	257,010	265,156	+3.2
Popular Sunday tabloids			
The *News of the World*	4,469,884	4,433,710	−0.8
The *Sunday Mirror*	2,284,985	2,217,587	−2.9
The *People*	1,956,977	1,870,638	−4.4
Sunday mid-market tabloids			
The *Mail on Sunday*	2,129,089	2,207,933	+3.7
The *Express on Sunday*	1,163,150	1,106,812	−4.8
Sunday broadsheets			
The *Sunday Times*	1,322,988	1,356,913	+2.6
The *Sunday Telegraph*	892,630	884,656	−0.9
The *Observer*	456,496	435,444	−4.6
The *Independent on Sunday*	275,810	305,519	+10.8

Source: Audit Bureau of Circulation

Diana, Princess of Wales, arrived at the right time for newspapers trying to compete with the three minute visual culture. At first, she gave the papers a fairytale to sell and then she gave them pure melodrama; a royal soap, an upmarket *EastEnders*, with villains, heroes, adultery, eating disorders, loyalty, disloyalty and extravagant emotions. Like *EastEnders*, the 'Diana soap' commanded a huge audience and the end of the story was a tragedy not just in human terms but in terms of media finance as well. Journalists and photographers who wept when they heard of Diana's death may well have been weeping from the tragic loss of a young life but they were also weeping for the loss of a lucrative income. It is obvious, but unfortunately true, that Diana photos and stories sold newspapers in alarming quantities; tabloid editors would say that a 'Diana' front page could bring them an extra 200,000 readers on the day. In September 1997, newspaper sales were unusually high because of the tragedy but, in October, the post-Diana slump in sales became evident. *Media Week* commented: 'The tabloids were the worst hit. After the extensive sampling at the time of Diana's funeral, tabloid sales have dropped away both month on month and year on year. October is usually a strong month, as papers spend in September to bring back holiday readers. But the *Mirror*, the *Star* and the *Sun* have all posted their lowest sales in 1997 in October.'[6] Indeed, among the popular tabloids, the *Sun* lost about four per cent of its sales but the biggest loser seems to be the *People* with about a four and a half per cent drop.

It is difficult to identify the 'Diana factor' in broadsheet sales variation because of the impact of continuing circulation wars which means that sales patterns are changing in line with cuts in cover price.

It is rather unjust to compare the October slump in sales with the surge in sales created by the tragedy in September and so in Figure 6.1 the October circulation figures have been compared with the average figures for the first six months of the year.

TYPES AND CHARACTERISTICS OF NEWSPAPERS

Most British newspapers are in two main formats.

■ Broadsheet or full text size

For instance, the *Telegraph*, *The Times*, the *Guardian*, the *Independent*. These papers have retained the format despite the fact that there is no evidence to suggest that changing to a new format would have injured their character. In France, Le Monde is a 'quality' tabloid. Over the last few years, however, local newspapers have been rapidly changing to tabloid format

■ Tabloid or half size

For instance, the *Sun*, the *News of the World*, the *Mail* and the *Mirror*. Tabloids lend themselves to bold poster style layout and, of course, cheaper full-page advertising and more regular single positions which appeal to advertisers who feel a product is more memorable in a spot on its own. The tabloid category can also be sub-divided as there is a split between the 'popular dailies' such as the *Sun* and the *Mirror* and papers such as the *Daily Express* and the *Daily Mail* which have both changed from broadsheet to tabloid in recent years; both of these papers have a strong 'middle of the road' (B,C1) readership and are called the 'mid-market' dailies

Structure

There is method in the way newspapers are structured or organised as far as their contents are concerned. Stories and features are not just dropped into pages where they will fit. There is an overall plan or model of which pages are devoted to what aspect of news. This is one part of the selection process. If you are a regular reader of a particular paper you expect to find certain types of story on certain pages whether it be home news, foreign news, sport, fashion or readers' letters. This may seem obvious but the way a newspaper is put together is very important in the discourse with its readers. Within news-papers there is also a fine balance between space for stories and space for advertising; this can sometimes become quite a battle between the editorial staff and the media sales staff who both want the prime slots in the paper – advertising usually wins.

Lay out

The layout of stories on a page varies from newspaper to newspaper. The front page of a newspaper is very important as it is that which will initially catch the eye of the reader before they even read the first paragraph of a news story. A newspaper is usually divided into a number of columns across the page – eight or nine in a broadsheet and about six or seven in a tabloid. Mast-heads reflect and attract the readership; a quick perusal of *The Times* and the *Sun* will reveal that the former's masthead is a serif and the latter's a sans serif typeface. One is also set in colour the other is black and white. The serif typeface gives the impression of tradition and establishment while the sans **serif typeface** gives a more modern message to the reader. This underpins the importance of font and typeface in presenting a message in mastheads, headlines, etc. Fonts and typefaces vary from publication to publication according to their particular style. However, body text in most newspaper publications is in a Times Roman serif typeface (7, 8 or 9 point size) because this is easier to read in small print than sans serif typefaces (see Figure 6.2).

Serif typeface

A typeface with embellishing tails on the end of the letter strokes.
Sans serif typefaces do not have these.

Examples of font and point size

- Times New Roman 8 point
- Courier 10 point
- *Shelley 24 point*
- Gill 14 point

Hard news and feature articles – what is the difference?

A news story has an inverted pyramid shape – in other words it is top heavy. All the important information is at the beginning for two reasons.

Figure 6.2 The layout of a page of news

- Most readers are skimming the news and they read a maximum of the first three paragraphs of any story, unless really interested
- The sub-editor always cuts a story from the bottom upwards and important information too far down in a story might get cut

Feature articles are longer and tend to have a more traditional story shape with a beginning, middle and an end. Features used to be more exclusive to periodicals but because broadcast news is now first with the hard news, features are more prevalent in the daily press. Newspapers have the most topical features; a rule of thumb is that the less frequently the publication hits the streets the less topical the features. There are numerous types of feature including the following:

- Investigative/expose
- Interviews/profiles
- Personal experience
- Travelogues

- How to
- Humorous pieces
- Columns
- Reviews
- Editorials

Bias and impartiality

By tradition, the British national press have never been impartial and impartiality is not required of them by law as it is in broadcast news. If there is going to be bias then perhaps there is some rationale for suggesting that the overt bias of the tabloid press is preferable to the covert bias of the broadsheet newspapers. Many would say that you know where you are with the popular daily tabloids such as the *Sun* and the *Mirror* who openly support certain political parties – 'We're backing Blair', the *Sun* during the election campaign – or make racial jibes – 'Achtung! Surrender – For you Fritz, ze Euro 96 Championship is over', the *Mirror* during the 1996 European Football Cup.

A useful study of press bias emerges from the press coverage of the departure of Michael Grade from Channel Four in January 1997. While at Channel Four Michael Grade had been ultimately responsible for the programming of such series as *Gaytime TV*, *Dyke TV* and *The Word* and this was considered by some newspapers to be reason enough on hearing of his resignation to call him 'Pornographer in Chief' (the *Daily Mail*) or 'The King of Trash TV' (the *Express*). The *Sun* – as ever guardian of the nation's morals – used the headline 'Mr Porn Quits as Boss of Channel Four – Good riddance, say MPs' and then added in a highly emotive editorial:

Mr Mucky

One man took TV into the sewers. He gave us gay Christmas, lesbian nights, Europorn and four-letter filth. Now Michael Grade has quit as boss of Channel 4. Decent people will not mourn his passing. Let's hope the airwaves smell a little sweeter.[7]

Editorials are the one area of a newspaper where judgements can be made but this editorial is not just making judgements on Michael Grade but also by implication making judgements on homosexuality and, by nature of the **discourse** saying that the reader is not a 'decent' person if they don't make the same judgements.

Conversely, on the same day (28 January 1997) the *Guardian*'s Andrew Culf reported Michael Grade's departure with the following headline: 'Channel defender who put the flair in Four' and went on to quote Channel Four staff as saying that Grade was an 'inspirational creative leader'; then, it listed 'high profile' British Film Industry successes such as *Four Weddings and a Funeral*, *The Madness of King George* and *Shallow Grave* that came into being with help from Channel Four financing agreed by Grade. Of course, this story is also skewed by opinion – albeit a very different one from that presented in the *Sun*.

'Mr Porn' or 'inspirational creative leader' – where is the truth? Of course, there is no finite answer but students and critics of the media should always pose the question. Look once again at the editorial from the *Sun* above. The paper is really saying that if you 'mourn' Michael Grade's departure from Channel Four you are not a 'decent' person; the reader is forced into agreement. A discourse depends on this 'agreement' between the institution and its audience.

Discourse

Roger Fowler calls discourse a 'socially and institutionally originating ideology, encoded in language'.[8] For example, tabloid reports on so-called 'youth crime' require the audience to share their view that youth crime is a serious problem and this is often underpinned by emotive and judgmental words like 'yob' and 'hooligan'. Calling a 'joy-rider' a 'victim of society' opens up a discourse that many tabloids are unwilling to consider.

Power without responsibility?

The arguments are currently being put forward once again that sections of the press need their activities curbing and the government is once again looking at tightening laws on privacy. However, on 14 February 1997, one event prompted another criticism of press treatment of individual rights when the *Daily Mail* printed this headline:

Murderers
The Mail accuses these men of killing. If we are wrong, let them sue us[9]

It then continued by naming five young men, who the *Mail* said 'despite a criminal case, a private prosecution and an inquest' now thought '. . . they had got away with the killing' of Stephen Lawrence – a black student who was stabbed to death at a bus stop in Eltham in 1993 in what was widely considered to be a racially motivated attack. The naming of these young men, who had not been found guilty of this crime in a court of law, laid the *Daily Mail* open to court action either for libel or for a possible contempt of court. The *Mail*, however, knew that, as there is no legal aid for libel actions and the youths named did not have large amounts of money, they were safe from prosecution. The Attorney General also decided that proceedings for contempt of court against the newspaper 'would not be justified'. This case undoubtedly poses a number of questions for the media student.

- Should papers be allowed to act as judge and jury in this way?
- What protection do libel laws offer to the man in the street in a case such as this?
- What might effect an Attorney General's decision about prosecuting a newspaper for contempt of court?

Another event which recently opened up the debate about 'power and responsibility' within the press was the Mandy Allwood/Paul Hudson story – August to October 1996. Mandy Allwood became the centre of media attention when it became known that she was expecting octuplets after fertility treatment. In this case, Ms Allwood and her partner Mr Hudson engaged the services of a publicity agent, Max Clifford, who put her story up for auction; there were some rumours that one paper had offered to pay her on a 'sliding scale' according to how many of the babies survived – more babies, more money – and yet medical opinion seemed to favour the selected abortion of some of the foetuses in order to save the rest. The papers were criticised for putting the 'big' story before the well-being of the mother but at the same time Ms Allwood and Mr Hudson seemed to have courted maximum media attention. Maureen Freely writing in the *Observer* after Ms Allwood had miscarried all eight of the babies commented on the complexity of this issue as it could not simply be seen as a straight case of the media taking advantage of the individual.

Proud Paul [Hudson] went on to hint [at a press conference] that he was hoping to name some of the babies after the characters in the space-age children's book he wrote. The title (hint, hint, are there any publishers listening?) was to be *Chunkmasters* – his personal slang word for children. It was at this point in the story that it started becoming hard to tell who was taking advantage of whom. The happy couple's ignorance of things medical and the workings of the media were worrying. They were apparently easy prey, but then again, they seemed to be working on an awful lot of angles.[10]

This case also poses a number of questions for the media student about the ethics of cheque book journalism and the part that a so called 'media victim' might play in their own downfall which brings us back to where the chapter began with the Diana story and the question of privacy.

In November 1995, Diana, Princess of Wales appeared on *Panorama* and gave an in-depth interview about her private life to journalist Martin Bashir. Two days before the programme was broadcast Lord Wakeham, Chairman of the Press Complaints Commission wrote: 'Privacy can be compromised if we voluntarily bring our private life into the public domain. Those who do that may place themselves beyond the PCC's protection and must bear the consequences of their actions.'[11]

THE PRESS COMPLAINTS COMMISSION

In 1990 the government set up a committee, led by David Calcutt, to look at the problems of press intrusion into personal privacy. The old Press Council had long been criticised for its ineffectiveness in dealing with complaints against the press and Calcutt's job was a difficult one as he only had two avenues open to him.

- To recommend government legislation on press activity
- To recommend properly regimented self-regulation by the newspapers themselves

Calcutt opted for the latter and in January 1991, the Press Complaints Commission (PCC) came into being with Lord McGregor as the first chairman of this new body. In 1993, the press once again came under fire for intrusive practices and Calcutt was reappointed to investigate and make recommendations. After deliberation, Calcutt was highly critical of the PCC as it was and made three recommendations.

- A code of practice for journalists and photographers
- A press complaints tribunal with a judge and two lay assessors
- New legislation to cover bugging and the use of telephoto lenses

The Code of Practice was eventually agreed by newspaper editors who were anxious to avoid the prospect of legislation which would facilitate press censorship. Within the Code of Practice, members of the press 'have a duty to maintain the highest professional and ethical standards' and editors are responsible for the actions of their journalists.

The death of Diana, Princess of Wales once again brought the behaviour of the press into question and there were numerous appeals for greater curbs on journalists and photographers to prevent them invading people's privacy or hounding them as there was a real fear that press attention would now be focussed on Diana's two sons, William and Harry. In September 1997 Lord Wakeham, current Chairman of the PCC, put forward new proposals to be considered by the Code of Conduct Committee. These proposals deal with intrusions into privacy while at the same time trying to safeguard the principle of journalism 'in the public interest'. They are:[12]

- To ban publication of pictures obtained illegally or through 'persistent pursuit' or stalking

- To encourage photo agencies to sign up to the Code of Practice
- To tackle the 'deeply intimidating' media scrum that builds up around the home or workplace of someone in the news
- To extend the arbitrary age limit of 16 on the protection of children to all those in full time education
- To ban payments for stories to those under 16
- To ban stories on the private life of children where the only justification is that their parents are famous
- To expand the Code's definition of private property to include such places as churches or restaurants, where people might rightly expect privacy
- To define private life in terms, for instance, of people's health, home life, family relationships and personal correspondence into which the press should not intrude without overriding public interest

A revised Code of Practice covering these proposals was ratified on 26 November 1997.

Code of Practice

1   Accuracy

i   Newspapers and periodicals should take care not to publish inaccurate, misleading or distorted material.
ii   Whenever it is recognised that a significant inaccuracy, misleading statement or distorted report has been published, it should be corrected promptly and with due prominence.
iii An apology should be published whenever appropriate.
iv   A newspaper or periodical should always report fairly and accurately the outcome of an action for defamation to which it has been a party.

2   Opportunity to reply

A fair opportunity for reply to inaccuracies should be given to individuals or organisations when reasonably called for.

3   Comment, conjecture and fact

Newspapers whilst free to be partisan, should distinguish clearly between comment, conjecture and fact.

4   Privacy

i   Intrusions and inquiries into an individual's private life without his or her consent, including the use of long-lens photography to take pictures of people on private property without their consent, are only acceptable when it can be shown that these are, or are reasonably believed to be, in the public interest.
ii   Publication of material obtained under (i) above is only justified when the facts show that the public interest is served.

Note – private property is defined as:

- Any private residence, together with its garden and outbuildings, but excluding any adjacent fields or parkland and the surrounding parts of the property within the unaided view of passers-by

- Hotel bedrooms (but no other areas in a hotel)
- Those parts of a hospital or nursing home where patients are treated or accommodated

5 Listening devices

Unless justified by the public interest, journalists should not obtain or publish material obtained by using clandestine listening devices or by intercepting private telephone conversations.

6 Hospitals

i   Journalists or photographers making enquiries at hospitals or similar institutions should identify themselves to a responsible executive and obtain permission before entering non-public areas.

ii   The restrictions on intruding into privacy are particularly relevant to enquiries about individuals in hospitals or similar institutions.

7 Misrepresentation

i   Journalists should not generally obtain or seek to obtain information or pictures through misrepresentation or subterfuge.

ii   Unless in the public interest, documents or photographs should be removed only with the express consent of the owner.

iii Subterfuge can be justified only in the public interest and only when material cannot be obtained by any other means.

8 Harassment

i   Journalists should neither obtain nor seek to obtain information or pictures through intimidation or harassment.

ii   Unless their enquiries are in the public interest, journalists should not photograph individuals on private property (as defined in the note to Clause 4) without their consent; should not persist in telephoning or questioning individuals after having been asked to desist; should not remain on their property after having been asked to leave and should not follow them.

iii It is the responsibility of editors to ensure that these requirements are carried out.

9 Payment for articles

i   Payment or offers of payment for stories or information should not be made directly or through agents to witnesses or potential witnesses in current criminal proceedings except where the material concerned ought to be published in the public interest and there is an overriding need to make a payment for this to be done. Journalists must take every possible step to ensure that no financial dealings have influence on the evidence that those witnesses may give. (An editor authorising such a payment must be prepared to demonstrate that there is legitimate public interest at stake involving matters that the public has a right to know. The payment or, where accepted, the offer of payment to any witness who is actually cited to give evidence should be disclosed to the prosecution and the defence and the witness should be advised of this.)

ii Payment or offers of payment for stories, pictures or information, should not be made directly or through agents to convicted or confessed criminals or to their associates – who may include family, friends and colleagues – except where the material concerned ought to be published in the public interest and payment is necessary for this to be done.

10 Intrusion into grief or shock

In cases involving personal grief or shock, enquiries should be carried out and approaches made with sympathy and discretion.

11 Innocent relatives and friends

Unless it is contrary to the public's right to know, the press should avoid identifying relatives or friends of persons convicted or accused of a crime.

12 Interviewing or photographing children

i Journalists should not normally interview or photograph children under the age of 16 on subjects concerning the personal welfare of the child or of any other child, in the absence of, or without the consent of a parent or other adult who is responsible for the children.

ii Children should not be approached or photographed while at school without the permission of the school authorities.

13 Children in sex cases

i The press should not, even when the law does not prohibit it, identify children under the age of 16 who are involved in cases concerning sexual offences, whether as victims or witnesses or defendants.

ii In any press report of a case involving a sexual offence against a child:

- The adult should be identified
- The word 'incest' should be avoided where a child victim might be identified
- The offence should be described as 'serious offences against young children' or similar appropriate wording
- The child should not be identified
- Care should be taken that nothing in the report implies the relationship between the accused and the child

14 Victims of sexual assault

The press should not identify victims of sexual assault or publish material likely to contribute to such identification unless there is adequate justification, and, by law, they are free to do so.

15 Discrimination

i The press should avoid prejudicial or perjorative reference to a person's race, colour, religion, sex or sexual orientation or to any physical or mental illness or disability.

ii It should avoid publishing details of a person's race, colour, religion, sex or sexual orientation unless these are directly relevant to the story.

16 Financial journalism

i Even when the law does not prohibit it, journalists should not use for their own profit, financial information they receive in advance of its general publication, nor should they pass such information to others.
ii They should not write about shares or securities in whose performance they know that they or their close families have a significant financial interest without disclosing the interest to the editor or financial editor.
iii They should not buy or sell, either directly or through nominees or agents, shares or securities about which they have written recently or about which they intend to write in the near future.

17 Confidential sources

Journalists have a moral obligation to protect confidential sources of information.

18 The public interest

Clause 4, 5, 7, 8 and 9 create exceptions which may be covered by invoking the public interest. For the purpose of this Code that is most easily defined as:

i Detecting or exposing crime or a serious misdemeanour.
ii Protecting public health and safety.
iii Preventing the public from being misled by some statement or action of an individual or organisation.

In any cases raising issues beyond these three definitions the Press Complaints Commission will require a full explanation by the editor of the publication involved, seeking to demonstrate how the public interest was served.

Press Complaints Commission
1 Salisbury Square
London
EC4Y 8AE

THE PRESS IN THE FUTURE

All new products require huge amounts invested into advertising campaigns to get them off the ground. This even holds true with new print media products; here, the change to electronic publishing has allowed greater opportunity for new publications as there is no longer a need for a huge publishing and distribution infrastructure. Newspaper or magazine pages can be composed on computer and sent electronically anywhere in the world. They are then printed locally in very little time at all. The biggest cost involved in setting up a new publication is the advertising necessary to gain a share in the market; this can be a prohibitive factor. New electronic publishing technology facilitated the birth of the *Independent* in the 1980s; the newspaper soon took a sizeable share of the broadsheet market which prompted Rupert Murdoch's organisation, News International, to move in to protect *The Times*. Murdoch started a circulation 'war' which included price cutting and a huge marketing campaign; this eventually saw the *Independent* brought to its knees as it did not have the financial backing to take on the wealth of the Murdoch empire. The *Independent* was ultimately rescued by the Mirror Group but this meant the loss of its 'independent' status.

The lesson that could be learnt from this is that new technology has facilitated cheaper production and publishing but to gain and keep readerships newspapers need plenty of financial backup; inevitably, Goliath-like conglomerates will beat the small independents if it comes to circulation wars because the conglomerates can sustain short- and long-term losses which cannot be sustained by the independents.

 THE VOICE: REPRESENTATION IN THE MEDIA

'Most of the Black population think that they are not represented by the mainstream media in the same way as their White counterparts and that if there were no racial discrimination there would be no need for a separate Black media.'
Ionie Benjamin, *The Black Press in Britain*[13]

There is no doubt that Black people in Britain have, over the years, been subjected to negative representation in the popular press. Benjamin's comment above is elaborated by Paul Gordon and David Rosenberg in their book on racism in the press, *Daily Racism*: 'Previous studies of press coverage of race relations from the 1970s have shown how media images of black people invariably stressed ideas that black people caused trouble and took white people's jobs and homes ... Such studies have argued that instead the media could have put forward images of the prejudice, discrimination and deprivation experienced by black people.'[14] It is useful to look at some of the representations of Black people which pre-empted the first issue of *The Voice* in August, 1982. Indeed, in 1981 and early 1982 there was a sequence of events which prompted an orgy of racist reporting in the British press:[15]

■ March 1981 – an 'angry but dignified'[16] group of several thousand Black demonstrators marched through Fleet Street to protest at the failure of the police to solve the New Cross fire (Jan. 1981) in which 13 young Black people had died. The *Sun* (March 1981) reported: 'Day the Blacks Ran Riot in London' and the *Daily Express* headlined on the same day: 'Rampage of the Mob.'

■ April 1981 – the Brixton riots, which were provoked by a huge police 'stop and search' campaign called 'Swamp '81', initiated headlines such as 'Battle of Brixton – 100 black youths in clash with the cops' (the *Sun*, 11 April 1981) and 'Bloody hatred in the Streets' (13 April 1981).

■ June 1981 – the murder of a white youth, Terry May, by black youths prompted this extreme and emotive headline from the *Daily Star*: 'Black Vengeance Mob Kills Helpless Cripple' and this one from the *Daily Telegraph*: 'Rampaging Blacks Kill Youth After Wrecking Pub' (both 3 June 1981). However, the murders of two black youths, Markland Chambers and Mian Azim, in the same year had received minimal coverage in the national press; in fact, one had no national press coverage at all.

■ March 1982 – London's official annual crime statistics are released after a great deal of adverse pre-publicity in which one senior police officer claimed that 80 per cent of all London muggings were committed by Black people – even though mugging was not a crime on the statute books. A number of newspapers greeted the release of the figures with headlines such as these: 'The Yard Blames Black Muggers' (the *Sun*), 'Black Crime: the alarming figures' (*Daily Mail*), (both 11 March 1982)

The Voice was launched in August 1982 and it is easy to see how the paper identified the need to vocalise 'the mood of young Black Britons... The frustration and anger that had erupted into riots in British cities was in urgent need of a voice'.[17] It became the first paper in Britain to specifically target a young Black readership; over 70 per cent of the readers are between 15 and 34. 'This was an unusual step, since popular papers as a whole target a social class rather than an age group.' Says Ionie Benjamin: 'Other early papers were said to have failed to appeal sufficiently to the average non-academic young Black.'[18]

The Voice *factfile*

- Ownership
  Voice Communications Group who are also involved with publishing and music management. They publish the magazines *Chic, Black Beat International, Pride Magazine* and manage Mica Paris and Lavine Hudson

- Cost – 65p

- Frequency – weekly

- Circulation – 42,501

- Readership – 191,254

- Readership profile by social class – A/B = 10%, C1 = 39%, C2 = 38%, D/E = 13%

- Readership profile by age – 15 to 24 = 39%, 25 to 34 = 31%, 35 to 44 = 13%, 45 to 54 = 9%, 55+ = 2%

- Newspaper content
  News stories, features, *live and kicking*, USA today, international/Caribbean news, *The Voice* interview, Young voices, soul stirrings, sports.

- Magazine supplement content
  Films round-up, previews, music, life and living, arts, fashion

- Advertising content
  General appointments, professional and executive, public and community, regional appointments, social, health and housing, legal and finance, secretarial and administration, sales, media and marketing, teaching appointments, engineering and technical, entertainment guide, classified, courses and training, fostering and adoption, travel, legal and public notices, hair and beauty classified, AM/PM listing, heart to heart classified

How does The Voice *speak for the Black community?*

The Voice sets out its **agenda** clearly; there are two full page advertisements for the paper which state that they are 'Fighting for Fairness and Equality' and 'Education in the Community'. In its 'fight for fairness' *The Voice* has traditionally campaigned for Black people who have suffered miscarriages of justice. Ionie Benjamin describes *The Voice* as a 'populist and campaigning paper' which was instigated by a campaign in the early 1980s to find the truth behind the case of Colin Roach, a young Black man who had supposedly walked into Stoke Newington police station and shot himself. They followed this by taking up the case of the **Cardiff Three**, three black men jailed for the murder of a prostitute; they succeeded in bringing this case to the public's attention and, after a long campaign for an appeal, the men were freed in December 1992.

The 29 September 1997 edition carries on the campaigning stance of the paper with two stories about the judicial system. One story on the front page (see Figure 6.3a) 'Hanging Case Victory Close' reports the case of the last man hanged for murder in this country, a Somali born sailor, Mahmood Mattan, whose case has just been referred to the Court of Appeal. A story on page two reports the inquest on a Gambian policeman who died after being sprayed with CS gas at Ilford police station. The headline 'voices' the plea of his family 'Police Must Ban Spray'. This story is followed up by an editorial on page ten which also calls for the banning of CS gas.

Agenda

Each media institution will prioritise its selection of news in terms of its ideology.

Cardiff Three

Steve Miller, Tony Paris and Yusuf Abdullah were jailed for life in 1990 for the murder of a Cardiff prostitute. There was no forensic evidence to link the men with the murder and the police case hinged on a 'confession' given by Mr Miller after persistent police interrogation even though he had denied the offence over 300 times. The Appeal Judge, Lord Chief Justice Taylor, described the tape recordings of the police interviews as 'almost passing belief'.

LOOKING FOR A JOB? We've got 'em **PAGES AND PAGES FOR YOU**

THE VOICE

BRITAIN'S *BEST* BLACK PAPER

ISSUE No. 774 SEPTEMBER 29, 1997   65p

❊ FREE INSIDE ❊ THIS WEEK

20-PAGE COLOUR SUPPLEMENT FOR WOMEN

LEWIS SCHOOL IN CASH CRISIS

'We can't go it alone forever'

EXCLUSIVE by Tony Snow

LENNOX Lewis has threatened to cut his multi-million pound funding of the college he set up to help excluded children unless government chiefs back their political rhetoric with hard cash.

The Lennox Lewis College (LLC) in Hackney, east London, accepts students not wanted by the mainstream education system.

Over the past three years Lewis and business partner Panos Eliades have personally ploughed more than £10 million into the college for expelled and special needs children.

LLC was set up just four years ago in a disused metal box factory in Hackney, east London.

The college, which has a majority Black intake, is an accurate reflection of alarming figures released by CRE last week which show that Black children are six times as likely to be expelled as their White counterparts.

Lewis vented his frustration to associates and insiders involved in the college last week before jetting off to the States to complete train-

Continued on Page 5

FRUSTRATED: Lennox Lewis.

Free with VOICE

woman2woman

Issue one September 1997

Let's talk about sex

How do you rate the first night?

❊FASHION❊HEALTH❊SEX❊TRAVEL❊HOME-And MUCH, MUCH MORE
This week and EVERY month - ONLY IN THE VOICE

HANGING CASE VICTORY CLOSE

ONE of the last men hanged for murder in this country, who always protested his innocence, could be on the verge of having his name cleared.

Somali-born sailor, Mahmood Mattan, was hanged 45 years ago at Cardiff Prison, south Wales, for the horrific murder of a local shop keeper. He always swore his innocence and

now his case has been referred to the Court of Appeal.

Last year his family and friends succeeded in having his body exhumed from the unconsecrated ground of the prison and moved to the Muslim section of Cardiff's Western Cemetery.

Many saw this as a change in the government's attitude towards Mahmood's conviction.

Mahmood's wife, Laura Mattan, now 69, told The Voice: "The family are ecstatic about the appeal. I'll be relieved and happy when it's all over, and we finally clear his name.

The family's solicitor, Bernard de Maid, said: "We are understandably optimistic that our application at the Court of Appeal will be successful. In fact, we fail to see how it can be

defended.

A statement from the Criminal Cases Review Commission, which took over responsibility of reviewing criminal cases from the Home Secretary, said: "Following a number of enquiries and submissions by the family's solicitors, the Commission believes that Mr Mattan's conviction should be re-considered by the Court of Appeal."

Figure 6.3(a) *The Voice*, 29 September 1997

4 VOICE September 29 1997

YOUR

BRITAIN'S BEST BLACK PAPER

Mobile phones: Cool or plain sad?

These days everyone seems to have a mobile phone. A recent survey found that a lot of men carry phones to attract women. But what do people really think of men and women with mobile phones? Are they still cool or just sad posers?

James Bailey, 33, bank clerk, Cricklewood, north London.
"I normally carry a mobile but I'm not impressed when I see other people with mobiles. I think you've got a few posers who make a phone call on the bus and talk loud for no reason."

Samantha Morris, 23, student, Brixton, south London.
"I've got a mobile myself. It's very useful if you're in a difficult situation and if you use the phone a lot. But I hate people who have for show."

Coral Robinson, 22, student, Islington, north London.
"A mobile is just an accessory of the 1990s. It's not anything to be impressed about. But I do think young guys, especially teenage guys, use them to attract girls."

Mamadou Diop, 33, assistant manager, Edgware, Middlesex.
"I've got a mobile phone but I use it only for business. Most people I see using it are just chatting to friends. They are living on council estates and can't really afford to have one."

Chris Wade, 17, student, Isle of Dogs, east London.
"A lot of people don't really need mobiles use them to impress other people. A small percentage of guys have one to attract women. I don't have a mobile. They don't appeal to me."

STUDENT DRAWS IN GRADUATION

Sole Black graduate nowhere to be seen on degree ceremony film

By Paul Macey

WHAT should have been a life-long memento for a successful university student turned into a 'non-event' when he was nowhere to be seen on his graduation video.

Twenty-six-year old Trevor Robinson left the University of Portsmouth in July after successfully completing a three-year Honours degree in engineering.

Proud

As a proud memento of his graduation day, he bought the university's specially commissioned video recording of the ceremony.

But when he sat back to watch it he was not among the almost one hundred students filmed receiving their degrees.

"I was angry and shocked that I was not on the video," said Trevor, of Leyton, east London.

"At the time I was supposed to be on the stage, all you could see was the audience. The announcement of my name was even rubbed out. Basically, there is no trace of me receiving my degree."

A letter accompanying the video from Interface Video Productions, of Salford, Greater Manchester, explained that a faulty camera – which could not be repaired at the time – was the reason for the omission.

Trevor, the only Black person on his course, remains less than satisfied: "I cannot believe that this has happened. From

UNEMPLOYMENT GAP CONTINUES TO WIDEN

UNEMPLOYMENT figures produced last week by the Labour Force Survey show that unemployment rates within African and Caribbean communities are three times higher than those amongst White people.

Of particular concern is the fact that whilst White unemployment fell there was an increase of 5,000 in Black unemployment between Spring 1996 and Spring 1997.

Figures also showed that almost 60 per cent of Black people who were in part time employment could not find permanent jobs, far more than the figure of 38 per cent amongst White people.

David Shire, director of the Black Employment Initiative believes that drastic action is needed to improve employment prospects for Black people.

"The prospect for closing the gap in employment opportunities is bleak unless the Government comes up with specific measures to tackle the endemic ethnic inequalities by the creation of long term secure jobs for all," he said.

STARS IN THEIR EYES

AN EXCITING new venture is due to be launched next month to help young musicians on their way to stardom.

The Starlight Music Academy, based in Peckham, south London, is looking for talented singers between the ages of 16 and 25 to take part in a nine-week training programme.

The course, which will start at the end of October, will offer tuition in singing, dance and studio techniques, as well as give an insight into how the music industry operates.

The course will end with a performance by the trainee artists to the public and music industry guests.

FIRST BLACK STAR FOR ROYAL BALLET

THE ROYAL Ballet began its new season of performances on Wednesday, featuring its first ever black dancer.

But while 19-year-old Jerry Douglas, (pictured left) from Sacramento, California, may be leading the way, he is taking it all in his stride.

"This is one of the biggest and best ballets in the world, I am delighted to be a part of it," he said. "People might see me as something of a pioneer, but you do have to work hard to get here."

Jerry came to London two years ago to study at ballet school. He was picked by talent spotters in the spring to perform at The Royal Ballet, which has moved from its home at The Royal Opera House in Covent Garden for two years while redevelopment takes place.

● *Jerry will appear in The Royal Ballet performances of Romeo and Juliet, Giselle and The Sleeping Beauty at Labatt's Apollo, Hammersmith, west London which runs until October 18. Voice readers have the opportunity to attend any matinee or evening performance at a 30 per cent discount. Contact The Royal Ballet Box Office on 0171-304 4000, quoting reference 'BR'. Tickets before discount start at £15.*

Figure 6.3(b)

September 29 1997 VOICE 5

A BLANK VIDEO

RUBBED OUT: *Trevor Robinson with his graduation video.*

what I can see I am the only person not on the video. What makes it doubly disappointing is that this was for my Mum who could not be at the ceremony as she lives in Jamaica. Now she will never see it."

An Interface Video spokesman told The Voice: "It would not be appropriate for us to talk about this issue without firstly talking to the client involved."

Apology

A spokesman from the University's marketing department said: "The video company has filmed our graduation ceremonies for two or three years now and we have had no problems with it. We are sorry that this has happened to this person and hope that the situation can be rectified in some way to his satisfaction."

Army steps up its anti-racism drive

Efforts to end race discrimination within the Armed Forces have been given a cautious welcome by the government.

In a progress report to the Commission for Racial Equality this month, the Ministry of Defence outlined a series of measures designed to achieve its policy of ethnic equality.

Proposals include equal opportunities training and steps to ensure that commanders are aware of their role in tackling racism in the ranks.

Dr John Reid, Armed Forces Minister, said: "We still have a long way to go. But these measures reflect considerable progress and the determination shared by ministers and service chiefs alike to make the Army more open, tolerant and representative of the society which it serves."

The report follows increasing revelations of racism within the ranks. Last month The Voice reported the case of two sisters who were racially abused by a group of soldiers from the Cheshire regiment at an army base in Cambridge. Despite hundreds of witnesses only one soldier has been disciplined.

CASH CRISIS FOR LEWIS SCHOOL

Continued from page 1

ing for Saturday's heavyweight clash against Andrew Golota in Atlantic City.

The sentiments of the world champ are shared by his partner Mr Eliades.

"Nobody is prepared to commit to funding the college. It has been left entirely up to Lennox and myself," he said.

"We are not prepared to go it alone forever."

Difficulty

Lennox is under no illusion about the difficulty of the task he faces on October 4 against title challenger Golota, but the fight to secure the future of his brainchild seems even tougher.

Liz Jones, LLC's principal, told The Voice: "Lennox has spared no expense on the college. This is a very personal issue to him and right now he feels totally disillusioned."

Charity

The two benefactors keep the college afloat singlehanded. It costs £750,000 a year to keep LLC afloat – the only state funding the college receives is a paltry £15,000 annual grant from the Single Regeneration Budget.

The college's status as both a charity and a private school mean that LLC is excluded from local authority funding. The unique status it holds means it does not fit into any neat funding category.

A spokeswoman for Hackney Council, who was unable to confirm if the college had applied for any mainstream funding, said: "We have our own provision for excluded pupils, but do refer some to Lennox Lewis College."

VOICE COVER GIRL WINS BEAUTY PRIZE

CORONATION: *Miss Jamaica UK tries out her throne.*

THIS stunning six footer has no trouble turning heads at the best of times, and her effortless good looks certainly paid off last weekend.

Nineteen year old La Donna Griffiths beat off 15 rivals to be crowned Miss Jamaica UK, at a glitzy ceremony at the Marriot Hotel in central London.

The mantle of Miss Jamaica UK was passed on to her by last year's winner, the equally dazzling Lisa Mendes.

Organiser June Daley, who conceived the event eight years ago told The Voice: "It has been our best year so far with an excellent calibre of girls who were all highly intelligent and were a credit to Jamaica."

La Donna will be no stranger to regular Voice readers. We first spotted her at Jamaica Expo in July and promptly put her on the cover.

HIGH CALIBRE: *Six-foot La Donna stands tall and proud.*   Pics: Corey Ross

Project's cash boost

A PROJECT offering support and friendship for young people with disabilities has received a welcome financial boost.

The Croydon Contacts 'Hard to Reach' project has been awarded £11,000 a year for the next three years from the council and local health authority.

It is now looking for people who are interested in providing one-to-one support in a range of pursuits, including shopping or going to the cinema.

Volunteers, who must be aged between 17-35 years old, will be offered full training and expenses.

Schools urged to tackle exclusion crisis

COMMUNITY organisations are calling on schools to urgently tackle the high rate of exclusions among Black children

The call has come amidst increasing concern that African Caribbean children, particularly boys, are bearing the brunt of an exclusions epidemic sweeping the country.

Respect

New figures show that children from the African Caribbean community are now four times more likely to be permanently excluded as their White classmates.

Although Black children make up only 2 per cent of the school population they represent over 8 per cent of all exclusions.

Research produced by the Children's Society last week shows that an estimated 250,000 days of schooling are lost every year through children being excluded from class.

Liz Jones, the head teacher of the Lennox Lewis college in east London, which takes on many permanently excluded youngsters, believes that exclusions can be lowered if pupils are treated with respect.

She told The Voice: "We base our philosophy on respect and treat students as adults. We show them that we believe that they have talent and can

succeed, given the chance. We have disciplinary measures but exclusion is certainly not a first resort."

A spokesman for the Commission for Racial Equality agrees there is no reason for the numbers to be so high.

Guidelines

"The issue of exclusion has always been high on the agenda for the CRE. Following successful work in schools in Birmingham we have developed guidelines of good practice which we believe, if adopted, will show that there is no reason for the rate of exclusions to be high."

Figure 6.3(c)

One news story, 'Race Watchdog "has no bite",' has the chief of the Commission for Racial Equality (CRE) criticising the organisation's lack of 'bite' when implementing standards for race equality in local government. Another story voices concerns about the continued 'unemployment gap' between African and Caribbean communities and White people. The newspaper speaks for its readers in these areas but it also offers its readers a voice in other ways; there is a letters page and a vox pop type 'Your *The Voice*' column (see Figure 6.3b).

The Voice employs a mode of address somewhere between a typical national mid market and a popular national tabloid; sometimes it talks about the needs of Welsh people being 'subsumed' and sometimes it talks about 'this stunning six footer' but it also occasionally slips into the voice of the young Black community in Britain. This is most evident in this edition's 'Woman2Woman' magazine, when *The Voice* asks 'Wanna be a sista on the couch? or invites readers to be 'this month's main man'. There is also a humorous columnist, Vasta-Man, who presents an irreverent and streetwise view of life, pokes fun at black stereotypes and successfully yokes together Caribbean cool and Noel Coward with sentences like: 'Dat night June and I 'n' I pledged our undivided love for one another under the exquisite Jamaican moonlight.'

How does The Voice *represent the Black community?*

The pages of *The Voice* are filled with positive images of the Black community and there are very few if any sorties out of this community. On front page, (Figure 6.3a) there is the Boxer Lennox Lewis talking about the college he has set up to help children who are 'not wanted by mainstream education'. This story is 'Lewis led' because Lewis, of course, is a positive representation for young black aspirations. It is worth imagining how this story could be reported in a national tabloid. Those publications might lead in on the fact that the college is mainly for Black children who have been excluded from mainstream schools. Instead of the headline 'Lewis School in Cash Crisis' they might say 'No cash for Black Tearaways' and they might only mention the Lewis connection in passing.

The story on page 4 (Figure 6.3b) about the 'First Black Star for the Royal Ballet' is also a positive image. It stresses that Jerry Douglas is a pioneer, in that he is the first black dancer to be accepted into this institution, but it is also a doubly positive image because it is also questioning traditional male stereotypes.

Nevertheless within this publication, which is seeking to present positive Black images back to the community it serves, there are some strange anomalies. For instance, there are at least three advertisements for hair relaxants: Hairwerks (*sic*), Arosci and Isoplus. There is also a beauty page letter on the problem of hair straightening. This could possibly send confusing signals to readers as it seems to be iconising a 'White' look.

 **FURTHER WORK**

Controls on news reporting
Is there a case for saying there should be greater controls placed on news reporting?

Mode of address
Look at the three pages from *The Voice* and see how many positive images of the Black community you can identify. Look at one of these stories in greater detail and see if you can rewrite it with headline for a popular national daily tabloid.

FURTHER READING

Curran, James and Seaton, Jean, *Power Without Responsibility*, Routledge, 1991.

Fowler, Roger, *Language in the News*, Routledge, 1991.

Benjamin, Ionie, *The Black Press in Britain*, Trentham Books, 1995.

Gordon, Paul and Rosenberg, David, *The Press and Black People in Britain*, The Runnymede Trust, 1989.

Notes

1 Quoted in *The Daily Mail*, 1 September 1997.

2 The *Guardian*, 23 September 1997, p12.

3 James Curran and Jean Seaton, *Power Without Responsibility*, Routledge, 1991, p72.

4 Information from Steve Peak and Paul Fisher, *The 1998 Guardian Media Guide*, Fourth Estate, 1997.

5 Steve Peak and Paul Fisher, *The 1998 Guardian Media Guide*, Fourth Estate, 1997, p24.

6 *Media Week*, 14 November 1997, p7.

7 The *Sun*, 28 January 1997.

8 Roger Fowler, *Language in the News*, Routledge, 1991, p42.

9 Quoted from *The Daily Mail*, 14 February 1997.

10 The *Observer*, 6 October 1996, p3.

11 Quoted in Steve Peak and Paul Fisher, *The 1997 Guardian Media Guide*, Fourth Estate, 1996, p17.

12 Itemised by Carol Midgley, *The Times*, 26 September 1997.

13 Ionie Benjamin, *The Black Press in Britain*, Trentham Books, 1995, p6.

14 Paul Gordon and David Rosenberg, *The Press and Black People in Britain*, The Runnymede Trust, 1989, p1.

15 See Paul Gordon and David Rosenberg, *The Press and Black People in Britain*, The Runnymede Trust, 1989.

16 Paul Gordon and David Rosenberg, *The Press and Black People in Britain*, The Runnymede Trust, 1989, p17.

17 Ionie Benjamin, *The Black Press in Britain*, Trentham Books, 1995, p69.

18 Ionie Benjamin, *The Black Press in Britain*, Trentham Books, 1995, p5.

CHAPTER 7 News

┌───┐
│ **CONTENTS OF THIS CHAPTER** │

- **What is news?**
- **News gathering**
- **News selection**
- **News bias**
- **The narrative of news production**
- **Case study: BBC1 *Nine O'Clock News*, Wednesday 27 August 1997**

└───┘

'A lot of BBC news looks stale and rather 1980s. We have got to get rid of over-paid, middle-aged anchors in suits sitting in state in huge empty studios. There is no resonance with anyone.'

A senior BBC programme maker commenting on plans to update BBC News[1]

There is no better place to start the study of news than with a quick glance at two popular TV programmes that satirise the idiosyncrasies of news production. *Drop The Dead Donkey* (Channel Four) and *The Day Today* (BBC2) offer the media student a useful, if exaggerated, introduction to many of the concepts being discussed later in this chapter. A brief acquaintance with Globelink reporter, Damian Day, as he dumps dead fish into a lake to 'enhance' an item on pollution or a battering from the authoritative hyperbole of *The Day Today's* nonsensical news items crystallises the concept of news as a manufactured product. No one would want to suggest that news reporters have the low ethical standards of a Damian Day or that news reports are the sum total of mode of address over content but a study of these programmes reveals a number of the ingredients present in news production 'recipe'.

WHAT IS NEWS?

Too often, we take the term 'news' for granted but what does it really mean? What *is* news? Many famous and not so famous people have defined the word news; few of them agree on an interpretation but, interestingly, few of them conflict. Here are a selection of definitions listed by F. W. Hodgson[2] with the addition of Lord Northcliffe's interpretation:

- 'News is people' (Harold Evans)
- 'Dog bites man – no interest. Man bites dog – news' (Anonymous)
- 'News is anything that makes a reader say "Gee Whiz" ' (An American editor)
- 'News is what someone somewhere wants to suppress; all the rest is advertising' (Lord Northcliffe)
- 'Fresh events reported' (*Concise Oxford Dictionary*)

The first definition is bound to be true. News is inevitably an entity that involves people and, certainly, the human aspect of news is enormously important. In Britain, the popular press have made people a priority and they have made famous people a top priority. Tabloid column inches are either groaning with stories that possess that particular person angle such as 'Tiny Tina Heart Op Tot', 'Harrow Housewife Harriet' or they are plastered with the exploits of Fergie, Madonna, Gazza, etc.

In the second and third definitions, the idea of dramatic surprise or unusualness is given importance. Certainly, the more quirky the story the more an audience will be engaged by it, even if this news has little future bearing on events or people in general.

Northcliffe's definition is one of the most thought provoking because he is clearly stating that essentially most news *is* advertising; many people working in a newsroom would probably agree. Press releases, press conferences and orchestrated 'media happenings' are the source of many news stories; this could take the form of a book review, political conference or **lobby briefing**. The 'real' news would be those stories that have remained hidden until uncovered by painstaking investigation; unfortunately, this definition might give many scandal stories a higher status than they deserve and devalue the worth of important news that comes from the orchestrated sources mentioned above.

LOBBY BRIEFING

The name comes from the 'lobby' of the House of Commons through which MPs pass when voting. Lobby correspondents are a select group of reporters who work within the House of Commons and are privileged to receive special briefings by the Prime Minister's press secretary. During Margaret Thatcher's Government, two newspapers, the *Independent* and the *Guardian* withdrew from briefings given by her Press Secretary, Bernard Ingham, because they felt the lobby system was too manipulatory as it allowed the government to speak without the source having to be revealed; in essence, any report which remains unattributed is difficult to verify and the two newspapers believed that the government were using the briefings to test public opinion on policies before they were being made official as well as to make comment on opposition policies and politicians. The anonymous nature of the briefings then allowed the government to deny the statements if they proved unpopular or unsubstantiated.[3]

The final definition, the dictionary delineation, seems to be the most useful for the media student. Every word within it is important to the understanding of the term *news*.

▪ Firstly, news must be new or fresh or at least have a fresh angle

▪ Secondly, news must be presented as something which is not mundane; it must be an event

▪ Finally, and most importantly the fresh event must be *reported* to become news

NEWS GATHERING

The news process requires that the event is related but first it must be gathered. If news agencies do not discover a story or if they find a story and then feel that it will not fit within their **news agenda** then the public will be left uninformed.

An event's newsworthiness often depends initially on the ease with which the story can be obtained. For obvious reasons, journalists tend to rely on the **primary definers** of an event to give them not only the factual details but also an idea of the news story's eventually angle and importance.

A good example of the importance of the primary definer is a comparison of two shipwreck stories which happened as 1996 drew to a close. One incident involved the British round-the-world yachtsmen, Tony Bullimore, adrift awaiting rescue thousands of miles from civilisation; the other involved several hundred Asians, allegedly trying to enter Europe illegally, who were missing presumed drowned a few miles off the coast of Greece. The former attracted saturation, blow-by-blow coverage on the British media because it involved a British yachtsman. The latter received no media coverage at all when it happened – it simply did not become news. The *Observer* was one of the only newspapers to pick up on the story at all and then on Sunday 12 January 1997 it commented:

'Massacre at sea
A lone yachtsman is pulled from the sea. The world gasps. Hundreds of immigrants disappear in the Mediterranean.
Was it murder? Who even cares?'

If the primary definer is not immediately credible, for any number of reasons, then that story will probably not be investigated or will not be thoroughly investigated. In the case of the illegal Asian immigrants, the primary source was the surviving immigrants none of whom spoke Greek – where they landed – and few of them spoke English well. The Greek authorities and journalists were initially sceptical of the scraps of stories about hundreds being drowned at sea. It was only when families of the dead in the Western world started reporting their relatives missing that the search for the missing and their story began.

The police are often primary definers of news stories. In the past, this has often ensured that crime news has presented a good police image. For instance, the initial reports of the London poll tax riot in 1990 laid the blame

News agenda

Each news production organisation will prioritise types of news in keeping with its ideologies.

Primary definers

The primary definers are usually people who have witnessed an event first hand; this is often the police or emergency services but it can be an ordinary eyewitness including a journalist, cameraman, etc. Whether or not a story becomes news often depends on the primary definers. If they hold credibility, as the police do, the story will be placed on the news agenda. Secondary definers are usually news agencies or journalists who manufacture the initial story into a news story.

almost entirely on the anti-poll-tax demonstrators. Much later, investigations alleged that the police were not without blame for the riot as they had used heavy-handed methods in trying to disperse the crowd. Unfortunately, most journalists relied on the version of events initially supplied by the police instead of tracking down other angles on the story and the poll tax protesters were presented as the day's villains.

News agencies

National international and global news agencies have a powerful influence over global news consumption. A relatively small number of huge news agencies supply much of the media in the Western world with initial news of major events and, as secondary definers, they are instrumental in angling the way an event should be perceived. (Sometimes news agencies are referred to as primary definers but perhaps it would be more accurate to refer to them as dominant secondary definers of news events.)

Major news agencies include the following.[4]

- AP – Associated Press is an American international news and pictures agency owned by a co-operative of US media companies
- Reuters – a hugely important, global supplier of news and information which took over the TV news agency Visnews in 1992, renaming it Reuters Television
- UPI – United Press International provides coverage of the Middle East, business news, sport, politics, etc.
- PA – the Press Association, which is owned by regional newspaper publishers in Britain
- UK News – a provider of news and pictures to 33 regional newspapers

If we take AP as an example of these, the importance of news agencies can be established. AP provides news and wire pictures to local daily papers throughout America. Many of these papers print the national and international stories as they stand. This means that millions of Americans are receiving the same slant on the same story. Even if a story is given more in-depth coverage, this coverage will undoubtedly be coloured by the definition of the item given by the news agency.

Although the following news organisations are not strictly agencies, they hold such an important place in global news gathering and dissemination that they must be acknowledged.

- CNN International – Cable News Network, a global news network owned by American, Ted Turner
- WTN – Worldwide Television News is owned by ITN, ABC (USA) and Nine Network (Australia)
- BBC News – now moving into digital 24 hours world-wide satellite news broadcasting
- ITN – Independent Television News owned by a consortium of: Carlton TV, Granada TV, the *Daily Mail* and General Trust, Reuters, Anglia TV and Scottish TV. ITN provides TV news but it also supplies news to IRN

(Independent Radio News) which serves independent radio stations throughout Britain

NEWS SELECTION

Once the story has been gleaned, it still has a long way to go before it hits the headlines or the TV screens as now it must be processed by the secondary definers and at this point a number of things can happen to a story; these range from significant changes to 'spiking' (ie being thrown out altogether). Every news agency and organisation sets an order of importance for their news dissemination. This set agenda is policed by the 'gatekeepers' within the organisation who are responsible for prioritising the selection of stories as well as prioritising the key elements within a story.

Gatekeeping is a useful metaphor for a process which allows some news through to the public while some is stopped at the 'gate'. In essence, everyone involved in news production plays a part in the gatekeeping process but particularly news editors and sub-editors who have the final say in the content of a news bulletin or a particular newspaper's daily news. A camera man, for instance, selects certain aspects of an event to shoot and not others; similarly, a journalist might choose to get one person's account and not another's. In the newsroom the story has to be selected by a news editor to be included in the bulletin/paper and then its position within the bulletin/paper will be decided. Sub-editors will often change a story to fit a space; video editors edit the length or sequence of the pictures we see. Choices are being made and so there must be criteria for this selection process.

News values

For many years news selection criteria were loosely categorised by journalists and media critics. Alastair Hetherington, a former editor of the *Guardian*, listed the criteria that governed his choices as follows:[5]

- Social significance
- Political significance
- Economic significance
- Human significance
- Drama – excitement, action
- Surprise – the unexpected
- Proximity – how close to home is the event
- Personalities – royalty, show business, politicians, actors
- Sex – scandal, crime
- Numbers – how many affected

One might be forgiven for thinking that this list covers just about everything. In essence, almost anything can be news; much depends on whether it can be manipulated into an interesting story for the particular target audience. However, in 1965, Johan Galtung and Mari Ruge in an academic study of news selection and structure arrived at twelve factors or news values which govern the news agenda.[6]

- Frequency

  The more similar the frequency of the event is to the frequency of the news medium, the more likely it is to be recorded (eg if a murder happens quickly and its meaning is established rapidly it is more likely to get in the news. If an item of news takes time to establish an understandable plot or evolves over a number of weeks it is less likely to be reported)

- Threshold/amplitude/numbers

  The size of an event will govern the amount of attention it is given. Obviously the bigger the better

- Unambiguity

  The simplicity of a story will also make it more attractive to the media as it will be easier for the journalist to investigate and easier for the audience to understand

- Meaningfulness

  Culturally relevant or culturally proximate events are more likely to make the news. The news audience is far more interested in events which have happened close to home or events which contain references to values, beliefs and attitudes that it shares

- Consonance

  Events which meet our expectations are more likely to become news

- Unexpectedness/surprise

  Conversely, events which hold a large element of surprise are also more likely to hit the headlines (eg man bits dog)

- Continuity

  Events which have initially been defined as news will continue to carry importance in news agenda (eg a war that starts with a big battle and then turns into minor skirmishes is more likely to get full news coverage even in the latter stages than a war which starts and continues as minor skirmishes)

- Composition

  Most news organisations try to balance their news output. Often, news editors will try and ensure that a balance of home and foreign news is preserved or that there is an element of lighter news within a news bulletin to make it less depressing. Hence, the **dead donkey** story at the end of news bulletins. These stories would not, in other circumstances be defined as newsworthy

- Reference to elite nations

  Other major Western nations such as the USA, Germany, France are more likely to get in the news even if it is perhaps only one person being killed than are Third World nations

- Reference to elite persons

  Events which contain references to stars, politicians, royalty, etc., are all more likely to become news

Dead donkey

This story usually ends a bulletin or is the filler at the bottom of a page. It is an insubstantial story at best humorous at worst mawkish – often trading on the British love of animals – which is included purely to give the news a balanced composition. It is also the first item to be dropped should an important story break. Hence the saying 'drop the dead donkey'.

■ Personalisation

Events which are personalised are more likely to be reported than those which have no specific individual concerned (eg large scale NHS stories about understaffing and operating theatre cancellations tend to become personalised as 'Tiny Tina Refused Heart Op' treatment if they are to become news)

■ Negativity

Bad news makes good news!

Nearly a quarter of a century after this list was initially defined there is a major new factor to consider.

■ Actuality

If a news station has some video, a newspaper has a picture or a radio station has a soundbite of an event then this story is more likely to be reported than it otherwise would or it might have a greater/higher priority within the paper/bulletin than it would otherwise deserve

A good example of the high value of actuality can be found in a comparison of the front pages of the *Sun* and *Today* on 18 November 1993 (see Figure 7.1).

In terms of standard news values, the story concerning the deaths of the school children should have higher news priority because of its amplitude; however, the only actuality is a picture of a similar minibus to the one that crashed. The *Sun* uses this story as its lead with the flare attack as its second lead but because *Today* has a colour picture of the flare gun attack at the football ground it prioritises the stories differently; the flare attack becomes the lead story. In tabloid news, actuality is all important.

Different news organisations prioritise these news values according to their particular agenda. The popular daily and Sunday newspapers place great emphasis on two news values – elite persons and personalisation. This manifests itself as their preoccupation with royals, soap and pop stars and the tendency to turn big issues into personal 'Tiny Tina' stories. Broadsheet newspapers tend to place a high value on composition. Often the front page of a page such as the *Independent* will provide home news stories balanced with some foreign news and a 'dead donkey' story.

NEWS BIAS

By following the news story through the production process via gathering and selection, it becomes clear that no news story is going to exist without being affected by personal/organisational bias or even bias created by commercial pressures. Broadcast news is legally required to be politically impartial and this was most evident in the run up to the last general election; the logistics of offering equal air time not just to the three major parties but to so many marginal parties proved a headache for broadcasters but provided the viewer with some unusually entertaining party political broadcasts.

Nevertheless, news is mediated, even on radio and television, and that does not happen in an ideological void; both the individual news reporter and the

ONLY 25P

TODAY

NEWSPAPER OF THE YEAR

WINDSOR

RISING FROM THE ASHES AT £8 A HEAD – Pages 26 & 27

THURSDAY November 18, 1993   TV: Pages 28-29   SL ★★★★

Nine kids die in crash

by IAN GALLAGHER

NINE children and a teacher were killed early today when their school minibus crashed into the back of a truck on a motorway.

Many of the youngsters were burned to death as their vehicle burst into flames after the impact.

Six others were critically hurt and police said the death toll could rise.

The crash happened on the M40 on the outskirts of Warwick at 12.30am.

A policeman said: "The scene is one of unbelievable carnage. There are bodies lying all over the place. Some of the children were trapped in the blazing wreckage and could not be reached."

Several motorists travelling behind the vehicle made heroic rescue attempts but were beaten back by the heat.

Outing

Police said the children were returning after an evening outing organised by their school.

It is believed the minibus was being driven by a teacher at the time of the accident.

"Our first indications are that the vehicle went into the back of a lorry involved in motorway maintenance," police said.

Some of the children were thrown out of the vehicle on impact.

Police say they think the minibus, travelling on the northbound carriageway near junction 15, hit the back of a parked Warwickshire County Council truck on the hard shoulder.

Emergency services battled through the night to free children trapped in the wreckage.

Every available ambulance in Warwickshire was mobilised to go to the scene and local hospitals were put on major alert.

One motorway officer said: "It is simply the worst accident I have ever seen."

TRAGEDY HITS WORLD CUP

FAN KILLED BY ROCKET

A flare explodes among the fans at Cardiff Arms Park before tragedy struck at last night's World Cup game   Picture: CHRIS TURVEY

Crowd horror as England, Wales go out

A SOCCER fan was killed by a huge firework at a World Cup match last night.

Horrified supporters saw the rocket explode in his face.

It streaked across Wales's Cardiff Arms Park pitch as Romania celebrated a 2-1 victory which put the home side out of the

by RICHARD CREASY

competition. First aid teams struggled in vain to save the stricken Welsh fan — aged in his sixties — in the north stand.

Police, who were treating the tragedy as murder, said the firework was similar to an emergency distress flare.

Millions of TV viewers tuned in to the end of the game when the BBC switched coverage from England's

doomed attempt to stay in the World Cup.

Firecrackers and flares sent clouds of smoke across the stadium throughout the match.

Scaffolder Peter Thomas, who was among the 40,000-strong crowd, said: "We saw the rocket coming in with a trail of smoke behind it.

"A couple of us ducked but it veered away and went into a group of

Turn to Page 4

Figure 7.1 (a) In *Today* 'actuality' gives a story top priority

THE Sun 20p

Thursday, November 18, 1993   20p   Audited daily sale for October 3,778,312

VALIUM TURNS JACKO INTO A CLINIC ZOMBIE

Jacko . . . he's in a daze

By PIERS MORGAN and MATT HORAN

MICHAEL Jackson has been left a "zombie" by treatment for his painkiller addiction, The Sun can reveal.

He is living in an "incoherent daze" after receiving large doses of Valium, sources inside London's Charter Nightingale clinic confirmed last night.

EXCLUSIVE

Doctors gave him the sedative to help him cope with withdrawal effects after his painkilling drugs were stopped.

Jacko is believed to have been hooked on one called DF-118, which contains dihydrocodeine tartrats.

It is understood the medical team have managed to break his painkiller habit and the star is now having to be weaned off Valium.

Jackson, 35, is said to be dazed in bed on the sealed-off fourth floor of the Marylebone clinic.

A team of doctors and
Continued on Page Four

World Cup fan killed by yob rocket

By TONY SNOW

A WORLD Cup soccer fan was killed last night when a hooligan fired a rocket into a crowded stand.

The firework shot across the pitch when the final whistle went in the Wales-Romania match.

It smashed into the victim's face as he sat with his horrified son.

The man, in his 60s, died instantly in a pool of blood in the North Stand of Cardiff Arms Park.

Witness Peter Curtis, 36, said: "I saw the rocket coming at a hell of a speed. It hit the man in the face and neck.

"He didn't stand a chance — it was like an Exocet. There was blood everywhere and people began panicking when he slumped to the ground."

The tragedy happened seconds after Wales lost 2-1 and crashed out of the World Cup. England are also out, despite beating San Marino 7-1.
Continued on Page 4

10 KIDS DIE IN M-WAY FIREBALL

2 am NEWS

Minibus hits 'warning' lorry

Carnage . . . children's Transit veered onto hard shoulder

By ANDY PARKER and TONY SNOW

TEN children were killed early today when their schoolbus burst into flames after hitting a lorry on the hard shoulder of the M40.

Some burned to death as rescuers tried to pull them from the wreckage.

The minibus hit the stationary council truck at Junction 15 near Warwick where it had been placed as a warning of roadworks ahead.

Motorist Patrick Molloy 27, said: "They were only young kids. We got about seven or eight out, pulling at anything we could. But then the flames drove us back. We kept trying but the flames were too hot and we could not get near.

"It was awful. But we had to leave them in there. There were about six or eight in the minibus that

we could not get out.

"There was nothing we could do for them."

added: "I had been driving behind the minibus. It was in the middle lane and then veered into the council truck.

"At first the fire was very small and then suddenly it flared up under the bonnet and spread so quickly.

"The Fire Brigade arrived not long after but it was too late. By the time
Continued on Page Seven

Figure 7.1 (b) In the *Sun* 'amplitude' ensures the minibus story is the lead

news agency/organisation have been conditioned by particular beliefs, values and attitudes and these will inevitably mould the underlying message. This inevitability leads Roger Fowler to suggest dispensing with the word 'bias' and replacing it with terms such as 'mediation' or 'representation' which will 'less provocatively cover the processes which leads to "skewing" and "judgement".'[7] When studying the news, then, it is useful to be aware of the internal individual/organisational bias or the outside influence of commercial pressures which might bias stories involving the following:

- Politicians and political issues/debates
- Social and ethnic groups and accompanying social issues/debates
- Elite nations and individuals

There is no doubt that the whole question of bias highlights the polysemic nature of many news texts. Over the years, there have been numerous complaints made by both major political parties claiming political bias in the BBC. There are often complaints that an interviewer has shown partiality in an unusually hard interrogation of a particular politician; the interviewer will then defend him/herself by using the argument that, far from creating bias against the interviewee, the hard interrogation technique often summons sympathy and support from the audience for the 'victim'.

SPIN DOCTORS

Spin doctoring was a term coined in the USA in the 1980s and it refers to someone whose job is to promote the positive image of a particular person, political party or business organisation within the media. Spin doctors are often instigators or at least the primary definers of an event and as such are able to initially skew the angle of the story to present their clients in the best light. Michael Deaver, Ronald Reagan's image maker, is considered to be the father of present-day spin because he managed to present a positive image of the then President by setting up well-choreographed photo opportunities while helping Reagan avoid situations such as press conferences, where he would have to speak off the cuff which was never his forte.

Today, spin doctors are enormously important and every major organisation has their own media spin physician; usually, this is the press spokesperson or public relations person. Labour's landslide victory in the 1997 General Election was considered by pundits to be attributable to Peter Mandelson, the Labour Party's spin doctor, rather than the Party leader, Tony Blair. In less than a year, Mandelson orchestrated a metamorphosis of the Labour Party which, in early 1996, still carried with it the enduring historic image personified by the northern, working class, flat-cap-and-ferrets trade unionist. By May 1997, the flat cap, ferrets *et al* were swept away and New Labour, a besuited, middle England businessman, had replaced them. John Wilson, however, believes that the power of the political spin doctor is 'over-rated'. He says: 'In the intensity of three weeks or a month of [Election] campaigning in Britain, people hear enough plain truth to overcome the gloss the parties prefer.'[8] Perhaps, the notion of 'spin' relies too heavily on the concept of the audience as passive receivers of media texts; spin doctors are not witch doctors and can only occasionally turn black into white but they are still pretty good on shades of grey.

THE NARRATIVE OF NEWS PRODUCTION

The news text is also moulded by a number of key narrative elements.

- The need for a complete story
- The need to convey authority and credibility
- The need to be presented in a certain form which is recognised within a particular medium

Story

Audiences are conditioned to reading texts that offer a complete story; even instant texts such as billboard advertisements set up a narrative (ie they create a need, offer an answer to that need and invite the consumer to complete the narrative with a purchase). Broadcast news, like other media texts, needs a story and often this has to be forced onto an event which, when initially reported, does not contain all three essential sections – beginning, middle and end. For instance, wars often drag on for years without reaching an end and murders are inclined to remain unsolved for some while at least. In presenting a news story, a news organisation will inevitably impose this structure and this, in turn, will manipulate the story.

On the day that Diana, Princess of Wales, died the news organisations' desire to give a sense of completeness to the story caused them to place blame for the tragedy entirely on the paparazzi. It later became apparent that this was not necessarily the case. The example of the poll-tax riots, mentioned above, also shows that a convenient perpetrator is good news for reporters seeking to round off a story.

THE FIVE WS

The key questions that should be answered in any news story are the five Ws: Who? What? When? Where? Why? In newspapers, hard news does not necessarily need to have an 'end' as stories are frequently edited from the bottom up and might lose any imposed ending. Nevertheless stories must answer the five Ws if they are to convey a sense of completeness if not closure. However, as the function of newspapers as the disseminators of hard news has been lost to the broadcast media, the greater emphasis is on feature articles which back up the hard news stories; these always have a clear sense of beginning, middle and end.

Authority and credibility

Much of the way a story is presented to us depends on the mode of the address of the institution where it originates. Mode of address is the way that a media text speaks to its audience in a variety of ways. For instance, the ITN *News at Ten* employs a mode of address that is direct and formal and by use of symbols such as the chimes and view of Big Ben creates an air of persuasive authority. The newsreader also uses received English, dresses formally and looks straight at the camera.

In the news media, there is significantly more than a particular mode of addressing the audience; there is always a highly structured discourse. A discourse is not just a mode of speaking to the audience but it also carries with it presumptions and values which close down other avenues of thinking.

Everything that surrounds the news discourse implies that the audience is not just being spoken *to* but being spoken *for*; news reporters and newscasters are trying to convey the impression that they are acting as an intermediary for the audience. Recently, when Jeremy Paxman was collecting an award for TV journalism, he said that his success lay with the fact that he asked the questions that the audience would ask if they had the opportunity.

The rhetorical mode of address adopted by news organisations also conveys the notion of power and authority over the audience. The audience is being called to attention by the declamatory style and the symbols and icons of authority within the news discourse and feels it is both being spoken 'for' and 'at'; it is, in essence, being placed in an unequal position within the discourse. This idea of an unequal balance of power sustained by a specific mode of address was described by Louis Althusser (1918–90) as 'interpellation'.[9]

Form and medium

The codes and conventions governing each medium, genre and form dominate the way every news story is told. Within print, hard news stories and feature articles are the norm (see Chapter 6).

Within the broadcast media, factual items vary in style and length and include everything from **soundbite** clips to wraps and features which are prepared for news bulletins; there are also longer radio, TV and even film documentaries. All these forms require the content to be manipulated in different ways and this will undoubtedly affect the message.

The boundaries of reality and fantasy are, however, becoming increasingly blurred as new hybrids of factual forms and fictional genres constantly evolve. (See also Chapter 1, Realism.)

Reconstruction

Reconstruction is now common practice in programmes such as *Crimewatch UK* and *999*. A reconstruction is supposed to be a carbon copy of actual events designed to make the audience believe they are watching or listening to what really happened; nevertheless, this form is still moulded by the desire to tell a 'dramatic story'.

Drama documentary

Drama documentary has some basis in fact but the story is openly dramatised; Jimmy McGovern's *Hillsborough* is one such example.

Docudrama

Docudrama is the new genre of fiction which is paraded in a factual form using documentary camera techniques and more naturalistic locations and acting; Ken Loach's *Cathy Come Home* is credited with being one of the first docudramas. This style is becoming more commonplace and programmes such as *This Life* (BBC2) and *ER* (Channel Four) have successfully utilised key elements of the genre.

Soundbite

This is a short clip of opinion from a relevant 'expert' or politician. They are often only about 10 to 30 seconds in length and are enormously important because their pithiness or use of rhetoric gives them a great deal of impact and makes them useful to news broadcasters who are always short of time. Many politicians are now trained to speak in sentences which could become suitable soundbites.

New news technologies

A number of new technologies have made a big impact on the way that news is gathered and disseminated.

▨ The Internet

The net has opened up the information superhighway to everyone and anyone – all major news agencies have web sites. People can taste the news as it happens without leaving the computer screen. Multi-media technology allows the user to have instant video and soundbites as well as digital images. This has possibly made the news more democratic as absolutely anybody can add a view to an event but it is also nearly impossible to regulate fully

▨ Satellite broadcasting

This form of broadcasting has opened up round-the-clock world-wide TV news from agencies such as WTN. The ramifications of this are huge. Some countries are not particularly impressed by the views presented by Western news agencies. Recently, there have been allegations in the British press that the BBC has 'softened' its attitude to human rights issues in China because it wants to introduce the BBC World satellite TV news service into that country

▨ Portable satellite transmission equipment

This equipment now allows reporters to send back news instantaneously from any part of the globe. The initial impact of these was felt in the Gulf War where CNN were sending back live reports and pictures as scud missiles bombed Baghdad. This technology has allowed even more priority to be placed on actuality as a news value. 'As it happens' news tends to beguile the audience into believing that they are viewing a relatively 'unmediated' event but despite the immediacy, the audience is still being presented with a partial, manipulated and selected account

 BBC1 *NINE O'CLOCK NEWS*, WEDNESDAY, 27 AUGUST 1997

All manufacturers of the news attempt to persuade the audience that they are being informed of what *really* happened. Notions of realism have already been discussed at some length but within the news genre the term 'realism' can be more usefully defined as a desire to create a credible source or believable narrative:

▨ Credible source
This is created by seeming to speak with an authoritative voice. The news source must command a sense of authority. The audience must be given a reason to believe this is a credible source by the use of symbols, icons, etc. that convey authority. These will not necessarily be the same across all news production because the target audience will determine the type and use of authoritative signifiers. For instance, in the *Big Breakfast* on Channel Four the news presenter wears a jumper not a jacket which makes him more credible to the young target audience whereas this would not be an option for Trevor McDonald on *News At Ten*

■ Believable narrative
This is created by seeming to offer a 'window onto the world'. The news story
must have factual backup in terms of actuality – on the spot reporters, video
footage of events, interviews, soundbites, etc. but this must also be joined
together in a seamless narrative using accepted conventions within a recognised
form so that the 'story' is created and the suspension of disbelief is not abruptly
halted

These aspects will now be considered in terms of the overall bulletin and then in
terms of one particular item within the bulletin.

Figure 7.2 Running order for the BBC *Nine O'Clock News*, Wednesday 27 August 1997.

Item	Description	Running time in mins (') and secs (")	Elapsed time
Opening headlines	◇ Controversial Diana, Princess of Wales interview with *Paris Match* ◇ Ex MI5 agent's allegations about secret files kept on potential subversives ◇ Rising house prices	38"	38"
1	Controversial Diana, Princess of Wales interview with *Paris Match*	3'20"	3'58"
2	Ex MI5 agent's allegations about secret files kept on potential subversives	2'51"	6'49"
3	Rising house prices	2'56"	9'45"
4	The creation of a body to oversee arms decommissioning in Northern Ireland	2'38"	12'23"
5	Volcano on Monserrat	3'	15'23"
6	Rise in cot deaths	23"	15'40"
7	The banning of herbal drug substitutes for ecstasy and cannabis	10"	15'10"
8	A plea for a new public enquiry into the sinking of the *Marchioness*	17"	16'07"
9	Mass action by opposition groups in Nigeria to bring down President Daniel Arap Moi	2'41"	18'48"
10	Two aeroplanes have a near miss over southern England	2'05"	20'53"
11	A conference on land mines in Oslo	3'58"	24'51"
12	European Cup Football	24"	25'15"
13	Planet Mars exploration story	31"	25'46"
Closure	Recapitulation of headlines plus a trail for Newsnight	1'28"	27'14"

Credible source: characters

In this bulletin, Michael Buerk, like all news readers must be credible and this is created in a number of ways. First of all, Buerk has a credible accent. He looks directly at the camera addressing the audience at home and speaks with received pronunciation and has no distinct regional accent or dialect. It is only within the last 10 to 15 years that regional accents have been heard at all on national news. However, some accents are still deemed more acceptable than others. For instance, there are numerous Scottish presenters such as James Naughtie (*Today*), Kirstie Wark (*Newsnight*) but few from Birmingham or the West Country. Michael Buerk is also dressed formally in sober suit and tie which adds to his air of credibility. The other reporters within the bulletin also carry credibility. They are named so we are made to feel less distanced from them and they also directly address the viewer and dress with authority.

Credible source: location/signifiers

It is one of the paradoxes of broadcast news that the credibility of the source is now enhanced by a virtual reality studio. The *Nine O'Clock News* studio is no exception. It is a steel blue which gives the air of formality or even clarity; the studio gives the impression of being large with uncluttered reflective surfaces which add to the meaning inferred from the huge 'mirror of reality' behind the reader. The virtual reality coat of arms with the motto 'Nation Shall Speak Peace Unto Nation' implies that this news has the authority to speak for this nation to other nations. It also implies the product is coming from an established source. The virtual 'lie' is given greater 'reality' by the fact that we can see the studio lighting gantries, etc.; this makes the audience feel that they are in a privileged position – participators in the studio bulletin or even part of the production team. Of course, this is all part of the discourse; the audience are both being spoken *to* with authority and spoken *for* with authority. The music which opens and closes the BBC bulletin is relevant too because it gives the bulletin immediacy and importance. The insistent almost telegraphic beat and drum role create a fanfare opening; this signifies a big event.

Believable narrative: structure

By examining the running order for the bulletin a number of important construction devices become apparent. The most notable thing about this bulletin – taken at random from the BBC output – is the remarkable balance between structure and content which adds to the seamlessness and consequent believability. How is this attained?

The need for a complete narrative is as important to the whole bulletin as it is for the individual items within it. Michael Buerk, the newsreader, holds the bulletin together and adds to the feeling of continuity as after each item we return to him for the next cue. The narrative of the bulletin is opened by the enigmas of the initial headlines; these serve to call the viewer to attention while also setting up questions which will only be answered later in the bulletin. The headline for the item on rising house prices (discussed in detail below) is a good example of the enigma and the direct call to the viewer: 'What your house is worth: the winners and the losers in the new housing boom.' This headline is addressing 'you' the viewer; it is not just any house but *your* house that is going to be discussed and it is saying that *you* could be a winner or a loser but *you* must wait until later in the bulletin to find out. In this bulletin, the headlines correlate with the first three stories but this is not always the case. Sometimes stories mentioned in the headlines are quite far down the bulletin order; this is another deliberate device to keep audience attention. The narrative is also strengthened by the length and positioning of certain items. The first five stories are all about three minutes long; then there are three short items with the shortest of all in the very centre of the bulletin, ie cot deaths (23"); herbal drugs (10"); Marchioness (17"). This structure gives pace and climax to the bulletin and grabs back those viewers whose attention may be beginning to wander. After these 'attention grabbers' there are three more long items and then the bulletin ends on two short items followed by a recapitulation of the main headline – giving pace, climax and a feeling of closure.

Figure 7.3 *Nine O'Clock News* item – the rise in house prices

Segment	Picture	Sound	Running time in mins (') and secs (")	Elapsed time
1	Close up head and shoulders of Michael Buerk seated in studio, to the right of frame, looking directly at camera; BBC news 'mirror' to left of picture showing house prices	Michael Buerk: 'House prices in some areas have gone up by as much as 25% . . . Anthony Browne reports'	20"	20"
2	Long shot – camera following Simon Hindley, first time house buyer, and estate agent walking towards, and moving inside, new house	Diegetic sound of the two people in shot discussing the house but with Anthony Browne, Economics Reporter, voice-over: 'The rise in house prices is drawing many first time buyers into the market. Simon Hindley has just bought his first home a newly built house in Maiden bower in West Sussex.' Change from voice-over to interview. Simon Hindley: 'Basically what I'm looking at is a long term investment . . .	18"	38"
3	Close-up, head and shoulders of Simon Hindley outside new house. He is not looking directly at camera but – we imagine – he is talking to reporter who is to left of shot and out of picture. Titling: Simon Hindley – first time buyer	'. . . I needed to get into the housing market when I could and so I might as well get in on a rising market as a dropping one. I hope it doesn't drop but it doesn't seem like it's likely to at the present time.'	10"	48"
4	Medium shot of new houses, panning to Wimpey sign saying houses 'All Sold'. Panning back to houses then blue screen and change to computer graphics showing map of England and Wales in brown on blue background with accompanying figures consecutively pinpointing percentage increase in house prices in certain areas. The voice-over fits precisely with the graphics. Shot changes to close up of a street full of 'For Sale' and Sale Agreed' signs. Camera tracks back along signs then picture fades under computer graphic overlay of graph depicting rise in house prices	Anthony Browne, voice-over: 'First time buyers have helped push up the price of newly built flats and maisonettes . . . in the first half of this year growth has steadied at about 9%.'	1'16"	2'04"
5	Quick close-up of carpenter at work in new house changes to medium shot of two people on a building	Anthony Browne, voice-over continues: 'House buying is getting more expensive . . . but	15"	2'19"

	site in protective helmets looking at site plans. Panning down a shot of their reflection in a puddle	the industry is playing down suggestions that the recovery might run out of steam.'		
6	Close-up, head and shoulders of John Anderson, Taywood homes, talking to reporter who is out of shot. Backdrop is a house in the process of being built. Titling: John Anderson, Taywood homes	John Anderson: 'I think there will be a sensible . . . market place over the next 18 months . . . it's still a good place to put your money.'	17"	2'36"
7	Close-up of developer's sale board cuts to head and shoulders close-up of Anthony Browne (with identifying titling) standing in front of housing development's sales centre	Anthony Browne: 'The housing industry is convinced that we are not seeing a return to the boom of the 1980s . . . of the 1980s . . . Anthony Browne, BBC news, Crawley.'	20"	2'56"

Believable narrative: content

There is high priority in this news bulletin to home news; although, it does present an overall balance of stories. There are 13 news items: nine home, three foreign and one 'space' item. There is care to present a spectrum of news to satisfy a range of audience segments; there is news on domestic social issues such as the cot deaths and herbal drugs as well as the more far reaching political and governmental issues such as arms decommissioning in Northern Ireland and the allegations against MI5. Parents, home owners, teenagers, Diana watchers, football fans *et al* are catered for and this amounts to a fair slice of the viewing population. The most important aspect of credibility within the bulletin is perhaps the way each item is put together and this will be discussed below by looking in detail at the item on house prices.

This is a useful news item to use as a study of TV news narrative because a discussion about house prices is not essentially a 'visual' story; therefore, this item, has to work hard to construct the visual narrative.

The narrative begins in the studio with Michael Buerk reading the cue. As he reads the cue about house prices the visual underpinning begins and a picture depicting house sale boards is seen in the 'mirror' at his right shoulder. The narrative moves from the studio cue to the 'actuality' of the estate agent showing the first time buyer round the new house. We take part for a moment in this viewing process as if we are accompanying the house buyer which adds to the feeling that this is a 'real' experience and then we are distanced again as the reporter begins his voice-over. Before the picture changes, the interview with the house buyer begins. There is a seamlessness here; the story flows so that the interview 'sound' begins before the interview 'image' appears on screen. This is a common convention of TV news reports – either the sound starts and the picture follows or vice versa; this softens the move from section to section and creates the illusion of a continuous narrative.

The voice-over then moves on to talk about the actual rise in house prices all over the country – thus keeping the interest of the maximum number of viewers. The only way that this rise in prices can be visually represented is through graphics and so the reporter's voice-over is accompanied by a highly sophisticated graphic representation of the change in house prices in the different areas around the country. At last the enigma of the headline ('What your house is worth') is beginning to be addressed but of course it is never satisfactorily answered.

The voice-over moves on to talk about the building industry and, predictably, the picture changes to a carpenter at work and once again the story is continually accompanied by underpinning images; this is followed by an interview with a representative of a housing developer to discuss whether houses are a good investment. This is set up with the same overlap as before so that the interview sound begins before the image. There is a feeling of balance created here; we have had the view of the buyer and now it is the turn of the builder. There is a completeness of narrative created by the belief that we have heard two sides of a story.

The narrative is completed by the reporter talking direct to camera with the backdrop of a recently built housing estate and a board saying 'Sale Centre'. Until this point, the reporter has been a disembodied voice but as the item comes to a close, this voice is given an identity and a location. We now know the reporter is *there* and, consequently, we should believe what we are being told. He reaffirms this with the authority of his sign off to camera '. . . Anthony Browne, BBC News, Crawley.'

FURTHER WORK

News values

In groups. Choose one broadsheet and one tabloid on the same day and compare the type and number of news stories covered. What news values are given greater priority by which paper? Why do you think this is?

News selection

Take a tape recorder into your local shopping centre and ask several people their view on a particular news topic. When you return to class listen to the answers then decide which answers you would choose to use for a news bulletin item on local radio and which you would choose to reject and why?

Believable narrative and credibility of source

Tape one local independent radio news bulletin and one local BBC radio news bulletin and compare them in terms of how they are creating believability of narrative and credibility of source.

FURTHER READING

Cohen, Stanley and Young, Jock, (eds), *The Manufacture of News*, Constable, 1973.
Fowler, Roger, *Language in the News*, Routledge, 1991.
Hartley, John, *Understanding News*, Routledge, 1982.
Wallis, Roger and Baran, Stanley, *The Known World of Broadcast News*, Routledge, 1990.

Notes

[1] Quoted in an article by Andrew Culf in the *Guardian*, 3 March 1997, p3.

[2] F. W. Hodgson, *Modern Newspaper Practice*, Heineman, 1989, p9.

[3] At the moment of writing, the lobby system is being reviewed by the Labour Government.

[4] Information from *The Guardian Media Guide*, 1997, edited by Steve Peak and Paul Fisher.

[5] *News, Newspapers and Television*, MacMillan, 1985, p8.

[6] Johan Galtung and Mari Ruge, 'Structuring and selecting news', in Stanley Cohen and Jock Young (eds), *The Manufacture of News*, Constable, 1973, pp52–61.

[7] Roger Fowler, *Language in the News*, Routledge, 1991, p12.

[8] John Wilson, *Understanding Journalism*, Routledge, 1996, p205.

[9] Louis Althusser, *Lenin and Philosophy and other Essays*, New Left Books, 1971, p163.

CHAPTER **8** The British Film Industry

'Which of the following films are British? 1 *A Fish Called Wanda*; 2 *Sense and Sensibility*; 3 *Emma*; 4 *Hamlet* and 5 *The English Patient*. The answer is none of them.

Why? Because *A Fish Called Wanda* – quintessentially British in humour and setting – was backed by American money. *Sense and Sensibility*, because too much of its post-production went abroad. *Emma* – adapted by an American writer and starring the American actress Gwyneth Paltrow – was paid for in dollars. *Hamlet*? Columbia put up the money. *The English Patient*, despite its 12 'British' Oscar nominations, is based on a Canadian novel and was financed once again by Hollywood. Does any of this matter? Despite certain unseemly compromises, are these films any less 'British' because of them? The answer is yes – right now it does matter.'

Rupert Widdicombe in *The Sunday Times*[1]

FILM PRODUCTION

What is a British film?

One of the problems of studying the British film industry[2] is the difficulty of defining exactly what a British film is. For example is a film made in Britain with a US director and Hollywood money British? Can co-productions with European countries also be classed as British? The *BFI Film and Television Handbook 1994* attempts to define precisely the term 'British film': 'feature-length films which are expected by their makers to receive theatrical distribution and for which either the financial or the creative impulse came from Britain. The guiding principle is to identify films which directly contribute to British film culture or to the culture of the British film industry.'[3] It is clear from this definition that some 'British' films will be more British than others.

British versus US film production

Film production in Britain takes place on a small scale compared to Hollywood. In 1996 the total number of 'British' feature films produced was 128 compared to an all time low of 24 in 1981. The small size of the British film industry compared to that of Hollywood can partly be explained by economics. In America, with its potentially vast audience, a Hollywood film can cover its costs even with moderate audiences by using the large network of cinemas. Further profits can then be taken from distribution in other countries, video and television deals, sales of sound track and merchandising. A British feature, however, if moderately successful would be unlikely to cover its costs from theatrical exhibition alone, due to the small size of the audience. A British film will also have difficulty in attracting audiences away from American films that have higher production values (the average budget of an American film made in Britain is £19.48m compared to that for a British film, £1.6m), recognised stars and substantial marketing campaigns.

The British film industry despite these problems is still a force to be reckoned with. Low budget films such as *Four Weddings and a Funeral*, *Shallow Grave*, *Trainspotting* and *The Full Monty* demonstrate the ability of British film-makers to make films that appeal to the home audiences, but which also are successful internationally.

BRITISH FILM PRODUCTION 1996[4]

The 128 'British' films produced in 1996 can be classified into four different groups.

Group 1
Films where the cultural and financial impetus is from Britain and the majority of personnel is British.
Number of films made: 53
Average cost: £1.6 million

Group 2
Majority British co-productions. Films in which, although there are foreign partners there is a British cultural content and a significant amount of British finance and personnel.
Number of films made: 20
Average cost: £5.0 million

Group 3
Minority British co-productions. Foreign (non-US) films in which there is a small British involvement in finance or personnel.
Number of films made: 30
Average cost: £3.7 million

Group 4
American films with a British creative and/or part financial involvement.
Number of films made: 18
Average cost: £13.2 million

Types of release for British films 1984–95[5]

Proportions of British films and British co-productions made in 1994 which achieved: (a) a wide release – opening on 30 or more screens around the country within a year of production; (b) a limited release mainly in art house cinemas or a limited West End release; (c) unreleased – a year after production.

Year	(a) %	(b) %	(c) %
1984	50.0	44.0	6.0
1985	52.8	35.9	11.3
1986	55.8	41.9	2.3
1987	36.0	60.0	4.0
1988	29.5	61.2	9.3
1989	33.3	38.9	27.8
1990	29.4	47.1	23.5
1991	32.2	37.3	30.5
1992	38.3	29.8	31.9
1993	25.4	22.4	52.2
1994	31.0	22.6	46.4
1995	23.1	34.6	42.3

FILM FUNDING IN BRITAIN

Financing films has always been a headache for British film-makers and over the years funding has been obtained from a number of different sources. The following extract from the *BFI Film and Television Handbook 1995* outlines the changes in the last ten years.

'In 1983 and 1984, at least half of all films were supported by British sources other than Channel Four, British Screen and the BBC (all of which are either state funded or perform a public service function). Since the ITV companies invested only modestly in feature films at that time, the assumption must be that equity was available from the film companies themselves. Indeed, in the early 1980s there was a host of properly capitalised British production companies willing to risk money in films – among them Handmade, Hemdale, Virgin, Goldcrest and, most importantly, Thorn EMI Screen Entertainment. Now there are none, unless one counts Polygram, which strictly speaking is Dutch. The latter day British producer, no matter how experienced, goes from project to project, raising money where he or she can and in the process giving away the bulk of the rights. Little or no value accrues to the producer or production company beyond the production fee, and even that is sometimes part-deferred. British film production, in other words, has migrated in the past ten years from being a small industry to being a cottage industry.'[6]

In the 1990s British producers have increasingly relied for finance upon European funding bodies such as the European Co-production Fund as well as the TV industry.

Raising the money

Figure 8.1 Sources of finance for the British film industry

Television	Television has become an important source of finance for the British film industry, with both Channel Four and BSkyB playing key roles; the BBC and ITV companies to a lesser extent. In exchange for funding the TV company usually receives the broadcast rights to the film after it has been distributed theatrically.
Channel Four	Since the early 1980s Channel Four has invested substantially in British film production in return for exclusive TV rights after theatrical distribution. Annual budget: £15 million. Recent films include: *Four Weddings and a Funeral* (Mike Newell, 1994); *Shallow Grave* (Danny Boyle, 1994); *Death and the Maiden* (Roman Polanski, 1995); *Brassed Off* (Mark Herman, 1996).
BSkyB	BSkyB recently made an unconditional offer to buy the pay TV rights to all British films that receive a theatrical distribution, on the same terms offered by British Screen (up to £350,000 per film). BSkyB also has TV distribution deals with American films made in Britain. Recent films include: *The Young Poisoner's Handbook* (Benjamin Ross, 1995); *Face* (Antonia Bird, 1997); *Twin Town* (Kevin Allen, 1997).
BBC	BBC films has a relatively small budget of £5 million a year to invest in British films. Recent films include: *The Van* (Stephen Frears, 1996); *Jude* (Michael Winterbottom, 1996); *Bring Me the Head of Mavis Davis* (John Henderson, 1997).
ITV companies	Most ITV companies do not invest in film production, but there is the possibility that if the government offers bigger incentives some will take the film-making plunge. One exception is Granada, whose film division made *August* (Anthony Hopkins, 1994) and *Jack and Sarah* (Time Sullivan, 1994).
British and European government	Since the 1920s it was recognised that in a market 95% dominated by American films, the British film industry would need state support. This support ranged from the Cinematograph Act of 1927 which set a quota for the number of British films to be shown in British cinemas (axed in 1982), to the Eady Levy (part of the 1957 Cinematograph Act) which imposed a levy on box office takings to be paid into the British Film Production Fund to help finance British films. In 1985 the Eady Levy was dropped in favour of a combined system of private and state finance administered by British Screen Finance. Unlike other European countries in the 1990s such as France, the British government provides relatively meagre support for British film producers, although national lottery money may have a substantial impact.[7]

Figure 8.1 Sources of finance for the British film industry – *continued*

British Screen Finance Ltd	British Screen finances projects that might have difficulty in attracting mainstream funding, but for which there is an audience. In the first five years it received £9 million which with other investments totalled £95 million. British Screen's contribution rarely exceeds £500,000 or 30% of the film's budget. Recent films include: *Fever Pitch* (David Evans, 1996); *Mojo* (Jez Butterworth, 1997).
British Film Institute (BFI)	The aim of BFI Production is to 'develop new talent and new ideas in UK film and television'[8] by part-funding low budget features, shorts and documentaries. A recent film that received funding from the BFI is *Madagascar Skin* (Chris Newby, 1995). In 1996, the BFI in conjunction with Channel Four produced three feature films: *Gallivant* (Andrew Kötting); *Stella does Tricks* (Coky Giedroyc) and *A bit of Scarlet* (Andrea Weiss).
European Co-Production Fund (ECF)	Set up by the British Government in 1991 with an overall budget of £2 million a year, the fund's aim is to enable British producers to collaborate in the making of films which could not be made without its involvement. The ECF offers commercial loans, up to 30% of the total budget, for full-length feature films intended for theatrical release. The film must be a co-production involving at least two companies, with no link of common ownership, established in two separate EU states. It is administered by British Screen. A recent film receiving such assistance: *The Tango Lesson* (Sally Potter, UK/France/Argentina/Japan/Germany, 1997).
National Lottery	On 6 June 1995 the government announced that up to £84 million of National Lottery funds will be put into the British film industry. Up to £70 million of this would be set aside to support British film production over five years. The money will be administered by the Arts Council which has already received Lottery grant applications worth £42.1 million from 89 film projects, and would make grants of up to £1 million per film (providing the film-makers can raise 50% of the film's budget from other sources and it has guaranteed UK distribution). Foreign film companies, such as Polygram, makers of *Four Weddings and a Funeral*, as well as British broadcasters such as Channel Four, the BBC and ITV, would also be able to apply for Lottery grants as part of consortia. The Arts Council lottery board would select films which it believed would be financially successful. Part of the proceeds of profitable productions would go back into a central fund and be used to finance other films. First film to be backed by National Lottery money: *The Woodlanders* (Phil Agland, 1997) backed by Channel Four and River films (budget: £4 million). Other recent films to receive funding include: *Wilde* (Brian Gilbert, 1997) and *Metroland* (Philip Saville, 1997).
Eurimages	An organisation based in France that provides finance (up to £500,000 per film) for feature-length fiction films and creative documentaries which are made by at least three countries.) *Jane Eyre* (Franco Zeffierelli, UK/Italy/France/US, 1995) and *The Tango Lesson* (Sally Potter, UK/France/Argentina/Japan/Germany, 1997).

Figure 8.1 Sources of finance for the British film industry – *continued*

Other funding	
London Production Fund	Aims to support and develop film, video and TV projects by independent film-makers living or working in the London region. Has an annual budget of approximately £200,000 (receives finance from Carlton Television and Channel Four).
Scottish Film Production Fund	Development funding of up to £15,000 is available for narrative fiction films with the aim of encouraging film production in Scotland.
Glasgow Film Fund	Administered by the Scottish Film Production Fund, the Fund aims to encourage production in the Glasgow area with finance for feature films of up to £150,000 (each film must have an overall budget of at least £500,000). Recent films include: *Shallow Grave* (Danny Boyle, 1994); *Small Faces* (Gillies Mackinnon, 1995); *The Near Room* (David Hayman, 1995) and *The Slab Boys* (John Byrne, 1997).
Film companies	In the 1990s there are no film companies that can fully finance film production on a large scale. The only likely contender PolyGram (Filmed Entertainment), involved in eight British films in 1994, is classed as a British producer, but is in fact part of an international conglomerate which is officially Dutch. Most British film companies are set up for the production of one film but five companies made more than one film in 1995 (World Productions, Polygram, Metrodome, Capitol, Handmade).
British studios	Unlike in Hollywood there are no studios in Britain that have enough money to finance British films independently. Studios such as Pinewood, Shepperton and Ealing are increasingly busy, but they are primarily utilised as production facilities for other (mostly American) companies.
American co-production	American involvement means that profits from films do not stay in Britain to finance further productions as a percentage will be exported to America. The film director Ken Loach has commented that American involvement might also limit the creative potential of a film.
If all else fails?	The director David Cohen financed *The Pleasure Principle* (UK, 1992) using a loan from the Nat West (total budget £200,000). Seventy per cent of the loan was guaranteed by the government under the Small Firms Loan Guarantee Fund. The cast was paid a fee and a share in the profits based on a points system. This type of funding is unusual, if not unique.

HOW HAVE SPECIFIC FILMS BEEN FUNDED?

British funded films

Four Weddings and a Funeral (Mike Newell, 1994)
Budget: £2.9 million (Polygram: £2.03 million/Channel Four: £870,000)
Distribution: distributed in Britain by Polygram

Four Weddings and a Funeral has been the most successful British film ever shown in the states taking $50 million at the box office. It subsequently took $40 million in Britain. Total worldwide distribution gross: $350 million. The film's success was helped by its release in the US which built up publicity for Britain (British audiences are more likely to see a film if it has been successful in the US) and publicity centred on Hugh Grant's girlfriend Elizabeth Hurley. It is worth noting that despite the profits made by *Four Weddings* Polygram's film division still failed to make an overall profit.

Trainspotting (Danny Boyle, 1996)
Based on: Irvine Welsh's 1993 novel *Trainspotting*
Production companies: Figment Films/Channel Four/Polygram
Distributor: Film Four Distributors Ltd
Budget: £1.7 million

Channel Four fully financed the £1.7 million budget of *Trainspotting* although pre-sales brought in £2 million. The film benefited from a clever marketing strategy including film trailers featuring scenes specially made by the cast and a powerful poster campaign.

Figure 8.2 *Trainspotting* – A British film-making Renaissance?   ©BFI

The Full Monty (Peter Cattaneo, 1997)
Production companies: Twentieth Century Fox/Channel Four
Budget: £2.2 million
Distribution: Twentieth Century Fox

The Full Monty has taken £120 million at the box office worldwide and was more successful than *Jurassic Park* in the UK. Fox spent a large amount promoting the UK release (initially £850,000) and to ensure good 'word of mouth' invited over 100,000 people to preview screenings before its official release date. Channel Four were initially involved in the development of *The Full Monty* but did not continue their financial support for the film and therefore did not reap the rewards from its success.

FILM DISTRIBUTION

'The whole objective of film distribution is to try and get the film into a cinema and hold it there.'[9]

What does a distributor do?

- Chooses which films to distribute
- Decides how many prints to make (if a film has limited appeal only a small number of prints will be struck)
- Negotiates where and when the film is to be released (the release pattern)
- Sends trailers and publicity material to cinemas
- Publicises the film through: posters, trailers, press/TV advertising, press releases, etc.

Typical release patterns for the UK

Films usually open in London where reviewers and the largest audiences are to be found. After screenings in London the film will be released in Outer London and selected cities, followed by a wider release across the rest of the country. This release pattern can often benefit films which do not have the budget for a saturation advertising campaign.

Blockbusters from America that benefit from large numbers of second-hand prints and large advertising budgets can be released across the country into as many cinemas as possible.

Art house and foreign films benefit from a more restricted release pattern, which carefully targets specialised cinemas. A release in a key London cinema is followed by a release in selected cities, followed by a release in a small number of other cities. This type of pattern allows maximum use to be made of a small number of prints.

Distribution now

The major players

The British market is dominated by five American distributors (UIP, Warner, Buena Vista, Columbia and 20th Century Fox), who were responsible for distributing films that took 76% of British box office takings in 1996. The five majors primarily handle American films and have relationships with the key cinema chains and multiplexes in Britain. Warner Bros. is the only vertically integrated company of the five making, distributing and exhibiting its own films, thus retaining maximum profits.

The independents

Although there are many more independent distributors in Britain (26 in 1996) they only took 24% of box office takings in 1996. The independents tend not to distribute American blockbuster films, handling British, art house, foreign and low-budget American films (although sometimes they get lucky,

Figure 8.3 Breakdown of 1996 British box office for releases by distributor[10]

Distributor	Number of titles	Box office (£)
UIP	29	94,669,115
Buena Vista	26	89,900,905
20th Century Fox	16	57,518,416
Columbia	13	41,593,200
Warner	20	38,178,590
Total (majors)	**104 (39%)**	**321,860,226 (76%)**
Entertainment	20	39,131,233
Polygram	21	31,875,282
Guild	15	13,391,257
Film Four	14	6,070,476
Rank	10	6,025,751
First Independent	9	2,687,785
Artificial Eye	19	2,461,912
Electric	8	1,622,882
Metro	10	294,917
Feature Film Co.	3	279,917
Timedial	1	109,219
Starlight	6	52,911
Gala	4	52,696
Arrow	1	25,572
ICA	5	25,328
Winstone	4	24,107
BFI	1	19,131
The Bruce PLC	1	8,300
BBC/Winstone	1	7,291
AFC	1	5,329
Contemporary	1	4,519
Barbican	1	4,194
Rank/Polygram	1	3,834
Blue Dolphin	1	3,783
NFT	1	2,984
Clarence	1	1,281
Total (independents)	**160 (61%)**	**104,191,889 (24%)**

for example Guild distributed *Terminator 2*, *Stargate* and *Judge Dredd*). Mostly, however, they need to work hard to get their films distributed in the circuits and multiplexes as they are in competition with the American majors. Independent distributors often have strong relationships with art house and independent cinemas.

British versus American films

The five major distributors are often unwilling to handle British films (as well as art house and foreign films) believing them to be unpopular with main-stream audiences. The lower budget and predicted lower box office takings of a British film would also dictate that only a moderate advertising campaign could be conducted and a limited number of prints struck. American films, however, have a number of key advantages.

- They have already been shown in the US and therefore audience trends can be easily predicted
- Audiences know what to expect as the films are classified into recognisable genres, contain well-known stars and have high production values
- If the film is supplied internally from part of a vertically integrated company profits will be higher
- Large number of second-hand prints are available from the US (the cost of striking new prints for non-US films is £1000 per print
- The original advertising ideas/trailers can probably be re-cast for the British market. Whatever the case the film will benefit from advance publicity from its US release

The British producer is more likely to have success with an independent dis-tributor who would have to carefully construct a more limited release pattern, targeting key cinemas in which the film might be a success. Like the majors and independents, the producer would still be keen to get the film into the chains and the multiplexes, but would be facing stiff competition from Ameri-can films. There are some distributors that specialise in distributing art house or foreign film, usually to specialised independent cinemas or regional film theatres. Some of these distributors have overcome the problems of gaining access to screens by buying or leasing their own cinemas. Artificial Eye, for example, controls the distribution to a small chain of London cinemas: Camden Plaza, Chelsea Cinema and the Renoir Cinema.

Video

Distribution companies acquire the rights to distribute films on video cassette and then arrange for their distribution. Video cassettes provide an important and growing source of revenue for the major film companies (76% of British house-holds own a video recorder). The majors have formed their own video arms.

- C.I.C. (Paramount and Universal)
- Warner Home Video
- Fox Video
- Buena Vista Home Video (Walt Disney and Touchstone)
- M.G.M./U.A. Home Video
- R.C.A./Columbia Pictures Video (UK)

WHEN DOES A FILM GO INTO PROFIT?

In order for a film to make a profit it has to make two and a half times its production cost. A British film that was made for £2 million would thus need to make £5 million at the box office in order to make a profit. Prints, however, cost £1,000 to make. A distributor wanting to open the film at 100 cinemas would thus have to add an extra £100,000 to the budget. The distributor would have to be fairly sure of his/her audience to spend this sort of money, bearing in mind that a British film in Britain is unlikely to take over £500,000 at the box office (note that many films do not just rely on theatrical distribution alone to make a profit. Money is also generated from the sale of international TV and video rights in advance of production).

EXHIBITION OF FILMS

'Saturday night at the movies who cares what picture you see.'

(Song by The Drifters, 1964)

'. . . there are countless people who would go to the cinema if the available films were not almost entirely directed at indiscriminating adolescents.'

Letter in the *Independent*, 1988[11]

'We have to aim for the majority rather than the minority.'

Booking controller at Cannon Theatres in reply[12]

'This is the multiplex experience: you walk into a foyer full of neon lights, TVs playing trailers and the sweet fuggy smell of popcorn. There are marble tiles, mirrored ceilings, a sweet-shop on one side, and a games arcade on the other. You queue up to sit in comfy seats with drink-holders attached, eat sweets, slurp on straws, make a mess all over the floor, and then leave without cleaning any of it up.'

Robert Butler describing the cinema experience at Warners in Bury, 1994[13]

1985 proved to be a key year for British cinema exhibition. Cinema audiences had fallen from their peak of 1,585 million admission since 1946 to a low of 53.8 million admissions in 1984, but in 1985 the downward trend reversed with 70.7 million cinema tickets being purchased. 1985 was also the year in which the first multiplex, The Point at Milton Keynes, was opened.

Since 1985 British cinema audiences have continued to increase, reaching 123.8 million in 1996, and substantial investments have been made by North American companies in British cinemas especially the purpose-built multi-plexes. In addition many of the existing cinemas have been refurbished and have had their technical facilities improved.

The developments since 1985 seem to have vindicated those analysts who found cinema exhibition wanting as a retailing entertainment business. They argued that there was an audience for films, but that it was put off by the old fashioned, unattractive and often unsavoury aspects of cinema-going (see quotations above). Such criticism is not voiced so often now, although it is not hard to chance upon lacklustre service, poor quality prints and inadequate sound. Also since many auditoriums have been divided up into smaller units the size of some screens leaves a lot to be desired.

In addition to the changes that have taken place some aspects of British cinema exhibition have remained constant: the ownership of cinemas continues to be highly concentrated and the feeling is expressed recurrently that both independent exhibitors and audiences would be better served by changes in the structure and practices of the industry.

Despite the dramatic changes in exhibition created by the multiplex cinemas – which promise choice, but tend to deliver a predictable diet of Hollywood imports – audiences seeking a wider range of films continue to be served by several distinct types of cinema. Set out below are the main types of exhibition outlets currently operating in Britain.

Different types of exhibition

Exhibition practices in Britain can be divided between mainstream cinemas such as the large chains, multiplexes and independent cinemas and non-mainstream, which includes art-house and repertory cinemas. Generally speaking mainstream exhibitors show films that originate from Hollywood and appeal to a wide audience. Non-mainstream cinemas, on the other hand, appeal to more esoteric tastes including foreign language films.

Mainstream cinema

Mainstream cinemas show Hollywood product 90% of the time. Occasionally they may show foreign or art-house films, but only say on a Sunday or Wednesday afternoon. The age of the audience is on average between 12 and 30.

Traditional cinema chains: majors

- ABC operates 211 screens on 80 sites
- Odeon operated by Rank Theatres (British) has 361 screens on 73 sites

The ABC and Odeon chains dominate exhibition in Britain. Over the last ten years they have improved the facilities that their cinemas can offer including more screens, complete refurbishment, computerised booking, trained staff and a wide range of food. These cinemas tend to be found in town centres and are therefore not as convenient for parking as the multiplexes.

Cinema chains: independents

There are several small cinema chains in Britain. They tend to show similar films as the multiplexes and the major chains, but usually get the prints after the big companies have screened them. The independent chains are more likely to show non-mainstream films than the major chains and multiplexes. The cinemas have also been upgraded in the face of competition from the major chains. Examples are:

- Charles Scott Cinemas (West Country circuit with cinemas at Bridgewater, Exmouth, Lyme Regis, Newton Abbot, Sidmouth and Teignmouth)
- Robins Cinemas (24 screens on 11 sites including Basildon, Bath, Camberley, Newbury and Durham)

Independent individual cinemas

Similar to the independent chains but usually locally owned and on a very small scale, mainly showing Hollywood films. Examples are:

- Plaza, Oxted
- Windsor, Broadstairs

Multiplex cinemas

- UCI (235 screens on 24 sites)
- Warner Bros. (161 screens on 17 sites)
- Showcase (197 screens on 15 sites)
- Virgin (137 screens on 20 sites)

American companies have invested heavily in multiplex cinemas based on the US model, offering a large number of screens and appropriately large portions of fast food. Multiplexes can make use of their screens in a number of different ways. For example, if a new blockbuster is released it could initially be put on more than one screen and the starting times staggered. Films can also be kept on for longer by moving them into one of the smaller auditoriums in the multiplex as audience demand falls.

A multiplex manager will always stress that his/her cinema can offer the audience a wide choice of films. In reality, however, 'choice' is usually limited to Hollywood product, with little change to see non-mainstream, foreign or even British films. Some multiplex managers try to promote non-mainstream film by dedicating one screen to this type of material, but this is not a widespread practice. Multiplex cinemas are often located in out of town shopping centres providing ease of access combined with shopping and other leisure activities (such as ten-pin bowling). Examples are:

- Showcase, Manchester (14 screens, seats 3,191)
- Warner, Newcastle-upon-Tyne (9 screens, seats 3,384)

Non-mainstream cinema (art-house)

Although a number of mainstream cinemas occasionally show non-mainstream films, these films are usually sidelined and are not promoted to the same extent as those from Hollywood. Non-mainstream films are most often shown at dedicated art-house cinemas that have links with independent rather than mainstream distributors (see distribution).

Independent first run art-house

Usually a single screen cinema (or small chain of single screen cinemas) that obtains sole British distribution rights to a film. Independents show films that are outside the mainstream including foreign films. Many of the key examples are in London. Cinemas will often include a bar or café and will have a completely different ambience to that of mainstream cinemas. The audience will be older (18 to 45), and educated to a higher level. Examples are:

- Renoir Cinema, Brunswick Square, London
- Screen on the Green, London

Independent repertory art-house (non-subsidised)

Show a programme of different films that draw on world cinemas, both past and present – although mostly the films shown have already been screened at first run cinemas. Example:

- Everyman, London

Independent repertory art-house (subsidised)

The National Film Theatre (NFT) situated under Waterloo Bridge on the South Bank complex (London), heads a chain of 41 regional film theatres (RFTs) that receive government support through the Arts Council. RFTs are often located in university towns and in some cases actually on university campuses (Cinema 3 at the University of Kent for example).

Usually based on a single screen, RFTs show similar material to the independent art-house cinema, but films are placed in carefully organised programmes (for example a seasons of films by Stanley Kubrick or a focus on African cinema). A detailed information sheet that gives the credits, reviews and historical background of the film supports each screening. Mainstream films are shown at RFTs (although rarely blockbusters), but only after they have already been shown at the chains and multiplexes first. Audiences for RFTs are similar in composition to the independents. Examples are:

- Cinema City, Norwich
- The Watershed, Bristol
- Harbour Lights, Southampton

Art-house multiplex

In September 1995 the refurbished Ritzy cinema in Brixton reopened. The cinema now has five screens (354, 189, 126, 109 and 84 seats) and can lay claim to being the largest art-house cinema in Britain. The Ritzy is part of the Oasis group with The Cameo (Edinburgh) and The Gate (London).

Non-theatrical exhibition

Although feature films are made with cinema exhibition in mind, only 10% of the audience will typically see a film in a cinema, with 20% seeing it on video or cable, with the majority of 70% seeing it on television. In fact theatrical exhibition might serve as a means of bringing films to the attention of the potential video and or television audience as much as providing the appropriate setting for the viewing of the film.

British exhibition and ownership

As already noted above, key features of the exhibition business in Britain are the concentration of cinema ownership and the involvement of USA film companies. There are two major cinema chains, ABC and Odeon, which operate traditional city-centre sites as well as a number of multiplexes. In 1997 ABC controlled 211 screens on 80 sites and Rank Theatres controlled 361 screens on 73 sites. Together the two chains account for 45% of admissions.

The multiplexes, which account for 34% of the market, have grown tremendously since 1985. In 1990 there were 65, in 1995 there were 79 with 706 screens and in 1996 there were 95 with 859 screens. More sites are under construction or planned. Between 1984 and 1994 over £600 million was invested in this sector predominantly by North American firms. The three main firms operating were:

- National Amusements (UK) which operates 14 showcase multiplexes with 181 screens
- UCI (United Cinemas International) UK which operates 23 purpose built multiplexes as well as the Empire and the Plaza in the West End of London with a total of 222 screens
- Warner Bros. Theatres (UK) which operates 16 multiplexes with 134 screens as well as the Warner West End Village with nine screens

These firms have been joined by Virgin Cinemas which operates 20 multiplexes and plans to open more than 20 new cinema complexes before 2,000 with an average of 15 screens each. In 1995 Virgin bought the MGM chain but significantly sold off 90 of the smaller cinemas to ABC in order to develop its multiplex sites further.

The involvement of USA companies in exhibition is important in itself, but is especially important in that Paramount and Universal who jointly own UCI and Warner Bros. are substantially involved in film financing and production and film distribution. Given the involvement of these firms in all three sectors of the film industry (production, distribution and exhibition) the power that this vertical integration gives these firms in the British exhibition business must be acknowledged.

The presence of vertical integration immediately places independent exhibitors, who are responsible for 21% of admissions, at a disadvantage when it comes to acquiring new releases. Independent exhibitors have always found it difficult to compete in the exhibition market because of the existence of special arrangements between major distributors and exhibitors. The government acted to weaken these arrangements after a report in 1994 by the Monopolies and Mergers Commission on the cinema industry, but as Vincent Porter points out in *On Cinema*[14] access to a film by an independent cinema owner may be restricted by the fact that only a certain number of prints of a film may be available as these are an important cost to the distributor.

Figure 8.4 Number of sites versus number of screens 1984–96[15]

Year	Sites	Screens
1984	660	1,271
1985	663	1,251
1986	660	1,249
1987	648	1,215
1988	699	1,416
1989	719	1,559
1990	737	1,685
1991	724	1,789
1992	735	1,845
1993	723	1,890
1994	734	1,969
1995	743	2,019
1996	742	2,166

Figure 8.5 Breakdown of 1996 British box office by country of origin[16]

Country	Number of titles	Box office £	%
US	154	329,596,913	77.36
Britain/US	19	61,402,504	14.41
Britain	22	19,876,675	4.67
British co-production	20	8,172,836	1.91
EU	28	2,770,321	0.65
Other co-production	12	2,047,045	0.48
Rest of world (English)	4	2,028,874	0.47
Rest of world (Foreign)	5	156,947	0.04
Total	**264**	**426,052,115**	

Social aspects of cinema-going

Despite predictions in the mid 1980s that cinema-going would gradually fade out as films became more freely available in the home, exactly the opposite has taken place, partly encouraged by the new multiplex cinemas. For many it is not the individual film that is of primary importance, but simply the act of going to the cinema as a couple or part of a group. The cinema can thus be seen as a social institution where people can share a common experience. It is significant that very few people go to mainstream cinemas by themselves (although this would be more common in art house cinemas).

Figure 8.6 Top 20 films at the British box office 1996[17]

Title	Country	Distributor	Box office (£m)
Independence Day	US	Fox	37,010
Toy Story	US	Buena Vista	22,164
Se7en	US	Entertainment	19,510
Mission Impossible	US/UK	UIP	18,351
Twister	US	UIP	14,901
Sense & Sensibility	US/UK	Col-Tristar	13,615
101 Dalmations	US/UK	Buena Vista	13,436
Jumanji	US	Col-Tristar	13,272
Trainspotting	UK	Polygram	12,331
The Nutty Professor	US	UIP	12,205
The Hunchback of Notre Dame	US	Buena Vista	10,676
Heat	US	Warner	9,598
The Rock	US	Buena Vista	8,234
Star Trek: Generations	US	UIP	7,270
DragonHeart	US	UIP	6,642
Michael Collins	US	Warner	6,464
Twelve Monkeys	US	Polygram	6,356
James and the Giant Peach	US	Guild	5,792
The First Wives Club	US	UIP	5,634
Phenomenon	US	Buena Vista	5,487

FURTHER WORK

Making reference to production, distribution and exhibition outline some of the problems that are currently faced by film-makers when attempting to make a British film.

How important is government support for the British film industry?

FURTHER READING

1996 BFI Film and Television Handbook, BFI, 1995.
1997 BFI Film and Television Handbook, BFI, 1996.
1998 BFI Film and Television Handbook, BFI, 1997.
Auty, Martyn and Roddick, Nick, *British Cinema Now*, BFI, 1985.
Barr, Charles, (ed.), *All Our Yesterdays*, BFI, 1986.
Cooke, Lez, 'British Cinema: Representing the Nation' in Jill Nelmes, (ed.), *An Introduction to Film Studies*, Routledge, 1996.
Curran, James and Porter, Vincent, (eds), *British Cinema History*, Weidenfeld and Nicolson, 1983.
Dickinson, Margaret and Street, Sarah, *Cinema and State: The Film Industry and the British Government 1927–84*, BFI, 1985.
Murphy, Robert, (ed.), *The British Cinema Book*, BFI, 1997.
James, Park, *British Cinema: the Lights that Failed*, B. T. Batsford, 1990.
Porter, Vincent, *On Cinema*, Pluto Press Limited, 1985.
Street, Sarah, *British National Cinema*, BFI, 1997.

Notes

1 *The Sunday Times*, 23 February 1997.

2 Statistical information in this chapter is taken from *BFI Film and Television Handbook 1996/1997/1998*, BFI, 1995, 1996, 1997.

3 BFI, 1993, p19.

4 Adapted from *BFI Film and Television Handbook 1998*, BFI, 1997, pp20–26.

5 *ibid*, p28.

6 BFI, 1994, p23.

7 The BBC programme *Scrutiny: The Road to Hollywood* gives an excellent insight into the government's attitude towards the British film industry.

8 *BFI Film and Television Handbook 1996*, BFI, 1995, p16.

9 Pete Buckingham from Virgin Vision interviewed on *The Media Show*.

10 Adapted from *BFI Film and Television Handbook 1998*, p39.

11 The *Independent*, 10 August 1988.

12 *ibid*.

13 The *Independent on Sunday*, 16 October 1994.

14 Pluto Press Limited, 1985, p25.

15 Adapted from *BFI Film and Television Handbook 1998*, p32.

16 *BFI Film and Television Handbook 1998*, p37.

17 *ibid*, p36.

CHAPTER **9**

The Hollywood Film Industry

CONTENTS OF THIS CHAPTER

- ■ **A global industry**
- ■ **Global media powerhouses**
- ■ **The Hollywood Studio System**
- ■ **The future of Hollywood**

'The American film industry has never remained in a particular stable state for any length of time. It has always had to struggle and manoeuvre to establish and retain control, to keep out competition, to survive economic problems of its own and others' making, and to counter or negotiate with the government over policies that would upset its preferred modes of operation.'

Jim Hillier in *The New Hollywood*[1]

A GLOBAL INDUSTRY

The Hollywood film industry has enjoyed a pre-eminent position amongst the film industries of the world for most of this century. It continues to attract film-makers from around the world and produce films that audiences around the world want to see. It has the marketing power to ensure that these audiences are aware of its films and the distribution networks to make them available. As a result the films produced in Hollywood tend not only to do well in foreign markets, but also to produce higher box office takings than the domestic film industries with which they are competing. In many instances the Hollywood studios also have a stake in cinemas in foreign markets as well as in the American market. As a result Hollywood plays a significant role on a global scale in all three of the main constituent parts of the film industry.

- ■ The production of films
- ■ The distribution of films
- ■ The exhibition of films

The screenwriter William Goldman has commented that, 'Not one person in the entire motion picture field *knows* for a certainty what's going to work. Every time out it's a guess – and, if you're lucky, an educated one.'[2] Although the position of Hollywood suggests that some pretty good guesses have been made, Goldman's dictum that 'nobody knows anything' does highlight the element of risk in the film industry. Such a risk is present for any product produced for a market but especially in the case of the products of the film industry; a lot rests on the success of each individual film for the following reasons.

- Each film is unique
- The number of films produced in a year is relatively small
- Films require a substantial level of investment

The success of the Hollywood industry rests upon the individual studios being well managed and having large financial resources to sustain 'flops'. The security of the individual studios is enhanced by their belonging to larger entities, which have a diverse range of business interests, and since the 1980s the Hollywood studios have increasingly become part of large companies or conglomerates specialising in media and entertainment.

GLOBAL MEDIA POWERHOUSES

The Hollywood studio Paramount was taken over by Viacom in 1994, resulting in the creation of an entertainment giant, the Viacom Entertainment Group, whose market value was estimated to be $18 billion. To this deal Paramount Communications, the owner of the film studio, brought:

- Paramount pictures (900 films)
- The cable channels USA Network and Madison Square Gardens (a regional sports network)
- The book publishers Simon & Schuster and Prentice Hall [3]
- Paramount Television, the most successful television production company in the USA and responsible for programmes such as *Cheers*, *Taxi*, and *Star Trek*
- Seven TV stations
- Basketball and ice hockey teams, and the rights to the Miss Universe Pageant

Viacom brought:

- The cable channels MTV and Nickelodeon, and the Showtime cable systems.
- Fourteen radio stations
- A television production company, Viacom Entertainment, and five television stations
- The international video rental chain, Blockbuster

The aim of the Paramount/Viacom deal in the words of Sumner Redstone, the chief executive of VEG, was to create a 'global media powerhouse' and the appeal of such a deal lies in the fact that a large group can control media texts and the means by which the texts reach audiences. For example, products such as *Star Trek* or *Beavis and Butthead* can be exploited in different audio-visual markets: cinemas, television, video, and video games. They can even be exploited in theme parks. The media conglomerate can also control the timing of the release of their products in these different markets and this enables them to develop a coordinated marketing campaign that creates the possibility of maximising revenue from their products. The size of the group also makes it possible to expand their activities. For example, the Viacom group will hope to build on the success of MTV and Nickelodeon with channels like VH1.

The commercial appeal of having control over the many manifestations of a media text has led to the creation of other media empires that include a Hollywood studio although Universal and Columbia and Columbia Tri-Star were taken over by Japanese electronics groups hoping to achieve **synergy**.

Warner Brothers

Warner Bros. is part of Time-Warner Inc., which was formed in 1990 when Time Inc. bought Warner Communications for $14.1 billion. The group owns, in addition to the Hollywood studio and its library, Time Magazine and extensive magazine interests; Home Box Office, the world's most successful pay television operation; and the Cinemax pay cable channels in USA.

Seagram

In 1995, Seagram, the Canadian beverage giant, took over MCA and its assets from Matsushita, the Japanese electronics group that had taken over MCA in 1990. Matsushita had not achieved the success it had hoped for from the combination of its hardware with North American software such as the movies of Universal Pictures. As well as the latter Hollywood studio Seagram acquired assets that included MCA Entertainment Group (Video), MCA Music Entertainment; MCA Television Group; and the MCA publishing group. In 1998 Seagram acquired Polygram another major music company from Philips.

Columbia

Columbia and Columbia Tri-Star were taken over by Sony in 1989 for $3.4 billion, but like Matsushita's experience with Universal, the Japanese purchase of part of the USA film industry has not resulted in the expected benefits and Sony's continued ownership must remain in doubt.

Twentieth Century Fox

Since 1985 Twentieth Century Fox has been part of News Corporation which owns Fox Television, has developed satellite broadcasting interests in Western Europe and South East Asia, and magazine and newspaper publishing interests. In Britain Rupert Murdoch's group owns the *Sun*, *The Times*, *The Sunday Times*, and the *News of the World*.

Walt Disney Company

The Walt Disney Company has been considered too big to be taken over and is, (at the end of 1996), the world's largest media group after its takeover of the ABC television network in 1995. Disney was the forerunner in the 1950s of the modern media conglomerate with its films, television programmes and the amusement parks, which exploited the characters in its films. Disney did not enter the ranks of the majors, however, until the 1980s. In the 1930s and 1940s its strategy was to release a small number of expensive films which

Synergy

The idea of synergy in business terms is that by bringing together a number of linked activities under the same roof, each operation will make the others stronger and more profitable than any one could be alone. The idea is exemplified by the purchase of Columbia by Sony. In Sony's annual report for 1990 it is stated that the company is 'one of the world's leading manufacturers of audio and video equipment, television displays, semiconductors, computers and such information-related products as micro floppydisk systems. Keenly aware of the interrelated nature of software and hardware, Sony is also bolstering its presence in the audio and image-based software markets through the CBS Records group and the newly acquired Columbia Pictures Entertainment, Inc.'[4]

yielded high profits. In the 1950s Disney focussed on television and the amusement parks which were the most profitable part of its business as well as films. New management in the 1980s saw the creation of Touchstone in 1984 and Hollywood Pictures in 1989 as well as increased output of new animations and the judicious re-releasing of past favourites in theatres and on video cassette.

THE HOLLYWOOD STUDIO SYSTEM

The current list of Hollywood studios consists of a number of names, Paramount, Warner Bros, Universal, Columbia, Twentieth Century Fox and Disney that have been associated with Hollywood since the 'golden age' of Hollywood in the 1930s and 1940s. Then, as now, the film industry was dominated by a small number of companies known as 'the majors' because of their important role in the film industry. Two groups of companies emerged after the introduction of sound.

- The 'Big Five': Paramount, MGM (Metro-Goldwyn-Meyer), RKO (Radio Keith – Orpheum), Fox (in 1935 it became Twentieth Century Fox), and Warner Bros.
- The 'Little Three': Columbia, Universal, and United Artists

These eight studios dominated film production in the USA and they had the best facilities and most sought-after performers and staff. The difference between the Big Five and the Little Three is that the big five owned cinemas whereas the Little Three did not. The Big Five had an especially strong market position because they were vertically integrated enterprises: they made films, distributed films and exhibited films. Vertical integration meant that they had a ready market for their films and that they could make money on everything that they produced. They could also cut their costs because they did not have to persuade exhibitors to rent their films. As a result they could specialise in marketing their films to the public. Douglas Gomery points out that the Big Five owned only 15 per cent of the cinemas in the USA but that they owned the majority of the first-run cinemas, the key houses in which films were first released and generated the most revenue.[5] As well as owning cinemas the Big Five were able to maximise their revenue by getting together and developing the run-zone-clearance system in which cities and towns in the USA were divided up into zones through which films had to pass in a set order. In each zone movie theatres had the exclusive rights to screen a film for a period of time or clearance (7 to 30 days) and that time had to elapse before the film could progress to the subsequent zone, of which there were up to eleven in the major cities. The virtue of this system was that it made it possible to charge different audiences different prices: the initial runs were charged more than the later ones. The possibility of staggering the audience also meant that the majors needed fewer prints, thus further increasing the cost-effectiveness of the system. Finally, the power of the majors meant that they were able to require smaller cinemas to book films in blocks of five or six. As a result an exhibitor would have to hire a number of films in order to screen the one that was wanted. Again this ensured a screening for the product of the studios and reduced the costs of selling their films, especially the lower budget ones.

Although Hollywood had become firmly established as the centre for North American film production by the 1920s, the centre for film distribution remained New York. Similarly important production decisions – the number of films to be made, the budget of the studio and the schedule of releases – were made on the East coast and then it was up to the head of the studio to put these decisions into operation. These heads of studios or **moguls** were responsible for the following tasks.

- Approving the initial idea for a film
- Approving the budget
- Assigning the director and the team of writers to a film
- Approving the final version of the script
- Supervising the casting of the actors and actresses
- Supervising the hiring of the other personnel
- Checking the progress of the film
- Supervising the final stages of editing

Moguls

The most powerful and most highly paid individuals in the studio system. Harry Cohn at Columbia, Louis B. Mayer at MGM, Jack Warner at Warner Brothers and Darryl L. Zanuck at Twentieth Century Fox all had very long careers. They were both respected and hated for their interventionist role in film-making that was based on an intuitive grasp of what the public wanted.

The heads of the studios were helped to carry out these responsibilities by the heads of production, although Darryl L. Zanuck performed both roles at Twentieth Century Fox from 1935 to 1956. In the Hollywood studios power was concentrated in the hands of these top executives, who were collectively known as the 'front office'. Although individual directors and stars that had established a reputation had a degree of personal power and therefore some control over their careers, they were employed on a contract, as was everyone else who worked for a studio. The stars were part of a highly developed division of labour that served the mass production of films and led to the description of Hollywood as the 'dream factory'. Joel W. Finler quotes Richard Zanuck who said that his father Darryl L. Zanuck, had a big chart under the glass top of his desk, 'and it had everybody that was under contract there. All the producers, and the directors, and the writers and actors and actresses. And it was so simple . . . Casting meetings would take all of about ten minutes. Not only casting, but putting the whole picture together. He would say, "Well, we've got Julian Blaustein as producer, he's available next week. Put him with Hathaway, he'll direct. And we've got Tyrone Power, he's going to finish his picture, give him a week off." And that was the end of it.'[6] The simplicity of this system did not always appeal to the stars for whom the contract system was a source of contention. A major reason for this was that if they were to refuse an appointed role in a film they would not be offered an alternative one during the production period of that film. As a result they lost income but what is more they had the time that they had been required to sit out plus a half again added to the time of their contract. In consequence a seven-year contract could become a ten or fifteen year one and the star would feel enslaved by the studio even if they enjoyed a luxurious life-style for their pains.

The end of the Hollywood studio system

The majors rode out the Depression years of the 1930s and although the Second World War hit their foreign markets it provided the most profitable years ever in the domestic market culminating in the most profitable year ever in 1946. Within a few years however the studio system had undergone a number of changes that resulted in a new industrial framework for film-making in the USA.

- The vertical integration of the industry was brought to an end in 1948 when the Big Five were required by the courts to divorce their exhibition holdings from their production and distribution arms because they were judged to be contravening the anti-trust laws. They had already agreed in 1940 to end their practices of block booking and blind selling but the ending of their ability to own cinemas hit at the heart of the system, especially as the theatres had provided collateral for bank loans

- The 1940s saw an increase in independent production as a result of the buoyant demand for films, the tax advantages of starting a private company rather than drawing a salary and the end of block booking and blind selling referred to above

- The stars began to seek more independence. For example, in 1943 Olivia de Haviland had taken Warner Bros. to court on the issue of the contract. She had been loaned to David Selznick for *Gone with the Wind* and when she returned to Warners she was suspended for refusing the roles that were offered her. She sued Warner Bros. and the result of the case was that contracts in future were limited to seven consecutive years and so stars could not be tied to a studio for an unpredictable number of years

- The costs of film production had been rising as trade unionism had achieved improvements in wages

- Foreign countries that wanted to prevent the export of dollars and thereby protect their balance of payments position imposed import duties on Hollywood films or restrictions on the repatriation of money from film rentals

- After the war the demand for films fell drastically as a result of competition from other forms of consumption and entertainment. Television emerged as a competitor in the late 1940s before establishing itself as the major form of leisure activity during the 1950s. New family commitments after the disruption of the war as well as population movement further depressed the demand for cinema

As a result the majors entered a period of retraction. They tried to maintain their audience by experimenting with 3–D and wide-screen but it fell by a half between 1947 and 1957 and between 1946 and 1956 4,000 theatres were closed. There were also huge staff cuts including producers, directors, writers and performers at the studios. Gradually the mass production of the film 'factory' was replaced by the package–unit system, the essence of which is that 'rather than an individual company containing the source of the labour and the materials, the entire industry became the pool for these. A producer organised a film project: he or she secured financing and combined the necessary labourers (whose roles had previously been defined by the standardised production structure and subdivision of work categories) and the means of production (the narrative **'property'**, the equipment, and the physical sites of production).[7] RKO finally disappeared in 1957 but the other studios continued to exist. Production activity did become more and more dispersed but the majors continued to dominate the film industry as producers and distributors of films. Meanwhile the theatre chains were divorced but they still dominated the exhibition sector. Douglas Gomery has termed this new

Property

Property in the film industry refers to anything that can be bought or optioned to form the basis or starting point for a film's narrative. It can therefore be a novel, for example, *Regeneration* (Gillies MacKinnon, UK/Canada, 1997) based on the book by Pat Thomas; a previous film, for example, *Twelve Monkeys* (Terry Gilliam, USA, 1996) based on *La Jetée* by Chris Marker; a magazine article, for example, *Top Gun* (Tony Scott, USA, 1986) or other sources such as short stories, plays, and non-fiction works.

Oligopoly

Refers to a market situation where a small number of firms have the power to control prices etc. The position of an oligopolist is often protected because the price of entry to the industry is too high for newcomers.

situation a 'bi-lateral **oligopoly**' replacing the 'mature oligopoly' (Tino Balio) of the pre-1948 era.

Gradually the studio system was replaced by individual productions wholly or partially financed by a studio. The studios, Columbia, Columbia Tri-Star, Fox, Paramount, Universal, Warner Bros. and Disney, continue to have a major role in film production and film-makers still need the Hollywood studios to make films. The studios however make deals and not films as in the studio era. The typical pattern for a deal is as follows:

- A film producer or agent will assemble the elements that she or he will use to attract the interest and subsequent funding of a film by a studio. These elements will include a property, a director, a screenplay and a star or stars and are known as the 'package'. Some producers and/or directors have a deal whereby they are given office space and administrative support by a studio and in return the studio has a 'first-look' at new projects. For example, Steven Spielberg's production company, Amblin Entertainment, had such an arrangement with Universal as did the directors, Joe Dante and Richard Donner with Warner Bros.

- Studio interest will result in a deal to produce and finance the film

- The project will be further developed: the director will be confirmed, the cast assembled, the screenplay worked on, and a production schedule drawn up

- The budget will be approved and all the costs vital to making a film, the 'above-the-line costs' will be finalised.

- The film will enter its pre-production phase in which a start date will be established, the heads of departments will be appointed and the 'below-the-line costs' will be finalised

Not only do film-makers need the financial resources of the majors to make their films but they also require their distribution networks – the deal will give the studio ownership rights and the rights to world-wide distribution. The huge costs of entry to the film distribution business make it very difficult for newcomers to enter this activity and successful independents are susceptible to being taken over by the majors. For example, in 1993 Disney took over the independent distributor Miramax that had been associated with films like *The Crying Game* and *Sex, Lies and Videotape* rather than the traditional family entertainment associated with Disney, thus exemplifying the conglomerates' continued need to grow and diversify.

HOLLYWOOD AND DIRECTORS

In the studio system producers, directors, writers, players, technicians *et al* were employed on contracts. The studios produced many films per month on what has been seen as an assembly-line basis. In these 'film factories' the stress was not on individual artistic expression. Typically directors were appointed to films. They were given a script to film with very little notice and they were not expected to play a role in the editing stage to any great extent.

However in 1954 the French critic Francois Truffaut argued in the film magazine *Cahiers du Cinéma* that the director ought to be the author (*auteur* in French) of her or his film. Truffaut and his fellow critics, Claude Chabrol, Jean-Luc Godard, Jacques Rivette and Eric Rohmer were to become film authors themselves in the late 1950s but before that they discovered *auteurs* working in Hollywood cinema. Chabrol and Rohmer for example produced the first full analysis of the films of Alfred Hitchcock and the group also celebrated John Ford, Howard Hawks and Vincente Minnelli. This approach to film criticism proved to be very influential on reviewers, film-makers and the marketing departments of the Hollywood studios.

Studios still exist but the circumstances in which films are made are very different. Long gone are the studio moguls and the distinctive house-styles of the different studios. The studios are part of conglomerates and they are all searching for that elusive blockbuster with the multi-media pay-off. Films are not overseen by studio producers but by production executives who move from studio to studio and agents and accountants have a more pervasive presence. Although film-makers are independent of the studios they are still subject to constraints, especially financial ones and because each film is subject to an individual deal, film-makers have to be deal-makers as well. Contemporary film-makers operate however in a context in which individual artistic expression is acknowledged and applauded.

THE FUTURE OF HOLLYWOOD

Entertainment is the USA's second largest export (after military hardware) and the majors are now part of conglomerates that are shifting towards a stress on entertainment and media. The media empires such as Time-Warner, Viacom and News Corporation have stakes in the following areas of activity:

- Television production
- Television syndication
- Cable distribution networks
- Home video distribution
- Record companies
- Publishing
- Theme parks

The 1949 legal decision that required the majors to divorce their theatres was reversed in 1985 and the studios have been purchasing cinema chains again although there have been some doubts about the financial sense of this strategy. A new form has supplemented this old kind of vertical integration: News Corporation, for example, owns Twentieth Century Fox but also the Fox

Broadcasting Television Network in the USA as well as BSkyB in Britain. The important point here is that there is more than one market for films now. In addition, while the run-zone-clearance system has long gone the majors are still able to charge different audiences different prices. The audience is segmented and can therefore be charged different prices for:

- Cinema screenings
- Pay per view television screenings
- Home video rental and sell-through
- Pay television screenings
- Network television screenings
- Independent television screenings

Whereas the majors were slow to catch on to the importance of television in the 1950s the contemporary majors have been quick to take advantage of new developments in television. Pay television stimulated film production and Home Box Office was a major financier of films in the 1980s. The majors did try to become directly involved in pay-cable but were legally barred from vertically integrating in this way. The majors did seize on the potential of video however and they are now marketing videos on a large scale. Video cassettes of feature films provide a reliable and lucrative form of income. Video allows the majors to exploit their libraries as well as see a greater number of their contemporary releases show a profit. It has been suggested that the income from video is more predictable than that from cinemas and that whereas before the development of video only two films in ten showed a profit it is now estimated to be seven in ten. Another market that has developed is that of electronic video games that can form a part of the merchandising essential for some films. As a result electronic games designers are now being incorporated very early on in the production cycle. Independent studios still play a role but they always have the problem of trying to compete with the majors and it is possible for a company like Orion to have many successful films and still eventually go under. Jim Hillier noted the emergence of 'neo-indies' from the mid 1980s onwards in response to the growing demand for films in the context of the growth of cinema screens, home video and pay-cable television as well as cutbacks in production by the majors and the availability of low-cost credit. The neo-indies were well capitalised from multi-national sources. They made their own films but used the majors for distribution. They often financed their own advertising and prints however, and this reduced the majors' distribution fee. They also retained the rights to foreign distribution, home video, television sales and cable sales, and were concerned to build up their own libraries of titles. Carolco, Castle Rock, Imagine Entertainment, Largo and Morgan Creek had a number of successes but Caralco collapsed in 1995 and Castle Rock was purchased in 1993 by Turner Broadcasting Systems (and later by Time-Warner).

Finally, the Hollywood studios have operated in many different contexts and have adapted to many different changes since the demise of the studio system. Recently MGM has been the least successful studio to survive from that era. It has made very few films in the 1990s and has suffered badly from a number of takeovers. What has remained the same however has been the global demand for the Hollywood-made feature film, which remains a dominant cultural artefact, however it is made available to audiences.

FURTHER WORK

Comparing past and present Hollywood

Examine the idea that the films made in the Hollywood studio era were works of collaboration whereas the films made in contemporary Hollywood are the products of individual creativity.

Compare and contrast the economic organisation Hollywood in the present with that of the past.

FURTHER READING

Gomery, Douglas, *The Hollywood Studio System*, MacMillan/BFI, 1986.
Balio, Tino, *The American Film Industry*, The University of Wisconsin Press, 1985.
Hillier, Jim, *The New Hollywood*, Studio Vista, 1992.
Schatz, Thomas, *The Genius of the System*, Simon & Schuster, 1989.
Wasko, Janet, *Hollywood in the Information Age*, Polity Press, 1994.
Bordwell, David, Staiger, Janet and Thompson, Kristin, *The Classical Hollywood Cinema: Film Style and Mode of Production to 1960*, Routledge, 1985.

FURTHER VIEWING

A Personal Journey with Martin Scorsese through American Movies (Connoisseur Video, 1997)

Notes

[1]   *The New Hollywood*, Studio Vista, 1992.

[2]   *Adventures in the Screentrade*, Futura Publications, 1985, p39.

[3]   Simon and Schuster has subsequently been acquired by the British company Pearson, owner of the *Financial Times*, Penguin Books and Pearson TV.

[4]   Quoted by Janet Wasko, *Hollywood in the Information Age*, Polity Press, 1994, p61.

[5]   *The Hollywood Studio System*, MacMillan/BFI, 1986, p18.

[6]   *The Hollywood Story*, Pyramid Books, 1989, p44.

[7]   David Bordwell, Janet Staiger and Kristin Thompson, *The Classical Hollywood Cinema: Film Style and Mode of Production to 1960*, Routledge, 1985, p330.

CHAPTER **10** Advertising

'Well, you only have to ask: is Chris Evan's personality the right fit with Kelloggs' brand personality? His risqué nature is at obvious dissonance with Kelloggs' family values personality.'

A comment from an insider at the advertising agency J. Walter Thompson when Kelloggs' withdrew sponsorship of Virgin Radio's breakfast show after the news that Chris Evan's was to become its new presenter.[1]

For the media student, the important aspect of advertising is not the product being sold but the 'images, dreams and ideal ways of life'[2] being used to sell those products. It is the underlying ideological messages that repeatedly surface in advertising and make it the 'central force in the reproduction of culture'[3] which demand consideration.

THE HISTORY OF ADVERTISING

Advertising is not a modern phenomenon; there were wall writings and town criers advertising theatrical and gladiatorial events in Greek and Roman times but modern types of advertising came into being in the 15th century with the printing press. This facilitated the printing of handbills which could easily be distributed in busy urban thoroughfares and market places. The 17th century saw advertising for New World products such as tea and coffee appear in the pages of Britain's local newspapers.

A significant event in the 18th century was the commencement of mass production in the pottery industry by Josiah Wedgwood; this scale of production made the use of a range of advertising gambits necessary (posters, handbills, newspaper advertisements) to interest new markets both at home and abroad. As mass production of goods became more widespread in the industrial revolution of the 19th century a need for more advertising and better marketing strategies was created. At this time, advertising was primarily directed at the middle classes; the working classes were not really targeted until the American company Singer brought their hire purchase scheme to Britain in 1860 and offered an affordable consumer opportunity to the low paid.[4]

As the century progressed and cities and towns increased in size, advertisements for goods and services began to adorn the side of horse drawn trams, vans and buses. Advances in photography and the invention of the metal plate, which allowed the reproduction of pictures on the printed page, opened up the possibilities of visual impact in advertising. The abolition of the so-called 'taxes on knowledge' during the second half of the 19th century enabled the growth of a cheap press which could reach a wide range of the population. This, and the Education Act 1870, increased literacy and gave advertising in newspapers and on handbills a wider audience.

Advertising agents had, until this juncture, been bulk buyers of advertising space which they then brokered to manufacturers or businesses but these new events prompted the emergence of creative advertising agencies who could sell the whole package – both advertising space and ideas. This led to the need for copywriters many of whom were initially poets or writers.[5] As mass production facilitated 'the collapse of the distinction, formerly so clear, between items of refined design possessed by the rich and the rough possessions of the poor'[6] many goods became affordable to the man in the street. Inevitably, society's goals shifted and, by the time the 19th century came to a close, consumption rather than production was the dominant ethic.

ADVERTISING IN THE 20TH CENTURY

In the 1920s, commercial radio in countries such as the USA and Australia created another medium for advertising and allowed more scope for sponsorship (see Chapter 13, Soap Opera). Cinema going also became increasingly popular in the early 20th century and, certainly by the mid 1930s, advertising for household goods and local firms was common. In the 1950s the introduction of independent TV brought the concept of the commercial break into people's living rooms and quickly became the most effective medium for advertising. Similarly, in Britain today, deregulation of the airwaves and the consequent growth in the number of independent radio stations means that commercial radio is the fastest growing advertising medium; indeed, in 1995 radio-advertising revenue increased by 213 per cent to £220 million.

Today about one third of a product's cost goes towards advertising but the function of that advertising has changed since the beginning of the century. Initially, when the markets were less competitive, advertising was used to help a product take a share of a particular market; now companies have to advertise to keep their share of the market. Economic rationalisation has produced markets dominated by just a few major manufacturers and these wealthy companies can fight off those newcomers to their particular markets by paying huge amounts in advertising which most newcomers cannot match. The detergent market, for instance, is dominated by Unilever and Procter and Gamble; new detergent products from small companies have little chance of survival if launched onto the market; the only significant intruders on this market in the recent past have been the ecological products which captured a corner of the market on the back of increased eco-consciousness.

In the 1980–90s, Channel Four became one of the biggest surprises in the advertising industry when they successfully delivered niche audiences with big spending power to the advertisers. From the outset, Channel Four had a requirement to target niche audiences and so it depended on a share of ITV's overall advertising revenue to keep it afloat; advertisers wanted mass audiences and so it was thought that Channel Four would never be able to gain enough advertising revenue to become financially independent. Traditionally, broadsheet newspapers have been financed by offering advertisers smaller but richer consumer groups but no one thought that the same formula would work in TV. Channel Four proved them wrong; clever programming and targeting has put it in a very healthy financial position. Unfortunately, Channel Four targeting does owe more to financial cynicism than liberal thinking than is widely realised. For instance, gay and lesbian targeting can guarantee an advertiser within such programming a high number of double income households; equally, alternative sports programmes such as *Trans World Sport* and *The American Football Big Match* are more likely to be viewed by the jet-set sport enthusiast with high earning power.

Today, advertising and marketing reaches into every corner of daily life: the ubiquitous 'bill stickers' is still in evidence despite the threat of prosecution; billboards, posters and neon lights demand attention from the passer by and LED screens at sports stadia offer the chance to buy yet another new first team football kit – sponsored of course. Bus, car park, theatre tickets and every other possible type of ticket have half price pizzas, new CDs or package holidays on offer. Homes are similarly invaded, be it by junk mail, hard sell telephone calls, commercial broadcasting, designer emblazoned clothing or simply by newspapers stuffed with classifieds, display ads, advertorials and leaflets and, of course, there is one more advertising method that is now on-line to daily private and public life.

The global billboard

Information superhighway

This relates to the exchange of information in cyberspace over the Internet or the World Wide Web.

One by-product of the **information superhighway** has been the opening up of the 'persuasion superhighway' via the World Wide Web (WWW). The WWW offers users a huge market place; already there are over 50 million pages on line and over 20 million users world wide. The potential market place is unlimited and so is the scope to change the nature of advertisements. Web pages offer multimedia interactivity to the user which means that web advertisements really can employ every visual and audio trick in the book. The opportunity that the WWW offers in terms of direct marketing has already been identified by the travel industry; it has found the size and segment of market targeted, as well as the interactive opportunities, particularly suitable for selling its services. The growth in this quarter over the last year has been nothing short of phenomenal. In January 1996, there were 5,000 travel related web sites but by 1997 that figure had increased to over 80,000. The on-line travel industry is currently worth 600 million dollars per year but this could grow to well over nine billion dollars by 2002. The WWW is also an effective medium for corporate advertising and all big businesses now have their own web sites – mostly offering a little information and a great deal of image. Even the British Monarchy is on-line.

Evidently, the WWW is going to revolutionise global marketing but the notion of global marketing is not new; Coca-Cola is a multinational corporation that has been 'teaching the world to sing' along with its advertising campaigns for a number of years but more companies than ever are now realising the benefits of global marketing. Levi, McDonald's, Nike and Pepsi-Cola are examples of global corporations that now treat 'the entire world as if it were a single entity and sell[s] the same things in the same way everywhere'.[7] The theory behind global marketing is that cultural boundaries may differ but there are similar market segments (see below) with the same needs and aspirations everywhere in the world. Corporations embarking on world-wide marketing need to employ an agency which is part of a global network if they are to 'realise true economies of scale'[8] – it would be enormously wasteful to have to hire the services of a different agency in every country. Omnicom, Saatchi World-wide, WPP and Interpublic are the big four global networks and most of the top ten agencies in Britain belong to one of these (see Figure 10.1).

Controls on advertising

There are numerous legal controls which cover all publishing and broadcasting and inevitably include advertising. These controls embrace libel laws as well as laws to do with racial or sexual discrimination. A common new phenomenon which is illegal but not that easy to prove is 'passing off'; this describes the process of packaging a new product to look like an established market leader. This allows the look-alike product to be bought on the back of the brand image created by market leader's advertising or it simply enables the look-alike to be bought in mistake for the market leader. This practice is most common when supermarket chains try to disguise their own brands as brand market leaders. As an act of 'goodwill' in 1994, Sainsbury's changed the packaging on their Classic Cola after complaints by Coca Cola that the packaging on Sainsbury's product was too similar. In October 1996, United Biscuits threatened the supermarket chain ASDA with legal action because the packaging on ASDA's chocolate coated Puffin biscuits looked too similar to United Biscuits' own market leader, Penguin.

For the most part, however, advertising is primarily controlled by self-regulation and this is policed by two main bodies:

The Advertising Standards Authority (ASA)

This was set up in 1962 by the Advertising Association to introduce self-regulation and thus minimalise government intervention. It is financed by a levy on advertising space and so remains independent of industry or government control although the chairman is appointed in conjunction with the Department of Trade and Industry. The job of this authority is to police print and cinema advertising by making sure that all advertisements adhere to the British Codes of Advertising and Sales Promotion. The basic rubric of these codes are that advertisements should be 'legal, decent, honest and truthful'.

The Independent Television Commission (ITC)

The ITC controls the frequency and content of advertising on Channels Three, Four, Five and satellite TV providers such as BSkyB. The Broadcasting Advertising Clearance Centre (BACC) clears new commercials and adjudicates on complaints for the ITC which operates by the following rules and codes.

■ **The ITC Rules on Advertising Breaks**

These cover the amount of advertising allowed per day – no more than seven minutes per hour on average – and where and when particular advertisements and advertisement breaks can be broadcast (eg alcoholic drinks cannot be advertised in children's programmes and ad breaks cannot be taken in broadcasts of religious services)

■ **The ITC Code of Programme Sponsorship**

This covers those programmes whose costs of production or transmission is met by an advertiser with a view to 'promoting . . . commercial interest'

■ **The ITC Code of Advertising Standards and Practice**

A comprehensive document which takes up the ASA requirement that all advertisements should be 'legal, decent, honest and truthful' and includes among many others the following prohibitions. Advertisements

– should not offend against 'good taste and decency'
– should not give misleading descriptions of or make unwarranted claims about a product
– should not be used for political purposes
– should not contain covert **subliminal** images to convey a message
– should not claim that alcoholic drinks are essential to 'social or sexual success'
– should not 'encourage or condone' dangerous driving
– should not contain elite persons endorsing 'medicinal products or treatments'
– should not 'exploit the superstitious'
– should not play on people's fears 'without justifiable reason'
– should not be called programmes and they should be 'clearly distinguishable' from programmes
– should not use the expression 'news flash'

> **Subliminal**
>
> Subliminal messages are usually split second screen images that appeal to the subconscious not the conscious mind; these can be a very effective means of persuasion if they are used without the knowledge of the receiver.

Over 700 advertisements were withdrawn for a variety of reasons in 1996 according to the Advertising Standards Authority. The five advertisements that caused the most complaints were as follows.[9]

■ Gossard – a woman wearing underwear with the slogan: 'Who said a woman can't get pleasure from something soft?' (321 complaints)

■ Conservative Party – Tony Blair's face with devil eyes superimposed with the slogan: 'New Labour, New Danger' (167 complaints)

■ Nissan – posters featuring a woman's body superimposed on a tonka truck with the slogan: '4 × 4 Play' (126 complaints)

■ Holsten Pils – a bottle of Pils with the slogan: 'Poncy arsed advertising? Get real' (94 complaints)

■ Benetton – three hearts with the words: 'White, yellow and black written on them' (87 complaints).

Advertising and editorial freedom

The mid 19th century saw the independence of the press increase because of the wealth brought to them by advertising. Until this point, many papers were dependent on financial support coming from political alliances. The growth of advertising revenue was the most important single factor in enabling the press to become such a powerful force. However, the reliance of the commercial media on advertising revenue also means that it is possible for large advertisers to exert control over media output. Watson and Hill say that this effect 'is rarely overt; rather it is a process of media people internalising advertisers demands'[10] and thus self-censoring any material which would offend advertisers, but it is not unknown for advertisers overtly to issue the threat of withdrawing advertisements because of programme/newspaper content as is evident from the Chris Evans/Kelloggs example quoted at the opening of the chapter. Recently, after some public debate over the judiciousness of the fashion industry's craze for 'heroin chic' catwalk models, Omega, the watch manufacturers, threatened to pull advertising from *Vogue* magazine if it continued to use these 'skeletal' models in their fashion pages. However, this threat by Omega's advertising director was ultimately overridden by its chairman who said it was 'not in anybody's interest to manipulate the editorial position of any given media'.[11]

Advertising organisations

The importance of the service provided by the modern advertising agency is indisputable. Years of market research have given agencies intricate knowledge of the relationship between brand image and consumer and now few big companies would try to reach the consumer without employing the services of an agency, although, **Benetton**, with its successful 'shock tactics' campaigns, has been a notable exception.

The Conservative Party was the first political party in this country to employ an advertising agency (Saatchi and Saatchi) to improve their image and the last election was notable for its presentation of this image. The Conservative campaign started with 'devil-eyed' Tony Blair and the slogan 'New Labour: New Danger'; it continued by representing Blair as a puppet sitting on the lap of Chancellor Kohl of Germany but, despite these dramatic images, New Labour's in-house spin doctors won the image battle. This does not alter the fact that advertising agencies are hugely important: the major advertising agencies have a lion's share of advertising output. The top ten advertising agencies in Britain in 1996 are given in Figure 10.1.

How do agencies work?

Advertising agencies offer a complete service from planning to production and the departments within agencies have quite a complex relationship. The client's point of contact within the agency is the account handling group; then, beneath this group are the five major departments housing the following functions:

- **Media** – they will decide on which media can be used when so that it will be the most effective for a campaign. This department has intimate knowledge of trends within the media in terms of popularity, readership, etc.

Benetton

Luciano Benetton launched a global campaign 'United Colours of Benetton' in 1984 to gain corporate recognition and increase his string of franchises. The campaign possessed a cultural vision of a multi-racial society living and working together in harmony. In 1990, the campaign had begun to lose momentum so 'shock tactics' were enlisted; the shock images included dying AIDS victims, bloody new born babies and a priest and a nun kissing and proved to be a winning formula as the media reaction to the shock images gave Benetton additional free publicity.

Figure 10.1 The top ten advertising agencies in Britain, 1997

Position	Agency	Global network
1	Abbott Mead Vickers BBDO	Omnicom
2	Ogilvy Mather	WPP
3	Saatchi & Saatchi	Saatchi Worldwide
4	J. W. Thompson	WPP
5	BMP DDB Needham	Omnicom
6	Grey London	Grey
7	Bates Dorland	Saatchi Worldwide
8	M&C Saatchi	–
9	Publicis	–
10	McCann-Erickson	Interpublic

Source: Campaign, AC Nielsen Register – MEAL Billings

- **Planning and research** – they will do market research to find out the client's share of the market and that of competitors
- **Creative** – this is the most important department as it is the source of a campaign's ideas
- **Traffic** – this department directs the work flow among departments
- **Print production and progress** – this department will deal with artwork and determine typefaces etc. for print and billboard designs

AUDIENCE SEGMENTATION

Of course, consumers have been put into groups since marketing began but it was not until the post-war economic growth in marketing and media that consumers were identified in terms of social class and this segmentation has remained important to the present day (see Chapter 5, p84 for social class categories). However, over recent years market research has moved away from demographic profiling (eg age, class, gender, geographical area, etc.) to psychographic profiling which categorises the consumer in terms of motivation and needs.

In 1954, Austrian Psychologist Abraham Maslow[12] put forward the idea of a hierarchy of human needs; his concept was that the needs within each stage of the hierarchy have to be satisfied before the next stage can be addressed. Starting at the lowest stage, the hierarchy is as follows:

- Physiological needs – food, drink, sleep, sex, relief from pain
- Safety needs – security, protection, freedom from danger, order
- Love and belonging needs – friends, companions, a family, being part of a group

- Esteem needs – respect, confidence based on the good opinion of others, admiration, self-confidence, self-worth, self-acceptance
- Self-actualisation needs – fulfil one's potential, develop one's potential, do what one is best suited to do, discover truth, create beauty, produce order, promote justice

Maslow's hierarchy influenced attitudes and research concerning the reasons for communication, motivation and behaviour and, in 1957, Vance Packard affected the marketing world more precisely when he identified eight hidden needs that advertisers attempt to engage when targeting consumers. Packard believed, 'Large scale efforts are being made, often with impressive success, to channel our unthinking habits, our purchasing decisions and our thought processes by the use of insights gleaned from psychiatry and the social sciences.'[15] His concern was to highlight the ways in which the public were being 'influenced and manipulated'[14] by identifying those hidden needs used by advertisers as the need for:

- Emotional security
- Reassurance of worth
- Ego gratification
- Creative outlets
- Love objects
- Sense of power
- Sense of roots
- Sense of immortality

The research into needs and motivation led to advertisers looking at the target consumer in terms of their desires and aspirations which brought them to look at specific lifestyles.

Young and Rubicam's Four Cs

Young and Rubicam, an American advertising agency, developed the Four Cs (Cross-Cultural Consumer Characteristics) categorisation of consumers in the 1970s; this method moved away from ideas of class to view consumers in terms of their personal aspirations. The Four Cs are:

- Mainstreamers

    At 40 per cent of the market this is the largest segment of consumers. This group seek security in conformity and tend to buy well-established brands such as Heinz Baked Beans or Kellogg's Cornflakes
- Aspirers

    This group's motivation is status and they tend to buy smart high tech and high fashion goods which will help give them a higher status image. Nescafé Gold Blend have successfully targeted this market
- Succeeders

    These are people who have climbed the ladder and now want to keep control of what they have. Car advertisements which emphasise power and control are aimed at this group
- Reformers

    This group want to make the world a better place. They tend to be educated professionals such as teachers, doctors, etc. These people buy eco-friendly products and healthy foods. Although this is a relatively small group of consumers they have an influential voice with manufacturers

In more recent times, a BBC *QED* programme, *It's Not Easy Being a Dolphin* (May 1988), identified another category of consumer, the Individual; this person responds to advertising which emphasises quirkiness or individuality. The enigmatic Guinness commercials with actor Rutger Hauer would be a prime example of a campaign targeting this consumer.

Lifestyles

In addition to the segments categorised above, admen are constantly identifying new segment 'sub-species'. They have pigeonholed any number of niche and not so niche consumer markets such as: opals (older people with active lifestyles), yuppies (young upwardly mobile professionals), dinkys (double income no kids yet), woopies (well off older people), lombards (lots of money but a real dickhead).

REPOSITIONING

Sometimes manufacturers will decide that a particular brand needs to change or add to its existing target consumer segment. A new advertising campaign will then be employed to present a new brand image which will attract the new consumer. One example of this is Rowntree's Walnut Whip which was repositioned in the early 1990s. The advertising agency, J. Walter Thompson, had to come up with a campaign that would give the chocolate a racier upmarket image so that it would appeal to the young female aspirer – the chocolate had traditionally been consumed by older women. The packaging was redesigned to give it a more modern feel and the new TV advertisement denoted well-dressed and glamorous female office workers being discovered in hidden corners of the office surreptitiously eating a Walnut Whip. The connotation of the advertisement was that Walnut Whips were a slightly sinful, self-indulgent, luxury eaten by glamorous upwardly mobile career women and if you bought this product you could buy into this lifestyle.

Analysing persuasion

It can be confusing when setting out to analyse advertisements as there are so many aspects to be considered. It may be helpful to conduct advertisement analysis as if using a zoom lens on a camera. Start with the distant perspective then zoom in to a close-up and then back out to the distant perspective again. In that way, the text can be examined for the following:

- Persuasive tools
- Signs
- Persuasive devices and ultimate meaning

Persuasive tools

In the initial distant perspective, the scrutineer is looking for some of the more obvious ploys being used to grab attention and create meaning such as:

- Humour

  Aspects of humour such as ambiguity and punning add layers of meaning to a text and will make it more satisfying to decipher and consequently more memorable. For instance, Guinness' 'Not everything in black and white makes sense'. The slapstick humour of the 'You've been tangoed' advertisements made them notable and imitable

- Repetition

  Slogans, images and brand names can be repeated and will give continuity and greater credibility to a campaign. Slogans remain in the memory long after the advertising campaign has finished. Everyone (above a certain age!) remembers that 'A Mars a day helps you work rest and play' or that 'Beanz Meanz Heinz'

- Shock tactics

  Luciano Benetton proved that shock tactics grab not only the attention of the consumer but also that of the media and in doing so increase the effectiveness of the campaign many times over

- Sex

  One of the most basic human needs and one of the most effective persuasive tools in advertising

In advertisements time/space are usually at a premium and some tools are well used because they enable the production of meaning in the minimum time/space available.

- Stereotypes

  These are useful in ads because they are easily identifiable and the stereotype tends to bring with it certain messages. They are a short cut that can add immediate meaning. Stereotypes tend to be accepted without much questioning; this often allows us to accept the message contained within the advertisement without much questioning

- Intertextual references

  Using other texts to create or add immediate meaning to an advertisement is a useful device. Recent TV car advertisements have parodied aspects of TV series and films such as *The Sweeney* and *Bullitt*

- Music

  This can be used in a number of ways as an attention grabber, as narrative short hand or as an emotive mechanism. Advertising executives have become extremely fond of using golden oldies in adverts as they summon up happy youthful memories. The product is then identified with those feelings

- Elite persons

  Famous people are used to endorse products and if the audience admire that person or aspire to be like them they will be more likely to buy the product. A good example of this is Gary Lineker and Walkers crisps

Signs

Moving in closer, it is possible to examine the advertisement for the following signs and from these signs some suggested meanings can be assembled. Although, the following signs refer to image based analysis, it is not difficult to apply the same guidelines to audio advertising.[15]

- Position signs

   The position of the camera which gives the viewer a particular point of view; this could be meaningful. For instance, if a picture is taken from a low angle then the viewer will look up at people within it; consequently, the person in the image will be imbued with authority

- Treatment signs

   The type/angle/strength of the lighting, overall colour of the image, focus, composition and framing all affect the meaning that we take from an image. For instance, our reaction to black and white and colour photos is usually different; black and white photos tend to convey a more 'documentary' feel

- Content signs

   People, objects, clothes, sounds, etc. It is self-evident that who and what the image contains will communicate this greatest part of the overall message

Persuasive devices

At this point in the analysis, the viewer moves out again to a distant perspective and it is possible to take an overall meaning from the narrative that has been surveyed.

- Reward and punishment

   These are probably the most important persuasive devices in advertising. Physical rewards are offered like 'buy one get one free' or the face cream that will keep you 'young looking' but more frequently they offer psychological rewards such as if you buy 'Moggy meat with vitamin plus' for your cat you will be a good owner because it will keep him healthier. The other side of the coin is often implied, ie if you don't use Moggy meat then you will be punished, as your cat will be unhealthy

- Needs, fears and aspirations

   Maslow's hierarchy of needs itemised earlier is relevant here. Advertisers play on the need to be safe, secure, part of a group, part of a relationship, etc. Insurance and pension schemes often use security and safety needs as a device. Fashion advertising often enlists the desire to be part of a group with slogans such as 'What the man about town is wearing'. People also need esteem and aspirations; they need to feel that they are important and that they can improve what they have. Opulent lifestyles are offered with products such as the Renault Clio (Nicole and Papa in their French chateau) and this presents the consumer with the opportunity of buying into a better life

- Value messages

  Many advertisements carry with them messages about life that cannot be denied and the advertiser will persuade the audience that if they do not buy the product then they do not agree with the message

ADVERTISING AND IDEOLOGY: HEINZ *A TOAST TO LIFE* CAMPAIGN

'These commercials show modern British families without any of the usual sugar-coated advertising fantasy. Heinz is a brand rooted in real life and we wanted a campaign which reflected those values in a new and arresting way.'

Robert Bailey, Heinz Marketing Director[16]

The Heinz *A Toast to Life* advertising campaign was launched in January 1997 and consisted of five 60 second television commercials. Initially, the advertisements were shown only in the Yorkshire and Tyne Tees TV areas to allow Heinz to gauge public reaction before being broadcast nationally.

In these advertisements, Heinz decided that it wanted to continue to show how its products 'sit at the heart of family life'[17] but the desire was to show Heinz at the heart of 'modern British' family life and this persuaded them to enlist the idea of using five different family 'types' which reflected the changing nature of the modern family. The family types and associated products were as follows:

- Latchkey kids – tomato ketchup
- Long distance lorry driver father – tomato soup
- Single mother – baked beans
- Teenage mother – salad cream
- Night worker father – spaghetti

The first three advertisements in the *Toast to Life* series are going to be discussed here but the 'lorry driver' will be subjected to the most detailed analysis.

First of all it is worth noting the repetitive aspects of the campaign which give it unity and of course greater memorability.

Music

This is the most noticeable and perhaps innovative aspect of the campaign; it is a distinctive black African soundtrack sung in Zulu by the Natal choral group, Ladysmith Black Mombazo. The song, *Inkanyezi Nezazi* (wise man), is loosely translated into English as follows.

From ancient time
Wise people call out to us
Children – oh children
Hear our words
You are a great family, all
Look up to the sky

You are the brightest star
Father, father, raise a cup
Drink fresh water
Break new bread
Be generous
Laugh loud – it is good

The words have no direct relation to what is being shown on screen but in translation they have the same 'worldly wisdom' effect which is characteristic of the proverbs which finish each advertisement. The song is also very harmonious which could indicate that we are all part of a human tribe trying to live in harmony. The song reached number 38 in the top 50 which highlights the advantageous cycle of the advertisement selling the song and then perhaps the song selling the advertisement.

Characters

All the advertisements were cast using a mixture of actors and ordinary people to give them greater 'realism'. The actress in the Baked Bean advertisement is acting with her own son. We are frequently given close up shots of these 'real' people to convey 'real' emotion such as weariness at the end of a hard working day, as in Figure 10.2.

Figure 10.2

Proverbs

The absence of dialogue and voice-over in *Toast to Life* means that a great deal of importance is placed on the anchorage of the music, the close-up of the product label which finishes each advertisement and the ultimate 'proverb'. The proverbs tend to imbue the advertisements with a gravity that suggests some universal truth

Figure 10.3

is being conveyed; that universal truth is then associated with the product. This lack of overt anchorage means that the texts are more polysemic – open to a variety of interpretations or readings – than most TV advertisements.

Shots

Aspects of filming are also repeated within the campaign. As the viewer we are constantly watching as if an intruder on a private moment, as if a precious moment has been captured. This is underpinned by the use of slow motion – as if time is slowing down – and by the use of well framed shots which suggest we are viewing a tableau (see the still in Figure 10.3, where we view the single mum at her daily work through an open door and the still in Figure 10.4, where we are watching the parents of the latchkey kids watching their children playing. This layering of 'viewers' distils the moment even further.

The use of soft focus to concentrate our attention on a particular part of the frame or to give the image a feeling of softness and warmth is also frequently used (see Figure 10.5)

Figure 10.4

How are ideological concepts of the family being explored within A Toast to Life?

In the tomato ketchup advert, the latchkey boy does take charge of the family and cooks dinner but when the parents arrive home you eventually see him revert to being a child again (Figure 10.6). There is a feeling that this is his correct role as it is the one the advertisement finishes on. We also 'accept' the mother going out to work as she is given a job in an important profession (nurse) that is predominantly considered a woman's job anyway. It is interesting to speculate whether this advertisement would work if the mother was a high powered business woman.

In the baked beans advert, the single mother lives in a nice middle class house in a seaside resort. She does do a menial job – chambermaid – but all the signs are that she is financially secure. This does not reflect the image of the deprived single mother living on the poverty line in an inner city high rise flat.

Figure 10.5

Figure 10.6

Detailed analysis – the lorry driver advertisement

Here, we will look at individual shots and sequences of shots and their potential meaning.

1 The advertisement opens (Figure 10.7) with the back wall of the cab of the lorry and its flags and memorabilia from a variety of sources, the most noticeable being the CMR (Country Music Radio) flag lettered in red. The shot pans left to a close-up of the driver; the camera stops with the driver to the right of the picture with the CMR flag clearly visible to the left of them. Although we are looking straight at the driver, it is a stolen glance at a thoughtful moment. The cab, the man's clothes – body warmer – and face present a working class stereotype. Accompanying this is the sound of a lone acapella voice. The lone driver, the lone voice, the obvious cold build up a picture of a life we would not like to share.

Figure 10.7

2 We are now given a view of the lorry driver looking out onto the road. Consequently, we transfer *our* feelings about the view onto the driver. We see the hazy glow of sunset in the top half of the picture – it is getting late – and a road which is deserted on our side but very busy on the other side. This adds to the feeling of loneliness. There is a cold blue pervading the lower part of the frame. The camera moves back to view the driver's hand and then his face in profile and we are moving outside the cab again. The driver's face is lit as if by the headlights of the oncoming cars. The lone acapella voice continues and underpins the driver's isolation.

3 The view is a reflection in a puddle of the driver getting down from the cab and he then puts on his jacket. The music changes and other voices join in as the driver acknowledges another man in a kiosk. Both men are glimpsed from behind the second man so that we view the face of the driver. The harmony of the acapella voices help to give the feeling that these two are united in their isolation. There is now a long shot of the lorry driver walking alone along a cold green subway with high walls. The high walls separate him from other people and accentuate the loneliness. He is also huddled against the cold. It is a bleak, cold, lonely picture. He arrives at a house which is framed by a fence. The gate leads to a path up to a well-lit welcoming front door to the right of the picture and the warm orange/red window to the left. The house is a welcome haven from the cold isolated exterior.

4 We move inside the house and view the man opening the door and entering. The first extreme close-up shows his hot breath on the cold air. Then from a point down the hallway the man and his wife are seen hugging and more voices join in the harmony (Figure 10.8). The woman does possess a sense of ordinariness; she is not thin or glamorous but 'warm and homely'. There is a warm reddish lighting and both characters are wearing red clothing; the shot is slightly out of focus adding to the softness and warmth of the shot. The low angle view suggests that we might be surveying this scene from a child's point of view. We feel relieved at this point that the man has found warmth, company, comfort.

5 The lone acapella voice is heard again as the man sits down at the kitchen table and rubs his face to indicate his weariness. The man is joined by the woman at the kitchen table and the view is split as we can also see the hall (Figure 10.9). Once, again we are snatching a glimpse of private moment. The kitchen is not 'designer' but full of the clutter of an 'ordinary home'. On the wall between the kitchen and hall is a clock which shows us that it is late, 9.30 pm – not the usual

Figure 10.8

time for someone to be coming home from work. As the couple sit together, the song moves back into harmony and the colours red and green predominate.

6 The next shot is the close-up of a hand opening a can of Heinz Tomato Soup. This is the first time the product has been identified. This is followed by a glance at the man in another room framed by the serving hatch (Figure 10.10). At this point, the emotion is intensified because we seem to be given the woman's eye view as she prepares the soup in the kitchen. We see the man pick up a football – this is obviously indexical of his son whom we see later. The man is lit from the front – the room is in the warm red glow of lamplight – and we see him smile as he throws the football in the air. He is obviously, thinking warmly about his son.

7 The next shot is from the man's point of view looking back through the hatch. We feel that he is looking admiringly at his wife as she stirs the soup (Figure

Figure 10.9

Figure 10.10

10.11). The foreground is light but she is soft focus suggesting warmth and even romance. It is a peaceful scene and the harmonious voices suggest the 'harmony' of this family life.

8   The music reaches a peak. We view the boy asleep as the light from outside the window shines over the boy's face and across his red bedspread. The boy is in the centre of the screen which underpins the idea that the boy is the centre of his father's life. The father kneels at his son's bedside and looks down at him; once again we are sneaking a glimpse of a private almost religious moment. Then there is a close-up of the boy asleep and then his father silhouetted in the doorway.

9   Then we see a close-up of a white bowl as hot red soup is ladled into it. Then, there is a shot of the full bowl in close-up with slices of bread surrounding it and in the background we view the man with the woman and the football – representing his son (Figure 10.12). This brings the family together even though the son is asleep.

10   Then, in close succession, we view the spoon going into the soup and the man looking lovingly at the soup and his wife in the same way that he has looked lovingly at the football and his son. We move out to view the man and the woman sitting at the table together; the music adds to the harmonious scene. As always, we feel as if we are sneaking a glimpse at a private moment.

11   The next shot is filmed from an interesting angle – low behind the sink (Figure 10.13). We view the woman as she completes the washing up and lovingly places the soup bowl beside her husband's beer glass. Then there is a close-up of the man lying in bed as the woman reaches over him to turn out the light. This reaffirms the messages of the previous frame – that she cares for him and looks after him. The music becomes quieter as the couple is viewed cuddled up in bed. Then the proverb emerges into view: 'And the man shall come home singing from the fields, for they have provided for their own'. This is followed by the soup label, full screen.

What is this advertisement saying?

Obviously, Heinz would like us to take the meaning that, even though this is an unconventional household, the tradition of Heinz and tomato soup is there to keep it together, safe and secure. Heinz offers warmth, comfort and belonging in a sometimes isolating world. This is not the only reading of this advertisement

Figure 10.11

however and its relative openness allows some variation. Here are some readings that have been suggested by a number of media lecturers and students:

'It reinforces the stereotypes of home life; the man comes home from work and is looked after and cared for by the wife. It is attempting to be multi-cultural by contrasting the music with the Britishness of the scene. It is an ordinary everyday product but it is implying specialness, care and love. The soup is satisfying on its own even after a full day's work.'

'What attracts attention is the contradiction – a song which would suggest a scene in rural Africa set against film in a very British working man's setting. No connection seems to be made. One is left feeling; am I missing something? Is the African song

Figure 10.12

Figure 10.13

talking about going home to a warm woman and hot soup? The association works at a deeper level, linking a tired old man with soup . . . not a turn on at all!'

'Heinz is trying to attract a wider target audience in this commercial – C2s and Ds. Many people would feel empathy with the characters represented here as they are more 'real' not 'super thin' models. The myth underpinned here is that a woman's place is in the home. The wife is waiting to make soup for the husband. She welcomes him home, washes up and tucks him up! Heinz is selling us the fulfilment of Maslow's needs: esteem, belongingness, safety. The advertisement is trying to persuade the viewer that a family has needs and values that Heinz can fulfil.'

'OK so the ''breadwinner'' drives lorries and comes home late but there is nothing that questions traditional views of the family in this advertisement. Heinz is saying that tomato soup brings: peace, safety, harmony, a haven from trouble, a special relationship with your child and a warm, loving, cuddly wife waiting to cook and wash up no matter what time you come home. The fact that the music is so essentially black and yet there is not a single black person in the advert makes this 'idyll' even more artificial. The proverb made me laugh; it was at one and the same time banal and esoteric and I just kept thinking of the philosophical wisdom of Eric Cantona.'

'It stresses the effect of the long working day on family life and the comfort Heinz can offer – indicated by the soothing background music. There is a traditional portrayal of gender roles within the family. The target group for the advert is perhaps C2s and Ds and the suggestion is that Heinz, and its convenience foods, can offer solutions to those people in difficult circumstances. In reality, a long distance lorry driver would probably want something more substantial at the end of the day. The proverb helps to stress the idea of the continuity of family life, struggles and traditional gender roles.'

FURTHER WORK

Ideology and image

'Advertising sells ideals but deals in ideologies'. Discuss.

Look at a Kellogg's breakfast cereal packet and try to identify what image that particular Kellogg's cereal is selling. Is it selling 'Kellogg's family values'? If so how?

Design a campaign

Design an advertising campaign for a new breakfast cereal that *does* 'fit' with Chris Evans' 'personality' and consequently could be promoted by him. Start by thinking of suitable qualities for your brand image; give the new cereal a name and then design the packaging, a full-page magazine advertisement and script a 30 second radio advertisement for it. Which publication would carry your magazine advertisement? Similarly, when and on what radio stations would you air the radio advertisement? When you have completed this assignment, write a justification of your decisions using other advertisements you have studied as a reference point/comparison.

FURTHER READING

Brierley, Sean, *The Advertising Handbook*, Routledge, 1995.
Burton, Graeme, *More Than Meets the Eye*, Edward Arnold, 1990.
Hart, Norman A., *The Practice of Advertising*, Heinemann, 1990.
Leiss, William, Kline, Stephen and Jhally, Sut, *Social Communication in Advertising*, Routledge, 1990.
Packard, Vance, *The Hidden Persuaders*, Penguin, 1957.

Notes

[1] The *Independent*, 10 October 1997.

[2] Jim Watson and Anne Hill, *A Dictionary of Communication and Media Studies*, Edward Arnold, 1997, p2.

[3] Stuart Price, *The Complete A–Z Media and Communication Handbook*, Hodder & Stoughton, 1997, p8.

[4] See Sean Brierley, *The Advertising Handbook*, Routledge, 1995.

[5] See Frank Jefkins, *Advertising*, Made Simple Books, 1992.

[6] William Leiss, Stephen Kline and Sut Jhally, *Social Communication in Advertising*, Routledge, 1990, p55.

[7] *ibid*, p171.

[8] Sean Brierley, *ibid*, p74.

[9] Steve Peak and Sean Fisher, (eds), *The Media Guide*, Guardian Books, Fourth Estate, p274.

[10] Jim Watson and Anne Hill, *ibid*, p3.

[11] The *Guardian*, 1 June 1996.

[12] A. H. Maslow, *Motivation and Human Personality*, Harper and Row, 1954.

[13] Vance Packard, *The Hidden Persuaders*, Penguin, 1957, p11.

[14] *ibid*, p11.

[15] See Graeme Burton, *More Than Meets the Eye*, Edward Arnold, 1990, p12.

[16] H. J. Heinz, Press Release, 5 January 1997.

[17] *ibid*.

CHAPTER 11 The Music Industry

'True, major record companies have long sought to horsefix the chart. The difference is now – thanks to strike teams, multiple formatting, the complicity of radio playlists, but mostly the fact that nearly every CD single costs £1.99p in its first week of release and £3.99 the week after – they succeed. How do we stop this madness? Well, fixing the price of singles and restricting the number of formats would be a start. After all, the Top 40 – and the Number One in particular – used to hold a sacred place in the hearts of British top lovers. Is it right that it should become merely a week-by-week guide to which sales teams deserve a pat on the back?'

Mark Sutherland in the *New Musical Express*[1]

'Not only are the major record companies vying to issue recordings of movie soundtracks which would once have been left to specialist labels, but also the film studios are increasingly building classical repertoire into their productions and even the storylines.'

Phillip Sommerich in *Classical Music*[2]

The music industry operates on an international scale and is dominated by five major companies belonging to conglomerates.

- ■ Sony Music Entertainment which is part of Sony of Japan
- ■ Warner Music International which is part of Time-Warner Inc. of the USA
- ■ EMI Music which is part of the British group Thorn-EMI
- ■ Bertelsmann Music Group (BMG) which is part of the Bertelsmann group of Germany
- ■ MCA, Music Entertainment which is part of the Canadian group Seagram. In 1998 Seagram bought Polygram, a music and film company, that was part of the Netherlands-based group, Philips. As a result of this acquisition the 'big six' of the global music market became the 'big five'.

The current configuration, then, is the product of mergers and continuing attempts to build up international media and entertainment empires. The conglomerates think and act globally and they search constantly therefore, for performers/personalities who possess global appeal. As a result of this strategy they try to identify regions in the world that are culturally receptive to their output rather than perceive of individual countries as completely separate markets.

THE OWNERSHIP OF COPYRIGHT

An important aspect of the operation of the major companies is their owner-ship of copyright. It is an important source of revenue, constituting about a third of their turnover. They are therefore, keenly interested in enforcing copyright in a world where innumerable recordings are reproduced illegally, where audio tapes are exchanged and copied by friends and where music is used extensively in public places.

Copyright exists to protect the originator of a musical composition and it is regarded as the 'intellectual property' of the composer. Anyone who wants to make use of the composition must seek the permission of the originator. The owners of copyright can receive revenue in three ways.

- If a recording of a composition is broadcast or played in public they will be due Public Performance Rights. In Britain the revenue due is collected by Phonographic Performance Limited

- If a part of a performance or broadcast is based on a piece of music or a record then they will be due Performing Rights. In Britain this revenue is collected by the Performing Rights Society

- If a new recording is made of a piece of music then they will be due Mechanical Rights. These monies are collected by the Mechanical Copyright Protection Society in Britain.

Songwriters and publishers

In the past it was common for the songwriter to give the copyright to a music publisher, who would have the job of contacting people who would want to use the song. This enabled the songwriter to get on with the creative work while the publisher got on with the job of 'selling' the material. Any user of a song would require a licence for which they would pay the publisher who would then pass on a share to the composer. Publishers were powerful because they had writers, including the best, under contract and because artists were continually seeking new material.

When artists were inspired by The Beatles, Bob Dylan and others to write more of their own songs from the early 1960s onwards, acquiring a song from a publisher was less vital. More writers began to keep their own copyright and become their own publishers. As a result publishers are now less likely to have successful songwriters under contract.

However because the ownership of copyright is an important source of revenue, the media conglomerates have been active since the 1980s in the purchase of song catalogues and the two largest music publishing companies currently are Warner/Chappell Music and EMI Music. The value of song cata-logues has also led to purchases by major stars such as Michael Jackson, who owns the copyright of Beatles' songs.

INDEPENDENCE IN THE MUSIC INDUSTRY

The audience for popular music is often much more aware of the label of a song than the name of the big company ultimately responsible for it. This raises the question of the nature of the relationship between the majors and individual labels. Keith Negus identifies three different ways in which the relationship is described:[3]

First, a clear distinction is made between the independent record company and the major corporation. Independents are evaluated very positively as innovative, authentic and closer to the audience. The majors are seen as conservative, glossy and manipulative of the audience. Negus points out that the problem with this model is that although some independent companies like Atlantic, Island, Rough Trade and Factory have made a distinctive contribution to the development of a range of different kinds of music, many independents desire commercial success or recycle music from the past. The picture also becomes less clear cut from the late 1980s onwards when the majors started to form their own 'indies'.

Second, three types of organisation are identified. There are the transnational corporations who are involved in both the manufacturing and distribution of recorded music. There are sizeable companies, which use the manufacturing facilities and distribution networks of the majors. Finally, there are the small independent companies that negotiate individual deals with manufacturers and distributors.

Third, Negus puts forward a model that he argues is based on recent changes in the music industry. He identifies a structure consisting of 'a web of major and minor companies'. This model suggests fluidity, flexibility and interaction. The large companies benefit from the musical creativity of the small companies, who in their turn benefit from the financial resources, manufacturing facilities and distribution networks of the majors. As in the film industry the small firms need the distribution facilities of the majors in order to gain access to foreign markets. Overall, this model is in line with Negus' analysis of the music industry as having become less centralised and hierarchical: the general direction of companies is decided at the centre but issues of musical creativity are decentralised.

Majors, independents and new technology

It seems likely that the majors will continue to consolidate their strong position in the global market, given their ability to sustain the rising costs of marketing. Meanwhile the independents will tend to be more susceptible to downturns in the economy if they are struggling or takeovers if they are more successful. However, the independents will continue to be responsible for some innovations as well as serving specialised markets for dance or blues music, for example, and they can take advantage of technological changes that make it easy to produce a record without huge capital investments. Matthew Collin discusses the lasting impact of acid house on music production and distribution in that since the late 1980s 'a self-supporting, *ad hoc* production network had developed around dance music, based on small-run white-label records, home studios using cheap technology and a distribution system hooked together by mobile phones. It was an independent alternative based on the same ethic of autonomy that punk rock had once propagated, but with a reach far wider than punk ideologues had ever dared to envisage, and one that catalysed an enormous, relentless output of recordings.[4]

Technological developments are, however, double-edged. The majors have been able to take advantage of technological change as well. The introduction of digital technology is leading to the demise of vinyl records and their replacement by cassettes and CDs. The latter are especially important, as the majors are able to earn their largest profits from them. While the majors are able to benefit from repackaging their own back-catalogues the independents cannot take similar advantage of the new digital technology nor are they in a position to acquire the back-catalogues of other companies to the same extent as the majors. Further to this Robert Burnett has coined the term 'the global jukebox' to highlight another potential outcome of digital technology.[5] In the near future subscribers will be able to have access to music of their own choice and of CD quality via cable, satellite, or telephone. Here, again, the ownership of the copyright will be the key to a company's success in responding to these new possibilities. It also might make it easy however for some artists to bypass record companies – the 'artist formerly known as Prince' announced in 1997 that all his new recordings would only be available to download from the internet for payment by credit card.

Anglo-American hegemony

The dominance of Anglo-American music raises questions about the development of culture in the world as a whole. For the USA music industry, overseas earnings are a bonus whereas for the British music industry they are a necessity. Both industries however play a significant role around the world in a number of respects. Firstly, in other countries the North American and the British charts are studied as an indicator of what to play on the radio or of what records to release. Secondly, the USA and Britain are the main centres of repertoire development. Thirdly, the major companies tend not to be concerned with developing talent around the world. These factors raise questions about Anglo-American cultural domination in the world.

R. Wallis and K. Malm suggest four possibilities when examining the relationship between cultures: cultural exchange, cultural domination, cultural imperialism and transculturation.[6] It is important to stress that these possibilities are not mutually exclusive and the authors suggest that all four coexist in a complex system of relationships.

Cultural exchange

Cultural exchange suggests sharing between equals. This sharing can take place through face-to-face interaction or through the intermediary of recordings. Many regional musics in the USA grew out of the meetings between one or more cultures. For example, the music of French speakers in Louisiana is called 'cajun' music and is based on the violin and accordion. Black musicians responded to this music and by mixing it with blues produced a new form called 'zydeco'. Exchanges can also take place at a great distance. For example, Djelimady Tounkara of the Super Rail Band of Mali recalls that he listened to the music of Chuck Berry on the radio and on recordings. He liked his style and he picked it up bit by bit just as aspiring guitar players like George Harrison of the Beatles or Keith Richard of the Rolling Stones did in Britain. An earlier example can be found in the 1920s and 1930s when French musicians began to play jazz in imitation of North American musicians. Distinctive players like Django Reinhardt then had an influence back on American and British guitar players. Such appropriations are not enforced and so fit the category of exchange rather than domination.

Cultural domination

Cultural domination entails the ability of one culture to suppress the culture of another and impose its own culture, usually within a framework of political and/or economic inequality. For example, missionaries in colonial Rhodesia (now Zimbabwe) sought to impose Christianity on the indigenous population and to eliminate their sacred ceremony, the Bira, which involved communing with the ancestors. Key figures in the ceremony were the **Mbira** players; they were able to facilitate communion with the ancestors, who would reciprocate the respect and care that their living successors were according them. In this context the Mbira was defined as a 'devil's instrument and denied a place in Christian worship. However, Mbira music was never eliminated. It lived on in rural Rhodesia and now in Zimbabwe not only does it survive in the traditional setting of the Bira ceremony but it is also being incorporated into contemporary popular music. One performer, Stella Chiweshe, has emerged at international level. Formerly Mbira players were male but Chiweshe adheres to the spirituality of Mbira playing and combines this with concert playing around the world.

Mbira

Consists of thin metal strips that are attached to a bridge on a solid, decorated wooden base. The strips have different pitches and are plucked with the thumbs (hence the name thumb or hand piano). The sound is made more resonant by using a hollowed out calabash.

Cultural imperialism

Cultural imperialism for Wallis and Malm involves cultural domination but also the transfer of money, resulting from the sale of records or the ownership of copyright, and/or the transfer of resources such as musicians, pieces of music or traditional instruments. This pattern, then, involves the movement of money and/or resources from the dominated culture to the dominating one. The authors offer the following illustrations of cultural imperialism: 'For example, there have been cases where pieces of music have been taken from small countries and copyrighted in the United States. To enjoy the financial advantages, many gifted artists have moved from Latin America and the Caribbean to the United States. Some, like Bob Marley, have transferred the right to collect copyright money for their creative work to a US copyright organisation.'[7] Concerns about cultural imperialism have often centred on the commercial activities of North American enterprises. For example, the growing impact of rock and roll in Britain in the mid 1950s was unwelcome to many commentators. Yet the British example illustrates two problems with the cultural imperialism perspective. Firstly, rock and roll was celebrated by a large segment of British youth. Secondly, a longer historical perspective indicates that not only was American music a source of excitement and a constituent of the identity of many young people but it also formed a basis for their own cultural production. So that, within a few years, British music began to have an impact in the USA with the result that British performers had hit records in the USA and a number of North American groups contrived to look and sound British. It could be argued therefore that cultural imperialism gave way to cultural exchange. This cultural exchange was also very important in the history of popular music in that it was successful on an international scale and laid the basis for a global popular music culture. This process, accompanied by the development and diffusion of the appropriate musical technology made possible the emergence of Wallis and Malm's fourth possibility, transculturation.

Transculturation

Transculturation emerged about 1970. It developed as a result of the establishment of transnational corporations, world-wide marketing networks and the spread of technology. In this view different cultures around the world contribute to a global musical culture that is not tied to any particular nation-state. In turn this global culture further influences music-making in particular territories and so on and so on, all made possible by the internationalisation of the music industry. The authors offer disco music as a transcultural music that developed from 1975 to 1978 but did not emerge from 'any special ethnic group'. On the other hand, reggae did emerge from a specific Jamaican culture in the late 1960s to become part of international music culture. In so doing such music can move away from its 'roots' and become another element in the contemporary musician's vocabulary. A similar case can be made for rap. Rap developed in the mid-to-late 1970s in the South Bronx of New York and as Dick Hebdige puts it 'did for poor blacks in America in the 1980s what reggae had done for the "sufferers" in Jamaica a decade earlier. It got them noticed again and it helped to forge a sense of identity and pride within the local community. Like reggae, the music later found an international audience. And then the sense of identity and pride that went along with rap became available to other people who listened to the music.[8] Hebdige's statement is a useful reminder that although from an industry perspective music is 'product' for audiences it is also something that moves them emotionally.

As Brian Longhurst suggests,[9] the concept of a transculture seems useful when discussing artists like Michael Jackson or Madonna who can be seen as forming part of a global culture. However, artists such as these point to the Anglo-American epicentre of transculture. Some artists are in a better position to replenish and refresh their music by incorporating influences from other cultures. Also, 'it is important to recognise the leading role of large corporations'[10] as Longhurst advises. Because of the continuing hegemony of the Western industry and artists it is necessary to maintain the element of power found in the cultural imperialism model even if a simple domination model is rejected.

The music industry and the other mass media

There are institutionalised links between the music industry and the other media industries as a result of the growth of conglomerates like Sony, Time-Warner and Philips. The aim is for their different activities to complement and enhance each other and a star such as Madonna, who has signed a $60 million deal with Time-Warner, personifies such synergistic intentions. Consequently, when the film *Evita* was released in 1996 it was accompanied by a soundtrack album and a single of a song from the film. Madonna is a prime example of a performer who possesses global appeal and who works in many different media: her contract promised six music albums but also two **Home Box Office** television specials, videos, files, books and merchandise.

Home Box Office

Cable service that began in the USA in 1972. In 1975 it became the first cable system to use satellite distribution. It was owned by Time Inc. and is now part of Time-Warner.

MUSICAL ACTIVITY AND THE MEDIATION OF MUSICAL PRODUCTS

From the evidence of advertisements, notices in pubs and shop windows, and listings in newspapers and magazines a great deal of musical activity takes place at the local level. Ruth Finnegan[11] in her study of music-making in Milton Keynes in the early 1980s revealed that a large number of people are involved in making all kinds of music – classical, brass band, folk, jazz, country and western, rock, pop and the music essential for different types of musical theatre. She estimates that at the time of the study there were several hundred musical groups in action and that there were hundreds of live performances each day. Overall, in this study of the 'hidden musicians', Finnegan estimated that between 6,000 and 7,000 individuals or five to six per cent of the population of Milton Keynes were actively engaged in music-making. She argues further that making music is an activity of prime cultural importance. Not only is it seen in a very positive light, but it is also an important aspect of many public occasions and ceremonies. Also at the individual level the practitioners 'can, and regularly do, experience a justified awareness of personal meaning and control'.[12] While music-making is not a major source of income for most of the participants it is a sociable activity which allows musicians and their audiences to share an aesthetic experience and a sense of community.

Recording companies

Local music exists for the most part at some distance from the music industry but if a performer or group of performers is taken up by the industry then at this point musical activities are transformed into musical products. Initially recording companies are responsible for mediating musical activities to a wider audience. Keith Negus uses the term 'cultural intermediaries' to characterise the activities of recording industry personnel. Recording companies are responsible for the creation of musical products and therefore they make decisions about who makes records and what is recorded. Negus also stresses that they play an active role in the creative process as well because artist and repertoire staff, record producers, and product managers all contribute to the final form of a recording, as do the visual styles of artists.

The media

The press, radio, television and film also play an important role in mediating musical activities to the public before, during and after artists have produced a record:

Radio

■ Radio is an important mediator of music and there is a great range of music to be found on radio in Britain. However, a lot of air time is dedicated to promoting recently released records through the use of playlists. An increasing trend in the 1990s has been the growth of stations dedicated to a restricted range of music, eg Classic FM, Jazz FM, Melody Radio, X-FM and Virgin Radio.

Television

Television is predominantly tied to music on the current charts such as *Top of the Pops* and *The Chart Show*, although from time to time programmes emerge that communicate a sense of music that is developing apart from the mainstream, eg *Ready Steady Go*, in the 1960s and *So it Goes* in the 1970s. *The Tube* and *Later with Jools Hollands* put a priority on live performances which had not been a key aspect of the television presentation of music even before the music video explosion.

The music press

The music press is especially important in drawing attention to new acts and has a close relationship with the music industry. 'The relationship between the music press and record companies has sometimes been characterised as one of symbiosis; dependent upon one another for their daily livelihood, the press officer and journalist mutually make each other's lives easier.'[15] The music press has become more diverse as the long-running newspapers *Melody Maker* and the *New Musical Express* have been supplemented by magazines such as *Smash Hits* (1978–), *Q* (1986–), *Mojo* (1993–) and *Metal Hammer* (1989–). Since the late 1960s the broadsheets have taken popular music seriously while the tabloids have tended to concentrate on personalities and extra-musical aspects of the business.

Film

Film and music have had a very long relationship. The first song hit from a film was 'Sonny Boy' sung by Al Jolson in *The Singing Fool* (1928). The introduction of sound in 1927 led to the development of the film musical of which 32 were made in 1929. The musical was firmly established by the early 1930s and this led to a search for material that resulted in Hollywood taking over many publishing houses. Warner Bros. for example, owned the copyright on material written by leading composers like Jerome Kern, Richard Rodgers, George Gershwin and Cole Porter. It soon became clear that popular songs were ideal for promoting a film. The Disney film *The Three Little Pigs* was able to benefit in 1933 from the national popularity of 'Who's Afraid of the Big Bad Wolf?'

In the Hollywood of the studio system all eight of the majors had music departments with composers under contract who, in the late 1940s, worked within the classical tradition. Many scores became more jazz-influenced, however, reflecting the number of films dealing with crime and violence. At the same time Bing Crosby was the most successful singer to star in films. He sang 'White Christmas' which remains the biggest selling song from a film for the 1942 film *Holiday Inn*. Judy Garland also featured in many of the MGM musicals of the 1940s that produced a number of the hits of the 1940s such as 'I Got Rhythm' and 'But not for me'.

In the 1950s the musical faltered except for those that were based on stage hits like *Oklahoma* or *South Pacific* and a division developed between scores based on classical music and those that were based on jazz or popular music. In the 1960s the latter began to take over but there was a resurgence of orchestral composition in the later 1970s and 1980s. An important figure was John Williams who worked on extremely popular films directed by Stephen Spielberg and George Lucas. In the 1990s music promotes films and films promote music whether it is rap (*Dangerous Minds*, featuring Coolio), pop (*Bad Boys*) or classical (*The Piano* with the music of Michael Nyman).

FURTHER WORK

Visual style

Discuss the importance of visual style in the popular music business with reference to music video and press coverage.

Development of form

Trace the development and transformations of a form of music in relation to the music industry and other media. For example, ska, folk-rock, heavy metal or acid house.

Is 'world music' a real phenomenon or a marketing category?

The influence of technology on the music industry

To what extent do technological developments undermine the major recording companies in the music industry?

FURTHER READING

Burnett, Robert, *The Global Jukebox*, Routledge, 1996.
Friedlander, Paul, *A Social History of Rock and Roll*, Westview, 1996.
Longurst, Brian, *Popular Music and Society*, Polity Press, 1995.
Negus, Keith, *Producing Pop*, Edward Arnold, 1992.
O'Sullivan, Tim, Dutton, Brian and Rayner, Philip, *Studying the Media*, Edward Arnold, 1994, pp145–154.
Palmer, Robert, *Dancing in the Street*, BBC, 1996.
Price, Stuart, *Media Studies*, Longman, 1993, pp403–419.
Shuker, Roy, *Understanding Popular Music*, Routledge, 1994.

FURTHER VIEWING

Dancing in the Street (ten part television series), BBC video, 1996.

Notes

1   *New Musical Express*, 1 March 1997.

2   *Classical Music*, 8 March 1997, p18.

3   *Producing Pop*, Edward Arnold, 1992, pp16–17.

4   *Altered state: The story of Ecstasy Culture and Acid House*, Serpent's Tail, 1997, p268.

5   *The Global Jukebox*, Routledge, 1996

6   'Patterns of Change' in S. Frith and A. Goodwin, (eds), *On Record: Rock, Pop and the Written Word*, Routledge, 1990.

7   R. Wallis and K. Malm, 'Patterns of Change' in S. Frith and A. Goodwin (eds), *On Record: Rock, Pop and the Written Word*, Routledge, 1990, pp160–180.

8   *Cut 'N' Mix*, Comedia, 1987, pp136–137.

9   *ibid*, p52.

10   *Popular Music and Society*, Polity Press, 1995, p53.

11   *The Hidden Musicians: music-making in an English town*, Cambridge University Press, 1989.

12   *ibid*, p304.

13   Keith Negus, *Producing Pop*, Edward Arnold, 1992, p125.

3

CHAPTER 12 Introduction to Genre

WHAT IS GENRE?

A genre is a particular type of media commodity. It has characteristic features that are known to and recognised by audiences because the same formula is reproduced again and again. It would be easy to think that the term genre only applies to media fiction such as westerns, crime drama, soaps and science fiction, but quiz shows, sports programmes, news bulletins and natural history documentaries are also distinguishable genres. However, the term genre is usually only applied to categories within the broadcast, film and print fiction media; the press have recognisable forms such as hard news and features but they are not referred to as genres.

Unfortunately, genres cannot be clearly defined as they are not static: they are subject to constant renegotiation between the industry and the audience. This means that, although audiences come to specific genres with specific expectations, they are willing to accept innovations within, or redefinition of, a genre; their subsequent response to that innovation will determine whether it is absorbed into the genre or ultimately rejected by the industry.

The term genre should not be applied to transgeneric aspects of style such as comedy, melodrama, naturalistic and epic; these enhance genres but are not genres within themselves even though they contain certain recurring components. When they are used, these aspects often create **subgenres** such as comic westerns and epic costume drama.

Within the media, genres have evolved to encompass the conventions of the medium itself. As a result, the western film is often quite different from the western made for TV. For instance it would be pointless to concentrate on the panoramic backdrop in a TV western, as this would be lost on a small screen. TV westerns have therefore tended to focus on character and dialogue rather than on scenic metaphor to create meaning.

Radio and TV tend to have more genres in common because they have similar modes of reception and are constantly demanding the audience's attention whereas film and print can usually rely on having gained that already. Broadcast genres also allow for more audience participation and control. Quiz shows, community access programming, audience comment, video/audio diaries and other forms allow the audience not only to take part but also to have a voice (albeit a small voice) within these broadcast genres.

Subgenres

Subgenres are subdivisions within a genre that become established through repetition. For instance, there are spaghetti westerns, Hammer horror films and science fiction space odysseys as well as crossgenres such as sci-fi spy thriller or TV crime soaps. The David Lynch serial *Twin Peaks* is a good example of a text that borrowed from a number of genres.

Why is genre attractive to audiences?

Audiences find genres satisfying because they know that certain expectations may be fulfilled and they find pleasure in predicting what will happen next. Creators of generic narratives depend on a certain amount of immediate communication with the audience. They want the narrative to be instantly attractive and they do not want to waste valuable time setting up characters and plot and so genres using key components that are quickly recognisable are particularly valuable. The audience know what to expect from a genre but at the same time they want to find something they don't expect as it would otherwise be boring. Thus any text in any genre is a combination of the familiar and the unexpected.

THE KEY COMPONENTS OF GENRE

Each genre has a recipe, which is comprised of a number of accepted ingredients. The recipe is not always exactly the same and, sometimes, particular ingredients are left out but there are always some of the accepted ingredients present that will allow the audience to recognise the product as a particular genre and consequently gain satisfaction from or make sense of the product.

The key components are as follows.

Stock characters

Genres nearly always have some key lead and supporting characters. Cop dramas often have a chief cop and his sidekick such as Morse and Lewis; quizzes tend to have a presenter and one or two glamorous hostesses.

Stock plots, situations, issues and themes

Certain plots are expected within genres; crime drama usually begins with a crime and then the story of the detection of the perpetrator is told. Plots in westerns are often concerned with a prolonged search for a particular character or characters. Stock situations can be found in most genres, eg the car chase in police series and detective stories; the neighbourhood party in soaps. Soaps also deal with recurring issues such as teenage pregnancy, divorce or infidelity. Such themes usually contain the dominant messages within a text but themes should not be confused with plot. Greed and power are themes that underlie the plots of many gangster films and good versus evil, jealousy, loyalty, etc. are important themes in a variety of genres. The horror genre relies heavily on myth and legends for both its plots and themes. Horror plots, concerning monsters, vampires, the devil, the zombies, etc., provide audiences with a means of **catharsis**: monsters, vampires and the like are often viewed as a metaphor for illness, death or simply the fickle finger of fate and the horror hero, in overcoming such threats, gives the audience reason to hope that their own worst fears can also be overcome. The science fiction genre has a number of similarities with horror in that it deals with similar metaphors; in sci-fi the 'monsters' are usually aliens invading (eg *Alien*, *Independence Day*) or even technology taking over (eg *Terminator 1* and *2*).

Catharsis

An ancient Greek term describing a purging of emotion experienced by the audience of tragedy who is empathetic to the action on stage.

Stock locations and backdrops

The craterous landscape or starry backdrop in sci-fi, the pub and the café in soaps, the mean streets and alleyways in cop thrillers; all of these locations are recognisable to the audience and will immediately communicate the type of genre.

Stock props and signifiers

These are often small items but sometimes they hold a great deal of significance. The ray gun is a stock prop in science fiction, Big Ben and the Houses of Parliament are used as signifiers of power and authority in news programmes. Certain sounds are also signifiers such as the creak of a door in a horror film.

Music

There are specific types of music for specific genres. News programmes tend to use an insistent repetitive monotone that builds to a crescendo. Soap opera music has a familiar, work-a-day quality.

Generic conventions

Within genres there are other sets of rules which are the result of certain agreements between industry and audience. In musicals, for instance, the audience happily accepts that characters will suddenly burst into song with full orchestral backing. In soaps, very short scenes, a dominance of head and shoulder shots and a lack of overall narrative resolution are acceptable to an audience where they would not be in a drama (although these conventions are being increasingly adopted by a number of genres).

Graeme Burton emphasises the 'tight relationship between the media industries that manufacture genre products and the audience which consumes them'.[1] Genres are good for media industries because their potential audience, and consequently their potential profit, can easily be assessed. In commercial broadcasting genres are particularly relevant because a genre audience can easily be packaged as a commodity to advertisers; programme planners will also know exactly where to schedule them because they appreciate the audience segment that different genres attract.

 **FURTHER WORK**

Identify TV genres
List as many genres as you can which are peculiar to TV. Then try to identify why this is so.

Analyse a show
Study one TV or Radio quiz show and see if you can identify where it utilises key components of the genre and where it is experimenting with new ideas.

FURTHER READING

Burton, Graeme, *More Than meets the Eye*, Edward Arnold, 1990.

O'Sullivan, Tim, Dutton, Brian and Rayner, Philip, *Studying the Media: an Introduction*, Edward Arnold, 1994.

NOTES

[1] Graeme Burton, *More Than meets the Eye*, Edward Arnold, 1990, p77

CHAPTER **13** Soap Opera

'If anybody has the right to get angry at *EastEnders* it is the people of the East End of London who for more than ten years now, have been collectively libelled by this series. Albert Square seems populated by hopeless alcoholics, juvenile delinquents, rapists, arsonists, murderers, serial adulterers, psychopaths and sad misfits. And that's just the Mitchell family.'

> Irish broadcaster, Eamonn McCann, commenting on numerous complaints accusing the BBC of negative stereotyping of the Irish in a series of episodes of *EastEnders* set in Eire.[1]

BACKGROUND

Where did soap operas come from?

Soap operas originated on American radio in the 1930s. The term was first used to describe daytime drama productions sponsored by major soap manufacturers. These daytime 'soaps', popular in America and Australia, targeted housewives but, initially, they didn't present the domestic backdrop familiar on today's TV soaps. Strangely enough, the central female characters were not usually housewives but women '...shown within a professional setting, such as the medical and legal worlds, but with the emphasis on the emotional aspects of the narrative'[2]. This emphasis on 'emotional aspects of the narrative' reveals the importance of melodrama, with its exaggerated appeal to the emotions, within the soap genre.

The history of the soap opera in Britain (see Figure 13.1) begins with the first transmission of *Mrs Dale's Diary* in 1948. This radio soap ran for over 20 years and doggedly reflected the dominant view that a woman's place was in the home supporting her husband. Interestingly, it met its demise in 1969 as the feminist movement gained strength and bra burning hit the headlines; bra burning was undoubtedly a step too far for Mrs Dale.

Early TV soaps which did deal with professional life often gave men the more important jobs and presented women as their satellites, undertaking the menial tasks. *Emergency Ward Ten*, a twice weekly 'medicated' soap, was no exception; female doctors were practically unheard of and the male doctors needed to do little more than walk on set wearing a white coat to have the nurses swooning into submission.

Crossroads for all the criticism it has taken in terms of production values and acting quality, was still one of the first soaps to present a strong professional female character (Motel owner, Meg Richardson). Several years earlier the soap *Compact*, in which the action centred on the production of a women's magazine, had begun to question presumptions concerning women in the workplace but still reinforced more negative female stereotypes than it questioned.

What makes a successful soap opera?

In the early 1960s, *The Newcomers* looked at life for one family moving into a London overspill community and did its best to examine some of the preoccupations of the army of people who were making such a move at that time. Perhaps, the picture of life in this 'modern' community where there was no history, no roots and no extended family was too much like the audience's own reality – many of whom had been similarly displaced – as its run lasted only four years.

Thirty years on, *Eldorado* seems to have failed for similar reasons. Primarily, viewers seemed unwilling to identify with a disparate bunch of expatriates who had everything including sun, sand, sex and Sangria but were still miserable; however the important unifying root of 'community' was also missing. In *Coronation Street* and *EastEnders* the ghost of Mancunian/Cockney communities long gone are ever present. Even in *Brookside*'s new suburb, the feeling of 'a Liverpool community past' is inescapable; *Eldorado* couldn't offer the viewer any sense of a rich communal past and this made their present directionless existence too bleak to identify with and thus too bleak to provide entertainment.

However, there is no set recipe for soap success; new soaps based on communities with a history are not always destined to go straight to the top of the British Audience Research Bureau (BARB) top 70. In 1985, two new soap operas hit the TV screens. *Albion Market* produced by Granada TV was broadcast on Friday and Sunday and was supposed to attract the same audience as *Coronation Street* (also Granada) but at the weekend. This soap was set in a covered market in Manchester and, for the most part, looked at working class working life. Unfortunately, this particular recipe was not a winner – *Albion Market* lasted only one year – but another soap that started in the same year is still running after more than a decade. *EastEnders*, produced by the BBC, had Albert Square and its market as its focal point and explored working class community and domestic life.

The focus of the most successful British soap operas such as *EastEnders*, and *Coronation Street* is community and domestic life. Forays are made into professional life but this is peripheral to the importance of family and community life. There is definitely, however, a move towards the professional/domestic focus in soap operas targeting young adults, such as *This Life*. Interestingly, in this programme, there is a move back to one of the original American/Australian radio soap preoccupations – the legal world.

Figure 13.1 A chronology of soap operas in Britain 1948–97

Duration	BBC Radio	Television	Focus
1948–69	*Mrs Dale's Diary*		Professional/domestic (Mrs Dale as supportive wife to Dr Dale)
1950 – present day	*The Archers*		Community/familial/domestic
1954–57		*The Grove Family* (BBC)	Familial/domestic
1957–67		*Emergency Ward Ten* (ITV)	Professional
1960 – present day		*Coronation Street* (ITV)	Community/domestic
1962–65		*Compact* (BBC)	Professional
1964–88		*Crossroads* (ITV)	Professional/familial
1965–69		*The Newcomers* (BBC)	Familial/domestic
1980 – present day		*Take the High Road* (ITV)	Community/domestic
1982 – present day		*Brookside* (C4)	Community/domestic
1985–86		*Albion Market* (ITV)	Professional
1985 – present day		*EastEnders* (BBC)	Community/domestic
1992–93		*Eldorado* (BBC)	Exile community/domestic
1995 – present day		*Hollyoaks* (C4) (soap serial)	Young community/domestic
1996 – present day		*This Life* (BBC) (soap serial)	Young professional/domestic

What do soaps provide for broadcasters?

Despite increased viewing choice, niche broadcasting and today's technical advances (eg the 'zapper' and the VCR) which have encouraged desertion from, or disruption of, network broadcast flow, programme schedulers still try to catch a large audience early on in the evening as people start their viewing. Soap operas are the most popular form of entertainment on British TV; this is held out by the BARB viewing figures for any week of the year. Those presented overleaf (see Figure 13.2) for the week of 22 December 1996, show that seven of the top ten programmes in that week were episodes of soap operas. With the promise of such a huge audience, it isn't surprising that soaps are used by the schedulers as 'bait' at the beginning of the evening.

Figure 13.2 British Audience Research Bureau (BARB), Top ten viewing figures week ending 22 December 1996, *Broadcast*, 6 January, 1997.

Place	Title	Day	Time	Viewers (millions)	Broadcaster/ Producer	Last year
1	*Coronation Street*	Mon	19.35	16.82	Granada	1
2	*Coronation Street*	Wed	19.30	15.96	Granada	2
3	*EastEnders*	Tues	19.30	15.76	BBC 1	6
4	*Heartbeat*	Sun	20.00	15.69	Yorkshire	34
5	*Coronation Street*	Fri	19.30	15.24	Granada	3
6	*EastEnders*	Mon	20.00	14.96	BBC 1	9
7	*EastEnders*	Thur	19.30	14.70	BBC 1	4
8	*Casualty*	Sat	20.10	13.61	BBC 1	5
9	*Coronation Street*	Sun	19.30	13.11	Granada	–
10	*National Lottery Live*	Sat	19.50	12.69	BBC 1	8

Granada recently increased the number of *Coronation Street* episodes from three to four per week which is a shrewd move when the following consequences are considered:

■ Granada gains revenue from the sale of the extra programmes in Britain and abroad

■ Networks gain revenue from the increased number of prime advertising slots within the additional soap episodes

■ Networks also increase their advertising revenue for rest of the evening because they can promise advertisers a larger 'inherited' market

KEY COMPONENTS OF THE SOAP OPERA GENRE

Conventions

Soaps have specifically agreed conventions.

■ Episodes are usually short but frequent. All of the major TV soaps in Britain (ie *Coronation Street*, *EastEnders*, *Emmerdale* and *Brookside*) last for half an hour and are on the screen at least three times a week (*Coronation Street* now goes out four times a week and in 'special storyline' weeks *Brookside* and *EastEnders* often go out five times)

■ Episodes usually contain a large number of very short scenes. These can range anywhere between five seconds and five minutes but they are usually one to two minutes in length

- There are always a number of storylines being presented at the same time. The storylines often intertwine but they can be self-contained. There is eventual resolution within individual storylines; although some stories take longer than others – after two years Grant Mitchell still does not know he is the father of Michelle's baby – but there is never any overall narrative closure
- British soaps are indefinite serials and are constantly on our screens – unlike series which are on for a number of weeks and have a self-contained storyline within each episode or serials which have a continuing storyline which is resolved over a set number of weeks

Characters

Although there are characters who are central to particular storylines, in classic soap operas there are no central characters *per se*. There is usually, however, an ensemble of characters; these are often stock characters associated with soap communities. *EastEnders* can provide examples of these stock characters, for instance the mother figure (Kathy Mitchell), the busybody (Dot Cotton), the villain (Nick Cotton) and the clown (Nigel), but the degree of stereotyping is much more fluid than it used to be and today's soap characters tend to amalgamate, or even move between stereotypes more easily than ever before. Grant Mitchell, for instance, moves between hero and villain with relative ease. Australian soaps in particular like to introduce bad characters such as Darren Stark (*Neighbours*) who eventually become good citizens of the community. Character motivation will be discussed later in this chapter but it is interesting to note that soap audiences seem to accept these 'reconstituted' characters with relative ease.

Locations

Most soaps utilise the domestic backdrop (Pauline Fowler's front room or Dot's flat) but the use of public spaces such as pubs (the Vic in *EastEnders*, the Woolpack in *Emmerdale*, the Rover's Return in *Coronation Street*) and cafés (Kathy Mitchell's in *EastEnders*, Roy and Gale's Café in *Coronation Street*) allows a space where characters – who are not necessarily friends – can meet. Streets, closes and squares are also useful public spaces particularly if they have a market or a shopping parade which allows characters to meet while going about their daily business.

Plots and themes

Soaps rely heavily on plots which reflect the domestic sphere and prevalent social rituals. Christmas, birthday and Christening parties are common, as are weddings, funerals and divorces. Plots often centre on relationships either romantic or familial but the soap audience know that underneath any happy resolution to a storyline there is always the threat of disruption at a later date. Consequently, characters such as Kathy Mitchell (*EastEnders*) can be happily married, then separated, then reconciled but the audience is prepared to accept that Kathy and Phil's story does not end there. Soap characters are inevitably recidivists.

In recent years, soaps such as *EastEnders* and *Brookside* have been prepared to explore serious social issues such as racial/homosexual/gender prejudice, AIDS, drugs, youth crime, rape and domestic violence and they have presented them before the watershed.

Another unique aspect of the soap narrative is the fact that stories tend to unfold in real time which mean that the characters' lives carry on between episodes when the cameras have stopped rolling.

WHO WATCHES SOAP OPERA AND WHY?

There is no doubt that soaps are watched by a predominantly female audience but it is significant that Australian soaps have a large teenage following because there is a higher proportion of young characters. Consequently, meeting places within these soaps are often younger haunts. For example, there is the coffee bar and the school in *Neighbours* and the beach and the school in *Home and Away*.

A number of critics have commented on the reasons governing who watches soaps and why. David Morley says soaps 'require the viewer to have a particular form of cultural capital – in this case in the form of being able to predict the range of possible consequences attendant upon actions in the spheres of the domestic/familial.'[3] This preoccupation guarantees that women will be the most empathetic with the soap world. Certainly, the female characters who deal with alcoholic husbands and errant teenagers are usually more morally responsible. The stoic mother figures such as Pauline and Kathy (*EastEnders*), Pippa (*Home and Away*) and Helen (*Neighbours*) are the only characters who can be relied on not to develop into some 'soap monster'.

Ien Ang argues that soaps offer 'fantasy positions' and 'fantasy solutions'[4] that the viewer can make use of in their everyday life. Certainly soaps seem to offer a desired reality to the audience – 'ordinary' people with familiar problems who can resolve these troubles within a relatively short space of time.

In soaps, the multiple storylines and open nature of the narrative mirror reality. Most media narratives, even news stories, offer a beginning, a middle and a resolution; our own lives are never quite as neatly packaged. Soap operas allow the viewer to make sense of this 'incompleteness' and to feel that they are not alone in experiencing it and its dissatisfactions.

Paddy Scannell says that long-running serials such as soaps present 'a past in common'[5] to vast sections of the public. They become a talking point – something that whole sections of society can relate to and they become part of other areas of the media such as the tabloid press. In fact, they don't only offer a 'past' in common but a 'present' in common as well. Often in the tabloid press, fact and fiction become blurred; headlines such as 'Bet Lynch could run your local' or 'Would you go into business with Dirty Den?' draw the viewer more and more into the belief that they are watching something real and relevant and also something that they can make a comment on.

Beyond soap?

The success of the soap opera has led to aspects of the genre being utilised in other radio and TV genres. In America, TV crime drama and hospital drama have been revitalised by the use of the ensemble cast, **narrative enigmas**, multiple storylines, pacey presentation, etc. *Hill Street Blues* was in the vanguard of this change; it altered the nature of crime drama on American TV and has directly influenced later series such as *NYPD Blue*.

Paradoxically, these interestingly gritty American TV hybrids such as *NYPD Blue* and *ER* have successfully employed conventions of realism that have never been associated with glamorous American TV soaps such as *Dynasty* and *Dallas*.

Narrative enigmas

Covert questions within the narrative which are being asked of the audience. Part of the satisfaction that the audience gleans from soaps is how easily they can answer or how accurately they can predict the answer to these questions. An example of this might be the speculation whether Phil Mitchell will stay off the bottle in *EastEnders* or whether *Neighbours'* Darren Stark is really a hero or a villain.

REALISM IN BRITISH AND AUSTRALIAN SOAP OPERAS

A good point of departure for any study of these two soap opera subgenres is the question of realism. The main contention is that Australian soaps are less concerned with the presentation of realism than British soaps and are consequently more artificial. Does this view change if the cultural context (ie a British audience reading a text which contains culturally unfamiliar, events, beliefs, attitudes, values, language) is removed? Indeed, could it be argued that *EastEnders* is more artificial than *Neighbours* when decoded by an Australian audience? Of course any discussion about the difference in meaning taken by different geographical audiences brings us back to arguments about defining audiences or defining the way that audiences receive media messages and these are dealt with in greater detail elsewhere.

The following case studies will concentrate on one episode from a British and one episode from an Australian soap opera and for the sake of accessibility two well-known soap operas *EastEnders* and *Neighbours* will be examined.

EASTENDERS – 8 PM, 23 JUNE 1997 BY JOANNE MCGUIRE

This episode has a number of preoccupations.

■ Grant Mitchell and Nigel Bates are nearing the resolution of their keep fit campaign – ie the race around the square

■ The community is being disrupted by the presence of a gang who are creating different problems for different characters: Simon and Tony are being persecuted by them because they are gay (Tony has been beaten up and a brick has been thrown through the window of their flat); Ian Beale is just about to be hit by theft (the gang leave the chip shop without paying) and vandalism (the gang throw red paint over Ian's window) and Robbie's pet Alsation 'Wellard' is also about to be 'dognapped' by the gang

■ Dot Cotton thinks that she has failing eyesight

Figure 13.3 Analysis of an episode of *EastEnders*

Scene	Characters	Location	Storyline	Duration in mins (') and seconds ('')
1	Nigel, Mark, Sanjay, Grant	The Square	Getting fit for the race between Grant and Nigel.	22''
2	Simon, Tony	Simon and Tony's flat	Gay bashing. Their relationship.	36''
3	Tiffany, Grant, Courtney	Upstairs in the Vic	Getting fit for the race.	30''
4	Sanjay, Simon, Gita	The market	Simon being late for work.	18''
5	Dot, Nigel	Dot's new flat	The race. Dot's eyesight.	1'16''
6	Pauline, Martin, Ruth	Fowlers' front room	Martin's police caution. The settlement for Arthur's death. Mark and Ruth fostering.	1'10''
7	Mark, Simon, Gita, Sanjay, the gang, Ruth, Ian	The market. . . . . .Fowler's front room	Gang vandalism and gay bashing. Mark and Ruth fostering.	2'02''
8	Simon, Sanjay, Gita, Mark, Dot	Market. . . Front door of Simon's flat. . . inside Simon's flat	Gay bashing. Relationships, prejudice, sexuality, HIV.	2'07''
9	Dot, Locum doctor	Dr Legg's surgery	Dot's eyesight.	1'50''
10	Robbie, Carol	Jacksons' front room	Ted Hills' court case for beating up Robbie.	35''
11	Simon, Tiffany, Courtney	Simon and Tony's flat	Tony and Simon's relationship. Gay bashing.	2'08''
12	Claire, Sonia, 'Wellard'	Outside and inside Kath's café	The race. . . (dognapping).	30''
13	Ian, the gang, 'Wellard'	Ian's chip shop. . . the square (café)	Gang theft. . . dognapping.	27''
14	Dot, Nigel	Dot's flat	Dot's eyesight.	1'04''
15	Claire, Sonia, Sanjay	The square (café)	Dognapping.	18''
16	Kath, Ian	Kath's café	Gang problem. Simon and Tony – gay prejudice.	53''

17	Robbie, Claire, Sonia	The portakabin. . . . . .the car lot	Dognapping.	37''
18	Simon, Tony	Simon and Tony's flat	Gay bashing. Their relationship.	1'02''
19	Ian, the gang	Ian's chip shop. . . outside Ian's chip shop	Gang vandalism.	6''
20	Sonia, Carol, Robbie	Jackson's front room	Dognapping.	59''
21	Tiffany, Grant, Peggy, Tony, Pauline, Ruth, Mark, Simon, Kath	The Queen Vic	Simon and Tony's relationship. Martin's police caution. The gang problem. Mark's first wife's death from AIDS.	2'22''
22	Sonia, Robbie	Jacksons' front room	Dognapping.	1'12''
23	Simon, Tiffany, Tony, Kath, Ian, Peggy, Pauline, Sanjay, Gita, Grant, Mark	The Queen Vic.. . . . the square	Simon and Tony's relationship. The gang problem – youth crime. Sexuality.	3'41''

The episode finishes with a lingering last shot of Simon's face; then, there is the familiar drum roll and the music begins. The camera pans across the map and zooms out. The music finishes with its final whistle.

■ Ruth and Mark Fowler are trying to become foster parents but Mark is worried that they might not succeed because of his HIV status

■ Martin Fowler has been caught stealing and is about to be cautioned by the police

There are other storylines – either touched on tangentially or unmentioned – that are still being resolved but they are on the back burner for this episode. These storylines include: The Grant – Tiffany – Lorraine love triangle, Joe Wicks' schizophrenia, menacing strangers looking for Dot, George Palmer's money laundering businesses, Gita and Sanjay's fertility treatment and Ted Hills' court case.

The episode begins as always with the familiar map of the Thames meandering through the East End of London. The opening shot is a close up of the river and as the camera moves out to reveal more of the map the map spins round until we are given a bird's eye view of a large area of this map of the East End. This is the denoted image but what readings can be made from this sequence? The primary connotation is that the Albert Square community and its characters are representational of communities everywhere. However, the inference is that we have a privileged position – a god-like, omniscient view of the action being played out before our gaze and this view gives us the option either to identify with that action, as part of a similar community, or to stand in judgement on that community from our superior 'god-like' position.

The music which accompanies the opening sequence is also important as it underpins and enhances the visual message. The music is pleasantly work-a-day. It is a simple repetitive melody that sounds oddly familiar and slightly nostalgic. It is the

Figure 13.4 Analysis of an episode of *Neighbours*

	Characters	Location	Storyline	Duration in mins (') and seconds (")
1	Madge, Harold *et al*	Wilkinsons' front room.	Carol concert.	42"
2	Karl, Susan, Mal	Kennedys' front room	Xmas turkey. Karl, Mal and Darren working on Xmas day.	48"
3	Madge, Toadfish, Philip, Ruth, Billy, Anne *et al*	Wilkinsons' front room	Carol concert. Billy and Anne. Philip and Ruth.	1'35"
4	Toadfish, Lance, the parrot	Kennedys' front room	Billy and Anne	55"
5	Madge, Toadfish, Philip, Ruth, Billy, Anne *et al*	Wilkinsons' front room	Carol concert Billy and Anne Philip and Ruth	1'39"
6	The turkey	Kennedy's garden.	The turkey.	3"
7	Madge, Harold	Bishops' front room	Harold and Madge	1'32"
8	Ruth, Anne, 'Bonnie'	Wilkinsons' front room	Billy and Anne's relationship. Absent father.	1'23"
9	Susan, Karl, Toadfish, Billy, Mal, Darren, Libbi	Kennedys' front room	Billy and Anne. Karl, Mal and Darren working on Xmas day.	1'45"
10	Lou, Madge, Harold	The Bishops' garden	Lou and Madge.	1'26"
11	Philip, Ruth, Helen, Hannah.	The Martins' kitchen	Ruth and Philip.	54"
12	Lolly, Anne, Helen, Marlene, Harold Madge *et al*	The Bishops' (interior and (exterior)	The Bishops' Xmas barbecue. Anne and Billy.	3'59"
13	Ruth, Philip, Lance	The Martins' kitchen	Ruth and Philip. Lance's reaction to this relationship.	1'07"
14	Harold, Madge, Lou *et al*	The Bishops' (interior and exterior)	The Bishops' Xmas barbecue. Lou v Harold. Karl, Mal and Darren working on Xmas day.	1'19"
15	Karl, Mal, Darren	Chez Ches	Accident – Mal hurt. Will Karl cope? (cliffhanger)	57"

This episode also ends with a single drum beat then the music begins and the screen is divided by the use of colour filters. There is an aerial view of Erinsborough starting with Ramsay Street but moving out and once again suggesting that this community is representative of communities anywhere. Once again, the viewer is placed in a privileged, omniscient position.

sort of melody that you might have heard someone whistle down the street before traffic noise killed off the art. Indeed, at the close of this sequence, it sounds as if the melody *is* being whistled.

The episode can then be broken down into individual scenes to see how characters, locations and storylines are utilised.

 NEIGHBOURS – 5.40 PM, 26 JUNE 1997

This episode is almost exclusively concerned with romantic relationships between the following people:

- Billy Kennedy and Anne Wilkinson
- Philip Martin and Ruth Wilkinson
- Howard Bishop who has returned after being absent with amnesia and is jealous of his wife's (Madge) relationship with Lou Carpenter
- One other storyline being pursued is that of Karl Kennedy who is working with his son as a builder after losing faith in his ability as a doctor

The credit sequence of *Neighbours* is split by the daily recap of the previous episode's 'cliffhangers'. The first part of the sequence is comprised of a series of 'moving snapshots' of the families who end up striking a pose with the first name of each character overlayed. These opening shots are significant because they present the participants in idyllic situations; everyone is smiling and having fun. There is no hint of the dissension that might follow. The shots also blur into soft focus at the edges, giving the opening a dream like quality; all this combines to put the viewer in the position of being a part of Ramsay Street as if watching another family having fun in the next door garden. After the cliffhangers the rest of the titles are placed over the beginning of the new action so there is often a few seconds without dialogue as the titles fade and the music plays out.

The music for this programme has the same bland-but-jolly, hummable melody as *EastEnders*. This adds to the general accessibility of the programme and the fun portrayed in the title sequence.

A comparison

Both soaps contain the stock locations of the genre and these are in evidence in both case study episodes; action takes place in private spaces such as the Fowlers'/Jacksons' front rooms (*EastEnders*) and the Wilkinsons'/Kennedys' houses (*Neighbours*) but it also takes place in public spaces such as Kathy's café (*EastEnders*) and Chez Ches (*Neighbours*). Nevertheless, more than double the number of locations are used in *EastEnders* and there is also more movement of characters from place to place which adds to the pace.

In terms of form, the *Neighbours* episode has 15 scenes and *EastEnders* has 23 – although in both of these episodes, scenes where action is continuous have been counted as one overall scene. *EastEnders* is longer and so could be expected to contain more scenes but even taking that into account there is a tendency shown here for *EastEnders* to have more short scenes than *Neighbours*. These short scenes, particularly at the opening of episodes, give more pace and immediacy.

Both soaps contain long scenes which carry mini-scenes within them. In *Neighbours* scene 12, the Bishops' Xmas Barbecue, there are nine mini-scenes and in the final scene of *EastEnders* there are numerous scenes between couples and trios which builds to the point where most of the regulars are gathered around the bar so that the audience see the reaction from other characters to Pauline's outburst on the reasons for youth crime and Tony and Simon's news of the gang's gay bashing attack.

This episode of *Neighbours* seems almost totally consumed with the presentation of relationships. Billy and Anne, Ruth and Philip and the Harold/Madge/Lou love triangle are the main stories although there is the story concerning Karl's crisis of confidence in himself as a doctor which is reaching its resolution. Tangentially, the problems of teen friendships and a son coping with his mother's new boyfriend are examined. Nevertheless, themes examined in this episode of *Neighbours* are rather lightweight and repetitive by comparison to those being examined in the *EastEnders* episode. Here, more storylines are being employed which adds to the pace and within these stories there is a greater preoccupation with **social realism**. For instance, the problem of youth crime is addressed from a number of angles. The audience is presented with the point of view of a number of victims such as Simon, Tony and Ian but these are juxtaposed with an examination of motive; we have Martin's police caution and Pauline's defence of the vandals in the last scene where she talks about pressures on the young such as bullying. This storyline also allows other themes to come into play; the gang are responsible for beating up Tony and thus discussions about prejudice against homosexuals can be introduced. Mark and Ruth's decision to foster a child also introduces a new angle to the HIV story. It has to be said that this particular episode (picked at random!) is a very well thought through piece of writing which allows a balanced view of a number of issues to be put in front of the viewer without resorting to trite stereotyping or easy resolutions. Not all episodes of *EastEnders* are as well-written as this one and it is often guilty of stereotyping; it is interesting to compare this episode with a series of episodes broadcast later in the summer of 1997 which placed the Fowlers in Ireland looking for Pauline's adopted sister; these latter episodes induced a wave of complaints (see opening quotation) and eventually an apology from the BBC because of negative stereotyping of the Irish which included an offensive hotel owner, a lecherous drunk and donkeys wandering the streets.

Social realism

There is a strong tradition of social realism in British TV drama and film. An influential movement was the British New Wave of the late 1950s and early 1960s which was in turn influenced by British theatre and novels. The tradition stresses a 'warts and all' revelation of working class life.

 **FURTHER WORK**

Compare two soap episodes

Individually look at two episodes of different soaps. Video them if you can and see what overall similarities/differences in terms of character, plot/theme, location, conventions you can identify. Then look specifically at the way individuals, groups or issues are represented within these soaps. Are teenagers/gender/ethnic or social groups viewed in the same way by both soaps, for instance?

Research a new soap

In groups, you are a team of television scriptwriters and researchers presented with the task of producing a treatment, a sample script (first 15 minutes) and a storyboard (showing the opening credit sequence) for a new kind of soap opera set in Britain, targeting the 16 to 25 year age group. This will mean looking carefully at the characteristics of popular British soaps and also conducting a modest survey of the soap opera viewing preferences of this particular target group.

FURTHER READING

Ang, Ien, *Watching Dallas: Soap Opera and the Melodramatic Imagination*, Methuen, 1985.

Buckingham, David, *Public Secrets: EastEnders and its Audience*, BFI, 1987.

Geraghty, Christine, *Women and Soap Opera*, Polity, 1991.

Goodwin, Andrew and Whannel, Gary, *Understanding Television*, Routledge, 1990.

Morley, David, *Television, Audiences and Cultural Studies*, Routledge, 1992.

NOTES

1   Tony Harnden, Irish Correspondent, *The Daily Telegraph*, Telegraph Group Limited, London, 1997, 25/09/97, p11.

2   Verina Glaessner 'Gendered Fictions' in Andrew Goodwin and Gary Whannel, (eds), *Understanding Television*, Routledge, 1990, p116

3   David Morley, *Television, Audiences and Cultural Studies*, Routledge, 1992, p129

4   Ien Ang, *Watching Dallas: Soap Opera and the Melodramatic Imagination*, Methuen, 1985, p134

5   As quoted by David Morley, *Television, Audiences and Cultural Studies*, Routledge, 1992, p261

CHAPTER **14** Crime Fiction

'The quality of the writing is first and foremost. We are storytellers – we have no real ambition beyond that. We exist to entertain, but we are able to incorporate all kinds of other elements. Occasionally, we tell a story about a bent copper, but we are not denigrating the Metropolitan Police as a whole. In any case, we are not PR agents for the Met, but we do behave responsibly in portraying them and there is an educative element in our work.

The subject matter is usually small scale; we trade in small coinage, not in big currency notes. It is one of the reasons for our durability.'

Michael Chapman, executive producer of *The Bill*.[1]

'As a breed, policemen are lukewarm about television police drama, chiefly because they watch it through a lens of different experience. Crime as entertainment is enjoyed by coppers only if the "believability factor" is present and *The Bill* apart, few of the recent series have had much of it. Wexford, Dalgleish and Morse present an image of policing as unfamiliar to a young, urban cop as *Dixon of Dock Green* was. The settings are modern, but their appeal is as beautiful, classy nostalgia. *Prime Suspect* (ITV) comes closest to capturing the atmosphere of the CID offices I grew up in: tough, taciturn and sexist; and *The Chief* (ITV) deserves respect for tackling the sometimes murky pressures of high command, even if its credibility was occasionally stretched.'

John Stalker, ex high-ranking police officer.[2]

BACKGROUND

Crime fiction quickly became a staple of TV programming as British Television developed and grew during the 1950s. The genre encompasses a wide range of programmes and new angles are continually being developed. Many programmes feature policemen, whether uniformed or in plain-clothes; others feature specialists who work alongside the police such as a forensic psychologist in *Cracker* or a pathologist in *Silent Witness*; others feature private investigators, from Sherlock Holmes to Hetty Wainthrop; and yet others focus on individuals who routinely encounter crimes and contribute to their solution such as Miss Marple or Simon Templar in *The Saint*. Beyond this, crime is an aspect of many single dramas on television as well as series which are not predominately concerned with crime such as soaps or hospital series like *EastEnders* or *Casualty*.

What does crime fiction provide for broadcasters?

The virtues of crime fiction for television producers and schedulers are as follows:

- It is diverse and can be guaranteed to appeal to a wide range of audiences – for example in April 1997 Agatha Christie's *Poirot* attracted 11.18 million viewers, *The Bill* attracted up to 10.75 million, *Hamish Macbeth* attracted 10.46 million, *Kavanagh QC* 9.61 million, *Crime Traveller* 8.88 million and *Cracker* 8.06 million viewers
- The audience might not be restricted to Britain, as in the case of *The Sweeney* or *Inspector Morse*
- Programmes that have a long life do not have to modify their costumes and sets continuously, etc.

Crime fiction narrative

The narratives of crime fiction can take a variety of forms. Early crime series like *Dixon of Dock Green* concentrated on investigating single crimes whereas *The Bill*, for example, combines two separate crimes which in the end turn out to be linked. The degree of complexity of the narrative is related to the length of the programme. For example, the two-hour time slot of *Inspector Morse* makes the exploration of characters and situations possible while slowly proceeding to the solution of the puzzle presented at the beginning of the episode. Some series like *NYPD Blue* have more than one crime being pursued at a time and plot lines may carry over several programmes in a series producing a hybrid between the serial and the series.

Crime fiction generally raises questions about representation and realism. As Alan Clarke puts it:

'The problem of the relationship between the fictional and what it portrays is particularly acute in the police series, where the referent is so clearly present in the world outside the series. However, all too often the criteria of reality imposed to assess the fiction are based on only a partial knowledge of that reality. Hence, with the police series, the authenticity of the series may actually be judged against the fictional presentation of the police in other series, the well-publicised views of certain leading police officers and the new reports – themselves constructed – of police actions.'[5]

For the reasons listed by Clarke, above, new crime series or individual crime dramas often receive a less than warm welcome. For example, senior police officers were disconcerted by the representations of police officers who had problems or vices in the early episodes of *Z Cars*; the National Viewers and Listeners Association (NVLA) criticised the representation of Regan in *The Sweeney* for his promiscuity; and the writer G. F. Newman has created controversy with his portrayals of police corruption and criminality in plays such as the *Law and Order* Series (1978) and the BBC film *Black and Blue* (1993). Disputes such as these draw attention to the fact that crime fictions offer interpretations of reality and that it is important to investigate the ways in which the different series and dramas present the police, criminals, the crime problem and the justice system.

CASE STUDIES

- *The Blue Lamp*
- *Dixon of Dock Green*
- *Z Cars*
- *The Sweeney*
- *The Bill*
- *Inspector Morse*
- *Between the Lines*

 THE BLUE LAMP AND DIXON OF DOCK GREEN

The Blue Lamp (feature film 1949)

Director: Basil Dearden (Ealing Studios)

Dixon of Dock Green (1955–76)

BBC1 shown on Saturday at 6.30 pm. The series was based on the character George Dixon in *The Blue Lamp*.

'...[*The Blue Lamp* is] less interesting as a thriller than as a cosy, rosy depiction of both the police and the society in which they function, ever ready to help the bobbies in their quest for justice. Very, very British, and not a patch on its far tougher, darker, Hollywood counterparts.'[4]

'...[*Dixon of Dock Green*'s] early mixture of everyday suburban station life, petty larceny, and homely moralising rarely strayed from its reassuring, never-never world of hearts-of-gold coppers and 'cor, blimey!' crooks.'[5]

The Blue Lamp starts with a 'real' newspaper story of a street murder that takes place in London. The words of Mr Justice Finnimore are played over a shot of the law courts. He refers to the 'disasters caused by insufficient numbers of police'. The solution obviously is to put more police on the beat. The film can thus be seen as an advertisement for the London police force, showing them as providing a good service that needs to be supported. The documentary style opening is also important for the audience as it establishes the film as being 'real', or at least providing a realistic framework to contain the fictional narrative.

The plot of *The Blue Lamp* is highly predictable, centring on the hunt for the criminals who not only carried out a robbery but also murdered a policeman – their capture is inevitable. *Dixon of Dock Green* later adopted the same single crime format. What is interesting about the narrative of *The Blue Lamp* is that the speed and pace of the last 40 minutes (after Dixon has died) is very similar to that of the modern crime series, which often starts with the discovery of a crime.

Representation of the police

'He was always correctly attired, properly dressed, his uniform spotless. Above all, George Dixon was honest. Any thought of corruption was impossible where he was concerned. He was a man of integrity who would not have devalued

Figure 14.1 *Dixon of Dock Green*, with Jack Warner as George Dixon ©BFI

himself or the force he was serving by bringing the possibility of dishonour to the uniform.'[6]

George Dixon and his colleagues are presented as idealised policemen seemingly without fault. In *The Blue Lamp* team spirit and comradeship are shown between the men through activities such as communal singing and darts matches. Colleagues are also invited to Sunday lunch. In both *The Blue Lamp* and *Dixon of Dock Green* there is no hint of the corruption or dishonesty that pervades many recent crime series.

It is significant that both *The Blue Lamp* and *Dixon of Dock Green* are concerned with uniformed police. More recent crime fiction (with the exception of *The Bill*) tends to deal with the role of plain-clothed police (*Between the Lines*, *The Sweeney*, *99–1*, *Taggart*). The police uniform from the 1970s onwards is a signifier of boring routine. In *The Blue Lamp* the uniforms of the police and the very title of the film signifies law and order. The wearer of the uniform represents the law. This perhaps explains how the police force presented in *The Blue Lamp* is as uniformly good as the law itself is unambiguous. Obviously the situation is reversed when the uniform is removed. In one episode of *Dixon of Dock Green* George Dixon discovers that a police constable is responsible for a series of robberies. Before taking him to the police station Dixon insists that the 'rotten apple' exchanges his police tunic for ordinary clothes, as he is no longer worthy of what the uniform signifies. Dixon's home life forms a key part of the film. It is clear that he has a happy marriage and that there is no conflict between his job and home life. Hanley, a new recruit, lodges with George Dixon and his wife filling the place of Dixon's dead son. We know relatively little of the home life of the other officers. This is also the case in modern police series such as *The Bill*, but the reverse is true of the longer crime series such as *Taggart*, *Prime Suspect*, *Inspector Morse* and *Cracker* in which the home life of the protagonist is very much bound up in the action of the plot.

In *The Blue Lamp* the world of the police is male-dominated, there is one female officer, but she is confined to the police station. Significantly, in later examples of crime fiction women occupy positions of importance.

Representation of criminals

In *The Blue Lamp* the representation of the criminals who shoot Dixon is unambiguous, they have few redeeming features and even lack the code of behaviour of the traditional criminals, who are prepared to help the police catch a murderer. The film does, however, attempt to place the young criminals in a social context, claiming that the disruption to society caused by the war is partly to blame for their behaviour. It is also significant that in *The Blue Lamp* crime is exclusively the preserve of the lower classes.

Realism

Modern day audiences of *The Blue Lamp* and *Dixon of Dock Green* may laugh at some of the objects and characters that they see. The technology looks dated and the language sounds incredibly formal. To contemporary audiences, however, *The Blue Lamp* was probably regarded as having a high degree of realism partly because of its close observation of police procedure as the case progresses. Obviously compared to *The Bill* it doesn't seem realistic at all, but in ten years time *The Bill* might also appear contrived and wooden.

Z Cars (1962–78)

BBC1 Shown on Wednesday at 8.30 pm. The series was set in the fictional location of Newtown, somewhere on Merseyside.

 Z CARS

'It was a TV first in its presentation of grim and gritty police procedure. The original cast ... established the policemen as ordinary men who drank, backed horses, and even vented their frustrations on their wives...'[7]

Z Cars, unlike *Dixon of Dock Green*, was not necessarily concerned with reassuring audiences that apart from a few bad apples society was essentially good (epitomised by Dixon's friendly to camera address at the end of each episode). This difference was also reflected in *Z Cars'* scheduling slot of 8.30 pm on Wednesday compared to *Dixon's* 6.30 pm 'tea-time' slot on Saturday.

Due to *Z Cars'* 50-minute length, crimes were usually resolved within each episode and allowed a number of different but related characters to be introduced.

Representation of police

The police in *Z Cars* are presented as 'real' people who have disagreements with their colleagues and frequently complain about their superiors (unheard of in *The Blue Lamp* and rare in *Dixon of Dock Green*). They also tend to pass personal judgement on suspects and their crimes, which sometimes results in conflict between the officers. In the episode 'Happy Families' (1964) there are also disputes between CID and the uniformed officers over responsibilities (in *The Blue Lamp* both groups work well together). The first episode featuring bad table manners provoked the Lancashire Constabulary to withdraw its support of the programme.

This more 'realistic' approach to the workplace is mirrored in the home life of the police. Work takes priority and clearly intrudes into the personal lives of the officers. In 'Happy Families' for example, Barlow states that police work is no nine to five job. The episode illustrates this point by showing the break-up of one officer's marriage. On the whole, however, the private lives of the police form a small part of the plots – they are mostly depicted in the context of work.

As in *The Blue Lamp* and *Dixon of Dock Green* women play no significant role. The

Figure 14.2 *Z Cars*: The new style of policing   ©BFI

only policewoman in 'Happy Families' is BD (whose job is to pass on messages to the Z Cars). The police force is still very much characterised as a male occupation.

Representation of criminals

The criminals in *Z Cars* have moved on from the Cockney crooks of *The Blue Lamp* and *Dixon of Dock Green* to 'criminals' who are more ambiguous in their nature and activities. In 'Happy Families' for example, the criminals are a middle class married couple with a son. On first impressions they appear to make unlikely suspects, but they are found guilty of having made and sold pornographic photographs (a very different offence to the more straightforward crimes committed in *Dixon of Dock Green*). The police officers also make moral judgements over the young woman who has posed for the shots, which cause the break-up of her marriage. In fact the episode as a whole positions the police as upholders of morality rather than upholders of the 'law'.

Realism

Z Cars broke new ground stylistically and was applauded for its greater realism. It was broadcast live but utilised back projection, filmed/taped inserts and had an average 15 sets per episode. The pace of *Z Cars* now seems slow to audiences used to the faster pace of modern crime fiction. This is in part due to much longer dialogue scenes than would be found in programmes such as *The Bill* (in 'Happy Families' one scene lasts over eight minutes).

THE SWEENEY

The Sweeney
(1975–78)

Thames TV, Euston
Films Shown on
Monday at 9.00 pm

'Screaming tyres and blasting shotguns were the mark of this crime series featuring a trio of Scotland Yard Flying Squad officers played by John Thaw, Dennis Waterman, and their boss, Garfield Morgan [. . .] full of tough language, sweeping action, and accurate location photography.'[8]

'Regan carried "shooters", gathered information from "snouts" went after "faces" who got involved in "capers" and usually ended up at a "blag" on some god forsaken trading estate where he made prodigious use of the word "bastard".

"They got the jargon right," says Harry Clement who, like Jack Regan, was a detective inspector in the Flying Squad in the 1970s, "but they ought to have done because the pair of them were often at Scotland Yard with the lads and we went drinking with them. We used the same language as the villains, you see." '[9]

Representation of the police

The 'police' in *The Sweeney* are in plain clothes, work undercover and are seemingly accountable to no one. They deal with crimes which are larger in scale (gangs as opposed to individuals) than in previous crime fiction. The protagonists in the form of Regan and Carter (John Thaw and Dennis Waterman) are frequently shown to be operating outside of the 'law', as their methods involving violence and intimidation are similar to those used by the criminals. All that is important in *The Sweeney* is the 'result'; if the rules get in the way, they are ignored.

The audience is shown little of the private life of Regan and Carter as most activities are related to the job in some way. In the episodes, 'The Placer' and 'Cover Story' for example, Regan sleeps with a suspect while working undercover. It is made clear that the job encompasses all parts of their lives. Overall, in this male dominated series women play very little part. They are usually only seen as objects of desire through male eyes.

Figure 14.3 *The Sweeney*: The stress on action　　　　　　　　©BFI

Bastard!

The Sweeney's radical new representation of the 'police' also included frequent swearing (it was shown after the 9.00 pm watershed). Regan and Carter refer to crooks and superiors alike as 'bastards' in every episode. Today this type of language is an accepted convention of crime fiction, but in 1976 it caused controversy in the press.

Representations of the criminals

The criminals in *The Sweeney* are portrayed as intelligent characters who can easily outwit the uniformed police. Gangs are often controlled by men with established positions in society. They are not afraid to use violence against the police, but Regan and Carter are equally unafraid to use violence in return.

 ## THE BILL

The Bill has become such a familiar landmark on the weekly TV schedule that analysis becomes problematic. In 1997, the successful format seemed a little tired partly due to the constraints placed on the narrative by the 25 minute time slot (resolution is usually achieved through unlikely coincidences in the plot). In 1995 an extensive advertising campaign was used to promote a one-off three parter, which allowed the development of a more complex plot.

Representation of the police

The police are presented as a team and usually work well together. There are familiar minor antagonisms within the team, which flare up when tension increases (annoyance with Reg for example). For the most part, however, good humour prevails. Overall the police are honest and do their work well, although attempts are made to show how mistakes in police work can happen. There is also antagonism between CID and the uniformed officers and in previous episodes problems between the higher and the lower ranking officers.

The Bill (1984–)

Thames TV (1984–92); Thames TV/Yorkshire TV (1993–). Shown on various weekdays, normally at 8.00 pm.

Figure 14.4 *The Bill*: Routine police work   © Carlton UK Television/Ronald Grant Collection

Of key importance in *The Bill* is the issue of law and order versus justice. The police have the job of enforcing the laws of the land. Frequently, however, the police find themselves in a situation in which they disagree with the law, but they still have to carry out their duty. In other words the legal system that underpins the role of the police is sometimes shown not to deliver justice. In *The Bill* it is the police helmet that symbolises the law (it is the badge in *NYPD Blue*) and it is a key feature of the opening credit sequence.

Women police officers are seen both on the beat, but also in positions of power (which sometimes creates problems in the team). It is normal to see women in *The Bill* and on the whole they are on equal footings with the men.

INSPECTOR MORSE

Inspector Morse (1987–92)

Central TV/Zenith Prod
Shown on Tuesday at 8.00 pm.

At nearly two hours long *Inspector Morse* is an indulgence. The audience are as interested in solving the crime as they are in watching John Thaw's performance as Morse (the ultimate extension of this is *Columbo* in which the audience is shown who has committed the crime at the start of each episode – the main pleasure is taken from Peter Falk's performance).

The pace of the action is sedate and the plot, resolved in each episode, often involves a number of different characters and story strands. Narrative space is also given to Morse's personal life. In each episode he has an affair – or just an unfulfilled desire – with a female character which never lasts beyond the episode.

Psychology rather than muscle prevails. The plots are all based in the leafy Oxford area and tend to deal with crimes centred on the wealthy and well educated and Morse is always keen to point out the hypocrisies of such people.

Figure 14.5 *Inspector Morse*   ©BFI

Representation of the police

Morse plays the role of the highly individual lone detective continually at odds with his Chief Inspector and superiors in general, which in a number of episodes get him 'taken off the case'. He likes opera, chateau-bottled wine and real ale. He is offset by his assistant Lewis (a lager drinker), who is depicted as plodding and methodical. The rest of the police officers are shown to be incapable of appreciating high culture and certainly unable to foil the intelligent criminal mind.

Morse himself is moralistic and passes judgement on criminals, police and society alike. He is aware that the law hasn't got the answer to all problems, although he is still obsessed with solving the crime. Morse is not above concealing evidence to avoid implicating those that he feels are legally guilty, but morally innocent. Above all Morse is concerned to expose those who preach one set of values, but live by another.

Although women play professional roles in *Morse* they are not a regular part of any of the police teams. At times they seem to be written into the plot so that Morse can fall for them.

Realism

Inspector Morse is highly stylised (some would argue that it is an exercise in style) employing long takes and smooth mobile camera shots that would not be out of place in a feature film. The sumptuous *mise-en-scène* is often used as a foil to the mess that lies beneath the surface of upper-middle class life. *Inspector Morse* does not initially 'feel' realistic as it does not employ traditional techniques to make it appear 'believable' (such as fast-moving hand-held camera), but its sheer length does allow room for the crime to be solved over several days. Many mistakes are made and the final outcome is not usually based on coincidences (more often legwork on the part of Lewis!). *The Bill* may 'appear' to be more real, but because of its fast pace we are often prepared to suspend our disbelief of the narrative.

 ### BETWEEN THE LINES – FROM BAD APPLE TO ROTTEN ORCHARD?

Between the Lines (1992–95)
BBC 1 Shown initially on Friday at 9.30 pm

'*Between the Lines* was not about Flying Squad roughnecks doing sub-*Bullitt* car chases through the East End. It wasn't about moody, introspective inspectors solving one case a month in provincial cities like Oxford and Leicester. It was mostly not about the police as good guys at all, but as mortal and fallible people under gigantic pressure, as a result of which some miraculously managed to stay good but a great many went to the bad.

A mark of its subtlety was that one often sympathised with the guilty rather than their investigators. On a less subtle note, the sexual exploits of its central character earned the series the nickname "Between the Loins".'[10]

Between the Lines is unique in that it deals solely with corruption and malpractice in the police force. In every episode the team from CIB (Complaints Investigation Bureau) respond to allegations concerning fraud, falsification of evidence and even murder. The series provoked much controversy because the police were only ever seen in a bad light – like a dream come true according to its writer J. C. Wilsher.

Representation

The representation of the police in *Between the Lines* is in almost total opposition to that of *Dixon of Dock Green* or even *The Bill*: while both are prepared to admit that occasionally a bad apple can be found in the barrel, in *Between the Lines* the whole orchard seems to be rotten. The investigations often reveal that an isolated spot of fraud or corruption is merely the tip of the iceberg and that whole police stations are often involved; police work and corruption seemingly go hand in hand. It is stressed, however, that corrupt policing can bring in results.

As the series progresses it becomes clear that virtually everyone is corrupt in some way including the highest-ranking police officers and government officials. Even members of CIB themselves are shown to be breaking rules. In the episode 'The Great Detective', for example, Harry tries to destroy vital evidence. In a later dramatic episode the CIB team commits murder in cold blood and get away with it. The audience, however are in no doubt that this was the right thing to do. What is interesting is that the boundary between the criminals and the police become blurred, as it is the police themselves that are under suspicion, being investigated in the same manner as the criminals.

Despite the nature of the series, *Between the Lines* does not outrightly condemn the police – corruption is viewed as a way of getting the job done. Those investigated by CIB are often shown to occupy the moral high ground – certainly compared to those that have called for the investigation. In 'The Great Detective', for example, an officer under suspicion of corruption is shown to have a successful record. He is also likeable, respected by his men and engages in charity work. Although *Between the Lines* is in many ways 'different' to other crime series, it also has its fair share of stereotypical criminals.

The characters

- ■ Tony Clark is well educated and does not gel well with traditional police culture. He remains an outsider, who refuses to tow the line, but will only bend the rules if there is justification

- ■ Harry Naylor is part of the traditional police culture and is very loyal. In 'The Great Detective' he is prepared to destroy evidence to protect his old 'guv'. If Clark were not watching he would probably bend the rules to breaking point. Naylor also moonlights as a security guard to help pay for his wife's cancer treatment which subsequently places him in a compromising position

- ■ Maureen Connell would rather do things 'by the book' than break rules. She has to cure Harry of his sexism before she can command his respect. Her lesbian affair, which provokes varied reactions from her colleagues, is further used to highlight the problems faced by women police officers in a male dominated institution

FURTHER WORK

Discuss the role of police in crime fiction

In crime fiction the police have become indistinguishable from the criminals. Discuss.

Have the representations of the police in TV crime fiction changed over time? Discuss.

Research a new crime fiction

In Groups. You are an independent television production team and you have been approached by Yorkshire Television who want you to submit an idea for a new TV crime drama series to fill the hole left in the schedules by the demise of *A Touch of Frost*. Yorkshire Television wants the following tasks included in the submission: a treatment, a storyboard for the opening credit sequence and a script for the first ten minutes of the initial episode.

FURTHER READING

Clarke, Alan, ' "You're nicked!" Television police series and the fictional representation of law and order', in Dominic Strinati, and Stephen Wagg, (eds.), *Come on Down? Popular Media Culture in Post-war Britain*, Routledge, 1992.

FURTHER VIEWING

Every week's TV schedules contain a number of crime fiction programmes including repeats from television programme libraries. Some examples from Britain include: *The Chief, Cracker, Crime Traveller, Hamish Macbeth, Heart Beat, Hetty Wainthrop Investigates, Kavanagh QC, Prime Suspect, Silent Witness, Taggart, Thief Takers, A Touch of Frost, Wycliffe*. Examples from the US include: *Columbo, Hill Street Blues, Homicide, LA Law, Murder One* and *NYPD Blue*.

NOTES

1 *The Guardian*, 10 October 1994.

2 *The Sunday Times*, 20 September 1993.

3 Alan Clarke, ' "You're nicked!" Television police series and the fictional representation of law and order', in Dominic Strinati, and Stephen Wagg, (eds.), *Come on Down? Popular Media Culture in Post-war Britain*, Routledge, 1992, p239.

4 Tom Milne, (ed.), *The Time Out Film Guide*, Penguin, 1989, p67.

5 Tise Vahimagi, (compiler), *British Television*, BFI, 1994, p48.

6 Alan Clarke, *ibid*, p240–241.

7 Tise Vahimagi, *ibid*, p113.

8 *ibid*, p226

9 Andrew Anthony, *The Observer (Preview)*, 3–9 March 1996

10 Sue Summers in *The Radio Times*, Issue 42, 15–21 October 1994

CHAPTER **15** The Western

```
┌─────────────────────────────────────────────┐
│  ╭─────────────────────────────╮             │
│  │  CONTENTS OF THIS CHAPTER   │             │
│  ╰─────────────────────────────╯             │
│                                              │
│  ■ Background                                │
│                                              │
│  ■ Case studies: Stagecoach (1939), Shane    │
│    (1953), Ride the High Country (1962),     │
│    A Fistful of Dollars (1964), The Outlaw   │
│    Josey Wales (1976), Unforgiven (1992)     │
└─────────────────────────────────────────────┘
```

'Though the cinema did not invent him, the cowboy has galloped through the imagination of the world because American films and American television have, for the past 70 years, saturated the world market.'

From: *The BFI Companion to the Western*[1]

'As long ago as 1911, a writer in the trade journal Nickelodeon dismissed the western as "a gold mind that has been worked to the limit".'

Edward Buscombe in *Sight and Sound*[2]

'Westerns draw their strength and their enduring interest precisely from their preoccupation with one of the central problems in modern history: the encounter between white America and the continent it has conquered.'

Edward Countryman in *History Today*[3]

'An image remains emblazoned in my mind of William S. Hart's face. He holds up a pistol in each hand, his leather armbands decorated with gold, and he wears a broad-brimmed hat as he sits astride his horse. Or he rides through the snowy Alaskan woods wearing a fur hat and fur clothing. What remains of these films in my heart is that reliable manly spirit and the smell of male sweat.'

Akira Kurosawa, *Something like an Autobiography*[4]

BACKGROUND

The western drew upon representations of the west in popular fiction, journalism, the theatre, prints, posters and paintings. It was quickly established as a popular genre following *The Great Train Robbery* (1903), which contained many of the elements of the genre and proved an inspiration to many other filmmakers. The peak year for the productions of westerns was 1925 when 227 were made. In 1950, 130 were made before the accelerated decline of the 1960s, which resulted in the trickle that are produced today. In contrast to the westerns produced now a large proportion of those produced in the past were inexpensive 'B' movies often organised into a series featuring the same character and geared to a young audience at a Saturday matinée. Television killed off this kind of production for the cinema but provided a home for a large number of western series (48 in 1959) until the 1970s when the genre all but disappeared from television as well.

The western is usually set after the **American Civil War** in the period 1865–1890 and draws upon the realities of North American history of the 19th century. Factors which provided fertile ground for drama are as follows:

- The movement of people westward across great distances and often inhospitable terrain – by 1848 settlers had reached the Pacific coast and further migration of, for the most part, white American-born people was stimulated by the discovery of gold in California
- The construction of railways across the continent and the introduction of the telegraph
- The resistance of the plains Indians to these incursions which robbed them of their livelihood which depended on the buffalo
- The creation of a new occupation, that of the cowboy who drove the cattle from the plains to the railroad tracks and who soon became the less glamorous ranch-hand
- The disputes about the use of the land that developed between those who wanted an open range for their cattle and those who wanted to fence off their farms

This period then, was one in which the modern USA emerged as the geographical and political unit that we recognise today.

A brief history of the western

In *The Great Train Robbery* we see the following:

- A railroad telegraph office
- A band of outlaws
- A robbery from the mail car of a train and the subsequent robbery of the train passengers, one of whom tries to run away and is shot in the back
- The escape of the outlaws from the scene of the crime on horseback
- The formation of a posse in a dance-hall, where the feet of a new arrival in the west are being shot at to make him dance
- The pursuit of the outlaws by the posse who eventually kill them all

Even if the way the film is put together is unappealing to the viewer in the 1990s this short narrative film assembles many of the elements to be found in hundreds of later westerns. Also, the fact that over a half of the film was shot in the countryside (although not in the west) anticipates the importance of landscape in the appeal of the western. The film does not have an individual protagonist, but this omission was more than made up for in the years to follow.

The western hero

The western hero emerges as a man who is typically a loner and who is always on the move. He travels on horseback across the largely uninhabited

---

The American Civil War, 1861–65

This brutal conflict was fought between the northern states, 'the Union' and the southern states, 'the confederates'. The north was more industrialised and urbanised and condemned the existence and possible extension of slavery. At this time black slaves in the south constituted a third of the population. The victory of the north 'the Yankees', in the war preserved the Union, consolidated the leadership of the north and ended slavery if not racial inequality.

Westerns do not tend to examine the war in any detail but tend to use it to contribute to characterisation as in *The Searchers* or *Shane* for example.

landscape and he travels light. He is appropriately dressed for such an existence and unencumbered by possessions. He is usually not bound by the
routine of everyday work and, as Robert Warshow puts it, 'even when he
wears a badge of a marshal or, more rarely, owns a ranch, he appears to be
unemployed.'[5] The gun in his holster represents the inevitability and necessity
of violence, which the hero has to engage in to enact justice or assert law and
order or his own honour. Although in many **'B' westerns** the hero is absurdly
perfect, even in the 1910s the hero was not so straightforward although
undoubtedly some distance away from the heroes in the 'spaghetti westerns'
of Sergio Leone.

Because the western hero is adapted to an unsettled life his interactions with
women tend to be awkward as women represent either the settlement and civil-
ising of the west, when not represented as a 'good time' saloon girl or 'madam'.

The western hero's interaction with the Indians is much less ambivalent than
his interactions with women. The variety of Indian life has not been depicted
by the western as the films tend to feature those Indians who actively resisted
the advance westward of the white settlers. The American Indian is very
rarely individualised in westerns, usually representing a savage threat to the
white protagonists. However, in the 1950s westerns started to treat Indians
more sympathetically and, more recently, *Dances with Wolves* (1990),
although centring on a white protagonist, presents an account from inside the
culture of the Lakota Sioux.

The western genre

Many of the 'B' westerns were undoubtedly formulaic and therefore predictable. However, throughout its history, the western has attracted the very
best filmmakers in Hollywood. This was especially noticeable from the mid-
1940s into the 1960s when directors such as John Ford, Howard Hawks,
Anthony Mann, Budd Boetticher and Sam Peckinpah and actors such as John
Wayne, James Stewart, Randolph Scott, Gary Cooper and Joel McCrea made
substantial contributions to the genre.

After the Second World War the western, like other genres, had to respond to
the growth of competition from television and the relaxation of censorship.
These developments led to a greater concern to create a visual impact unat-
tainable on the small screen as well as a more explicit treatment of sex and
violence. In addition, social and cultural change led to a questioning of the
western and its representations of the 'wild west' and the men and women
that populated it.

'B' western

'B' films were primarily
made as programme
fillers in a double bill.
They had lower
production values and
more predictable plots
than 'A' pictures.

CASE STUDIES

- *Stagecoach* (1939)
- *Shane* (1953)
- *Ride the High Country* (1962)
- *A Fistful of Dollars* (1964)
- *The Outlaw Josey Wales* (1976)
- *Unforgiven* (1992)

STAGECOACH (1939)

Director:	John Ford
Country:	US
Length:	96 mins

Cast

Dallas:	Claire Trevor
The Ringo Kid:	John Wayne
Buck Rickabaugh:	Andy Devine
Hatfield:	John Carradine
Dr Josiah Boone:	Thomas Mitchell
Lucy Mallory:	Louise Platt
Sheriff Curly Wilcox:	George Bancroft
Mr Samuel Peacock:	Donald Meek
Henry Gatewood:	Berton Churchill
Luke Plummer:	Tom Tyler

Other key westerns directed by Ford

My Darling Clementine (1946)
Fort Apache (1948)
She Wore a Yellow Ribbon (1949)
Wagon Master (1950)
Rio Grande (1950)
The Searchers (1956)
Sergeant Rutledge (1960)
The Man Who Shot Liberty Valence (1962)
Cheyenne Autumn (1964)

Figure 15.1 *Stagecoach*: Indian attack at end of film   ©BFI

'Impossible to overstate the influence of Ford's magnificent film, generally considered to be the first modern western. Shot in the Monument Valley which Ford was later to make his own, it also initiated Wayne's extraordinary fertile partnership with the director, and established in embryo much of the mythology explored and developed in Ford's subsequent westerns.'[6]

'...The exteriors, shot in Monument Valley, transformed the look of the western forevermore. The interiors at Dry Fork and Apache Wells were innovatively shot with a low-angle camera that required sets with ceilings two years before *Citizen Kane*. The film also made a star of unknown John Wayne, lending the post-war western its most important player.'[7]

Historical time of action

The action of the film is probably 1865 – as clearly the civil war has just ended – on the Arizona border. The attacks by Geronimo and his Chiricahua band of Apaches are historically accurate.

Genre

The way in which *Stagecoach* is structured assumes that the audience has a wide knowledge of the western genre. There is little that is spelt out; it is assumed that the locations, events and characters are familiar.

The film has been termed a 'classic' of the western genre by critics because of its conventional narrative structure; its use of location; its approach to law and order and its range of 'typical' characters including the protagonist Ringo.

Ideology

All films are based on conflict. In the western it is the clashing of different ideologies that is captured. On one level the western could be seen as the ideology of the individual versus the ideology of the collective (usually associated with the town). On another it is that of democracy versus a corrupt class system (in the film most of the respectable characters are corrupt). Finally there is conflict between the traditional way of life and that of a progressive society.

Representation of western hero

Ford establishes Ringo as the protagonist visually by using a dramatic tracking shot, ending on a close-up when he first appears from the Prairie. Despite being immediately arrested it is apparent that Ringo is no criminal. He has a moral code, which treats all equally. He is unsophisticated and naive, but also strong willed – on the stagecoach what he says goes. Ringo, however, also believes that in order to achieve a just society violence must play a key role. He is contrasted with the other less tolerant and prejudiced characters (Gatewood and Hatfield).

The other characters

Hatfield belongs to the world of southern aristocracy, although he is now a gambler (he is also alleged to have shot another man in the back). He is set aside from the other characters by his flamboyant clothes and exaggerated manners. He is clearly not suitable for the new, classless, world of the west and is the only traveller that is killed in the stagecoach.

Dallas is clearly defined as a 'good' character – her actions towards Lucy Mallory show her to be sensitive and kind (the original 'tart with a heart'). She is the object of social prejudice from the others.

Curly is representative of the law; he has a great respect for Ringo (he used to work with his father) and will not administer the law without justice. Curly lets Ringo escape at the end of the film, believing that justice has been done (even though there is a $500 reward for Ringo's recapture).

Representation of violence

Unlike the Italian westerns, the actual shoot out at the end is not shown, although the build-up is efficiently handled (Leone's version would probably last ten minutes). Ringo's ability is unquestioned (he has three bullets), but the violence is not played upon or aestheticised; it provides a resolution of one of the key narrative strands.

There is, however, plenty of action in the fight with the Indians, although the violence here is clearly linked to the building of tension and suspense.

The law

The law is represented by Curly, who rides the stagecoach in order to recapture Ringo. Despite Ringo's identification as a 'criminal', Curly approves of his moral outlook. Curly legitimises Ringo's revenge on the Plummer brothers and lets him escape over the border to start a new life with Dallas. The 'real' criminal, however, (Gatewood) is handcuffed immediately on arrival at Lordsburg. The law then, is not shown to be black and white – there is room for ambiguity.

Binary oppositions

Jim Kitses in 'Authorship and Genre: Notes on the Western'[8] has pointed out that the western operates on a series of oppositions based on the wilderness versus civilisation:

The Wilderness		Civilisation
The Individual		**The Community**
freedom	↔	restriction
honour	↔	institutions
self-knowledge	↔	illusion
integrity	↔	compromise
self-interest	↔	social responsibility
solipsism	↔	democracy
Nature		**Culture**
purity	↔	corruption
experience	↔	knowledge
empiricism	↔	legalism
pragmatism	↔	idealism
brutalisation	↔	refinement
savagery	↔	humanity
The West		**The East**
America	↔	Europe
the frontier	↔	America
equality	↔	class
agrarianism	↔	industrialism
tradition	↔	change
the past	↔	the future

Many of the oppositions listed above can be applied to *Stagecoach*. For example, at the end of the film when Dallas and Ringo ride off into the sunset Curly exclaims: 'they're saved from the blessings of civilisation'. The film then is clearly critical of 'civilisation' – towns are unfriendly places, the characters associated with them are either fanatically moralistic or corrupt. Civilisation is contrasted with the wilderness which is associated with individual freedom, but also with savagery (the Indians).

Importance of landscape

Stagecoach established Monument Valley as a vital signifier of the western genre. John Ford used the location in most of his other westerns. Monument Valley has subsequently become a cliché – but film directors such as Ridley Scott have played on this. For example, in *Thelma and Louise* two women attempt to elude the law (and men), in a landscape evocative of Monument valley – this is clearly ironic as the setting connotes the world of the western – this is a man's world.

Representation of Indians

The Indian attacks are not contextualised – they are essentially motiveless. The Indians also remain uncharacterised – no words are spoken – the stagecoach is merely pointed at (the audience know what to expect). The Indians form part of the landscape. Only a few westerns from this period provide a more sophisticated view of Indian life and values.

The town

In *Stagecoach* the line between the town (civilisation) and the wilderness is clear: where the town ends the wilderness immediately starts. The town is a place that corrupts men and women, or makes them intolerant to others. The wilderness is associated with democracy. The name Lordsburg is ironic – it is where retribution is delivered, but it is also a den of iniquity.

Importance of music

The music in the film is based on popular folk tunes – which links the film to the world of Western US popular culture, rather than the sophisticated culture of the Eastern states. The music also serves as another signifier of the western.

 SHANE (1953)

Director:	George Stevens
Country:	US
Length:	118 mins

Cast

Shane:	Alan Ladd
Marian Starrett:	Jean Arthur
Joe Starrett:	Van Heflin
Joey:	Brandon de Wilde
Wilson:	Jack Palance

'. . .Superficially, this is a western, but from Shane's knightly costume, from the way his horse canters, from the Agincourt music, it's all too recognisable as an attempt to create a myth.'[9]

'*Shane* is often taken to be a distillation of the whole western genre. . .'[10]

Historical setting

The film is set in Wyoming in the 1890s, nearly 30 years later than *Stagecoach*. The struggle in the wilderness is no longer concerned with the Indians, but between different types of white settlers.

Genre

Shane, like *Stagecoach* is a classic western, but it also has mythical qualities, reinforced by the enigmatic figure of Shane, as well as by the use of landscape, 'grand' and 'operatic' music and the careful manipulation of the Technicolor film colour balance which softens the look of the film. The opening images show the West to be a kind of paradise, a far cry from the wild west of *Stagecoach* where it would be impossible to imagine anyone living off the land.

Representation of the western hero

Shane is an outsider to the world of the film: he appears from nowhere at the start of the narrative just in time to prevent trouble at Starrett's farm. The audience never knows much about him, although his murky past as a gunfighter is hinted at. At the end of the film he rides off alone towards the sunrise, having killed the Ryker brothers but also having 'educated' Joey.

The attraction between Shane and Marion presents another reason why Shane can't stay with the settlers even though the relationship is not consummated. The fight between Starret and Shane at the end of the film is really about Marian – by winning the fight Shane loses Marian.

Figure 15.2 *Shane*: The western hero can never settle   ©BFI

Shane acknowledges at the end of the film that, like Ryker and Wilson, he is outdated, there is no place for him in the new society.

Dress

On arrival Shane's clothes mark him as different, he wears smooth, butter-coloured buckskins and rides a well-groomed chestnut horse (compare to Starrett who is dressed in worn and stained work clothes). Shane later buys work clothes, but for the fight at the end changes back into his former garb, which contrasts with Wilson's almost completely black outfit.

Masculinity

The film plays with the idea of masculinity. Shane is laughed at in Grafton's bar for not being a 'man' – he is buying soda pop for Joey – and one of Ryker's men tries to make him 'smell like a man' by throwing whisky over him. When Shane does not retaliate Joey is disappointed as his hero has let him down. At the end of the film, however, Shane's actions in the gunfight fulfil Joey's wildest expectations.

In *Shane* the gun is a signifier of masculinity; even Joey has an unloaded gun. Shane makes it clear, however, that it is the person using the gun rather than the gun itself that is significant, claiming that 'a gun is just a tool like any other'. Shane, like Ringo, believes that in order to achieve peace violence must be met with violence.

The other characters

- Joe Starrett is the strongest of the settlers and holds them together. He passionately believes in community values and in family life (he got married on Independence Day)
- The Ryker brothers – although depicted as thoroughly nasty – do put forward arguments to explain their actions and the audience momentarily has sympathy for their claim to the land

Narrative

Shane begins with what has now become a cliché of the western: an outsider arriving in the small community. The stranger also happens to be an ex-gunfighter who wants to put his former life behind him. Shane helps Joe Starrett to win his battle against the cattle ranchers, but this also means that Shane has to leave the settlement after the shoot out at the end of the film. It could be argued that *Shane* is also 'about' the process of Joey growing up, as much of the film is from Joey's point of view.

The law

It is significant that no representative of the law makes an appearance in the film. It is made clear early in the film that there is no Marshal for a hundred miles. The community is therefore isolated from conventional ways of dealing with problems, leaving the achievement of justice to the western hero.

The town

The town in *Shane* is a threatening place. It is where Torrey is killed (although it is clear that Grafton himself is essentially a good man). The look of the town in *Shane* has subsequently become a cliché of the western.

 RIDE THE HIGH COUNTRY (1962)

(aka *Guns in the Afternoon*)

**Other key
westerns directed
by Peckinpah**

*The Deadly
Companions* (1961)
The Wild Bunch (1969)
*The Ballad of Cable
Hogue* (1970)
Junior Bonner (1972)
*Pat Garrett and Billy
the Kid* (1973)

Director: Sam Peckinpah
Country: US
Length: 98 mins

Cast
Gil Westrum: Randolph Scott
Steve Judd: Joel McCrea
Heck Longtree: Ronald Starr
Elsa Knudsen: Mariette Hartley
Billy Hammond: James Drury:
Joshua Knudsen: RG Armstrong
Judge Tolliver: Edgar Buchanan
Sylvus Hammond: LQ Jones
Henry Hammond: Warren Oates

'Scott's and McCrea's farewell western is characterised by a nostalgic sense of the passing of the Old West; a preoccupation with the emotionality of male bonding and of the experiential 'gap' between the young and old; and a fearful evocation, in the form of the Hammonds, of these preoccupations transmuted into brutal and perverse forms.'[11]

Historical time of action

The historical time of action of *Ride the High Country* is around 1900. There are motorcars and uniformed police on the street. Steve Judd nearly gets run over by a car in the opening sequence.

Representation of the western hero

The days of *Stagecoach* and *Shane* are long in the past and the heroes have aged considerably. There is an air of disillusionment and the western heroes seem to belong to a bygone age. Steve Judd rides into town thinking that the crowds are

Figure 15.3 *Ride the High Country*: Traditional values under threat ©BFI

waving at him, but he is quickly told to move aside to let a camel versus horse race continue. The race could be seen as a metaphor for the new society replacing the old – the camel does not belong in the West, it is a new immigrant. Judd is dressed in worn clothes (a far cry from the garb of Shane) and looks old. Later at the bank close-up shots of his frayed cuffs are shown and he needs glasses to read the contract. He is clearly a displaced figure in the new West.

Gil Westrum is dressed up as the 'Oregon Kid' in a fairground side show. He wears an over-the-top wig and beard. Not surprisingly (as he is using a scattergun) he is able to out-shoot all that come to his stall. Judd clearly disapproves of this form of cheating. Westrum himself is creating a myth of the West. The wilder the myth, the more money he will make.

Another central character is Heck Longtree, who has yet to learn the values of the other two men. It is his transformation during the film that forms a key theme. Much is made of the fallen status of the older men. The idea of transporting gold for a bank in their younger days would have been beneath them (as would walking around in all-in-one underwear). Westrum asks Judd what he has gained from his way of life, as clearly he has no material possessions. Later it is established that Judd's girlfriend left him to marry a wealthy rancher – life on the hoof has not brought reward.

The law

The law is now in uniform (for example there is a policeman on the street), but also there is the law of the miner's court. The law in Coarse Gold also takes the form of the drunken judge who performs the marriage ceremony. If the law were followed in Coarse Gold, Elsa would not have been allowed to leave. The gun, however, (administered by the likes of Steve Judd) is still the only law that will bring justice.

The town

The mining town of Coarse Gold distils the worst aspects of 'civilisation'. The characters that inhabit it seem to be without morals. The Hammond brothers are shown to be vicious without any redeeming features. They are essentially a product of greed. It is interesting to contrast this negative representation of settlers in *Ride the High Country* with the more positive one in *Shane*.

A FISTFUL OF DOLLARS

Other key westerns directed by Leone

For a Few Dollars More (1965)
The Good, the Bad and the Ugly (1966)
Once Upon a time in the West (1968)

Director:	Sergio Leone
Music:	Ennio Morricone
Country:	Italy/Germany/Spain
Length:	95 mins

Cast

The Stranger:	Clint Eastwood
Ramon Rojo:	John Welles (Gian Maria Volonte)
Marisol:	Marianne Koch
Silvanito:	Pepe Calvo
John Baxter:	Wolfgang Lukschy
Esteban Rojo:	Sieghardt Rupp
Benito Rojo:	Antonio Prieto
Consuela Baxter:	Margaherita Lozano
Julian:	Daniel Martin
Brono:	Carol Brown
Rubio:	Benny Reeves (Benito Stefanelli)
Chico:	Richard Stuyvesant
Piripero:	Josef Egger

'The term "Spaghetti Western" was first coined by American critics of the Italian western, and was intended as a pejorative; back home in Italy, the films came to be known – rather defensively – as "macaroni westerns". This started a craze among film journalists for applying culinary labels to "inauthentic" or "alien" westerns: "sauerkraut western" (produced in West Germany), "paella westerns" (international co-productions shot in Spain), "camembert westerns" (produced at Fontainebleau), "chop suey westerns" (made in Hong Kong) and, most recently, "curry westerns" (financed and made in India).'[12]

'The Cowboy picture has got lost in psychology ... The West was made by violent uncomplicated men, and it is this strength and simplicity that I try to recapture in my pictures'[13]

'...Its [*A Fistful of Dollars*] Latin ambience (family clans, church bell towers, the rituals of the bullfight), together with an emphasis on how the characters look (cigars, ponchos, interesting faces) were superimposed on the visual clichés of the American western, and the result was to change the history of the form. The music (traditional themes rearranged for electric guitar and shouting voices) was also influential.'[14]

Historical time of action

The time of action seems to be the early 1860s during the civil war, a step back in time in terms of American westerns of the 1960s such as *Ride the High Country*. The setting of the film is meant to be the south west of the USA an arid part of America on the Mexican border, but the film was in fact shot in Spain.

Western hero

The 'man with no name' as played by Eastwood is essentially an anti-hero. The traditional western hero acts to see that justice is done, but the 'man with no name'

Figure 15.4 *A Fistful of Dollars*: Emphasis on the violent hero   ©BFI

steps back from the human struggles he comes across and acts to ensure his own survival and material gain. If justice has been achieved by the end of the film it seems to be coincidental. Whereas Shane, for example, shows restraint and seeks to avoid a fight when whisky is thrown over him, the 'man with no name' seems to delight in ordering three coffins before confronting the men who have shot at him on his mule.

Genre

A Fistful of Dollars relies on audience knowledge of the generic codes of the American western. Sergio Leone, by thwarting some expectations and fulfilling others, both creates humour and revitalises the genre. For example he pays exaggerated attention to key aspects of iconography (such as clothes, mannerisms and weapons) whereas the traditional American western also stressed what the hero stood for.

Ideology

Christopher Frayling argues that '. . .since the *Dollars* films were made outside the Hollywood production system, they could involve a transcription of the traditional western 'codes' – without being subject to the usual ideological constraints.'[15] For example, an official representative of the law (Baxter) is present but although he wears the badge of a Sheriff it holds no significance. The law is the law of the gun.

Representation of violence

The violence of Leone is about the build-up and rituals of a shoot-out, not the shoot-out itself. A good example is the seven minute shoot-out at the end of *The Good, the Bad and the Ugly* in which Leone swiftly cuts together close shots of faces, eyes, guns and boots.

At the end of the film there are few characters left alive aside from the coffin-maker, who gleefully starts measuring up the bodies. The deaths themselves are not dwelt upon and certainly don't have the same significance as in *Shane*.

Film form

The film is highly stylised. Leone makes use of a number of different techniques such as fast cutting, zoom lens, mobile camera and innovative use of music. Ennio Morricone's atonal score, which includes shouting voices and electronically simulated sounds, was considered groundbreaking at the time.

 THE OUTLAW JOSEY WALES (1976)

Other key westerns directed by Eastwood

High Plains Drifter (1972)
Pale Rider (1985)
Unforgiven (1992)

Director:	Clint Eastwood
Country:	US
Length:	134 mins

Cast

Josey Wales:	Clint Eastwood
Lone Watie:	Chief Dan George
Laura Lee:	Sondra Locke
Terrill:	Bill McKinney
Fletcher:	John Vernon
Grandma Sarah:	Paula Trueman
Rose:	Joyce Jameson

'...the film demonstrated Eastwood's ability to recreate his first starring role, as the mythic man with no name of the Italian westerns, and to subtly undercut it through comedy and mockery.'[16]

Historical time of action

The film is set during and after the Civil War.

Representation of western hero

Josey Wales has many similarities with Eastwood's other characters – in particular 'the man with no name' of the *Dollars* trilogy. He is, however, conscious of playing the role and through various actions (the spitting for example) acknowledges that the audience knows what to expect. It is significant that, unlike his 'man with no name' character, Josey Wales is motivated by revenge. The audience is shown his family killed during the Civil War at the start of the film, thus giving a clear motivation for his actions.

The end of the film returns him to where he started with a new family, despite the fact that the last image of the film is of Wales riding off into the sunset.

The law

Ultimately Wales avenges the death of his wife. He achieves this outside the law and this is justified because of the nature of the crime. However, the murderers themselves are recognised to have been dehumanised by the civil war. Overall the message is one of reconciliation.

Representation of Indians

Both of the main Indian characters in the film are unusual. Lone Watie at first attempts to capture Wales for the reward money, but is unable to 'sneak up on him' as he has lost his 'Indian' skills and identity by trying to integrate himself into the

Figure 15.5 *The Outlaw Josey Wales*: Reassessing the role of the indian in the Western   ©BFI

culture of the white man (for example, he wears white man's clothes). He complains that the white man has taken away the land of his people. As the film progresses Lone Watie abandons his 'white' clothes and starts to re-acquire his Indian skills again. His political critique of white man's society is under-cut by Josey Wales falling asleep mid-sentence.

The other key Indian figure, the female who is rescued by Eastwood, is shown to be both independent and strong. She has no qualms about shooting a man dead and is handy with a knife. Despite being depicted as victims the Indians are shown to be able to fight back and have strong values (values shared by Eastwood and his 'family'). Ten Bears is another positive figure who is a man of honour. He claims that, unlike the treaties of the American Government, his word can be trusted. Ten Bears also compares himself to Wales – both are 'great warriors'.

Ideology

The film supports notions of equality, honour, justice and family values. It is significant, however, that violence still forms a key part in the emergence of a new order based on tolerance between and within all ethnic groups. This is illustrated by the odd collection that Wales gathers on his journey that eventually come to live together. It could be argued that the film comments on the simple distinctions between good and bad and the stereotypical treatment of the Indians.

UNFORGIVEN (1992)

Director/Producer: Clint Eastwood
Country: US
Length: 130 mins

Cast
William Munny: Clint Eastwood
Sheriff Little Bill Daggett: Gene Hackman
Ned Logan: Morgan Freeman
English Bob: Richard Harris
WW Beauchamp: Saul Rubinek
The Schofield Kid: Jaimz Woolvett

'Of all the major genres, the western is the most concerned with American history, with representing the establishment of social and national order and, crucially, with defining dramatically the terms of such an order. Challenging the conventions of the western thus offers the opportunity to query the dominant order at its source.'[17]

'In common with some other revisionist westerns, *Unforgiven* casts older actors, often with lengthy association with the genre, as embodiments of traditional western values. This tendency is perhaps most clearly demonstrated by two Sam Peckinpah films: *Ride the High Country* (1962) and *The Wild Bunch* (1969). In these films the values of the 'old' West are nostalgically mourned, but in *Unforgiven* the destructive attitudes of the older generation are forcefully attacked.'[18]

Historical time of action
The film is set in 1878 at a time when the mythology of the wild West was only just being established.

Dedication
The film is dedicated to 'Sergio and Don' referring to the film-makers Sergio Leone and Don Siegel both of whom played a significant role in Clint Eastwood's career.

Figure 15.6 *Unforgiven*: Eastwood character comes out of retirement   ©BFI

Representation of western hero

The film plays on the audience's expectations of Clint Eastwood as a western hero: firstly he is seen wrestling with his pigs in the mud while his two young children look on; secondly it is revealed that he has difficulty shooting a gun and mounting his horse and thirdly it becomes clear that Eastwood had been, in his past, a cold-blooded drunken murderer responsible for killing women and children. In the final shoot-out, however, Eastwood satisfies the audience's desire for a violent enactment of justice.

Myth

The film suggests that the mythology of the West is a construction by introducing the figure of WW Beauchamp who produces lurid accounts of the wild West. What 'actually' happened depends on to whom he is speaking. For example, English Bob's self-aggrandising account of his role in a famous shoot-out is completely undermined by the account of Little Bill. At the same time the stories about Will Munny are shown to underplay his exploits. In the final shoot-out at the end of the film, however, his actions take on mythic proportions. The Schofield Kid is also used to comment on the mythology of the West. He promotes himself as a hardened gunfighter, but when he does finally get to kill someone he realises the enormity of what he has done and vows that he will never kill again.

The law

The law in *Unforgiven* is shown to be either corrupt or inadequate. At the start of the film a prostitute is cut up by a cowboy. The only 'punishment' demanded by the Sheriff, Little Bill, is that the cowboy must bring the 'owner' of the prostitute (Skinny) horses in payment for the 'damaged goods', while the woman who has been cut receives no justice. Unusually for a western the women are not satisfied with this enactment of male justice and they seek further retribution outside the law. The revenge, however, is one that can only be administered by the male gunfighter. The town of Big Whiskey, like the town in *Shane*, ironically has strict rules and morals; this is the product of the tyrannical rule of Little Bill, a reformed gunfighter.

 **FURTHER WORK**

Formula versus the unexpected

'Although genre texts give pleasure by presenting the familiar elements of a formula, it is the text that offers an unexpected variation that gives greater pleasure.' Assess this view of genre films.

The true spirit of the West

'In that film the true spirit of the western is lacking.'[19] [Anthony Mann referring to *For a Few Dollars More*] 'The Cowboy picture has got lost in psychology', he said, 'The West was made by violent uncomplicated men, and it is this strength and simplicity that I try to recapture in my pictures.'[20] Discuss.

Discuss critically the statement that 'all westerns are the same.'

'Westerns are often criticised as being made to too rigid a formula but they are, in fact, complex in content and style.' Discuss this point of view with reference to at least two films that you have studied.

FURTHER READING

Buscombe, Edward, (ed.), *The BFI Companion to the Western*, BFI, 1988.

Buscombe, Edward, *Stagecoach*, BFI, 1992.

Buscombe, Edward, 'The Western' in Nowell-Smith, Geoffrey, *The Oxford History of World Cinema*, Oxford University Press, 1996.

Cameron, Ian and Pye, Douglas, *The Movie Book of the Western*, Studio Vista, 1996.

Cawelti, John, *The Six-Gun Mystique*, Bowling Green University Popular Press, 1971.

Cook, Pam, *The Cinema Book*, BFI, 1985, pp64–72.

Fenin, George and Everson, William, *The Western: from Silents to the Seventies*, Penguin Books Ltd, 1978.

Frayling, Christopher, 'The American Western and American Society', in Davies, Philip and Brian Neve, (eds), *Cinema, Politics and Society in America*, Manchester University Press, 1981, pp136–162.

Frayling, Christopher, *Spaghetti Westerns: Cowboys and Europeans from Karl May to Sergio Leone*, Routledge & Kegan Paul, 1981.

French, Philip, *Westerns*, Secker & Warburg/BFI, 1973.

Hayward, Susan, *Key Concepts in Cinema Studies*, Routledge, 1996, pp411–423.

Kitses, Jim, *Horizons West*, Secker & Warburg/BFI, 1969.

Warshow, Robert, 'Movie Chronicle: The Westerner', in Gerald Mast, Marshall Cohen and Leo Braudy, *Film Theory and Criticism: Introductory Readings* (4th edition), Oxford University Press, 1992, pp453–466.

Sight and Sound has a number of relevant articles. See especially the following:
   October 1992 (Vol. 2, Issue 6)
   June 1993 (Vol. 3, Issue 5)
   August 1996 (Vol. 6, Issue 8)

FURTHER VIEWING

The Iron Horse (John Ford, 1924)
High Noon (Fred Zimmerman, 1952)
Apache (Robert Aldrich, 1954)
The Searchers (John Ford, 1956)
Once Upon a Time in the West (Sergio Leone, 1968)
The Shootist (Don Siegel, 1976)
The Wild Bunch (Sam Peckinpah, 1969)
Young Guns (Christopher Cain, 1988)
Posse (Mario Van Peebles, 1993)
Wyatt Earp (Lawrence Kasdan, 1994)

NOTES

[1] Edward Buscombe, (ed.), *The BFI Companion to the Western*, BFI, 1988, p15.

[2] Edward Buscombe, 'End of the Trail' in *Sight and Sound*, Autumn 1988, Vol. 57 Number 4, p243.

[3] Edward Countryman, 'Westerns and United States History' in *History Today*, March 1983.

[4] Akira Kurosawa, *Something Like an Autobiography*, Vintage Books, 1983, p36.

[5] Robert Warshow, 'Movie Chronicle: The Westerner', in Gerald Mast, Marshall Cohen and Leo Braudy, *Film Theory and Criticism: Introductory Readings* (4th edition), Oxford University Press, 1992, p455.

[6] Tom Milne, (ed.), *The Time Out Film Guide*, Penguin, 1989, p561.

[7] Edward Buscombe, (ed.), *The BFI Companion to the Western*, ibid, p301.

8   *Horizons West*. Secker and Warburg, 1969.

9   Pauline Kael in *Cinemania 96*, Microsoft (CD–ROM).

10 Edward Buscombe, *ibid*, p297.

11 Edward Buscombe, *ibid*, p293.

12 Christopher Frayling, *Spaghetti Westerns: Cowboys and Europeans from Karl May to Sergio Leone*, Routledge & Kegan Paul, 1981, pXI.

13 Sergio Leone quoted in *Cinemania 1996*, Microsoft (CD–ROM).

14 Edward Buscombe, *ibid*, p290.

15 Christopher Frayling, *ibid*, p160.

16 Tom Milne, *ibid*, p440.

17 Leighton Grist, 'Unforgiven' in Ian Cameron and Douglas Pye, *The Movie Book of the Western*, Studio Vista, 1996, p294.

18 Leighton Grist, *ibid*, p301.

19 Quoted in George N. Fenin and William K. Everson, *The Western: From Silents to the Seventies* (2nd edition), Penguin, 1973, p347.

20 Biography of Leone in Baseline's 'Encyclopaedia of Film' in *Cinemania 1996*, Microsoft (CD–ROM).

CHAPTER **16** Gangster

' "The public enemy" is not a man nor is it a character – it is a problem that sooner or later we the public, must solve.'

Foreword to *The Public Enemy* (1931)

'Every incident in this picture is the reproduction of an actual occurrence, and the purpose of this picture is to demand of the government: "What are you going to do about it?" '

Foreword to *Scarface* (1932)

'You need people like me so you can point your finger and say "that's the bad guy".'

Tony Montana in *Scarface* (1983)

'As far back as I could remember I always wanted to be a gangster.'

Henry Hill in *Goodfellas* (1990)

'Don't want to burn no one even when I know I should. That ain't me now, all I want is to get my seventy-five grand and get out.'

Carlito Brigante in *Carlito's Way* (1993)

BACKGROUND

Classic gangster films

Little Caesar (Mervyn Le Roy, 1930)
The Public Enemy (William Wellman, 1931)
Scarface (Howard Hawks, 1932)

The gangster film is a strand of the crime genre that encompasses a large and diverse body of films. Its classic era is recognised to have lasted only four years, from 1930–34, but films featuring agents of law and order, who seemed very like gangsters, followed in the later 1930s. Film noir-influenced gangster films continued through the 1940s and into the 1950s. The most notable development after this period was the resurgence of the gangster film in the 1970s following the release of *The Godfather* in 1972. More recently the 1990s have produced a number of much-discussed and sometimes controversial films that have attracted a younger audience. These films such as: *Goodfellas* (1990), *Boyz N The Hood* (1991), *New Jack City* (1991), *Reservoir Dogs* (1992), *Pulp Fiction* (1994), *The Usual Suspects* (1995), *Heat* (1996), *Casino* (1996) and

Donnie Brasco (1997) contain a range of criminals from different ethnic groups and backgrounds.

The illegal supply of alcohol during **prohibition** and the associated violent activities of the criminals involved, provided the subject matter for the gangster films of the 1930s. Prohibition proved to be highly unpopular and, for many, the gangsters provided a valuable public service.

These films were also made during the **depression** (1929–34) which deeply affected the lives of many Americans. The flamboyant life style of the gangsters during this period of economic decline encouraged the public to view them as heroes – it was clear that crime did pay. The gangsters could thus be seen as fulfilling the **American dream**, not by the traditional route of hard work, but through criminal activities.

Realism in gangster films

The way in which the gangster films realistically reflected contemporary society also impressed audiences. Realism was heightened by the following means:

- The use of film scripts directly based on contemporary news stories as well as the inclusion of events that would have been familiar to the public, such as the St Valentine's Day Massacre
- Employing journalists to work on the scripts – for example, the reporter Ben Hecht wrote the script for *Scarface* (1932)
- The adoption of a semi-documentary style of film-making
- Making full use of the recent conversion of cinema to sound – this enabled the gangster film to take full advantage of sound effects and sharp colloquial dialogue

The success of the gangster films with audiences was matched by their popularity with the studios that produced them (in particular Warner Bros.) as they were relatively inexpensive to make, mostly utilising cheap sets, and they appealed to the largest group of cinema-goers – the urban working class.

The representation of the gangster in Hollywood films, such as *Scarface*, made the authorities anxious. The films, which depicted lavish life styles, charismatic protagonists and extreme violence were accused by a number of bodies of glorifying the gangster and *Scarface* encountered numerous censorship problems.

The gangster and his world

The American gangster in Hollywood films is usually depicted as working class and a member of an immigrant group, eg Italians in the 1920s and Cubans in the 1980s. Depicted as likeable and powerful figures they are driven by the desire for wealth and status, but rarely achieve acceptance outside their own ethnic world.

The genre dictates that the gangster will always be successful, enjoying an excessive materialistic lifestyle. He is, however, ultimately doomed, falling victim to either the authorities or other gangsters. This rise and fall structure is common to the films of 1930s as well as more recent gangster films.

Prohibition

Refers to banning of the manufacture and sale of drinks containing over 0.5% alcohol. Formalised in law by the Volstead Act of 1920 which was repealed in 1933.

The depression

The American depression was part of a world-wide economic slump provoked by the collapse of the Wall Street stock market in 1929.

American dream

Refers to the belief that in America there is the opportunity for anyone, regardless of social background to be successful, financially or in public life.

The city is the natural habitat of the gangster. In terms of his origins the city offers few legitimate openings, but is a rich source of criminal opportunities for the enterprising individual. For this reason the gangster is seen as pursuing the American dream of individual success and material advance. Ultimately, however, the city is a battleground between the criminals and the representatives of law and order. In the later gangster films of the 1930s and 1940s the focus shifts from the criminals to the law enforcers.

CASE STUDIES

- *The Public Enemy* (1931)
- *Scarface* (1932)
- *Scarface* (1983)
- *Goodfellas* (1990)
- *Carlito's Way* (1993)

 THE PUBLIC ENEMY (1931)

Director:	William Wellman
Producer:	Darryl Zanuck
Production Company:	Warner Bros.
Screenplay:	Kubec Glamson and John Bright
Length:	84 mins

Cast

Tom Powers:	James Cagney
Gwen Allen:	Jean Harlow
Matt Doyle:	Edward Woods
Mike Powers:	Donald Cook
Paddy Ryan:	Robert Emmett O'Connor
Putty Nose:	Murray Kinnell

The foreword of *The Public Enemy* states that: 'it is the ambition of the authors ... to honestly depict an environment that exists today in certain strata of American life, rather than glorify the hoodlum or the criminal.' The film concludes with the claim that' 'The end of Tom Powers is the end of every hoodlum. ''The public enemy'' is not a man nor is it a character – it is a problem that sooner or later we the public, must solve.' These statements justify the film by offering the audience a realistic portrayal of criminality, while at the same time defusing those critics who were keen to censor gangster films.

The film-maker's response to such critics was to claim that they were exposing the violent activities of the gangster to the public and the title of the film itself, *The Public Enemy*, suggested that it was necessary for the public to confront this contemporary phenomenon. The choice of charismatic protagonists, such as James Cagney and Paul Muni, however, ensured that audiences identified with the gangster rather than the forces of law and order. By 1934 the establishment of the Hollywood Production Code, along with other factors, ended the classic phase of the gangster film.

Figure 16.1 *The Public Enemy*: Urban environment of the gangster   ©BFI

Like many other gangster films *The Public Enemy* is about the rise to power of its central character Tom Powers, who becomes involved in criminal activities while still a child. It is noteworthy that Tom, unlike Tony Camonte in *Scarface*, does not rise to the top or share Camonte's ruthless desire to be successful. The realism of the film is immediately established in the opening shots that utilise **stock footage** of urban scenes as well as by stating the exact time of action: 1909. The dating of events in the film is kept up: 1915, 1917 and finally 1920 as the film closely follows, in semi-documentary style, Tom's criminal activities. The use of newspaper front pages at key moments supplies the audience with plot information, but also heightens the realism of the film. It is, however, the graphic portrayal of violence, including the machine gunning of Matt that gives a hard edge of authenticity to the film. The bleak ending in which Tom's wrapped body is delivered home demonstrates the eventual fate of every gangster in this and subsequent films.

In addition to realism *The Public Enemy* helped to establish other conventions of the genre such as the iconography and the use of stock characters. The iconography includes the expensive clothes that Tom and Matt acquire after their successful warehouse raid (which are in stark contrast to their street car uniforms) as well as the flashy car obtained at the same time. There is also the emphasis on guns, although more recent gangster films give this greater status. The characters established included amongst others the tough talking protagonist (it is worth debating the extent to which Cagney established the archetypal screen gangster), loyal side-kick, deceitful partner in crime, Irish cop and gangster's mother.

The film also made full use of the new sound system enabling audiences to experience gun fire, explosions and fast-paced dialogue as well as surprising them with the use of off-screen sound. For example, when Tom and Matt are at the safe house they jump at a loud sound like gun fire outside the window – revealed to be a coal truck unloading. Later the next day when Tom and Matt leave the house a noise makes them jump again, but they relax when they realise it is the same truck. It is precisely at this point that the machine gun is turned on them both. Earlier in

Stock footage

Footage held in a library that film-makers could insert into their own original footage. For example, rather than sending a film crew to Paris, stock footage of the Eiffel Tower could be used.

the film, when Tom kills Putty Nose, the audience do not see the event. They only hear a gun shot and the last gasp of the victim trying to sing the final word of the song as he slumps over the piano.

The film never deals explicitly with the reasons for Tom's criminality, although his over-bearing police-officer father is one factor to consider. The depiction of Tom's lower-middle class background is significant as clearly he does not need to steal to survive. Later in the film just before killing Putty Nose Tom tells him: 'You taught us how to cheat, steal and kill', Matt continues: 'If it hadn't been for you we might have been on the level'. Although Tom is only half serious in his accusations, a serious point is being made here about the influence of his social environment. Overall, however, the gangster depicted in *The Public Enemy* is an aberration of his own making and, despite some attempt to link his behaviour with external factors, the film is not critical of the ideology of American society.

Foreword to Scarface

This picture is an indictment of gang rule in America and of the callous indifference of the government to this constantly increasing menace to our safety and our liberty. Every incident in this picture is the reproduction of an actual occurrence, and the purpose of this picture is to demand of the government: 'What are you going to do about it?
The government is your government. What are YOU going to do about it?'

 ## *SCARFACE* (1932)

Director:	Howard Hawks
Producers:	Howard Hughes and Howard Hawks
Production company:	Caddo Company. For United Artists
Screenplay:	Ben Hecht *et al*
Length:	90 mins

Cast

Tony Camonte:	Paul Muni
Cesca:	Ann Dvorak
Poppy:	Karen Morley
Lovo:	Osgood Perkins
Rinaldo:	George Raft
Gaffney:	Boris Karloff

Scarface shares a number of similarities with *The Public Enemy* including the following:

- Iconography

- A rise and fall narrative structure

- A foreword that attempts to galvanise the public into action as well as promising realism

- A title, *Scarface, The Shame of the Nation* (later simply shortened to *Scarface*) that indicates a moral stance against the gangster

Whereas *The Public Enemy* starts with childhood games, *Scarface* begins with a cold-blooded murder. The scene comprises a two minute 45 second travelling shot that eventually reveals the silhouette of Tony Camonte poised to kill Costillo, the boss of the criminal underworld. The scene highlights the paradox of the gangster's acquisition of power: in order to be successful he must separate himself from others, but being alone makes him vulnerable to attack.

Scarface is about the meteoric rise to power and subsequent fall of Tony Camonte, based on the real life character Al Capone, America's most notorious gangster. It is immediately clear that Camonte is in a different league to Tom Powers in *The Public Enemy*. He will kill to climb to the top and apart from his downfall at the end of the film he is also highly successful. Surrounded by the material fruits of his criminal activities in his lavish new flat, Camonte registers the significance of the slogan for Cook's Tours across the street: 'The World is Yours'. The irony of the slogan is only apparent at the end of the film when Camonte lies dead on the street beneath it – he has caused his own destruction.

Figure 16.2 *Scarface* (1932): Camonte and his new machine gun   ©BFI

Despite his murderous activities Camonte is hugely likeable, appearing to regard the whole business of being a gangster as a game. Note, for example, his look of delight when he obtains a machine gun for the first time. The audience get no explanation of Camonte's social background or how he became drawn into crime. This makes it easier to regard his activities as a natural part of his personality and thus his appeal to audiences is increased. Rather than creating a figure to be despised the director, Howard Hawks, created a hero (Capone himself liked the film).

Scarface, like *The Public Enemy* was also successful because of its realism. Hawks used Ben Hecht, a reporter, to write the screenplay as well as obtaining advice direct from members of the criminal underworld. Devices such as the use of newspaper front pages to convey plot information add further authenticity to the film. It is the level of violence in the film that is, however, the most striking to a modern audience. Hawks graphically depicts the killing of numerous people by machine gun, complemented by furious car chases and arson attacks. The film also includes reconstructions of recent events known to the public such as the St Valentine's Day Massacre. Finally, the sound track adds weight to the images with the screeching of tyres, machine-gun fire and the screams of victims.

Not surprisingly *Scarface* had problems with the censors. It was finally passed for release after many cuts and with a different ending, in which Camonte is hanged for his crimes, but even this version was banned from release in New York. The distribution that the film eventually received, however, made it a commercial success.

SCARFACE (1983)

Director:	Brian de Palma
Producer:	Martin Bregman
Production Company:	Universal
Screenplay:	Oliver Stone
Musical score:	Giorgio Moroder
Length:	170 mins

Cast

Tony Montana:	Al Pacino
Elvira:	Michelle Pfeiffer
Gina:	Mary Elizabeth Mastrantonio
Frank Lopez:	Robert Loggia
Manny Ray:	Steven Bauer

Figure 16.3 *Scarface* (1983): The 1980s ultra-violent gangster   ©BFI

Brian de Palma's 1983 remake of Hawks' *Scarface* updates the story in a number of ways. The film is set in Florida in the early 1980s and deals with the problems associated with drug smuggling. Tony Montana is one of a large group of Cuban undesirables, expelled by Castro, who quickly rises to prominence in the criminal underworld. On arrival in America, Montana claims Castro's communist regime has held him back and he demands the opportunity to make money. He is motivated not by the need for power, but by materialism. He quickly realises that expensive clothes and cars also give access to beautiful women. Although both films focus on the gangster's overwhelming ambition to succeed, they have very different attitudes towards the American dream. For example, in Hawks' version, Camonte's material success is not condemned, only his methods of achieving it. In de Palma's *Scarface*, however, the notion of the American dream itself is criticised.

Montana eventually makes enough money to buy anything he wants, but then starts to question his achievements. In the restaurant scene in the second half of the film Montana voices his realisation that the American dream is flawed: 'Is this it, is this what it's all about . . . You fifty, you got a bag for a belly . . . you got a liver that got spots on it . . . Is this what it's all about? Is this what I work for?' Later in the same sequence he accuses the other wealthy diners of being no better than him, claiming that they hide their crimes behind a facade of respectability. His disillusionment with the ideology of American society is reinforced by Elvira who says to Montana: 'We're losers not winners'. American society in the film is thus shown to be rotten to the core, with a corrupt police force and a government that allows the trafficking of drugs for political gain. Compared to the other characters in the film, however, Montana is probably the least corrupt, maintaining a code of conduct that includes honesty and loyalty.

As in Hawks' version of the film, Montana is responsible for his own downfall. His death involves a literal fall from the balcony of his absurdly opulent house, landing at the base of 'The World is Yours' statue. That Montana seems invincible in this scene, remaining standing even when riddled with bullets, demonstrates how, over time, the gangster has acquired mythical status.

The gangster films of the 1930s were mostly conventional in style and form. Later films, made by directors such as Scorsese, de Palma and the Coen Brothers, turned visual style into a key element of the genre. Critics of de Palma's *Scarface* claim it is excessively concerned with visual style at the expense of characterisation and narrative progression. The iconography of the genre remains familiar, subject to necessary updating: an arsenal of powerful weapons including the rocket launcher that Montana wields at the end of the film replaces the machine-guns of *Scarface*, 1932. Fast cars, extravagant clothes, vast mounds of money and cocaine and over-the-top interiors also litter the film. De Palma makes full use of the *mise-en-scène* to emphasise material excess in virtually every shot. In one scene, in which Montana is sitting in a vast circular bath, the camera pulls right back making him look insignificant and powerless. This device is used at other points in the film, when characters are placed in vast, sparsely decorated sets, which reflect the emptiness of their lives.

The early gangster films were based on recent history and included events that would have been familiar to most Americans. *Scarface* 1983 continues this tradition of realism as it is based on a key event in modern American history. The semi-documentary style that includes use of stock footage and printing dates and locations on screen contributes to the realism of the film. *Scarface* also continued the tradition of depicting graphic violence including a sequence in which Montana is attacked with a chain-saw.

 ### *GOODFELLAS* (1990)

Director:	Martin Scorsese
Cinematographer:	Michael Ballhaus
Production Company:	Warner Brothers
Based on the book *Wise Guy* by:	Nicholas Pileggi
Screenplay:	Nicholas Pileggi & Martin Scorsese
Length:	139 mins

Cast

Henry Hill:	Ray Liotta
Jimmy Conway:	Robert de Niro
Tommy DeVito:	Joe Pesci
Paul Cicero:	Paul Sorvino
Karen Hill:	Lorraine Bracco

A short credit sequence is followed by the statement 'This film is based on a true story' printed on the screen. The opening sequence which follows sets the tone for the rest of the film. It introduces three of the main characters in the film: Henry Hill, Jimmy Conway and Tommy De Vito. They are travelling in a car at night in New York in 1970. They look weary and slightly dishevelled. They hear a knocking noise coming from the car and they stop to investigate. In the red glow of the rear lights they identify the noise as coming from the boot. Henry approaches the boot cautiously while Jimmy holds a spade and Tommy draws an enormous carving knife from inside his jacket. Inside the boot is a man wrapped in a sheet. His head and part of his chest are exposed and covered in blood. Tommy steps forward and stabs him several times and then Jimmy shoots him at close range four times. Henry moves forward from his position as an onlooker and shuts the boot. As he does so his voice-over says, 'As far back as I could remember I always wanted to be a gangster.' As he slams the boot shut the song *Rags to Riches* begins and plays over a freeze frame of Henry. After a further brief credit sequence the film cuts to a close-up of Henry whose voice-over says: 'To me being a gangster was better than being President of the United States.' The film then cuts back to the beginning of the story in East New York, Brooklyn, 1955.

These opening scenes draw attention to the viciousness of the way of life in the film depicts as well as the way in which the story is told. *Goodfellas* depicts the rise and fall of the main character, Henry Hill, and in this way is typical of the gangster genre. Henry, however, does not achieve the stature of Tony Camonte or Tony Montana. As an Irish-Italian he cannot be a full member of the Mafia, but psychologically he always remains on the fringes of the criminal activity. In the end he saves himself by turning state's evidence and is condemned to live in anonymity as an 'average nobody'. This is a fate almost worse than death as Henry is attracted to the mob for the 'action' and the respect that the life attracts. This life centres on making money in an ordered if illegitimate manner which enables Henry to revel in the fact that he is living better than those around him. Although the film does not stress the economic necessity of being a gangster for Henry, as it does for Tony Camonte, it is presented as an easy option, which Henry wants to enjoy without getting his hands too dirty. In this way he is different from Jimmy who takes pleasure from robbing and being expansive with the proceeds and Tommy who enjoys exercising his psychopathic tendencies.

As a film *Goodfellas* owes a lot to the director Martin Scorsese who is Italian-American, which could be regarded as some guarantee of the authenticity of the representations in addition to the fact that the film is based on a factual account by Nicholas Pileggi. More importantly though, like many of Scorsese's films, *Goodfellas* deals in a non-moralistic way with characters that are both attractive and repellent and it contains scenes that are both amusing and disturbing. Scorsese uses a whole range of cinematic devices such as: long takes, slow-motion, freeze-frames, the voice-overs of both Henry and his wife Karen and direct address to the camera. Popular music is used constantly both as a counter-point to the images and a means of denoting the time periods of the events depicted.

In conclusion, *Goodfellas* communicates the excitement and attraction of being a gangster but the male camaraderie and material success the life provides seems ultimately shallow and unfulfilling.

***CARLITO'S WAY* (1993)**

Director:	Brian de Palma
Producers:	Martin Bregman, Willi Baer and Michael S Bregman
Production Companies:	Universal Pictures & Epic Productions
Screenplay:	David Koepp
Based on the novels:	*Carlito's Way* and *After Hours* by Edwin Torres
Length:	139 mins

Cast

Carlito Brigante:	Al Pacino
Dave Kleinfeld:	Sean Penn
Gail:	Penelope Ann Miller
Benny Blanco:	John Leguizamo
Steffie:	Ingrid Rogers
Norwark:	James Rebhorn
Pachanga:	Luis Guzman

Carlito's Way opens with the murder of the central character, Carlito Brigante. Surprisingly the scene establishes the fate of the gangster before the flashback narrative begins. The audience are therefore made aware that despite all his efforts, he will never escape from the city. The only escape is death. The scene also establishes the importance of style in de Palma's gangster films, in its use of slow motion, unusual camera-angles, subjective point-of-view shots, music and voice-over.

The time and place of *Carlito's Way* are clearly printed on the screen at the start of the flash-back sequence: New York, 1975. Carlito is a small time Puerto Rican gangster, who has acquired notoriety before his imprisonment. The choice of Al Pacino to play Carlito is significant as audiences will also recognise him as the character Tony Montana in *Scarface*. His actions in *Carlito's Way* therefore acquire additional resonance for devotees of the genre. The narrative begins when he is released from prison in 1975 on a technicality, after only five years of a 30 year sentence. He makes it clear to Kleinfeld, his lawyer, that he no longer has any criminal ambition, desiring only to save enough money to buy into a car hire business in the Bahamas. Despite Carlito's conscious effort not to become involved in crime he swiftly finds himself being sucked back in.

In many ways the film attempts to demythologise the gangster. Carlito wants to escape his past and is not proud of his previous life as a gangster. He accepts that Benny Blanco (a truly nasty piece of work) is merely a younger version of himself. The gangster characters in the film as a whole are shown not to be exotic or even charismatic, but cheap low-life. Carlito himself is aware that he is one of the few survivors of the gangster lifestyle; the rest are either dead or in prison. All the characters are shown to be unable to escape their environment. This message is reinforced by the fact that the action of the film is confined to just a few blocks in the city. The resolution of the narrative is also more decisive than in *Goodfellas* and closer to the endings of the 'classic' gangster films of the 1930s.

In Carlito's world no one can be trusted. The reason Carlito is released from prison early is that the law is proven to be corrupt, as is Kleinfeld who is disloyal to friends and clients alike. He steals from Tony T. before murdering him, and promises to bear false witness against Carlito for crimes he did not commit. Finally, Carlito's death is caused by Pachanga's treachery. The only person with any loyalty or values in the film is Carlito. It is his loyalty to Kleinfeld, however, that seals Carlito's fate. It is obvious that Carlito no longer has a place in the new order and can thus be seen as a tragic figure.

Carlito's Way is easily identifiable as a Brian de Palma film. Trademarks include the following:

- The fast-paced 'set-piece' ending of the film, which rivals that of *The Untouchables*
- The use of inventive editing (for example the scene in which Benny Blanco is thrown down the stairs)
- The littering of the *mise-en-scène* with palm trees as in *Scarface*

The film retains, however, some of the traditional elements of the gangster films such as an emphasis on guns. The opening sequence, for example, takes the audience by surprise with a gun shot after complete silence, accompanied by a close-up slow-motion shot of the gun that fired the shot. What is lacking, however, is the material excess of both *Scarface* (1983) and *Goodfellas*. The myth of the gangster high-life is stripped bare.

 **FURTHER WORK**

Why are *The Public Enemy* and *Scarface* considered to be 'classics' of the gangster genre?

Compare and contrast the two different versions of *Scarface* using the following points as a guide:

- Themes of the gangster film
- Narrative patterns
- Iconography
- Visual style

To what extent do *Scarface* and *Carlito's Way* break with the conventions of the gangster genre?

Do contemporary gangster films glamorise the gangster to a greater extent than those in the past?

 FURTHER READING

Cook, Pam, *The Cinema Book*, BFI, 1985, pp85–92.

Griffith, Richard, 'Cycles and Genres' in Nichols, Bill, (ed.), *Movies and Methods Vol. 1*, University of California Press, 1976.

Mitchell, Edward, 'Apes and Essences: Some Sources of Significance in the American Gangster Film' in Grant, Barry, (ed.), *Film Genre Reader II*, University of Texas Press, 1995.

Reid, Mark A., 'The Black Gangster Film' in Grant, Barry, (ed.), *Film Genre Reader II*, University of Texas Press, 1995.

Roddick, Nick, *A New Deal in Entertainment: Warner Bros in the 1930s*, BFI, 1983.

Shadoian, Jack, *Dreams and Dead Ends*, MIT Press, 1977.

Solomon, Stanley J., *Beyond Formula: American Film Genres*. Harcourt Brace Jovanovich, Inc, 1976.

Warshow, Robert, 'The Gangster as Tragic Hero', in *The Immediate Experience*, Atheneum Books, 1970.

Warshow, Robert 'Movie Chronicle: The Westerner' in Mast, Gerald, Marshall Cohen and Leo Braudy, *Film Theory and Criticism: Introductory Readings* (4th Edition), Oxford University Press, 1992.

Sight and Sound has a number of relevant articles. See especially the following:
    November 1991 (Vol. 1, Issue 7)
    August 1996 (Vol. 6, Issue 8)
    November 1995 (Vol. 5, Issue 11)
    May 1997 (Vol. 7, Issue 5)

FURTHER VIEWING

Underworld (Joseph Von Sternberg, 1927)
Little Caesar (Mervyn Le Roy, 1930)
G-Men (William Keighley, 1935)
Angels with Dirty Faces (Michael Curtiz, 1938)
The Roaring Twenties (Raoul Walsh, 1939)
Al Capone (Richard Wilson, 1959)
The Rise and Fall of Legs Diamond (Budd Boetticher, 1960)
The Godfather (Francis Coppola, 1972)
Mean Streets (Martin Scorsese, 1973)
The Godfather Part II (Francis Coppola, 1974)
Once Upon a Time in America (Sergio Leone, 1984)
The Untouchables (Brian de Palma, 1987)
Miller's Crossing (Joel Cohn, 1990)
The Godfather Part III (Francis Coppola, 1990)
Reservoir Dogs (Quentin Tarantino, 1992)
A Bronx Tale (Robert De Niro, 1993)
Pulp Fiction (Quentin Tarantino, 1994)
Casino (Martin Scorsese, 1996)
Heat (Michael Mann, 1996)
Donnie Brasco (Mike Newell, 1997)

CHAPTER **17** Film Noir

Whoever went to the movies with any regularity during 1946 was caught in the midst of Hollywood's profound post-war affection for morbid drama. From January through December deep shadows, clutching hands, exploding revolvers, sadistic villains and heroines tormented with deeply rooted diseases of the mind flashed across the screen in a panting display of psychoneuroses, unsublimated sex and murder most foul.'

From: *Life* magazine[1]

' "Film noir" is literally "black film", not just in the sense of being full of physically dark images, nor of reflecting a dark mood in American society, but, equally, almost empirically, as a black slate on which the culture could inscribe its ills and in the process produce a catharsis to relieve them.'

Alain Silver and Elizabeth Ward in *Film Noir: An Encyclopedic Reference Guide*[2]

BACKGROUND

Unlike the western genre and the gangster genre, film noir was not a term used by the Hollywood film industry itself. The term was first employed by French critics after the Second World War. They found it remarkable that a number of Hollywood films, some of which had been delayed by the war, presented a much darker vision than expected from the North American film industry. These films had a pessimistic perspective both on American society and the chances for individual fulfilment within it. This trend produced a body of films, from the early 1940s to the late 1950s, that counteracted the American Dream. They introduced a dark and distinctive noir universe with a pervasive air of corruption and despair. For this reason the enthusiasm of the French critics was not matched by their North American counterparts who regarded film noir as 'an aberration of the American character'[3] and less American than the western or the gangster film.

The noir universe and its protagonists

Film noir is characterised by a wide range of wrongdoing, immorality and criminality. Private eyes and policemen populate these films and their occupations bring them into contact with a wide range of criminals, gamblers, hustlers, war veterans and women who are both attractive and dangerous. These protagonists are predominantly inhabitants of the city, and are to be found in its offices, police stations, nightclubs and places of entertainment. They live in hotels, apartments, tenements and occasionally big mansions but, more importantly, they are single men and women and not members of conventional families. In keeping with the anonymity of the city they give little away and favour quick-witted and fast-talking encounters with the people they meet.

WOMEN IN FILM NOIR

Often a contrast is drawn between the conventional woman who is chaste, straightforward and honest and the *femme fatale* who is sexually alluring, manipulative and devious. The male hero is ineluctably drawn to the *femme fatale* as a result of her sexual attraction as well as the operations of chance. A classic instance of this occurs in *Double Indemnity* in which insurance salesman Walter Neff colludes with Phyllis Dietrichson in the murder of her husband. Neff is stimulated to commit this crime by the sexual attractions of Phyllis which prompt him to fulfil his long-standing dream of outwitting the omniscient invincibility of his boss Barton Keyes and the insurance company for which he works.

The cinema has always taken an interest in crime and criminals but an essential feature of film noir is the lack of control enjoyed by its protagonists. This lack of control is exhibited by the characters in a number of ways.

- They cannot repress their desires despite the consequences
- They often fail to impose themselves on events
- If they are successful it is often at great cost to themselves and others
- They are presented as the victims of circumstance or of forces beyond their understanding or reach

As a result a film noir narrative often ends in failure, defeat or even death.

The noir universe and visual style

The lack of control experienced by the protagonists is expressed through the visual style of many film noirs. J. A. Place and L. S. Peterson in their article, 'Some Visual Motifs of Film Noir'[4], state that: '...film noir creates a visually unstable environment in which no character has a firm moral base from which he can confidently operate. All attempts to find safety or security are undercut by the antitraditional cinematography and mise-en-scène.'

Film noir has a distinctive approach to lighting which departs from the conventional high key, low contrast three-point lighting system and involves the following methods:

- Low key lighting in which the intensity of the fill light is not sufficient to eliminate the shadows created by the hard, direct key light and which results in a high contrast between light and dark in the image. Sometimes a fill light is not used at all which creates an even more exaggerated shadowy effect
- The use of the key light in unconventional positions below, above or behind and to one side of the performer
- The use of night-time shooting which gives a very black look to any areas of the image that are not illuminated

Chiaroscuro

A combination of two Italian adjectives: *chiaro* meaning light and *scuro* meaning dark.

This **chiaroscuro** lighting suggests a world out of kilter and was often suitably complemented by an unconventional approach to *mise-en-scène*.

- The protagonists are often not as prominent in the frame as other elements of the composition
- The protagonists are often placed in a frame within the frame by windows, stairways or other features of the urban environment

The camera also participates in this unsettling vision.

- The camera adopts unusual angles or positions
- It uses wide angle lenses which provide a distorted image in close-up and depth of field for long shots which aim to stress the insignificance of the noir protagonist in the setting

Place and Peterson argue that it is the remarkable style of film noir that ultimately creates its characteristic 'moods of claustrophobia, paranoia, despair and nihilism.'[5] However, not all the films regarded as film noir have a pronounced anti-traditional visual style. After the Second World War a number of noir films assumed more of a documentary style as filmmakers took advantage of developments in camera, filmstock and sound technology. These developments had military purposes initially but made for more flexible and mobile film-making in peacetime.

Narrative and narration

The effect of the visual style is to intrigue and disconcert the audience. As a result it works well with the typical noir narrative which often consists of a confusing set of events involving seemingly unconnected characters. The noir protagonist is often trying to make sense of these events and the links between characters. Sometimes the protagonist is recalling past events and the story unfolds in flashback with an accompanying voice-over narration. Flashbacks are often seen as an important element of the noir genre as they can convey a sense of entrapment but it is not essential for a noir film to have a flashback narrative structure. Many of them did but the majority of noir films have a conventional narrative structure even if the motivation of the characters and the events depicted within them are removed from the American mainstream.

The renaissance of film noir

According to Foster Hirsch, 'film noir constitutes a body of striking work that represents the American film industry in its most neurotic, subversive, and visually provocative phase.'[6] The French critics recognised these qualities but it was not until the late 1960s that critics in the USA began to catch up and adopt the term film noir as a tool of analysis. Since then the term has been used extensively by critics. It has also become a common summary word for reviewers and has, as a result, lost precision. For example, *Men in Black* (Barry Sonnenfeld, 1997) was described in a local paper preview as 'a light-touch noir comedy with an agreeable elegance about it'.

A number of noir films were made during the 1970s and 1980s and film noir has also proved a source of inspiration to many new film-makers who have continued the noir tradition with some vigour into the 1990s. They have been attracted by its visual style and the possibility of making a good crime thriller on a low budget, just as many of the film-makers of the 1940s and 1950s had been.

CASE STUDIES

- *Farewell My Lovely* (1944)
- *Build My Gallows High/Out of the Past* (1947)
- *Chinatown* (1974)
- *The Hot Spot* (1990)
- *The Last Seduction* (1994)

 ***FAREWELL MY LOVELY* (1944)**

Director:	Edward Dmytryk
Producer:	Adrian Scott
Production company:	RKO
Screenplay, based on the novel by Raymond Chandler:	John Paxton
Special effects:	Vernon L Walker
Art direction:	Albert S D'Agostino, Carroll Clark
Length:	95 mins

Murder My Sweet was the eventual USA title to avoid the confusion arising out of the fact that Dick Powell was known as a singer and dancer rather than a tough guy.

Cast

Philip Marlowe:	Dick Powell
Mrs Helen Grayle/Velma:	Claire Trevor
Ann Grayle:	Anne Shirley
Amthor:	Otto Kruger
Moose Maloy:	Mike Mazurki
Mr Grayle:	Miles Mander
Mrs Florian:	Esther Howard

Many film noir are based around a central character who is an investigator. In most cases the investigator is a policeman or a private eye, who is often a former policeman. In *Farewell My Lovely* the main character is private eye Philip Marlowe, the creation of Raymond Chandler on whose novel the film is based.

Raymond Chandler (1888–1959)

Chandler was an important source for film noir as were fellow crime writers, Dashiell Hammett, and James M. Cain. These writers were popular in the 1930s and had been published in France in a detective series entitled *Serie Noire* and *Fleuve Noire*. Films connected with these writers include a number of key films such as *Double Indemnity* and *The Postman Always Rings Twice* based on novels by Cain; *The Big Sleep* and *The Lady in the Lake* based on novels by Raymond Chandler; and *The Maltese Falcon* written by Hammett.

Figure 17.1 *Farewell my Lovely*: Marlowe with Ann Grayle and her father   ©BFI

The private eye in film noir, and in the fiction on which it is based, operates on his own – usually on a shaky economic basis. His resources are his wits, courage, stubbornness and experience of the streets and life in general. The world in which the private investigator operates is often hostile and full of corruption but he struggles to assert some morality. In facing this world he is outwardly world-weary and cynical but he is concerned to achieve a measure of justice, however minimal. He has to make a living but he is not completely mercenary. He operates on the fringes of the law but he is on the side of good. His typical method is to confront people to obtain information using humour and streetwise banter. As John G. Cawelti puts it, 'The hard-boiled detective investigates through movement and encounter; he collides with the web of conspiracy until he has exposed its outlines.'[7] This method often gets him into trouble and it can be contrasted with the more considered approach of Sherlock Holmes, Poirot or Morse, who proceed by gathering information and posing hypotheses.

In *Farewell My Lovely* Marlowe is an independent operator who works from a bare office and remarks on the sorry state of his finances, 'My bank account was about to crawl under a duck'. During the film his finances improve as he progresses through typical noir territory: Florian's Bar; Mrs Florian's seedy apartment; a night club with a floor show; Amthor's tasteful apartment; the Grayle mansion and beach house and the interrogation room of the police station where the film begins. In these various locations he meets a whole range of characters from the noir universe.

- Moose Malloy, the slow-witted 'heavy'
- Amthor, the cultivated, intelligent and manipulative criminal

■ Marriot, a minor character, coded as gay

■ Mrs Grayle/Velma, the dangerous and attractive femme fatale. Her sexual attractiveness is made clear in comparison with the ordinary woman – her stepdaughter Ann, whose attractiveness is homely and personable

Visual style and narrative

Before the credits there is a shot from above of a large table with a desk lamp on it. This lamp throws a bright, glaring light onto the surface of the table but the room around the table is in shadow, as are the men seated around it. This shot moves slowly down and into the harshly lit table surface under the credits until there is a dissolve into the first shot of the film proper, a close shot of the harshly illuminated table top. Over this shot there is a rapidly spoken statement:
'I remember you as a pretty noisy little fellow, son. All of a sudden you get quiet.'
and the rhetorical questions:
'You lost your book of answers or are you just waiting for your lawyer?'
'Maybe you don't think murder looks so good on you?'
in quick succession.

The camera then pulls back to reveal four men seated around a table in a dimly lit room. The light sources come from below and to the side and cast shadows across their faces. The camera is behind and to one side of one man who has a huge bandage wrapped around his head and covering his eyes. This man is being interrogated by three policemen. This situation, the characters and their dress, the aggressiveness of their language and the lighting scheme point to film noir. Firstly, the visual style of this opening scene establishes the mood of the film and many succeeding scenes are set at night and characterised by the use of heavy shadows. Two distinguishing features of the film's visual style are as follows:

■ A black pool which spreads from the edges and fills the screen each time Marlowe is rendered unconscious

■ A nightmare sequence after Marlowe has been drugged by Amthor's henchmen

Overall, the film is a good example of film noir's approach to lighting and *mise-en-scène*. For example, near the beginning of the film Marlowe is sitting in his office with his back to the camera with his reflection in the lower half of the sash window. As he sits there his reflection is joined, in the top half of the window by a reflection of the head and shoulders of Moose Malloy lit harshly from the side and thereby producing a disorienting and threatening three-shot.

Secondly, in narrative terms the opening scene raises questions in the minds of the audience. The main question that arises is, 'What train of events has led to this situation?' and the film begins to reveal this in flashbacks introduced and commented on by Philip Marlowe. (Because Marlowe is present in every scene and the story is told from his point of view the film is a clear example of restricted narration.) He reports on the visit of Moose Malloy who hires him to find Velma Valento. The initial enigma that is posed concerns the whereabouts of Velma. This question, however, declines in importance as the narrative unfolds and other questions become more important or pressing such as the issue of the jade necklace supposedly stolen from Mrs Grayle. In the end the questions raised and the characters introduced do turn out to be linked. This is a typical feature of such narratives and also a major source of audience pleasure. The audience is placed in the same position as Marlowe who throughout the film is trying to make sense of what he sees and hears. Both Marlowe and the audience want to know more to fill in the gaps in their knowledge. All films deliver information to the audience and this process involves the giving of some facts and the withholding of others. In films like *Farewell My Lovely*, however, knowledge is especially important because the plots themselves are concerned with the accumulation of facts and evidence. In this context it is cataclysmic that Marlowe is rendered unconscious three times in the film because the audience can only know what he knows. This fact is important because early on in the film Marlowe is duped by Mrs Florian. She pretends to be hiding a photograph of Velma and is caught out doing so by Marlowe. Towards the end of the film, however, it becomes clear that a trick has been played on Marlowe and therefore on the audience as well.

Themes

The deception of Marlowe by Mrs Florian is typical of film noir as things are often not what they seem. In *Farewell My Lovely* for example Ann Grayle pretends, unconvincingly, to be a reporter before being quickly unveiled by Marlowe. More seriously, the smooth Jules Amthor conceals his activities behind a professional front, and Velma Valento, the show girl, has become Mrs Helen Grayle, the wife of a wealthy and aged widower. This manipulation of appearances is an important theme in film noir, as is the existence of corruption beneath an unrevealing surface. The theme that sets the plot in motion, however, is Moose's obsession with Velma, which is matched by Mr Grayle's obsession with her and Marlowe's search to find out what is going on beneath the surface (motivated by his desire to protect his reputation). *Farewell My Lovely*, then, has the iconography, the visual style, the narrative structure, and the themes of the classic period of film noir. At the end of the film Marlowe and Ann Grayle are taking a taxi ride together but this conventional ending belies the darkness of the events that precede it.

 BUILD MY GALLOWS HIGH (1947)

(USA title: *Out of the Past*)

Director:	Jacques Tourneur
Producer:	Warren Duff
Production company:	RKO
Screenplay:	Geoffrey Homes (Daniel Mainwaring) based on his novel *Build My Gallows High*
Director of Photography:	Nicholas Musuraca
Length:	95 mins

Cast

Jeff Bailey/Markham:	Robert Mitchum
Kathie Moffett:	Jane Greer
Ann Miller:	Virginia Huston
Whit Sterling:	Kirk Douglas
Joe Stefanos:	Paul Valentine
Meta Carson:	Rhonda Fleming
Jim:	Richard Webb
Fisher:	Steve Brodie
Leonard Eels:	Ken Niles
The Kid (Jimmy):	Dickie Moore

At the end of *Farewell My Lovely* Philip Marlowe has his eyes bandaged but he leaves the police station in a taxi with Ann Gray and the prospect of a developing romance. Jeff Markham, the private eye in *Build My Gallows High*, however, is dead, killed by his former lover, Kathie Moffatt, who seconds later is herself killed by the police.

At the beginning of *Build My Gallows High* Jeff Markham has changed his name to Jeff Bailey. The 'Mysterious Jeff Bailey', as his girlfriend calls him, is the proprietor of a small garage with one employee, a deaf-mute young man, called Jimmy. He has tried to escape from his past, which has left him devastated and emotionally impaired. Although he has a girlfriend, Ann Miller, it is significant that he only communicates directly with Jimmy who is similarly unable to express himself freely to others.

Figure 17.2 *Build My Gallows High*: Jeff confronts Kathie ©BFI

Although Markham has tried to leave behind the traumas of the past he is forced to revisit them and eventually becomes a victim of them. As a film noir protagonist he is doomed by his past: he ends up a victim even though he is able to act masterfully and extricate himself from an attempt to frame him for a murder. Markham/Bailey can be contrasted with a western hero like Shane, who is also trying to escape the past. The western hero, however, is able to employ his abilities, even with great reluctance, to achieve a positive outcome before moving on. The film noir hero is often unable to escape because he is still in thrall to the events and relationships of his past life.

The film opens with the invasion of the present by the past. Joe Stefanos, Whit Sterling's henchman, drives into the small town of Bridgeport in order to summon Markham to Whit. Joe's dark clothes and hat mark him out as an outsider in contrast to Jeff who is seen beside a lake with Ann. He is dressed for fishing and is visually integrated into the landscape. On being required to travel to Whit Sterling's place by Lake Tahoe Jeff Bailey is forced to re-enter the noir universe: he leaves at night dressed in a trench coat and hat rather than his comfortable outdoor outfit. Ann accompanies him on his journey and Jeff recounts what is happening in his past.

Narrative

Build My Gallows High has a complex narrative which is often difficult to follow. It contains four main sequences.

- The opening sequence in Bridgeport: Jeff is summoned to Whit and sets out with Ann
- A flashback sequence: Jeff is hired by Whit in New York to trace Kathie; he becomes her lover in Acapulco; back in San Francisco they are seen by Jeff's ex-partner Fisher who follows them and is shot by Kathie

- After discovering that Kathie has returned to Whit, Jeff receives his instruction which leads into a sequence in San Francisco: he meets Meta Carson who introduces him to Leonard Eels, a tax lawyer who has been employed by Whit but who is threatening to expose him to the authorities. Although Jeff's ostensible task is to obtain the documents which incriminate Whit he soon realises that he is being set up for the murder of Eels, which is actually committed by Joe Stefanos. What is more Jeff learns that there is a document, signed by Kathie, in Eel's safe which incriminates him for the murder of Fisher. Jeff does, however, obtain the tax records from the office of the Sterling club

- The final sequence in Bridgeport and Lake Tahoe: Whit recognises that Jeff has a hold over him and is willing to turn Kathie over to the police for the murder of Fisher; Kathie shoots Whit and she and Jeff plan to leave together; Jeff alerts the police who lay an ambush on their escape route

The twists and turns in the narrative match its duplicities and deceptions and they are complemented by the way in which the characters play with language. For example, Joe Stefanos says to Jeff that 'No one ever thought more of you than Whit' and Jeff replies, 'Or more about me' and Jeff matches Whit's 'You just sit and stay inside yourself. You wait for me to talk. I like that' with the reply 'I never found out much listening to myself'. These two exchanges, however, reveal the importance of visual style because although at the *verbal* level Jeff holds his own at the *visual* level he tends to have less dominance in both scenes. His failure to dominate the frame parallels his inability to achieve final mastery over the predicament in which he finds himself. This point is further underlined by the performance of Robert Mitchum who plays the role of Jeff with laconic resignation.

Femme Fatale

Although Jeff is pitted against Whit Sterling and his employee Joe Stefanos the key figure in his downfall is Kathie Moffatt. She is the classic *femme fatale*: she is beautiful; she cannot be trusted; and is prepared to kill to survive. Her allure is sexual and she mesmerises Jeff on their first meeting. She is associated with the power of the sun and the moon and the sea as Jeff says: 'And then I saw her, coming out of the sun' and 'She waited until it was late and then she walked in out of the moonlight, smiling'. It is a visual attraction (Kathie asks 'Did you miss me?' Jeff replies 'No more than I would my eyes') and involves the rejection of rationality. On the beach at Acapulco Kathie asks 'Who do you believe?' and Jeff replies 'Baby I don't care.'

Such representations of the *femme fatale* have a strong element of misogyny in that she attracts the male protagonist but also causes his downfall. Characters like Kathie Moffatt are unpredictable and devious and do not have any clearly stated motivation. They do have power over the male protagonist, however, and this has led to commentators interpreting film noir as an expression of male insecurity.

 ### *CHINATOWN* (1974)

Director:	Roman Polanski
Producer:	Robert Evans
Production company:	Long Road/Paramount
Screenplay:	Robert Towne
Length:	130 mins

Cast

J. J. Gittes:	Jack Nicholson
Evelyn Mulwray:	Faye Dunaway
Noah Cross:	John Huston
Hollis Mulwray:	Darryl Zwerling
Katherine Mulwray:	Belinda Palmer
Escobar:	Perry Lopez

Yelbyrton: John Hillerman
Ida Sessions: Diane Ladd
Mulvihill: Roy Jenson
Loach: Dick Bakalyan
Walsh: Joe Mantell
Duffy: Bruce Glover
Man with the knife: Roman Polanski

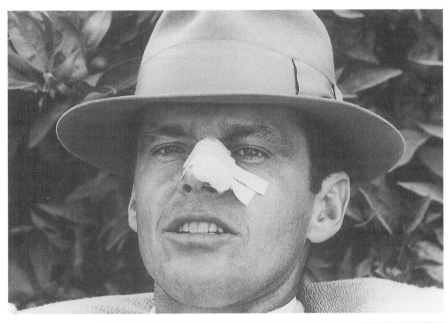

Figure 17.3 *Chinatown*: The ineffectual Gittes   ©BFI

John G. Cawleti in his article 'Chinatown and Generic Transformation'[8] states that *Chinatown* invokes the myth of the private eye, but then proceeds to undermine this myth. He defines a myth as '... a pattern of narrative known throughout the culture and presented in many different versions by many different tellers...' Cawelti then outlines the elements of the myth of the hard-boiled detective before going on to examine the ways in which the film undermines this myth.

The myth

The elements of the myth of the private eye are listed below:

- The private eye is an individual operator who has no great wealth or income. He is streetwise, lives on the edge of society and has no family attachments

- At the beginning of the story he is hired to find out something which seems straightforward, but leads him on to discover a whole web of deception

- He pursues justice which the police are not able to achieve within the letter of the law

- He becomes involved with a *femme fatale* during his investigations

- In the end he is able to uncover the connections between seemingly unconnected characters and, despite a number of fatalities, to ensure that justice is done

Chinatown has a number of these traditional elements but destroys the expectations that the audience brings to the genre and thereby demythologises it.

Undermining the myth

▨ J. J. Gittes is a more successful small businessman than the typical private eye. He has two assistants and a secretary. Moreover, his affluence is built upon matrimonial cases which traditionally the hard-boiled detective tries to avoid because they are demeaning

▨ At the beginning Gittes is hired by a woman who calls herself Mrs Mulwray to investigate whether her husband Hollis Mulwray is faithful to her. There is nothing unusual about this opening (it resembles the opening of *The Maltese Falcon*, for example) but as the plot proceeds he uncovers more and more corruption and degradation involving crime, politics and incest

▨ Gittes knows the tricks of the trade and he uses his skills and quick thinking to try to see that justice is done. However in the end he is impotent and cannot control the depredations of Noah Cross or prevent the death of Evelyn Mulwray with whom he has become emotionally involved. Almost half way through the film Noah Cross, played with engaging menace by **John Huston**, warns Gittes that 'You may think you know what you are dealing with, but believe me you don't'. Such a statement from a powerful figure to the private eye is commonplace, but usually the private eye is able, eventually, to understand the situation and provoke a conclusion. Gittes sets out to help Evelyn and her sister/daughter Katherine to escape the clutches of Noah Cross who fathered both of them. He fails on both counts: Evelyn is killed and Katherine is lead away by Noah Cross

▨ At the end of the film Gittes is lead away by his two associates, Walsh and Duffy. He is crushed by the events which re-establish *Chinatown* as a place where the inexplicable and inadmissible happen. Gittes tells Evelyn early in the film that when he was a policeman in Los Angeles he tried to stop a woman getting hurt, but ended up ensuring that she was hurt. The end of the film involves therefore the enactment of Gittes' darkest fears: the return of the past

John Huston (1906–87)

As a director and a screenwriter Huston was involved with a number of influential noir films, including one of the first and most famous, *The Maltese Falcon* (1941).

Roman Polanski (1933–)

Polanski is a film and theatre director and actor. He is notable for his visceral treatment of violence and sexuality and highly controlled command of cinematic expression. Director of:
Knife in the Water (Poland, 1962)
Repulsion (UK, 1965)
Cul-de-sac (UK, 1966)
Rosemary's Baby (USA, 1968)
The Tenant (France, 1976)
Tess (France/UK, 1980)
Frantic (USA, 1987)
Bitter Moon (France/UK, 1992)
Death and the Maiden (UK/USA/France, 1995)

In conclusion, *Chinatown* fulfils Polanski's desire to evoke the world and period of Dashiell Hammett and Raymond Chandler but it also reflects his urge to disturb the audience. In Robert Towne's screenplay Evelyn Mulwray kills her father and Katherine is successfully helped across the Mexican border by Gittes. Polanski's ending allows evil to triumph and this takes the film beyond the usual pessimism and darkness of film noir. Even before Gittes' failure at the end of the film however, Polanski undermines the heroic stature of the private eye. Gittes is flashily dressed and uncharacteristically flippant. He over-reacts when another customer riles him in the barber shop and then is made to look stupid when he is telling a sexually explicit joke in front of Mrs Mulwray. Later in the film his authority is undermined when he viciously slaps Evelyn's face only to reveal her as a hapless victim of incest. To cap it all Gittes has his nose slashed by one of Noah Cross's minions and spends some time in the film with a large bandage across it. Significantly this scene was not in the original screenplay and the actor wielding the knife is **Polanski** himself.

📖 THE HOT SPOT (1990)

Director:	Denis Hopper
Producers:	Paul Lewis and Deborah Capograsso
Production company:	Orion
Screenplay:	Nona Tyson and Charles Williams
Based on the novel:	*Hell Hath no Fury* by Charles Williams
Length:	120 mins

Cast

Harry Madox:	Don Johnson
Dolly Harshaw:	Virginia Madsen
Gloria Harper:	Jennifer Connelly
Lon Gulik:	Charles Martin Smith
Frank Sutton:	William Sadler
Sheriff:	Barry Corbin
George Harshaw:	Jerry Hardin

Figure 17.4 *The Hot Spot*: The look of the 1950s ©BFI

The film starts with the arrival of a stranger (Harry Madox) in a small Texas town. He finds himself a job as a car salesman and subsequently becomes involved with two women: the blonde *femme fatale* Dolly (the wife of his new boss), and her antithesis, Gloria, who also works at the car showroom. The plot revolves around the themes of deception, malpractice and corruption and manipulation. The robbery of the bank by Madox is a central event in the film, leaving him open to blackmail. At the end of the film, instead of escaping to a new life in the Caribbean, Madox is forced to stay with Dolly.

The Hot Spot is a retrospective film in a number of ways. It is based on Charles Williams' 1952 novel *Hell Hath no Fury* and was scripted for film in 1961, with the role of Harry Madox originally being written for Robert Mitchum. The director, **Denis Hopper** has a long history of performing, as well as directing, notably in David Lynch's *Blue Velvet* (1986) which has clearly influenced *The Hot Spot* and its depiction of small town America.

Despite being made in 1990, *The Hot Spot* does not have the look or feel of a modern film. The *mise-en-scène*, iconography and improvised blues based sound track which meanders and trickles behind the slow moving narrative, makes it difficult to place the film in the present day. The locations, cars and clothes all seem to indicate the 1950s.

The Hot Spot is unusual for a film noir.

- The opening shots are of desert landscape and the sun
- The main character is alone and isolated in this landscape

Denis Hopper (1936–)

Director of:
Easy Rider (1969)
The Last Movie (1971)
Out of the Blue (1980)
Colors (1988)
Chasers (1994)
Performer in (selective):
Rebel Without a Cause (Nicholas Ray, 1955)
Easy Rider (Denis Hopper, 1969)
True Grit (Henry Hathaway, 1969)
Apocalypse Now (Francis Coppola, 1979)
Rumble Fish (Francis Coppola, 1983)
Blue Velvet (David Lynch, 1986)
Red Rock West (John Dahl, 1993)
True Romance (Tony Scott, 1993)
Speed (Jan De Bont, 1994)

■ The succeeding action is predominantly set in a small, nameless, Texas town, whereas the typical noir is set in the city

■ It is filmed in colour

As the film progresses, however, it is clear that the small town produces the same sense of claustrophobia and constriction as the city. On his arrival in the town Madox visits a strip joint which helps to establish a seedy mood. Visually the town is reminiscent of an **Edward Hopper** painting and the noir look of earlier black and white films is recreated by the use of film stock that emphasises heavily saturated colours, and gives an oppressive feel to the film.

The characters within the town are physically isolated from each other, but yet very aware of each other and on display. The Harshaw Motors set, for example, has two glass offices which are raised from the ground and face each other. The visibility of the characters is, however, misleading as many of their activities are concealed from others. This leads characters to observe each other illicitly. Dolly's neighbour, for example, spies on her with binoculars and Sutton makes his living taking illicit photographs. This theme of voyeurism is also highlighted in the strip club where the men gaze at the dancers. Ironically, the only person who can 'see through' the web of deceit and corruption is the blind man who picks Madox out in an identity parade, claiming that he gives off: 'a little bleep, like a tea kettle.'

Madox has a number of similarities with noir protagonists of the 1940s and 1950s. He is in his mid-thirties, seemingly rootless and a drifter. He hints at a shady past, claiming that 'my life has just been a series of jams over floozies' and at the end of the film he acknowledges the inevitability of his fate: 'I've found my level, and I'm living it.' He is essentially weak-willed and self-destructive and cannot resist the charms of Dolly, despite knowing that she means trouble. Whereas traditional noir protagonists commit crimes because of a woman, Madox robs the bank without prompting. His motivation for committing the crime is not revealed to the audience and it is difficult to imagine what he will do with the money.

Dolly is an archetypal *femme fatale*. She uses her sexuality to get what she wants – in the case of her husband using it literally to murder him. The first meeting between Dolly and Madox is sexually charged and the exchange of dialogue is reminiscent of scenes between Walter Neff and Phyllis Dietrichson in *Double Indemnity*. Dolly has clearly married her husband for money and is prepared to murder him for it. Whereas Gloria is associated with light, water and the forest, Dolly is associated with darkness and the stuffed animals that decorate her house. Her bedroom is significantly in the form of a cage. It is also clear in the sexual encounters with Madox that she is in charge. When Madox first enters Dolly's bedroom, for example, she holds a gun to his head while she unzips his fly. The ending of *The Hot Spot* is a key example of how the noir genre has changed over time. In films of the 1940s and 1950s such as *Farewell My Lovely*, *Out of the Past* and *Detour* the *femme fatale* is killed. In *The Hot Spot*, however, Dolly escapes justice and gets both the money and the man. It is significant, however, that despite her increased power, the power of the *femme fatale* is still only defined by the weakness of men.

The Hot Spot could be analysed as a modern film noir, but it could also be examined as a **post-modern** film in its studied references to earlier noir films. Robert Ebert's review of the film supports this view, claiming that the film is best appreciated by a sophisticated viewer and that the average filmgoer will think:

'it contains clichés and stereotypes. Only movie lovers who have marinated their imaginations in the great B movies from RKO and Republic will recognise *The Hot Spot* as a superior work in an old tradition – as a manipulation of story elements as mannered and deliberate, in its way, as variations on a theme for the piano.[9]

Edward Hopper (1882–1967)

Hopper, an American artist, was concerned with the way in which urban landscapes isolate individuals. His paintings portray people in everyday work settings, but often they only form a small part of the picture as they are dwarfed by their environment. Key pictures include: *New York Pavement* (1924), *House at Dusk* (1935), *The Sheridan Theatre* (1937) and *New York Office* (1963).

Post-modern

The term post-modernism can be applied to all of the arts. It refers to the way in which new artefacts can be constructed by making reference to existing ones. To be effective it relies on the audience possessing extensive knowledge about the original material the new artefact is based on. Quentin Tarantino's *Pulp Fiction* (1994), for example, is best appreciated by audiences who have seen a wide range of films.

THE LAST SEDUCTION (1993)

Director:	John Dahl
Producer:	Jonathan Shestack
Production company:	ITC Entertainment Ltd
Screenplay:	Steve Barancik
Length:	110 mins

Cast

Bridget Gregory:	Linda Fiorentino
Mike Swale:	Peter Berg
Clay Gregory:	Bill Pullman
Frank Griffith:	J. T. Walsh
Harlan:	Bill Nunn

The director of *The Last Seduction*, John Dahl (1956–), has been a key figure in revitalising the film noir genre in the late 1980s and 1990s. His previous noir films including *Kill Me Again* (1989) and *Red Rock West* (1993) pay homage to the classic noir films of the 1940s and 1950s. In *Kill Me Again*, for example, the central characters have archetypal noir roles, such as: a down-at-heel private eye (Val Kilmer), a beautiful, but deceitful female client (Joanne Whalley-Kilmer) and a psychotic and sadistic boyfriend (Michael Madsen). The plot is torturous, with a number of twists, ending with the death of the *femme fatale*. These familiar elements are used self-consciously, and the audience's attention is drawn as much to the visual style of the film as to its content.

The Last Seduction opens in traditional noir style in the city (New York), with a drugs deal that nets the heavily indebted Clay Gregory $700,000. His wife, Bridget (Linda Fiorentino) steals the money and runs away to Beston, a small town near Buffalo, where the main action of the film is set. There she becomes involved with the well meaning, but dim-witted Mike, whom she persuades to murder Clay. At the end of the film, however, it is Bridget who ends up killing Clay, leaving Mike to take the blame. The last scene of the film shows Bridget driving away in a chauffeur driven limousine, destroying the only piece of evidence that could prove Mike's innocence.

Beston, unlike the unnamed town in *The Hot Spot*, is wholesome, friendly and not tainted by corruption. Its inhabitants, however, are shown to be small-minded, unsophisticated and constricted by their environment. Beston certainly has a claustrophobic feel to it and the audience can understand Mike's desire to escape to New York. The use of the small town setting also enables Dahl to comment humorously on differences between city and town life. When Bridge first arrives in Beston, for example, her 'New York' approach of ordering a drink at a bar is met with immediate hostility from the barman. For Bridget, living in Beston is like living in hell.

Bridget is an extreme reincarnation of the traditional *femme fatale*, often dressed entirely in black, including her underwear. She is ruthless in her desire for money, and manipulates men using her sexuality to fulfil her financial ambitions. She is portrayed as tough, cynical and selfish, and she shows her contempt of American family values by stubbing out her cigarette in 'Grandma's' apple pie. Bridget also turns the tables on traditional male/female representations on screen. For example, she initially sleeps with Mike to fulfil her immediate sexual appetite, but does not want any ties, or even to know his name. Later, Mike complains that Bridget only treats him as a sex object and demands love in addition. Unlike Dolly, in *The Hot Spot*, Bridget has no need for men as security, only as a means to an end. The film offers no alternative 'good' female figure to counteract Bridget, aside from Trish, Mike's transvestite wife. The lack of any positive role models in the film, lead the audience to regard Bridget's activities as almost legitimate. Her behaviour is consistent throughout the film, although the motivation for her actions is never

Figure 17.5 *The Last Seduction*: Bridget calls the shots ©BFI

revealed, and she shows no remorse when she murders her husband and frames Mike.

The men in the film are shown to be weak-willed, cowardly, greedy, easily duped and naive. The drugs deal in the film's opening sequence, for example, establishes Clay's lack of character and for the rest of the film his efforts to recover the money from Bridget are easily thwarted. None of the men can be favourably compared with the traditional noir protagonist in other noir films, such as Walter Neff in *Double Indemnity* who, despite being ultimately weak-willed, is at least aware that he is being manipulated by the femme fatale.

 FURTHER WORK

'In film noirs, sex, greed and power tend to displace love as the motivating feature of "romantic relationships", marriages tend to be bleak and unfulfilling, and the family is viewed in a consistently negative light. The films probe the darkest areas of the psyche (obsession and neurosis are common preoccupations) and focus in particular on male sexual anxieties and on the pathology of male violence. Their view of the legal system is frequently highly critical, and figures of the establishment are often shown as corrupt. Overall, they portray a society in which the American dream of success is inverted, alienation and fatalistic helplessness being the dominant moods, and failure the most frequent outcome.'[10]

To what extent do the films that you have studied exemplify this description of film noir?

FURTHER READING

Cameron, Ian, (ed.), *The Movie Book of Film Noir*, Studio Vista, 1992.
Crowther, Bruce, *Film Noir: Reflections in a Dark Mirror*, Columbus Books, 1988.
Hirsch, Foster, *The Dark Side of the Screen: Film Noir*, Da Capo Press, 1986.
Krutnik, Frank, *In a Lonely Street: Film Noir, Genre, Masculinity*, Routledge, 1991.
Barton Palmer, R., *Hollywood's Dark Cinema: The American Film Noir*, Twayne Publishers, 1994.
Silver, Alain and Ward, Elizabeth, (eds.), *Film Noir: An Encyclopedic Reference Guide*, Bloomsbury, 1988.

FURTHER VIEWING

Double Indemnity (Billy Wilder, 1944)
The Big Sleep (Howard Hawks, 1946)
Gilda (Charles Vidor, 1946)
The Postman Always Rings Twice (Tay Garnett, 1946)
Crossfire (Edward Dmytryk, 1947)
The Lady from Shanghai (Orson Welles, 1948)
In a Lonely Place (Nicholas Ray, 1950)
Kiss Me Deadly (Robert Aldrich, 1955)
Farewell My Lovely (Dick Richards, 1975)
Dead Men Don't Wear Plaid (Carl Reiner, 1981)
Body Heat (Lawrence Kasden, 1981)
The Postman Always Rings Twice (Bob Rafelson, 1981)
Trouble in Mind (Alan Rudolph, 1985)
Blue Velvet (David Lynch, 1986)
Kill Me Again (John Dahl, 1989)
Wild at Heart (David Lynch, 1990)
The Grifters (Stephen Frears, 1990)
After Dark My Sweet (James Foley, 1990)
One False Move Carl Franklin, 1991)
Light Sleeper (Paul Schrader, 1991)
Red Rock West (John Dahl, 1993)

NOTES

1 Article in *Life* magazine of 1947 quoted in Thomas Schatz, *Hollywood Genres: Formulas, Filmaking and the Studio System*, Random House, 1981, p11.

2 Taken from the book *Film Noir: An Encyclopedic Reference Guide*, by Alain Silver and Elizabeth Ward, published by Bloomsbury Publishing Plc., 1988, p1.

3 Paul Schrader, 'Notes on Film Noir' in Barry Grant, (ed.), *Film Genre Reader*, University of Texas Press, 1986, p181.

4 In Bill Nichols, (ed.), *Movies and Methods Vol 1*, University of California Press, p338.

5 J. A. Place and L. S. Peterson, 'Some Visual Motifs of Film Noir' in Bill Nichols, *ibid*, p326.

6 *Film Noir: the Dark Side of the Screen*, Da Capo, 1983 p209.

7 'Chinatown and Generic Transformation in Recent American Films' in Barry Grant, (ed.), *Film Genre Reader*, University of Texas Press, 1986, p185.

8 *Ibid*, p184.

9 *Cinemania* 1996, Microsoft (CD–ROM).

10 Michael Walker, 'Film Noir: Introduction' in Ian Cameron, (ed.), *The Movie Book of Film Noir*, London: Studio Vista, 1992, p38.

4

CHAPTER **18** British Cinema of the 1940s

BACKGROUND

Key themes in British cinema of the 1940s are as follows:

■ representation of the British nation
■ representation of class
■ realism.

Both the documentary and fiction film-makers of the 1940s attempted to provide representations of the British at war that would bolster the morale of the people and, in some cases, persuade other countries to join the war effort. The nation was, however, represented differently by individual film-makers: some seemed to anticipate a more classless society after the war whereas others saw the value of the pre-war class structure. Surprisingly, the concerns of the post-war films are often similar to those of war-time, showing a nostalgic desire to retain the war-time spirit of community.

HUMPHREY JENNINGS (1907–50)

Prior to his involvement in documentary film-making Jennings has been involved in Surrealist painting which subsequently influenced his film-making. Many of his films do contain bizarre/surreal images, but it is the way in which he juxtaposes images to create meaning that is perhaps more important.

Jennings was a founder member of Mass Observation an organisation set up in 1936 to observe and record the social habits and customs of the British people – in particular that of the northern working class.

Select filmography
Spare Time (1939)
Britain Can Take It (1940)
Heart of Britain (1941)
Words for Battle (1941)
Listen to Britain (1942)
Fires Were Started (1943) fiction
A Diary for Timothy (1945) fiction

THE CROWN FILM UNIT

The Crown Film Unit was in fact a reincarnation of John Grierson's GPO film unit which had produced highly regarded documentaries in the 1930s such as *Coalface*, *Nightmail* and *Housing Problems*. Grierson, as the pioneer of the British documentary film was critical of the studio bound fiction films that mostly featured the upper classes, supported the status quo and did not deal with real life events. The constraints placed upon the Crown Film Unit by the Ministry of Information in the 1940s would have been familiar to Grierson as throughout the 1930s all his films were made under sponsorship.

CASE STUDIES: DOCUMENTARY

- *Britain Can Take It* (1940)
- *The Heart of Britain* (1941)
- *Listen to Britain* (1942)

Britain Can Take It, *The Heart of Britain* and *Listen to Britain*, all directed by Humphrey Jennings were made during the Second World War (1939–45) by the Crown Film Unit for the Ministry of Information. All three films are powerful pieces of **propaganda** utilising carefully selected and juxtaposed images of the nation. *Listen to Britain*, however, unlike *Britain Can Take It* and *The Heart of Britain* does not make use of a voice-over that directs the audience to an interpretation of the images; instead the audience are left to provide their own 'reading' of the film.

Propaganda

This is a term used pejoratively with reference to any film that consciously attempts to persuade an audience towards certain beliefs and values.

BRITAIN CAN TAKE IT (1940)

US release title: *London Can Take It*
Directors: Humphrey Jennings, Harry Watt
Narration/introduction: Quentin Reynolds (American Journalist)
Music: Vaughan Williams (a London Symphony)
Length: 10 mins

Britain Can Take It served the dual purpose of helping to boost morale at home and persuading the Americans to join the allies as it was also exhibited in the US. Its narrator, Quentin Reynolds, an American journalist working in London was something of a catch as he gave the impression that the film was not simply British propaganda but an independent American production. It is interesting to note that the film was a success in the US and taken on by Warner Brothers for a nation-wide release and it did appear to help sway public opinion in favour of Britain. It was also favourably received at home.

The film starts with an image of St Paul's Cathedral and ends with one of Westminster Abbey, thus introducing the notion that Christianity itself, as well as Britain, is under attack from the Nazis. The style of the voice-over is at times jokey and understated, conveying a feeling of calmness and lack of panic. At the same time the commentator is not neutral, claiming for example, that the Nazis bomb houses, churches, hospitals and workers' flats, while the RAF bomb strategic targets such as munitions works, aeroplane factories and canals. Both London and Britain are also personified which encourages the audience to think of the destruction in human terms, for example:

'London raises her head, shakes the debris of the night from her hair and takes stock of the damage done'.

The devastation caused by the blitz provided Jennings with ample opportunity for capturing surreal images which centred on the way in which life continued as normal in the midst of destruction. For example, the delivery of milk after the bombing, the lines of people walking to work and the bus services. It is significant, however, that the damage shown tends to be limited as in many of the shots the buildings are mostly intact and certainly no bodies are seen.

The people of London are depicted overall as unified and resolute against the enemy although it is interesting to note that with the voice-over turned down the film could be read in a variety of different ways.

 ## THE HEART OF BRITAIN (1941)

Director: Humphrey Jennings
Length: 10 mins

The Heart of Britain, with its concentration on the North of Britain, is clearly a very different project from the London-centred *Britain Can Take It*, despite sharing broadly similar themes. *The Heart of Britain* establishes the countryside as a vital part of British national identity as well as emphasising the importance of the production capabilities of the industrial north. The film opens with images of the northern British countryside (Yorkshire, Derbyshire and Cumberland) combined with shots of the cathedral towers of Durham, Liverpool and Coventry, which serve to bind church and land together, but also convey a sense of history. Jennings then introduces industry as the third element of the equation, showing how the industrial working class form a key part of Britain's past and future greatness.

The middle-class voice-over strongly informs the audience how the images are to be interpreted, but the film is interspersed with to camera interviews by various workers which bring a sense of freshness and authenticity to the film. The role of women in war-time is also emphasised (although this is the most unconvincing part of the film for present day audiences), showing their work in industry and other war-related activities.

Jennings makes use of a performance of Beethoven's Fifth Symphony to show that the British have respect for pre-war Germany, but not for the new Nazi order. At this point in the film the voice-over is temporarily suspended (giving a foretaste of the style of *Listen to Britain*) and the music and images of bomb-damaged houses and churches, and still standing church spires are allowed to speak for themselves.

In the last section of the film Jennings uses a mass performance of the Hallelujah chorus of Handel's *Messiah* (also a German composer) to reinforce the notion of unity and to establish that God is on the side of the British. The voice-over further emphasises that it is the workers that will win the war: '... with all the skill of their hands, the tradition of their crafts and the fire in their hearts'. The last shots of the film juxtapose images of church spires, planes and countryside in a brief montage sequence which allows all the elements to be seamlessly drawn together.

LISTEN TO BRITAIN (1942)

Directors/Script/Editor:	Humphrey Jennings, Stewart McAllister
Producer:	Ian Dalrymple
Length:	20 mins

Figure 18.1 *Listen to Britain*: Unity and calm in war-time   ©BFI

Listen to Britain like *Britain Can Take It* was partly made for export to Canada and America where it was hoped to sway public opinion in favour of joining the war effort. The film is in the form of a complete day in the life of Britain and it is this 24-hour cycle (it starts at 12 o'clock midday) which is the main structuring principle of the film. *Listen to Britain* is also highly experimental, using a **montage** of images and sounds without a voice-over. The film should therefore be classed as an open rather than a closed text as the audience construct their own meanings from the images and sounds, rather than being told how to interpret them. It is this sense of openness that makes it difficult to identify the film as propaganda, but it is still successful however, in putting forward a positive and determined picture of Britain at war and even for modern audiences stirs up feelings of patriotism.

Montage

Montage comes from the French word meaning to mount; it means the assembling of bits of footage to form a whole.

The film opens with images of the natural world: a tree and a field of corn moving in the wind both of which (as in *The Heart of Britain*) establish the importance of the countryside to the identity of Britain. The Blackpool dance floor sequence, in which everyone moves together as one around the room, is also used early on to establish the complete unity of the British people. At the break of dawn the BBC World Service announces 'This is London calling' which further emphasises the BBC's role in bringing the people of Britain together as well as those in other countries.

The music used in the film is a mixture of popular and classical. In the Flanagan and Allan sequence Jennings once again emphasises the unity of the British people by showing everyone whistling along to the songs. The music of Flanagan and Allan flows almost seamlessly on to the Mozart concert at the National Gallery by cutting on the same musical note thus joining the two different musical events together. The choice of this particular concert is significant as, like the composer, the pianist, Myra Hess, is a German. Jennings is once again keen to demonstrate how it is possible to be against fascism, but not against the culture of pre-war Germany – in this way Britain is shown to be a fair and tolerant country. The concert is endorsed by the presence of the Queen, but Jennings is also keen to show the diversity of people enjoying the music.

The finale of the film is held together by *Rule Britannia* (the only **non-diegetic** part of the sound track) and returns to images of corn and fields juxtaposed once again between images of factories and smoking chimneys. Jennings is clearly trying to unite the two together to emphasise the absolute centrality of rural England to its identity but also to acknowledge the necessary reality of industrialisation. The final image of the film, however, is of a long shot of the countryside taken from on high with the camera eventually pulling upwards to focus on the sky and clouds thus ultimately favouring the natural over the industrial. In narrative terms it provides a sense of complete closure, as the film ends where it starts with shots of corn fields – it is also 12 o'clock midday. The 'natural' cycle of the film suggests that the rhythms of British life are themselves entirely natural and timeless and should not be disrupted.

Non-diegetic

Refers to any elements that remain outside the world of the film such as voice-overs, credits and mood-setting music that does not directly originate from the world of the film.

JOHN GRIERSON (1898–1972)

Grierson has been called the 'father of documentary' first coining the term 'documentary' in 1925 in a review of the Robert Flaherty film *Moana*. The phrase 'the creative treatment of actuality' refers to the belief that documentary film-makers should use the real world as a source, but that they are also required to interpret and shape this material in order to reveal the truth.

CASE STUDIES: FICTION

- *In Which We Serve* (1942)
- *Fires Were Started* (1943)
- *Millions Like Us* (1943)
- *The Wicked Lady* (1945)
- *Passport to Pimlico* (1949)

IN WHICH WE SERVE (1942)

Directors:	Noel Coward/David Lean
Producer:	Noel Coward
Screenplay and Music:	Noel Coward
Editors:	David Lean and Thelma Myers
Production Company:	Two Cities
Distributors:	British Lion
Length:	114 mins

Cast

Captain E. V. Kinross:	Noel Coward
Ordinary Seaman Blake:	John Mills
Chief Petty Officer Hardy:	Bernard Miles
Mrs Kinross:	Celia Johnson
Mrs Hardy:	Joyce Carey
Freda Lewis:	Kay Walsh
A young Stoker:	Richard Attenborough

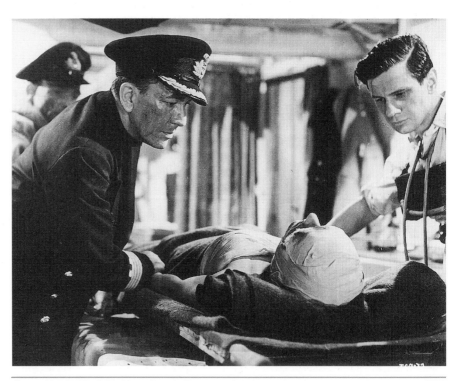

Figure 18.2 *In Which We Serve*: Captain Kinross with an injured man   ©BFI

'Personally I have always believed more in quality than quantity, and nothing will convince me that the levelling of class and rank distinctions and the contemptuous dismissal of breeding as an important factor in life, can lead to anything but dismal mediocrity.'

Noel Coward, Director[1]

The opening of *In Which We Serve* which shows the complete process of building a destroyer, concentrating on the skill of the workers and using a quickly-edited sequence focusing on machinery, is reminiscent of the style of 1930s documentaries.

Otherwise the film is conventional in style and form although audiences were impressed by the realism of the naval battle sequences.

In Which We Serve supports the view that society is hierarchical, stable and unified; everyone in the film seems to know their place and respects their betters. The crew of the *Torrin* can be seen as a metaphor for British war-time society, a self-contained world in which order prevails. No comment is made on pre-war society; it is assumed that after the war society will return to its pre-war state; there is certainly no feeling that change is needed.

The film is structured around flashbacks from three different people's viewpoints as they await rescue: Captain Kinross, Walter Hardy and AB Shorty Blake. Kinross is clearly a member of the upper middle class (loosely based on Lord Mountbatten). Walter Hardy, his wife and her mother belong to the lower middle classes, while Shorty Blake and his family belong to the working class. Coward is keen to point out the basic similarities between the three groups: chiefly their family values, loyalty and love of the HMS *Torrin*. The way in which each of the groups is represented, however also points out their differences – they obviously belong to different classes.

Coward essentially shows the upper classes to possess classic leadership qualities: rational judgement, eloquence, wit and an ability to interact with all, while the working classes are depicted as being eager to please their betters, loyal, 'salt of the earth' types and unsophisticated. All, however, have equal importance in defeating the common enemy. They are also literally in the same boat and for much of the film they all face death together as the German planes shoot at them in the water. None of the characters question their relative positions despite the clear material disparities between the three groups. It is accepted that Britain is a country made up of very different groups of people who are categorised according to class. In the central part of the film Shorty Blake and his new wife (Freda) and Captain Kinross and his wife meet on a train. Shorty and Freda are subsequently shown swigging from bottles in their compartment while the Kinross's have a white-linen lunch in the dining car. The material differences between the two are shown to be both natural and accepted.

In Which We Serve highlights the importance of teamwork through a number of key sequences.

- The building of the boat
- The loading of the ammunition when the ship is under attack

The rigid chain of command involved in team work could be seen as mirroring the rigid class structure in Britain with the King/government on top of the pile giving orders.

As in other war-time films communal leisure activities (such as singing 'Roll out the Barrel' at the music hall) are also valued. These are similar to those shown in *Listen to Britain*, but in *In Which We Serve* the activities tend to be more class-bound with each class enjoying separate activities.

The film is also keen to show that it is not just those who are fighting that lose their lives, but also those left at home (*Millions Like Us* also plays heavily on this theme), although curiously the role of those at home seems not to be an active one. None of the women actually seem to play a part in the war work; their role is to maintain the family (the future of Britain) and to wait.

The film also supports the notion that everyone should make sacrifices and that everyone will experience loss in war-time. It is not just those away fighting that will suffer, but also those at home such as Kath Hardy and her mother. The reaction to the deaths is restrained and accepting and there is no sense that the state could be to blame in any way (Kath decides not to use the air-raid shelter or to go to the country to escape the bombing). Despite the loss and grief there is no sense of anyone becoming disillusioned with the war (no one seems tired and they certainly don't complain) – it is a war that everyone wants to fight.

In the Navy everyone must be prepared to sacrifice their life, no one must desert their duty. Richard Attenborough plays the young stoker who leaves his post and is subsequently held up as an example of cowardliness by Kinross – eventually, however even he is made a hero.

In Which We Serve, like many of the British war-time documentaries, supports the idea that rural England is worth fighting for: the Kinross picnic in the countryside shows rural England to be a paradise completely removed from the war which is taking place in the skies above. It is certainly an England that seems worth preserving.

 FIRES WERE STARTED (1943)

(aka *I was a Fireman*)

Director:	Humphrey Jennings
Photography:	C. Pennington-Richards
Sound:	Ken Cameron
Music:	William Alwyn
Editor:	Stewart McAllister
Producer:	Ian Dalrymple
Script:	Humphrey Jennings, Maurice Richardson
Production company:	Crown Film Unit
Length:	80 mins

Cast

Walters:	Philip Wilson-Dickson
Johnny Daniels:	Fred Griffith
Barrett:	William Sansom
Sub-officer Dykes:	George Gravett
J. Rumbold:	Loris Rey
S. H. Jackson:	Johnny Houghton
B. A. Brown:	T. P. Smith

Despite its status as a fiction film it would seem that Humphrey Jennings' *Fires Were Started* with its use of 'real' firemen, real locations and documentary style conforms to John Grierson's vision of documentary films as 'the creative treatment of actuality'.

Fires Were Started reflects the theme of unity to be found in many of the other films of the 1940s. The first part of the film introduces the fire-fighting team of a London sub-station – most of the actors were actual voluntary war-time fire-fighters borrowed for the duration of the shoot. It is quickly made apparent that the crew are from different walks of life and classes, yet they all work well as a team, although there is some tension between them. This sense of unity is reinforced by the arrival of the new man Barrett who is middle class and was an advertising copy writer before the war. He is initially regarded suspiciously by the others on arrival at the station, but is subsequently accepted by all the men. Barrett later binds the group together further by playing 'One Man went to Mow' on the piano as the fire crew get ready for the night ahead.

The narrative of the film emphasises unity, as fire fighting as an activity relies on teamwork – the job cannot be done by an individual. Much of the film therefore concentrates on the men working together, not just in the warehouse fire, but also before and after in the preparation and cleaning of equipment. The long build-up in the opening sequences (including scenes at the homes of the firemen) gives depth

Figure 18.3 *Fires Were Started*: The spirit of war-time Britain   ©BFI

and individuality to the characters and also allows Jennings to reunite them through communal singing, sleeping and eating.

The warehouse fire forms the dramatic central part of the film in which the fire crew are stretched nearly to breaking point. The section also allows the audience to be shown how the crew is monitored and supported by the central control station, linked by telephone to numerous other centres across London. Women play a key part in the running of the control station and in one scene after the control station is partially bombed they immediately carry on with their work as though nothing has happened. There is little mention made of the Germans; the fire-fighters have a professional job to do – there is no time for complaining.

The death of Jacko near the end of the film highlights the fact that in war-time sacrifices inevitably need to be made. Despite the enormous sense of loss, it is also made clear that Jacko's death was not in vain as the fire is extinguished, the rest of the fire crew have survived and the munitions ship is saved. The fire crew as a whole could be seen as a microcosm of Britain at war (in the same way that the crew of the HMS *Torrin* stands in for the British nation). The almost surreal image of the shiny munitions ship at the end of the film could be seen as a metaphor for the continuing fighting spirit of England.

MILLIONS LIKE US (1943)

Directors/Scriptwriters:	Frank Launder & Sidney Gilliat
Producer:	Edward Black
Production Company:	Gainsborough Pictures
Length:	103 mins

Cast

Celia:	Patricia Roc
Fred:	Gordon Jackson
Jennifer:	Anne Crawford
Gwen Price:	Meg Jenkins
Annie Earnshaw:	Terry Randall
Charlie Forbes:	Eric Portman
Jim:	Moore Marriot
Charters:	Basil Radford
Caldicot:	Naunton Wayne
Phillis:	Joy Shelton

Figure 18.4 *Millions Like Us*: The contribution of women to the war effort   ©BFI

Millions Like Us centres on the war-time lives of those on the home front. Unlike those in *In Which We serve* the three main characters all contribute to the war effort. The film acknowledges, however, that many are not initially keen to carry out this work and that people are often fed up with war-time discomforts. Jim Crowson (the father) for example complains to his daughter Celia '. . . coming home to an empty house, no fire in the grate, her out on the tiles, no supper, no bed made, I could pass away in that bed and nobody might know for weeks' but when Celia says that she will try to stay at home rather than help the war effort he exclaims, 'Oh no you won't, if the country needs you it needs you. Nobody is going to say I'm not patriotic.' Thus underneath the gripes, most are shown to be fiercely patriotic. Eventually, however, only Jim Crowson is left at home as his son, daughters and daughter-in-law are assigned posts elsewhere. What is interesting here is that the film allows dissatisfaction about the war to be expressed, but underneath there is still a firm resolve about fighting the enemy. The sequences also highlight the importance of the family unit and how sacrifices are being made by everyone in war-time. Celia's placement is not what she was expecting, having dreamt of joining the Land Army and having romantic liaisons with officers. She is however, disappointed to be assigned to a munitions factory in Stockford making aircraft components.

Social change

Millions Like Us deals with the issue of class explicitly. Early in the film two officers (Charters and Caldicot) are shown in a first class train compartment reassuring each other that they won't be disturbed, but at this point an avalanche of evacuee children pour into the carriage. This incident demonstrates that pre-war class distinctions and privileges have been swept away by the war.

At the factory, issues of class are once again confronted using four key figures: Celia Crowson, Gwen Price, Jennifer Knowles, Annie Earnshaw and Charlie Forbes. Jennifer Knowles is a member of the upper middle class and is initially disdainful of everyone else she meets. She is unsuitably dressed, arrives by taxi and smokes using a cigarette holder. She sets herself aside from the other members of the group asking if it would be possible to have a single room at the hostel. She seems only concerned with putting herself first and is not fully integrated into the group until the end of the film.

Gwen Price is the daughter of a Welsh miner and has attended the University of South Wales. She is politically aware and makes comments on living conditions in pre-war society (comments which would be considered to be politically dangerous in films such as *In Which We Serve*). She is impressed by the standard of accommodation offered by the hostel:

'Where's the long bare dormitory with 'the Lord shall provide' framed on the wall as a reminder that nobody else will. Where's the rows and rows of iron bedsteads with rusty knobs and little enamel pots under them – takes a war to do it.'

In the same sequence she tells Celia about her background:

'Dad's a miner, a wonderful time we had on the dole – if you don't know when you're well off I do. I was brought up in a distressed area, you know, lovely damp patches of fungus blossoming on the wallpaper, and a bath in a zinc tub in the kitchen Saturday nights – dizzy luxury that was. So if someone suddenly develops a social conscience I'm not going to sneeze at it.'

The message is that the war has brought social change that was unimaginable before the war – overall the film questions whether the changes will be maintained after the war.

Annie Earnshaw is working class, blunt, straightforward and speaks her mind. She ends up sharing a bedroom with Jennifer Knowles whose habits and mannerisms she finds extremely funny. In fact she is able to see straight through the airs and graces that Jennifer puts on. Jennifer in her turn finds some of Annie's habits strange, such as wearing her underclothes to bed. The sequences at the hostel show initially how the two have little in common and certainly don't understand each other.

Charlie Forbes the supervisor at the factory is lower middle class and well aware of the pre-war social conditions of Britain. He is both attracted and repelled by Jennifer. He criticises her outlook and values and at the end of the film refuses to even contemplate marrying her because he is afraid that after the war the class barrier will be raised again putting their relationship under threat. He hopes for a new (Labour) government:

'The world's roughly made up of two kinds of people – you're one sort and I'm the other. Oh, we're together now there's a war on – we need to be. What's going to happen when it's all over? Shall we go on like this, or shall we slide back – that's what I want to know. I'm not marrying you, Jennifer, until I'm sure.'

Despite the differences between the individuals at the hostel, as the film progresses they grow to understand each other. The factory itself serves to bind them together as a whole and communal values develop. There are shots of masses of people travelling to work by different methods of transport followed by a closely edited sequence of shots showing the complete process of building a plane – starting with the production of the small components. These shots serve to reinforce the message that despite the different nature of the tasks and the different nature of the people fulfilling them, all share a common aim.

Notions of community are enhanced further by the dance sequence at the hostel (reminiscent of Jennings' films) in which even Jennifer is eventually forced to join. At the end the camera pulls back to show everyone dancing in one huge circle. When the factory is under attack teamwork is emphasised as factory control directs operations and the fire crews put out the fire. It is significant that Fred proposes to Celia in the cosiness of a full pub with pint glasses being passed between them – the private thus becoming the public.

At the end of the film after Celia has heard that Fred has died in action Gwen encourages her to join the communal singing ('Waiting at the Church') and becomes part of the community again. It is also worth noting that in the background Jennifer Knowles is also joining in with the singing and has finally been absorbed by the group.

THE WICKED LADY (1945)

Director:	Leslie Arliss
Producer:	R. J. Minney
Script:	Leslie Arliss, Gordon Glennon, Aimee Stuart
Editor:	Terence Fisher
Production company:	Gainsborough Pictures Ltd
Length:	104 mins

Cast

Captain Terry Jackson:	James Mason
Barbara Worth:	Margaret Lockwood
Caroline:	Patricia Roc
Sir Ralph:	Griffith Jones
Kit:	Michael Rennie
Hogarth:	Felix Aylmer
Cousin Agatha:	Martita Hunt

As a film *The Wicked Lady* sits uneasily with the likes of *In Which We Serve*, *Millions Like Us* and *Fires Were Started* – indeed in terms of realism and representation it appears to be in opposition to them. *The Wicked Lady* is not about the different classes pulling together in times of hardship, in fact it isn't about hardship at all. The main characters belong to the ruling class and the working class are heavily stereotyped with strong accents and slow speech. The film is set in the 17th century, far removed from the austerity of post-war Britain allowing characters to behave in

Figure 18.5 *The Wicked Lady*: Escapist melodrama   ©BFI

ways that would not be acceptable or possible in the present day. The film is not about sacrifice, it is about fulfilling individualistic desires (in a way it could be compared to *Passport to Pimlico* which also has similar themes). Ultimately it demonstrates that these individual/selfish desires can only end in disaster – despite the fact that a great deal of fun is had along the way. *The Wicked Lady* allows the audience to live out their desires and fantasies of individual freedom vicariously, but returns them safely to their home lives at its close.

The film could be classed as a woman's film in the sense that it appeals to a female audience and concentrates on female protagonists. It also depicts the central character (Barbara) as strong, independent and more than a match for any man – although at the end of the film the more meek and mild Caroline wins the day.

 ***PASSPORT TO PIMLICO* (1949)**

Director:	Henry Cornelius
Producer:	Michael Balcon
Associate producer:	E. V. H. Emmett
Script:	T. E. B. Clarke
Editor:	Michael Truman
Production company:	Ealing
Length:	84 mins

Cast

Arthur Pemberton:	Stanley Holloway
Connie Pemberton:	Betty Warren

Shirley Pemberton:	Barbara Murray
Duke of Burgundy:	Paul Dupuis
Professor Hatton-Jones:	Margaret Rutherford
Frank Huggins:	John Slater
Molly:	Jane Hylton
Wix:	Raymond Huntley
P. C. Spiller:	Philip Stainton
Fred Cowan:	Sidney Tafler
Hermione Baddeley:	Edie Randall
Garland:	Frederick Piper
Bert Fitch:	Charles Hawtrey
Coroner:	Stuart Lindsell
Straker:	Naunton Wayne
Gregg:	Basil Radford
Inspector Bashford:	Michael Hordon
Bassett:	Arthur Howard

Passport to Pimlico is chiefly about a desire to recapture the collective spirit of war-time England. It is set at a time (probably summer 1947) when communal values are being challenged by individualist capitalist ones. There is still a strong sense of community in the film, but the people of Miramont Place are divided between the new entrepreneurs and those keen to retain war-time values. Pemberton (politically to the left) wants a public leisure centre to be built on the bomb site. Wix, the bank manager (politically to the right), thinks that the land should be sold off to businesses for short term profit – the explosion of the bomb disrupts proceedings.

The subsequent discovery of the treasure and the document proclaiming that Miramont Place belongs to Burgundy brings rapid change. The locals suddenly realise that they are not bound by the rules of England – they can make up their own. Wix the bank manager is able to assert himself over his superiors and even the local policeman indulges in an after-hours pint. In the same scene everyone in the

Figure 18.6 *Passport to Pimlico*: Desire to re-capture war-time spirits   ©BFI

pub defies the authorities by merrily tearing up their ration cards and identity papers and throwing them into the air. The next day the consequences of their actions become apparent: illegal trading, lawlessness and near mob rule. The atmosphere of the previous night has completely vanished and Pemberton is keen to rejoin the nation and embrace its rules. Wix, while handing out loans to the traders, disagrees and wants to remain independent.

The British Government allows events to escalate and eventually puts up a boundary around Miramont Place. It is this part of the film that sums up the whole. The siege culture, the self-enforced rationing, the communal meals at fixed times, the hardship and lack of water this time do truly recreate the values and comradeship brought about by the deprivation of war-time. Much humour is derived from the newsreels proclaiming for example the 'Wix Aid Plan' and the 'Pimlico Line' and comparing the siege of Miramont Place to Britain's role in the Second World War. A true sense of community is felt as everyone helps each other. The different positions taken by Wix and Pemberton now seem irrelevant – there are other considerations to be thought of. Hundreds of people turn out to help the people of Burgundy by throwing food over the barbed wire fence to replace the stocks lost in the flood. At the end of the film the people of Miramont Place are more than happy to re-embrace rationing and identity cards and to be accepted back into the fold – a firm sense of community re-established.

 **FURTHER WORK**

Documentary

Discuss how the images and commentary of *Britain Can Take It* have been carefully selected and placed together to show the strength and resolve of the British people.

'*Listen to Britain* is not propaganda, it is art?' Discuss.

Both *Listen to Britain* and *The Heart of Britain* are forms of persuasion. Which of the two is more successful and why?

Fiction

Compare and contrast the representation of British character and society in films made during and after the war.

To what extent could *Millions Like Us*, *In Which We Serve* and *Fires Were Started* be described as 'realistic'.

Was *The Wicked Lady* an escapist fantasy or a film which had a bearing on post-war society?

 FURTHER READING

Aldgate, Anthony and Richards, Jeffrey, Britain Can Take It: the British Cinema in the Second World War, Basil Blackwell, 1986.

Higson, Andrew, ' "Britain's Outstanding Contributions to the Film": The documentary-realist tradition' in Charles Barr, *All Our Yesterdays: Ninety Years of British Cinema*, BFI, 1986, pp72–97.

Higson, Andrew, *Waving the Flag: Constructing a National Cinema in Britain*, Oxford University Press, 1995.

Murphy, Robert, *Realism and Tinsel: Cinema and Society in Britain, 1939–1948*, Routledge, 1989.

Murphy, Robert, (ed.), *The British Cinema Book*, BFI, 1997.

 FURTHER VIEWING

Men of the Lightship (David McDonald, 1940)
One of Our Aircraft is Missing (Michael Powell and Emeric Pressburger, 1942)
Went the Day Well? (Alberto Cavalcanti, 1942)
The Bells Go Down (Basil Dearden, 1943)
The Life and Times of Colonel Blimp (Michael Powell and Emeric Pressburger, 1943)
This Happy Breed (David Lean, 1944)
A Canterbury Tale (Michael Powell and Emeric Pressburger, 1944)
Brief Encounter (David Lean, 1945)
Hue and Cry (Charles Crichton, 1947)
The Blue Lamp (Basil Dearden, 1949)

NOTES

[1] Quoted in Anthony Aldgate and Jeffrey Richards, *Britain Can Take It: the British Cinema in the Second World War*, Basil Blackwell, 1986, pp191–192.

CHAPTER 19 British Cinema of
the 1950s and 1960s

'Here at last is a film [*Saturday Night and Sunday Morning*] which not only in the contemporary fashion is about the working class, but of and for the working class ... It shows uncompromisingly that Arthur's weaknesses – and his developing strength – spring not from selfishness and irresponsibility but from the oppression and sheer frustrations of being a worker under the present social set-up.'

Nina Hibbin in the *Daily Worker*[1]

'... just that little bit too bland and rosy to be altogether true.'

John Russell Taylor (on *Every Day Except Christmas*)[2]

'It was when we were filming it that they were producing an effect on the entire population of Britain, for better or worse, which badly needed to be documented. I think that they were the first to give a confidence to the youth of the country which led to the disappearance of the Angry Young Men with a defensive mien. The Beatles sent the class thing sky high: they laughed it out of existence and, I think, introduced a tone of equality more successfully than any other single factor that I know.'

Dick Lester (on *A Hard Day's Night*)[3]

BACKGROUND

The historian Arthur Marwick[4] uses the term **cultural revolution** to characterise the social changes which he argues began in the 1950s and continued throughout the 1960s. He identifies three main elements in this period of accelerating social change:

■ sections of the population that had only led a meagre material existence previously enjoyed a rise in their standard of living

■ new technologies, especially in communications and transport, became more widely available

■ 'an attack, of unprecedented breadth and intensity, on established social controls, traditional hierarchies, and received assumptions' was set in train.

THE 'CULTURAL REVOLUTION': A CHRONOLOGY

1955 The introduction of commercial television Principle of equal pay for male and female teachers accepted

1956 The introduction of the Premium Savings Bond scheme; *Look Back in Anger* at the Royal Court

1957 *The Uses of Literacy* by Richard Hoggart published; Wolfenden Committee recommended that homosexual acts between consenting adults in private be legalised.

1958 Campaign for Nuclear Disarmament founded and film *March to Aldermaston* made by Free Cinema group

Eighty per cent of the population could receive BBC and ITV

1959 *Room at the Top*

1960 End of National Service; contraceptive pill introduced

1961 First issue of *Private Eye*

1962 First *Beatles'* record

1963 Mary Whitehouse began her Clean Up TV campaign

1964 Pirate station Radio Caroline begins broadcasting; Mods and Rockers clash at Clacton and Margate; Labour government elected

1965 Race Relations Act; Capital Punishment suspended

1966 *Time* published 'Swinging London' edition

1967 London School of Economics occupied by students; Abortion Act; Sexual Offences Act legalised homosexual acts; end of pirate radio and launch of Radio 1, 2, 3, 4; first mass demonstration against the Vietnam war

1968 Age of majority lowered to 18

1969 Divorce Reform Act; abolition of capital punishment; Isle of Wight festival

1970 Women's Liberation Conference at Oxford; Conservative election victory; Equal Pay Act

Harold MacMillan (1894–1986)

Conservative Prime Minister from 1957–63.

Karl Marx (1818–83)

As a communist, Marx believed that capitalism was based on the exploitation of the working class. He thought that this exploitation would become more severe and predicted that the working class would unite to overthrow the oppressive economic and political system.

The rise in the standard of living reflected a period of relative economic stability and full employment. In 1957 the Conservative Prime Minister, **Harold MacMillan** stated 'Most of our people have never had it so good'. Some commentators thought that the economic changes signalled the end of the working class as a force which would overthrow capitalism as predicted by **Karl Marx**. Others thought that the working class were disappearing as a distinctive group or at the very least were now fully integrated into society. This view was justified by reference to a number of changes that had taken place since 1945: the establishment of the Welfare State, increased educational opportunities, slum clearance and home building programmes as well as the new material affluence. The film-makers of Free Cinema and the New Wave offered their own interpretations of the new affluent society. They presented positive portraits of distinctive working class experiences in their documentaries, but the fiction films stressed the constraints and inhibitions of these experiences. The working class people in these films, however, are generally working, unlike many of the characters in the films of the 1980s and 1990s who live in a harsher economic climate.

The notable development in terms of communications was the growth of the mass media, especially television. Many commentators thought that this growth would mean that people became more reliant on the media for their knowledge and opinions about the world and less on the people around them in the local community. This trend would also be strengthened by the fact that old communities were being broken up and new areas of residence were being developed. The film-makers of the New Wave tend to present a jaundiced view of television, in particular, as it represents the emergence of a culture based on commercialism rather than individual or collective creativity. This negative view of television can be contrasted with the positive view of radio presented in *Listen to Britain* (Humphrey Jennings, 1942). As Charles Barr argues, the radio in this film – and in others – is an aspect of the unity of the nation whereas in films such as *Saturday Night and Sunday Morning*, *The Loneliness of the Long Distance Runner* and *A Kind of Loving*, television divides young from old and male from female.

Finally, the films of the late 1950s and early 1960s register changes that are taking place, but also seem to give warning of further changes to come. The energy of the predominantly young male characters seems to be searching for an outlet and there is a feeling that the new material stability is not enough. As Arthur Seaton says in *Saturday Night and Sunday Morning*, 'There's a lot more in life, Bert, than me mam and dad have got.'

FREE CINEMA

Free Cinema was a name given to a series of six programmes of short films shown at the National Film Theatre between 1956 and 1959. These programmes were organised by **Lindsay Anderson**, Karel Reisz, Walter Lassally and John Fletcher whose work, as well as that of other British and European film-makers, was represented. The aim of Free Cinema was to allow film-makers to have creative freedom and to be free from commercial demands. As contributors to film journals, Anderson and Reisz were critical of British films, the British film industry and British film culture. According to the introductory notes which accompanied the third Free Cinema Programme (May 1957), British films possessed the following characteristics:

- They were class-bound
- They did not respond to contemporary life
- They did not fulfil a critical role
- They were dominated by the culture of London and the South-east
- They ignored the rich cultural diversity of Britain

The film industry was seen as being geared only to the mass commercial market and film critics and reviewers were accused of not considering cinema as an art. With very limited resources Free Cinema set out to remedy this situation.

Lindsay Anderson (1923–94)

Was born in India where his father was an officer in the British Army. He was educated at Oxford University where he was a co founder of a film journal, *Sequence* (1947–52) which was groundbreaking in its treatment of popular cinema. He continued to write about cinema for journals and newspapers and was to later write a study of John Ford's films. In the 1950s he directed a number of short films, five episodes of the Robin Hood series for television as well as television commercials. He also directed in the theatre notably, at The Royal Court Theatre, London, where innovative plays like *Look Back in Anger* were premiered.

CASE STUDIES

- *Every Day Except Christmas* (1957)
- *We are the Lambeth Boys* (1959)
- *Saturday Night and Sunday Morning* (1960)
- *A Kind of Loving* (1962)
- *This Sporting Life* (1963)
- *Carry on Cabby* (1963)
- *Goldfinger* (1964)
- *A Hard Day's Night* (1964)

EVERY DAY EXCEPT CHRISTMAS (1957) AND WE ARE THE LAMBETH BOYS (1959)

Every Day Except Christmas

Director:	Lindsay Anderson
Producers:	Leon Clore and Karel Reisz
Length:	40 mins

We are the Lambeth Boys

Director:	Karel Reisz
Producer:	Leon Clore
Length:	50 mins

Karel Reisz (1926–)

Was born in Czechoslovakia and came to England at the age of 12. He was educated at Cambridge University. He wrote for *Sequence* and *Sight and Sound* and made friends with Lindsay Anderson when they were both making documentaries. He published a study of editing in 1953 and made *Momma Don't Allow* with Tony Richardson in 1956. He went on to make feature films in Britain and Hollywood.

Every Day Except Christmas and *We are the Lambeth Boys* reflected an interest in and respect for the working class whether at work or leisure. They were financed by the Ford Motor Company for whom **Karel Reisz** was working. He had become head of the Ford Motor Company's TV and Films programme in 1956. This position enabled him to make some documentaries of his own choice. Although these carried Ford's name, they were not primarily advertisements for its products.

Every Day Except Christmas was not planned in any detail. Elizabeth Sussex reports that the shooting was improvised although about five months was spent editing the footage to produce a very controlled piece of work.[5] It starts in a market garden in Sussex and follows the journey of a lorry laden with lettuces, mushrooms, and roses through the night to Covent Garden. While most people are asleep the market awakes: produce is unloaded and displays of fruit and flowers and built up. At 4.30 am the flower market workers take a break in a café amongst the early morning customers. After this break the more local produce of ordinary vegetables arrives; salesmen and buyers strike deals and finally the purchases are transported away from the market.

The film follows the daily cycle of work which takes place every day except Christmas day. In a number of respects it can be seen as employing an organic metaphor.

- Firstly, there is a daily cycle that has to be completed. This is based on the perishable quality of the produce that comes from all over England and from abroad

- Secondly, the film records the process of building up the displays which 'take shape and grow'. The camera even participates in this process, panning rhythmically as the produce is unloaded or passed from person to person

- Thirdly, the film suggests that the workers control their own pace of work. They know what has to be done and they get on with it without, seemingly, any supervision or any kind of friction other than ordinary everyday banter

- Finally, the soundtrack completes the world of the film. It provides a range of natural sounds, whistling, singing, fragments of conversation, folk-influenced music, and a subdued and mellow voice-over commentary by Alun Owen. In its use of sound it could be compared with *Listen to Britain* by Humphrey Jennings, who was admired by the director, Lindsay Anderson

Overall, the film celebrates the unheroic, but necessary labour depicted in the film. It affirms the importance of a group of workers who are unacknowledged, but who do something on which everyone depends. In this way it could be interpreted as a socialist film. The film is not, however, easy to interpret politically, because it can also be read as a conservative film. The film does not, for example, enquire into how the work is rewarded and suggests everyone has their part to play in society. Elizabeth Sussex in her study of Lindsay Anderson offers a humanistic reading. She applauds the film because it is affectionate and personalises the workers: 'These are people who work, not working-class people'.[6]

A potential problem for a modern audience is that although the film is dedicated to individuals and a number are referred to in the commentary, the workers are not accorded the privilege of speaking for themselves. No doubt this was determined by the budget and available technology, but it does give the impression of a view from the outside.

We are the Lambeth Boys was the second film in Ford's *Look at Britain* series. Karel Reisz, the director, visited about 40 youth clubs before he found one to his liking. Along with Walter Lassally and John Fletcher he visited the club, Alford House in Kennington, London, for six months and this possibly explains why the boys and girls of the club betray little awareness of the camera. John Russell Taylor describes *Every Day Except Christmas* as 'just that little bit too bland and rosy to be altogether true'[2] and the same can be said of *We are the Lambeth Boys*.

The commentary of the film places the group as part of 'the rowdy generation that's forever in the headlines'. This phrase is used ironically, because the film wishes to challenge the notion of young people as a problem. This is achieved by showing them socialising both inside and outside the club. They are allowed the freedom to express a range of views, but on the whole the film's voice-over commentary tends to speak for them.

A point of view is also implicit in its use of sound and images when it is contrasting the work and leisure activities of the young people. After the first sequence based mainly at the club a second sequence looks at school and work. This sequence starts with a school assembly attended by two of the boys. The assembly starts with a hymn *The King of Love my Shepherd Is* and this sombre music continues as the film cuts to a number of boys and girls at work. The conviviality and collective activity of the club scenes is replaced by individual activity which is often isolated in the frame. The use of music, editing, camera positions and framing thus creates a contrast for the audience, but the film does not explore how the young people think about or experience the differences between their work and leisure. In making these contrasts, the sequence demonstrates that documentary films often have a point of view which is stated implicitly in the use of film form.

THE BRITISH NEW WAVE

A number of the participants of 'free cinema' went on to make the feature films that became known as the British New Wave (1959–63). The films in this group continued the concern to portray aspects of working class experience. The film directors, Lindsay Anderson, Karel Reisz and **Tony Richardson**, were certainly not working class. They were, however, able to benefit from a number of recent successful novels and plays by writers who had experience of working class life in the Midlands and the North of England. The films emphasise an examination of character and are distinguished by strong performances by a number of emerging actors and actresses: Alan Bates, Tom Courtenay, Julie Christie, Albert Finney, Rachel Roberts and Rita Tushingham. The films also place the characters in real locations and this authenticates the claim that these films have a reality often lacking in the British cinema of the time.

Tony Richardson

Was born in Shipley, Yorkshire. He was educated at Wadham College, Oxford. He was a BBC television producer before becoming a theatrical producer at the Royal Court Theatre, where he also directed *Look Back in Anger* written by John Osborne. He subsequently co-founded Woodfall Film Productions with Osborne in 1958.

Key films of the New Wave

Look Back in Anger (Tony Richardson, 1959) from the play by John Osborne
Room at the Top (Jack Clayton, 1959) from the novel by John Braine
Saturday Night and Sunday Morning (Karel Reisz, 1960) from the novel by Alan Sillitoe
The Entertainer (Tony Richardson, 1960) from the play by John Osborne
A Taste of Honey (Tony Richardson, 1961) from the play by Shelagh Delaney
A Kind of Loving (John Schlesinger, 1962) from the novel by Stan Barstow
The Loneliness of the Long Distance Runner (Tony Richardson, 1962) from the novel by Alan Sillitoe
This Sporting Life (Lindsay Anderson, 1963) from the novel by David Storey
Billy Liar (John Schlesinger, 1963) from the novel by Keith Waterhouse and the play by Keith Waterhouse and Willis Hall.

THE REPRESENTATION OF GENDER AND THE ROLE OF WOMEN

Women had an important role to play in the economy during the Second World War but many had to relinquish the jobs that they had occupied as they were designated 'men's work'. Their post-war role was to return to the home and concentrate on child-care. In the post-war period, however, childbirth tended to be safer and women tended to have fewer children so, as a result, raising a family took up less of a woman's lifespan and this led to an increase in the number of married women returning to work. Between 1951 and 1961 the proportion of married women at work increased from one quarter to one third but women still tended to be identified with the domestic sphere. There were a number of reasons for this:

- married women tended to work part-time

- their work was often seen as a supplement to their husband's wage

- some commentators pointed to the dangers of women not being at home for their children referring to the concept of maternal deprivation or by predicting an increase in juvenile delinquency.

Perhaps the major economic role visualised for women was as consumers, specially of the more widely available consumer durables such as washing machines, vacuum cleaners and refrigerators which promised to reduce the drudgery of household tasks. It was not until the later 1960s that a thorough-going analysis of gender began to emerge.

SATURDAY NIGHT AND SUNDAY MORNING (1960)

Director: Karel Reisz
Producer: Harry Saltzman
Production company: Woodfall
Screenplay: Alan Sillitoe (from his own novel)
Length: 89 mins

Cast
Arthur: Albert Finney
Doreen: Shirley Ann Field
Brenda: Rachel Roberts
Aunt Ada: Hylda Baker
Bert: Norman Rossington
Jack: Bryan Pringle

Figure 19.1 *Saturday Night, Sunday Morning*: Don't let them grind you down   ©BFI

The central character of *Saturday Night and Sunday Morning* (made by the film company **Woodfall**) is Arthur Seaton, a young lathe operator in the Raleigh bicycle factory in Nottingham. The roar of machinery anticipates the pre-credit sequence of the film which reveals the shop floor of the factory, pans across it and tracks in to Arthur at his machine. He is introduced by means of a voice-over. This is barked out by the actor Albert Finney and it is surely the most aggressive ever recorded in British cinema. He is unreservedly combative in his attitude to work, the other workers around him, the foreman and life in general. He derides the older generation in the factory and later he criticises his own parents for their placid

Woodfall

Woodfall films (1958) was founded by John Osborne, Tony Richardson and the American Harry Saltzman (who left in 1961 and subsequently became involved with the James Bond films) and continued to make films throughout the 1960s.

accommodation to life. He scoffs at Jack, a fellow worker, who aspires to a higher position in the factory hierarchy and who is unaware that Arthur is having an affair with his wife, Brenda. Arthur Seaton stands out from and clearly distinguishes himself from the people around him.

Although Arthur is self-centred and uninterested in the point-of-view of anyone else, the audience can identify with his desire not to be ground down by the demands of work. It is this work that hangs like a pall over the rest of the film. It requires physical effort, repetition, and a grim calculation about the amount produced by his piece-work. Leisure is an escape from all of this. It releases new energies for a drinking competition, his adulterous affair with Brenda, a spot of fishing with his cousin, Bert, or a new sexual liaison with Doreen, the young woman he meets in a pub.

In terms of the representation of gender the film draws a clear distinction between male and female. The women in the film are mainly presented in relation to Arthur's activities and in this respect men and women are shown to have very different roles in the home. For example, both Mrs Seaton and Brenda serve Arthur at the kitchen table: he sits while they stand and serve. The film also indulges in some misogynistic pleasure at the expense of Ma Bull. Arthur shoots this stereotypical busybody with an air-rifle as she stands sentinel at the back entry to the terraced houses. The women in the film are not, however, totally passive: Brenda seeks her own sexual pleasure with Arthur, and Doreen has a degree of assertiveness and confidence.

The film has an episodic structure but nevertheless it is Arthur's pleasure seeking and its consequences that provide the film with its narrative momentum. The fairground scene and the subsequent beating-up of Arthur by two soldiers are the culmination of Arthur's experiences outside work and the audience is led to anticipate such an outcome from the narrative elements that are assembled prior to this sequence. The fact that the film does centre on Arthur has led some commentators to argue that the film is a study of an unusual individual, rather than a general examination of working class life in the 1950s. In terms of British cinema, however, the film has a lot to offer in its use of locations and its attempt to document the language, dress and lifestyle of a particular place and time. Other characters in the film also suggest a range of responses to the circumstances in which they find themselves. Bert, for example, shares some of Arthur's attitudes, but he is much more solid and does not understand Arthur's generalised anger at the world.

A KIND OF LOVING (1962)

Director:	John Schlesinger
Producer:	Joseph Janni
Screenplay:	Willis Hall and Keith Waterhouse
Length:	112 mins

Cast

Vic Brown:	Alan Bates
Ingrid Rothwell:	June Ritchie
Mrs Rothwell:	Thora Hird
Mr Brown:	Pert Palmer
Mrs Brown:	Gwen Nelson
Christine:	Pat Keen
David:	David Mahlowe
Jeff:	James Bolam
Whymper:	Leonard Rossiter

The main character of *A Kind of Loving* is Vic Brown. He works as a draughtsman in Whittaker's factory in a northern town. Like *Saturday Night and Sunday Morning* the film focuses on the relationship of the main character to women. Vic is close to his sister Christine, whose marriage to David opens the film. Close to his heart, literally though, is the book of pin-ups he carries in his inside jacket-pocket. To fulfil his sexual desires he pursues Ingrid Rothwell and he eventually seduces her in the front room of her mother's house. The resultant pregnancy forces the couple into marriage. Unfortunately it also forces them into the home of Mrs Rothwell whose exclusive relationship with Ingrid alienates Vic. After Ingrid suffers a miscarriage the couple decide to leave Mrs Rothwell's house, to get a flat and attempt to start their relationship again.

Like *Saturday Night and Sunday Morning*, the film has a strong sense of place created by the location shots of the factory, the streets, waste ground, a football match and the park where Vic and Ingrid meet. There are indications that the urban landscape is changing, but the social relationships in which Vic finds himself seem to be oppressively permanent. Like Arthur Seaton he longs for something beyond the life he knows. He speaks of going to Paris but this remains an unfulfilled ambition. After a drunken altercation with Mrs Rothwell, Vic goes to the railway station where he spends the night. The next morning, however, he ends up at his sister's house rather than catching a train.

A Kind of Loving also comments on contemporary culture and the relationship between class, gender and the mass media. In a scene soon after the couple return from their honeymoon Vic is being served his breakfast by Ingrid and he reveals that he has two tickets for a brass-band concert, in which his father is playing the trombone. **Ingrid** is not at all keen on going as 'it's all old-fashioned' and 'more for elderly people who clonk about in big boots'. Mrs Rothwell is busying herself around the kitchen during this brief argument but she draws it to a close by siding with her daughter. With her back to Vic she states that it is necessary to make sacrifices when you are married. Vic rejoins that they are going anyway. Inevitably, the next scene reveals two empty seats at the concert, before cutting abruptly and dissonantly from the brass band to the electronic organ of the Spot Cash Quiz on the television in the Rothwell sitting-room. This sequence suggests that the traditional, collective working-class culture is being replaced by the trivial, commercial output of television with its emphasis on individual consumption rather than collective production. The new emerging culture based on consumerism is, in addition, equated with women. Similarly in *Saturday Night and Sunday Morning* it is Doreen who is keen on a new house whereas Arthur would be happy with an old one.

Like *Saturday Night and Sunday Morning* the ending of *A Kind of Loving* is relatively open. It is more subdued than the earlier film but there is the same feeling that the male protagonist will adjust, however awkwardly, to marriage and its responsibilities.

Ingrid

Ingrid reveals that she was named after the film actress Ingrid Bergman in *For Whom the Bell Tolls*. When Vic says that he has read the book of the film, Ingrid replies that she has 'not got much time for reading'. The film thus equates Ingrid with popular film and Vic with literary culture.

THIS SPORTING LIFE (1963)

Director:	Lindsay Anderson
Producer:	Karel Reisz
Screenplay:	David Storey (from his novel)
Length:	134 mins

Cast

Frank Machin:	Richard Harris
Mrs Hammond:	Rachel Roberts
Weaver:	Alan Badel

Johnson:	William Hartnell
Maurice Braithwaite:	Colin Blakely
Mrs Weaver:	Vand Godsell
Judith:	Anne Cunningham
Len Miller:	Jack Watson

Figure 19.2 *This Sporting Life*: Main protagonist, Frank Machin ©BFI

This Sporting Life, directed by Lindsay Anderson, is set in Halifax, West Yorkshire. It is grimmer and less humorous in outlook than *Saturday Night and Sunday Morning* and was not a commercial success at the box office. Like *Saturday Night and Sunday Morning*, *This Sporting Life* was based on a novel by a northern writer, David Storey, who had been a professional rugby player.

The film is about repression and enclosure in a northern town, themes that are broadly similar to *Saturday Night and Sunday Morning*. The central character Frank Machin, a coal miner and amateur rugby player, is drawn into the world of professional rugby by the offer of money. He soon realises, however, that material wealth will not bring the respect or acceptance that he desires from either the working or middle classes. The other key character Mrs Hammond, a widowed landlady, is hemmed in and constricted by the local working class community and suffers from her own guilt about her husband's death.

The working class in the film are depicted as cold, uncaring and distant and lack any of the warmth of the characters in *Saturday Night and Sunday Morning*. Mrs Hammond's neighbours, for example, watch events sullenly without comment. The enclosed nature of society makes change seem unlikely and both Frank and Mrs Hammond can be seen as victims of circumstance.

The film is also concerned with issues of wealth, power and control. The cheque, for example, that Frank accepts from the rugby club is signed by Weaver, the same man who refuses to pay compensation to Mrs Hammond (her husband died at Weaver's factory) and it is clear that Weaver uses his position in society to manipulate others. Frank eventually realises that despite his desire to resist and fight, he is essentially a mere pawn in a game. At the end of the film he is powerless to prevent the death of Mrs Hammond.

This Sporting Life also draws upon the **myth of rural England**. A key sequence in the film is when Frank takes Mrs Hammond and her children to Bolton Priory in the Yorkshire Dales (a place with historical as well as rural connotations for the film). Away from the constrictions of the house, the tensions between them visibly relax. The release, however is short lived.

Despite using 'real' locations, the overall feel of *This Sporting Life* is surrealistic/expressionistic rather than realistic. The scenes on the rugby pitch and the hospital are particularly striking. There is also great attention given to framing and *mise-en-scène* which are often used to reinforce the scene of enclosure. Note, for example, how Frank is very closely framed in Mrs Hammond's house, almost filling the screen. The film also employs a flashback structure that enhances the sense of foreboding right from the start.

Myth of rural England

The myth of rural England was popularised in the films of the Second World War in which the public were encouraged to believe that it was the countryside that was being fought for rather than the towns and cities. Broadly speaking, however, the countryside is viewed as a means of escape and self-fulfilment.

CARRY ON CABBY (1963)

Director:	Gerald Thomas
Producer:	Peter Rogers
Length:	88 mins

Cast

Charlie:	Sidney James
Peggy:	Hattie Jacques
Pint Pot:	Charles Hawtrey
Sally:	Liz Fraser

Figure 19.3 *Carry on Cabby*: Mocking the war of the sexes   ©BFI

The *Carry on* films are interesting in that they depict relationships between classes, whereas the films of the New Wave tend to dwell on relationships within the working class. In the opening sequences of *Carry on Cabby* Charlie makes jokes at the expense of an aristocratic old lady and her chauffeur, before cutting them up at the lights in his cab. The scene establishes a tone of antagonism between the working and middle classes that informs the rest of the film. The cabbies generally mock the mannerisms of the wealthy at the slightest opportunity, but surprisingly do not complain about the material disparity between the different classes. The middle and upper classes are mostly shown to be humourless, individualistic and lacking the wit, charm and team-spirit of the working class. Overall the working class are shown to be happy and proud of their position in society and appear to be financially well off. Charlie, for example, has enough money in the bank to enable his wife to buy 15 new cars.

Charlie is depicted as honest and fair and it is made clear that he would always look after his workers properly. As a result the film does not present a meaningful role for trade unions, because there appears to be little call for the protection that a union offers in Charlie's taxi firm. The union official depicted in the film is also shown to be pedantic and absurd in his application of rules. There is, however, a role for collectivism in the film as Charlie's cab firm could be seen as a metaphor for a war-time society in which community values and social cohesion were upheld. Note, for example, the way in which the cabbies work as a team at the end of the film to capture the criminals. Everyone plays a part in the military style operation, except the police, who arrive too late to be useful. The young criminals who represent the new generation are shown to be both individualistic and stupid and could obviously do with a lesson in war-time team work.

The women in *Carry on Cabby* are at times shown to be strong and independent and more than a match for the men. Peggy, for example, sets up her own highly successful cab firm that almost forces Charlie into bankruptcy. She does, however, need to be rescued by the male cab drivers at the end of the film when taken hostage by the young criminals. She also decides to give up her new cab business when she finds out that she is pregnant, as the whole Glam Cab operation was only a means of getting Charlie's attention.

The Glam Cabs are successful, however, partly because they have new cabs and a loyal work force, but mainly because the women drivers use their sexuality to grab the fares from the male cabbies. The women also use their bodies to get men to carry out tasks. The vicar, for example, gets underneath a broken down cab to repair it because he is rewarded with a good view of his lady driver's legs. In keeping with the spirit of the *Carry on* series sex is, however, confined mostly to innuendo.

Context of *Goldfinger*

Tensions between East and West were heightened by the building of the Berlin wall in 1961 and the Cuban missile crisis of 1962. Increased resources on both sides were put into armaments and a programme of espionage.

GOLDFINGER (1964)

Director:	Guy Hamilton
Producers:	Harry Saltman and Albert R. Broccoli
Screenplay:	Richard Maibaum
Production design:	Ken Adam

Based on Ian Flemming's novel: *Goldfinger*

Cast

James Bond:	Sean Connery
Pussy Galore:	Honor Blackman
Goldfinger:	Gert Frobe
Felix Leiter:	Cec Linder
Q:	Desmond Llewelyn
M:	Bernard Lee
Jill Masterson:	Shirley Eaton
Tilly Masterson:	Tania Mallet
Moneypenny:	Lois Maxwell
Oddjob:	Harold Sakata

Goldfinger, with its quick paced action format, international locations and high production values was very popular with audiences, becoming the fastest money-maker in the history of cinema.[7] Clearly the British had got the formula right (with American money) and the film was one of many that were internationally successful in the 1960s.

Goldfinger is preoccupied with the traditional educated upper classes. James Bond is public school educated, knows his wines and how to dress correctly for all occasions and is endowed with the good looks, style and wit that enable him to be at ease in all social circumstances. The villains that Bond deals with are also predominantly wealthy and highly educated and usually involved in crimes that are on an international scale. The only remotely working class member of the cast is Bond's caddie who is visibly impressed at how Bond handles himself.

This is a very different world from that of the New Wave. The locations in *Goldfinger* include London, Kent, Switzerland and America, although some scenes were shot using back-projection and strategically-placed American street furniture. The Britain that is depicted is southern-centred, traditional and stable with conservative values. It is effectively controlled by the old-school-tie establishment working from oak-panelled rooms. There is no sense of internal conflict within the nation and the villains tend to be foreigners threatening the hegemony of Western capitalism. The foreigners in *Goldfinger* are from the East (Korea/China) and are for the most part weakly characterised. Overall the British are shown to be the only ones capable of solving international problems, partly through using charm, wit and sexuality. The Americans are also involved in joint operations, although they clearly lack the vital 'Brit' element possessed by Bond.

The representation of women in Bond films has both positive and negative points. In the opening sequence of *Goldfinger* Bond uses a woman as a shield against an attacker. He subsequently causes the death of Jill Masterson, who cannot resist Bond's charms, and he also contributes to that of her sister Tilly Masterson. Women can to some extent therefore be seen as victims in *Goldfinger*. The film contains almost as many sexual puns as *Carry on Cabby* and there are a number of similarities in terms of the representation of women. The key female character in the film is Pussy Galore who is intelligent, skilful and independent. She can easily repel the charms of Bond, but eventually even she falls for him – luckily just in time to save the day. What is important is that Bond's sexuality brings results.

It is significant that unlike other films of the 1960s *Goldfinger* does not deal with the new generation at all. Bond himself is hardly a young man and those around him, such as Q and M, are much older. The film is a celebration of traditional British values that belong to the Second World War rather than the 1960s.

 ## *A HARD DAY'S NIGHT* (1964)

Director:	Richard Lester
Producer:	Walter Shenson
Production company:	UA/Proscenium
Screenplay:	Alun Owen
Length:	83 mins

Cast

John Lennon
Paul McCartney
George Harrison
Ringo Starr

Paul's Grandad:	Wilfrid Brambell
Norm, the group's manager:	Norman Rossington

At the end of *Billy Liar*, Billy Fisher has the opportunity to go to London with the irrepressible and free-wheeling Liz. He cannot, however, make the break. *A Hard Day's Night*, in contrast, starts with a train journey to London after The Beatles have been chased through the streets by fans. It is as if the energy suppressed in the New Wave films bursts out in *A Hard Day's Night*, although the cheerful exuberance of this film seems to have little in common with the darker moods of the New Wave.

Janet Thumin states that *A Hard Day's Night* is part of a group of films (which includes *Goldfinger*) that have the following elements in common:[8]

- They emphasise the theme of personal liberation and freedom, especially in relation to the young and the new
- The offer excitement and spectacle, but also enquire into the relationship of the individual to class, nationality and power
- They exhibit an 'overt celebration of the pleasures of the text itself'

Beatlemania exploded in the autumn of 1963 and *A Hard Day's Night* draws on the excitement of this phenomenon. The film stresses the newness of The Beatles and the fact that their success is based on their own musical creativity. It is significant in this respect that the film does not contrast them with other emergent musicians, but with a range of entertainers who are following familiar and well-worn paths. The Beatles have made a break with this showbiz past and its staid routines.

Alun Owen, who wrote the screenplay, wanted to depict the pressures and constraints of celebrity and the way in which the group is ushered from train to taxi to hotel room retains this idea. The film does not, however, reveal much about the normal work routine of a group of musicians but instead presents The Beatles as a spectacle: the film audience can get close to the stars and enjoy the complete performance of a number of songs. In this sense the film is exploiting their recent success. The film, however, also reveals attitudes that The Beatles were held to exemplify. Throughout the film they collide with the older generation and established ways of doing things. For instance, on the train journey down to London they get into an argument with an upper middle class Englishman, complete with bowler hat and umbrella, and the following exchange takes place:

Commuter: I fought the war for your sort
Ringo: I bet you're sorry ye won
Commuter: I shall call the guard
Paul: Ah . . . but what? They don't take kindly to insults you know!

This exchange illustrates a humorous dismissal of the past and a humorous deflection of a threat from the older generation, and throughout the film, the jokes and word plays show great presence of mind and an unwillingness to conform to what is expected either linguistically or socially. The reference to the war suggests that the past does not have any potency for or relevance to the young generation.

The disruption of convention in the plot is matched by the style of the film. It is continually restless in terms of the cinematography, the editing and the movement of the performers within the frame. There is an improvisatory feel which suited the subject as well as the predilections of director Richard Lester. The style is playful and self-conscious. For example, the group mimic Lionel Blair and his dancers who are on stage rehearsing and then, in imitation of the Hollywood musical, Lennon yells out 'Hey kids I've got an idea. Why don't we do the show right here? Yeah!'

FURTHER WORK

Character representation

Compare and contrast the representation of the working class in *Carry on Cabby*, *Saturday Night and Sunday Morning* and *This Sporting Life*.

What role does the narrator play in *We are the Lambeth Boys*? To what extent does the narration shape our ideas about the main characters.

Free Cinema

'The films made under the banner of Free Cinema had an immediacy and freshness that in part stemmed from their documentary form'. Discuss the statement in relation to *We are the Lambeth Boys* and *Every Day Except Christmas*.

The use of sound and image

Compare and contrast *Listen to Britain* and *Every Day Except Christmas* in their use of sound and image.

The representation of Britain

Discuss the representation of Britain in *Goldfinger*. How would you explain the popularity of such representations?

FURTHER READING

Bennett, Tony and Woolacott, Jane, *Bond and Beyond: The Political Career of a Popular Hero*, MacMillan, 1987.

Hewison, Robert, *In Anger: Culture in the Cold War 1945–1960*, Weidenfeld and Nicholson, 1981.

Hewison, Robert, *Too Much: Art and Society in the Sixties, 1960–1975*, Methuen, 1986.

Hill, John, *Sex, Class and Realism: British Cinema 1956–1963*, BFI, 1986.

Murphy, Robert, *Sixties British Cinema*, BFI, 1992.

Murphy, Robert, (ed.), *The British Cinema Book*, BFI, 1997.

Street, Sarah, *British National Cinema*, Routledge, 1997.

FURTHER VIEWING

I'm Alright Jack (John Boulting, 1959)
Sapphire (Basil Dearden, 1959)
Carry on Regardless (Gerald Thomas, 1960)
The Brides of Dracula (Terence Fisher, 1960)
The Servant (Joseph Losey, 1963)
Carry on Spying (Gerald Thomas, 1964)
Thunderball (Terence Young, 1965)
Catch us if you Can (John Boorman, 1965)
Alfie (Lewis Gilbert, 1966)
The Spy who came in from the Cold (Martin Ritt, 1966)

NOTES

[1] Quoted in John Hill, *Sex, Class and Realism*, BFI, 1986, p204.

[2] *Directors and Direction*, Eyre Methuen, 1975, p80.

[3] In Alexander Walker, *Hollywood, England: The British Industry in the Sixties*, Michael Joseph, 1974.

[4] *Class: Image and Reality in Britain, France and the USA since 1930*, Fontana/Collins, 1981, p290.

[5] Elizabeth Sussex, *Lindsay Anderson*, Studio Vista, 1969, p34.

[6] *ibid*, pp34–35.

[7] Tony Bennett and Janet Woolacott, *Bond and Beyond: The Political Career of a Popular Hero*, MacMillan, 1987, p30.

[8] *Celluloid Sisters: Women and Popular Cinema*, St Martin's Press, 1992, p74.

CHAPTER **20** African Cinema

'With the advent of information highways, we are promised unheard-of possibilities for the circulation and use of images. So there will be a profusion of channels, but what of their content? How many specific views and awarenesses, imaginations and memories, different visions and dreams will survive this announced revolution? Will encounters between real authors and real audiences be possible and fertile?

Are cinemas still to be born, such as those of Africa, going to be brought to a premature end forever?'

Gaston Kaboré in *Écrans d'Afrique*[1]

'In the francophone parts of Africa, film-makers follow a European notion of what African cinema is like; that is a kind of censorship. Instead of making a personal film about my grandmother, I'd ask myself, "What do the French like? Something exotic!" There should be a national film policy to help African film-makers build up an archive of national memory. Film-makers are trying to make their own personal films on video in Ghana; they will use any instrument to ingrain their humanity. This is happening in Mozambique and Ethiopia; it can be very powerful, especially if film-makers begin to realise their capacity to affect society, even if some of these videos are an imitation of *Dallas*, with some witchcraft thrown in for good measure.'

Haile Gerima in *Index on Censorship*[2]

'The film-makers have come to understand the potential and importance of African people seeing images of themselves, seeing their own image. This offers the possibility of a certain unity in Africa, that is to say a unity in terms of culture.'

Med Hondo quoted in *Monthly Film Bulletin*[3]

'We should not be talking about African cinema, but African cinemas. We are many countries, with creative artists operating differently. The vision people had of us corresponded to their fantasies, but things are changing. Filming in South Africa gave me a new freedom, I had confidence in the technical crew, I enjoyed working with professional actors I could push more than amateurs. South Africa possesses a development we don't have but we were independent before them. We must take from each other now, especially in films. We can't consider language as a barrier.'

Idrissa Ouédraogo quoted in *Black Film Bulletin*[4]

INSTITUTIONS

Africa is a diverse continent but, as the above quotation from Med Hondo indicates, there is a desire among film-makers to unite Africa in terms of culture. This desire is part of the tradition of pan-Africanism which found expression in pan-African conferences in London, Paris and New York in the first quarter of this century and which led to the formation of the **Organisation of African Unity (OAU)** in 1963.

THE ORGANISATION OF AFRICAN UNITY (OAU)

The Organisation of African Unity was founded in Addis Ababa and the Charter of Unity signed there included the following statement.

The organisation shall have the following purposes:

- To promote the unity and solidarity of the African states

- To coordinate and intensify their cooperation and efforts to achieve a better life for the peoples of Africa

- To defend their sovereignty, their territorial integrity and independence

- To eradicate all forms of colonialism from Africa

- To promote international cooperation, having due regard to the Charter of the United Nations and the Universal Declaration of Human Rights

The OAU accepted that the new African states would be based on the old colonial boundaries and the new nation-states were consolidated on this principle despite the fact that they were originally established without regard to ethnic composition. A number of factors however militated against these states engaging in concerted cooperative efforts across Africa.

- A strong central state was seen as essential for economic development and to unite the diverse ethnic groups contained within each territory. The position of the state

and the new leaders was further enhanced by what Michael Barratt Brown identifies as a shift from democracy towards authoritarianism in the 1960s and 1970s in order to achieve these goals:

- The new states looked abroad to the West or to the USSR or China for aid and armaments

- Colonial patterns of trading were maintained

- The colonial languages of either English, French, Portuguese, or Arabic remained dominant, a factor which also separated the educated elites from the mass of people within these countries.

The OAU was prominent in the struggle against apartheid in South Africa and has played a role in numerous crises (eg the civil wars in Somalia and Angola in 1991). It has created a secretariat, an African Development Bank and an African Development Fund. Political and economic integration, however, seem distant goals. In a sombre assessment of the impact of the OAU, Kidane Mengisteab comments that African countries have not succeeded 'in advancing their political integration by jointly defining their interests in the global system and harmonising their position and foreign policies, or in mastering the political will to propel their economic integration.'[5] Mengisteab recognises though that the OAU might be important in future attempts to deal with the severe crises facing many African countries.

The Pan-African Federation of Film-makers

The pan-African spirit is widely shared by film-makers and in 1970 a number of them from 33 African countries formed the Pan-African Federation of Film-makers or FEPACI (Fédération Panafricaine des Cinéastes). This body has political observer status at the OAU and on its inauguration in Carthage FEPACI was committed to the following aims:

- The political, cultural, and economic liberation of Africa
- To fight against the Franco-American monopoly of film distribution and exhibition in Africa
- The encouragement of the creation of national cinemas[6]

FEPACI lost some of its impetus according to Manthia Diawara after its second congress in Algiers in 1975 but was revivified at an international conference held at Niamey, Niger in 1982. The manifesto produced at the Niamey congress established the following general principles.

- The viability of cinema production is tied to the complementary viability of the other four main sectors of cinema, namely the exploitation of cinema theatres, importation of films, distribution of films, technical infrastructure and training
- There cannot be any viable cinema without the involvement of African states for the organisation, the support, the stabilisation of cinema and the encouragement and protection of private and public investment in cinema
- It is not possible to have a viable cinema industry on a national level in Africa. The development of national cinema should take into consideration regional and pan-African cooperation by integrating cinema to political and economic ties that already exist between states
- At the present stage of development of audio-visual facilities in the world and particularly in Africa, television should be complementary to cinema
- It is possible to finance African film productions from the present revenue from the millions who patronise cinemas in Africa. What is required is a strategy that will ensure that part of this revenue legitimately returns to the production of films. Production should not rely solely on patronage[7]

The Niamey discussions indicated a more favourable attitude to private entrepreneurial involvement in African cinema than in the past when there was more of a stress on nationalisation. Also, there was an appreciation of the necessity for countries to cooperate rather than try to build a film industry on a national basis alone. The manifesto and the discussions at Niamey nevertheless revealed that much work had still to be done. FEPACI continued to play its role but its funds have always been limited and at the sixth congress in Ouagadougou in 1997 FEPACI was still struggling financially despite its standing both within and without Africa. Distinguished film-makers continue to participate but membership is based on the affiliation of national associations and many of these are inactive. As a result an Advisory Commission was set up at the congress to reorganise the Federation.[8]

The role of film festivals

One successful development for African cinema has been the growth of festivals. The two main festivals are the Festival Panafricaine du Cinéma de Ouagadougou (FESPACO) and the Journées cinématographique de Carthage (JCC). The FESPACO takes place in Ouagadougou, the capital of Burkina Faso, which has become the administrative centre of African film-making. It began in 1969 as La Semaine du Cinéma Africain on a small scale and has gone from strength to strength. The cinema in Burkina Faso has been helped by supportive political leaders: Thomas Sankara who took over in 1983 after a series of coups (he changed the name of the country from Upper Volta to Burkina Faso) was a lover of the cinema as an art and also recognised the potential for publicity from the FESPACO. After his death following another coup in 1987 his successor, Blaise Campaoré, has continued to support the cinema if in a less ostentatious manner. In 1997 Burkina Faso provided 200 million CFA (African Francs) out of the total budget of 700 million CFA for the fifteenth FESPACO, an event which was attended by '5,000 producers, distributors, directors, festival directors, actors, dignitaries and journalists' and at which 200 films were screened attracting audiences of 400,000.[9] FESPACO also came to the aid of FEPACI in 1985 when the ninth Pan-African Film Festival played host to the third congress of the FEPACI. Since then it has benefitted from the hospitality of this festival as well as the biennial festival at Carthage, the JCC.

The importance of these festivals was emphasised by a seminar held jointly by FEPACI and FESPACO in 1994. Sambolgo Bangré states that this meeting noted their historic role 'in the promotion of African cinema, the diffusion of images of the continent's film-makers, the strengthening of the bonds of solidarity between the peoples of Africa and the assertion of African cinemas in the face of that of the North.'[10]

In addition to FESPACO and JCC and other festivals in Senegal, Zimbabwe, South Africa, Côte d'Ivoire and Ghana a large number of festivals dedicated to or featuring African films have emerged in Europe and North America. This has increased awareness and appreciation of African cinema but Khaled L. Hagar for one expresses doubts about their efficacy in getting more films made:

'Most of the African film-makers, who are continually asked to attend, feel that these festivals do not meet their needs. They travel from one festival to the other, meeting the same people, spending one or two years showing the same films without making any significant contacts or progress for the future.'[11]

FILM PRODUCTION

Film production has a long history in Africa but until the 1950s it was dominated by the colonial powers. The popular entertainment cinema of Egypt was an exception. From the 1930s onwards the Egyptian industry produced 40 or 50 films a year although production fell in the mid-1990s. In the years since independence however no African country has been able to match the output of the Egyptian industry. Lizbeth Malkmus and Roy Armes report that only

Figure 20.1 Poster for the Festival Panafricaine du Cinéma de Ouagadougou 1995

Algeria, Iraq and Morocco have an output of 50 films in total. Senegal, Nigeria and Tunisia have produced 25 to 50 since independence but of the rest only a few have reached double figures.[12] This fact is not surprising given the resources that can be made available for cinema in relatively poor countries. Also many countries have small populations, which makes it difficult to sustain a national cinema industry.

It it possible to distinguish two main types of production. On the one hand, there are the genre films with popular appeal e.g comedies, melodramas and thrillers. These films have local stars and serve a small local market on a small budget. In the main these films are only seen in Africa, although films made in countries like Nigeria and Ghana are available outside of Africa on video. On the other hand, there are the films that are distributed and exhibited outside of Africa. These films, which vary greatly in style and content, seek to engage with African realities whether of the past or the present. In industrial terms they have the following characteristics:

- In the UK they are usually screened at film festivals, in 'art-house' cinemas, or on television, typically on BBC 2 or Channel Four
- They require the intense personal commitment of the director who is typically involved in the financing, marketing and distribution of the film as well as every aspect of the filmmaking. For this reason a director who makes a successful first feature may have to wait years to make a second and even established directors have long gaps between films
- They are predominantly made in countries that were formerly French colonies, Francophone (French-speaking) countries such as Burkina Faso, Mali and Senegal. These countries have been more productive than the Anglophone (English-speaking) countries that were formerly British colonies
- They are made on a low budget but are typically international co-productions.
- Post-production work is often undertaken abroad because of the lack of facilities in Africa.

African cinema however faces the major problem that African screens are dominated by films from the Hollywood, Bombay and Hong Kong film industries and there is no African company which distributes African films throughout Africa to combat this powerful competition. African cinema does not have a distribution system for foreign markets either but African films are screened in selected cinemas and on television channels such as Channel 4 in the UK, La Sept in France or ZDF in Germany, reflecting the involvement of such channels in the finance of African films. Taking into account film festivals, art-house cinemas and television it may be easier to see African films abroad than in Africa itself.

CASE STUDIES

- *Yaaba* (1989)
- *The Silences of the Palace* (1994)
- *Sarraounia* (1986)
- *Mapantsula* (1988)
- *Hyenas* (1992)

YAABA (BURKINA FASO/FRANCE/SWITZERLAND, 1989)

Director and Screenwriter:	Idrissa Ouédraogo
Cinematographer:	Matthias Kälin
Music:	Francis Bebey
Editor:	Loredana Cristelli
Length:	90 mins

Cast

Yaaba:	Fatima Sanga
Bila:	Noufou Ouédraogo
Nopoko:	Barry Roukietou
Kougri:	Adama Ouédraogo
Tibo:	Amade Touré
Poko:	Sibidou Ouédraogo
Razougou:	Adame Sidibe
Koudi:	Assita Ouédraogo
Taryam:	Ousmane Sawadogo

Yaaba represents an African community untouched by urban life or colonial invaders. It features Bila and his female cousin, Nopoko and their involvement with Sana, an old woman, who lives as an outcast from their village in Burkino Faso and is designated a witch. In the opening scene the two children are visiting the grave of Nopoko's mother. They are placed in the foreground of the shot and they are joined in the background by Sana who is also visiting a grave and like them performing a simple ceremony of remembrance. When the children eventually begin to play hide and seek Sana helps Nopoko outwit Bila in the game. These scenes thereby establish a link between the old woman and the children and between the audience and the main protagonists. Although the opening scenes appear inconsequential they establish a vantage-point from which the audience views the subsequent events. They make it harder for the audience to accept that the blaze in the granary in the subsequent scene is the result of Sana's witchcraft because the audience has been introduced to her as a dignified person. As the film progresses, vantage point is an important issue.

- It enlists the audience's support for the main protagonists, Bila, Nopoko and Sana

- It enables the director, **Idrissa Ouédraogo**, to present both a sympathetic portrait of village life and a judicious reflection on the superstitions of the villagers and the charlatans who take advantage of them

The use of space

Yaaba makes subtle use of the space within the village and the space outside the village. It is important that Bila, Nopoko and Sana meet outside the village because such a meeting would be impossible within the village as Sana is regarded as a witch

Idrissa Ouédraogo (1954–)

Is an acclaimed director from Burkina Faso. He trained in Ouagadougou, the USSR and France.
Director of:
Yam Daabo (1986)
Tilai (1990)
Samba Traore (1993)
Cri du Coeur (1994)
Kini and Adams (1997)

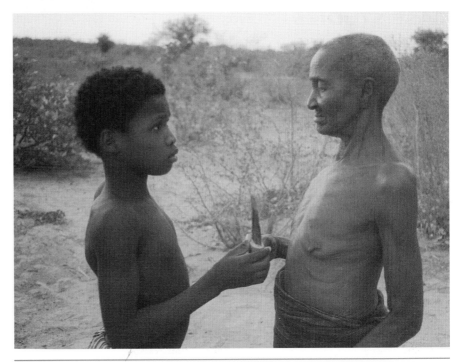

Figure 20.2 Scene from *Yaaba*: Bila shows Sana the knife that has scratched Napoko

©Ronald Grant Collection

by the majority of the villagers. Inside the village the children are much more subject to adult demands, supervision and discipline. Outside the village adults are still present though. For example, Nopoko's father, Tibo, breaks up a fight between Bila and some other children from the village. However, the recurrent deep shots of the landscape suggest, metaphorically, a space where it is possible to question the order of the village and the knowledge of the villagers.

The village itself is portrayed as a functioning unit that exists in harmony with nature and has the means to survive physically. The people are poor but not dejected. They squabble and argue but they are not riven by conflict. The children do come into conflict with the adults but the film emphasises that they offer hope for the future.

The issue of knowledge

Bila and Nopoko are able to see Sana as a person in an open unprejudiced way. They do not see her as a witch. She lives in exile because she is an orphan and this ensures that she will not have any children of her own. She literally has no place in the social world and for this reason it is very important when Bila calls her 'Yaaba' or grandmother. The relationship established between them enables Sana to pass on her knowledge and wisdom to Bila who in turn can pass it on to Nopoko. Sana sees that after being cut by a knife Nopoko is suffering from tetanus, not from having had her soul stolen. Sana travels to Taryam who is able to supply her with a mix of herbs which eventually cures Nopoko. The film is therefore able to place value on traditional medicine while at the same time rejecting another traditional healer who is only able to diagnose the operation of witchcraft. Sana also exemplifies an attitude of tolerance towards others which Bila mimics and passes on to Nopoko.

Yaaba, then, presents a positive humanistic portrait of an African culture. It is set in a real village and the language used in the film is Moore, which is spoken by the Mossi ethnic group and is one of the main languages in Burkina Faso. A number of factors contribute to the timeless feel of the film.

- It opens and closes with a shot of the spirited children running away from the camera into the distance
- It has a slow pace due to the prevalence of long shots, long takes and static framing – frequently, for example, the camera holds a shot and there is a delay before any character enters the frame
- It shows no evidence of the impact of urban life or other cultures

The fact that the film has this timeless quality has lead some commentators to criticise *Yaaba* and films like it for not examining contemporary African realities. It has also been pointed out by Françoise Pfaff writing from an anthropological perspective that the film has no mention of polygamy, castes, ethnic rivalry and the extended family structure, all of which can be found in rural Burkina Faso.[13]

 ## *THE SILENCES OF THE PALACE* (France/Tunisia, 1994)

Director and Screenplay:	Moufida Tlatli
Adaptation and Dialogue:	Nouri Bouzid
Cinematography:	Youssef Ben Youssef
Editing:	Moufida Tlatli, Camille Cotte, Kerim Hammouda
Music:	Anouar Brahem
Length:	127 mins

Cast

Khedija:	Ahmel Hedhili
Alia (young):	Hend Sabri
Alia (adult):	Ghalia Lacroix
Khalti Hadda:	Najia Duerghi
Lotfi:	Sami Bouajila
Sidi Ali:	Kamel Fazaa
Si Béchir:	Nichem Rostom
Jneina:	Sonia Meddeb
Houssine:	Kamel Touati
Sarra:	Khedija Ben Othman

Moufida Tlatli and Nouri Bouzid worked on the successful Tunisian film, *Halfaouine* (Ferid Boughedir, 1990) which looks at the passage of Noura, the young adolescent hero, from boy to man. The film intended to lift the veil on Tunisian society and succeeded in doing so from a male perspective. *The Silences of the Palace* has similar intentions but is concerned to present events from a female perspective.

In *The Silences of the Palace* Alia reflects on events in her life culminating in the year 1956 when she was 16 and **Tunisia** achieved independence. As a child she lived in the palace of the Bey, Sidi Ali, where her mother was a servant and where she was born illegitimately. The film makes it clear that Sidi Ali is her father but the fact cannot be acknowledged by any of the inhabitants of the palace – it is one of the important silences of the palace.

At the beginning of the film Alia is singing at a wedding ceremony, after which she joins Lotfi, her lover, in his car and they drive home. It is revealed that she is pregnant and that the next day she is to have an abortion. At home she hears of the death of Sidi Ali and the next day revisits the palace that she left ten years before. This visit provokes the flashbacks that form the body of the film.

Tunisia

The Tunisian film industry faces two typical problems: Tunisia has a small population (8.4 million) and exhibition is dominated by films from abroad. Since 1966 however the biennial film festival at Carthage has stimulated the local industry as well as providing a forum for African film-making generally. The current film generation reject the Egyptian cinema as a model preferring the international 'art-cinema' of the 1960s.

Figure 20.3 *The Silences of the Palace*: Alia finds solace and beauty in music   ©BFI

The use of space

The film focuses on the women who work at the palace and the way they are physically and socially separate from the princes and princesses for whom they work. The women occupy the kitchen and they relax there and entertain them-selves as well as perform all the necessary domestic duties. Even though it is predominantly a female space it is one which can be encroached on by males. For example, a scene opens with Alia sitting in the middle of a semi-circle of women who are singing. Firstly, Sherif the husband of one of the women, Habiba, comes through the ground-floor door. He totters in and amid much laughter he joins the women and proceeds to fondle three of them. This drunken fumbling and hilarity is interrupted by Houssine, the son of Khalti Haddi who draws Sherif from the group of women. As they leave Sidi Ali enters from the first floor and asks Khedija to bring some refreshments upstairs. Sidi Ali's entrance completely subdues the mood and one of the women comments that they will keep her all night. Khedija prepares a tray and Alia follows her upstairs and observes her placing a tray on the table for Sidi Ali who is playing the lute. This sequence reveals the way in which the women are subject to male authority even by males in the same social class. The male invasion of this space is underlined by Tlatli's use of long takes and panning shots as the men come and go to and from the different levels of the house. It also shows the desire of Alia to discover the secrets of the palace and what this means for her mother and therefore what it might mean for her in the future.

The lack of status

Alia is poised between being an adult and being a child – she is shocked and mortified by her first period. She is also poised between the world of the beys and the world of the servants. Firstly, she is friends with Sarra the daughter of Si Béchir. They were born in the palace on the same day and have been friends since they were little. Secondly, she sings and plays the lute and her talents are recognised especially by Sidi Ali. There are many silences in the palace but music is very significant for all the inhabitants. Singing and playing the lute are more than a means of entertainment for Alia: it enables her to escape from her troubles and she sees music as a way of escaping from the drudgery of the kitchen. The fact that she is poised between these different worlds is illustrated by the sequence in which she observes her mother dancing for the princes and princesses and their guests despite her mother forbidding her attendance. In a scene which emphasises the males' enjoyment of her mother's performance Alia and Sarra watch secretly through a glass partition. Disconcerted Alia leaves Sarra watching and goes downstairs to the bedroom of Jneina, the wife of Sidi Ali. She puts a record on and then goes to a mirror and applies some make-up. Then she puts on a silver robe from the wardrobe over the top of her nightdress and then in imitation of her mother starts to dance tentatively and awkwardly. Then, as if reverting to being a child again, she spins around and around until she falls back on the bed.

Throughout *The Silences of the Palace* there is a strong feeling of enclosure: Alia never leaves the palace and the continual use of mirrors intensifies the claustrophobia. The mirrors also put an emphasis on looking, which is a key aspect of the film. The opening shot of the film is a tight close-up of Alia's face as she looks apprehensively to her right, then ahead, and then to her left. In her role as a female singer she is isolated both from the male band and the indifferent audience. She is an onlooker who can also have no social location because she has no acknowledged father and therefore no name.

The film suggests parallels between the political situation in Tunisia and the relationships within the palace: the beys do not fulfil the proper requirements of rulers because they operate on behalf of the French and similarly Sidi Ali does not fulfil the proper role of a father. As Khalia Haddi says to Alia when she visits the palace as an adult: 'Is a father simply a name? A father is sweat, pain and joy. An entire life, daily care.' Also, the cycle of relationships within the palace is broken: Jneina, the wife of Sidi Ali is barren and Khedija aborts the child that is the result of her rape by Si Béchir and this lack of progeny coincides with the end of French Colonial rule.

Independence does not however guarantee freedom for Alia but at the end of the film she decides to have the baby she is carrying and this represents both a coming to terms with the past and a realisation that she has to decide her own destiny.

SARRAOUNIA (FRANCE, 1986)

Director:	Med Hondo
Production company:	Soleil Ô with the participation of the Ministères Français de la Culture et des Relations Extérieures, Ministères de l'Information et de la Culture du Burkina Faso
Cinematography:	Guy Famechon
Editor:	Marie-Thérèse Boiche
Based on a novel by:	Abdoulaye Mamani
Length:	121 mins

Cast

Sarraounia:	Ai Keita
Captain Voulet:	Jean-Roger Milo
Baka:	Aboubakar Traore
Colonel Klobb:	Jean Edmond

Figure 20.4 *Sarraounia*: communal celebration of a military victory ©BFI

Ousmane Sembène (1923–)

Is a venerated figure in African cinema. He was a novelist but became a film-maker in order to reach a larger audience. His film *Borom Sarret* (1963) is often taken as the first black African film. Nwachukwu Frank Ukadike says that although Hondo and Sembène 'differ in both their approach to and style of filmmaking, their goals were the same – to facilitate the freedom of the oppressed with social justice and equality in every area of life.'[14] Director of: *Xala* (1974) *Ceddo* (1977) *Guelwaar* (1993)

Mohamed Abid Hondo was born in Mauritania but since 1958 has lived in France. Initially he worked in the theatre but like **Ousmane Sembène** he saw the potential of cinema to reach and politicise a larger audience.

Sarraounia celebrates resistance to colonialism in the past and by implication in the present. It is set in the years 1898–99 and centres on the conflict between Sarraounia, the Queen of the Aznas and the French colonial troops led by Captain Voulet. Although the conflict between the stately African queen and the manic French Captain is personalised, the film depicts the movements of large forces across the African landscape. The film, for example, gives little access to the life and thoughts of Sarraounia herself but concentrates on her as a leader and orator. She is a powerful woman who seeks independence for her people from the colonists from the north and the Moslems to the east.

A key scene occurs in the second part of the film as the Aznas prepare to defend the walled city of Lugu. This scene confirms that Sarraounia, her people and her supporters have a spontaneous social order. There is a hierarchy but it is regarded as legitimate. This is in contrast to the French army that requires the constant imposition of discipline or the offer of inducements by the white officers to keep the black soldiers in line. All the lower ranks in the French army are black and the film emphasises that the great struggles in Africa involve black people fighting black people. As one of Sarraounia's allies in the battle says: 'Our worst enemy is black and speaks our tongue.'

As Sarraounia addresses her troops she is shot against the sky and against the troops on the ground and on the ramparts. She speaks with dignity as she asserts that they will fight for the honour of the Aznas. As she moves, the camera, positioned at a low angle, travels with her for over a minute. As she speaks she is accompanied by drummers who punctuate the pauses in her address. Her voice is resonant and has a musical lilt as she says: 'I did not give you a son, but I shall leave you more than life. I will leave the Aznas a name ...' Sarraounia stresses the importance of leaving a name rather than going to heaven as the Fulanis, whom they defeated earlier, believe. It could be argued that the film itself is putting this idea into practice. In this way the film-maker is the modern equivalent of the griot who sings the praises and celebrates the deeds of Sarraounia in the film. This oral tradition records the history and thereby maintains the continuity of the culture. As Sarraounia says, 'Our musicians and their grandsons will sing our name.'

 ## *MAPANTSULA* (SOUTH AFRICA, 1988)

Director:	Oliver Schmitz
Screenplay:	Oliver Schmitz and
	Thomas Mogotlane
Cinematography:	Rod Stewart
Editor:	Mark Baard

Cast

Panic:	Thomas Mogotlane
Pat:	Thembi Mtshali
Buma:	Peter Sephuma
Stander:	Marcel Van Heerden
Ma Mobise	Dolly Rathebe

Mapantsula maintains the spirit of political activism found in *Sarraounia* but in the context of the black township of Soweto and Johannesburg. The film was made and set in turbulent times; current events included those listed below:

- Rent boycotts in Soweto

- School boycotts

- A state of emergency

- The detention of political activists

- The 'neck-lacing' (a tyre placed around the neck and set on fire) of black politicians, policemen and others judged to be collaborators with apartheid

- A ban on newspapers, radio and television from reporting demonstrations and strikes

The film suffered from censorship by the Publications Control Board because of its depiction of such contemporary events. It was banned from cinemas although it was screened three times at a film festival and had a large circulation on video.

Figure 20.5 *Mapantsula*: At 'an illegal gathering'. Ma Mobise confronts the police ©BFI

The main character is Panic, a petty criminal who models himself in terms of dress on the Hollywood gangster of the 1950s. This enables the film-makers to use an entertainment format to make a political comment. The film moves between the present in which Panic is imprisoned in a cell with a number of black political activists and the past in which he thinks back to the events that have led up to his incarceration with such unlikely cell-mates.

As a police informer, vicious criminal and insensitive human being Panic is an unlikely protagonist even if his robberies can be read as political in the context of apartheid. The impact, however, is all the greater at the end of the film when he refuses to inform on Buma, an organiser for the South African Domestic Workers Association. As Thomas Mogotlane, the co-writer of the screenplay explains '*Mapantsula* doesn't set out to be a political film in the preaching sense. It is a slice of life – a few weeks in the world of an irresponsible black man who becomes caught up in the political drama almost by accident.'

By taking this black man as the main character the film is able to illustrate the deep divisions between black and white and the extreme contrasts in their living conditions. It does however, show a range of responses to life amongst the black population and highlights the deep division between the political activists and the non-elected members of the community council, who are accused of living comfortably off apartheid.

The virtue of the film is that it presents a black perspective on South Africa, and therefore felt for one member of the audience of one of the three initial screenings (it has subsequently been screened in the 1990s) '. . . like the first truly South African film.'[15]

HYENAS (FRANCE/SENEGAL/SWITZERLAND, 1992)

Director:	Djibril Diop Mambety
Music:	Wasis Diop
Editor:	Loredana Cristelli
Cinematography:	Matthias Kälin
Length:	105 mins

Cast

Dramaan Drameh:	Mansour Diouf
Linguère Ramatou:	Ami Diakhate
Mayor:	Mamadou Mahouredia Gueye
Geana:	Djibril Diop Mambety
Teacher:	Issa Ramagelissa Samb
Khoudia Lo:	Faly Gueye

Djibril Diop Mambety (1945–98)

He was a student and then an actor and director for the Daniel Sorano Theatre which is the national theatre company of Senegal. He began work on his first film in 1964 and wished 'to count amongst those who advance cinematic writing'.
Director of:
Contrast City (1968)
Badou Boy (1970)
Parlons grandmère (1989)
Touki Bouki (1973)
Le Franc (1993)
Before his death he had completed shooting *La Petite Vendeuse de Soleil*.

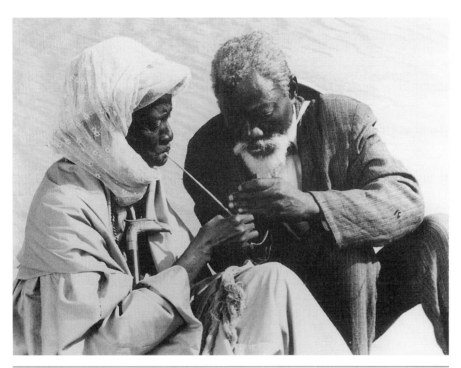

Figure 20.6 *Hyenas*: Dramaan Drameh solicitously attempts to light Ramatou's pipe   ©BFI

Hyenas is an adaptation by Djibril Diop Mambety of *The Visit*, a play by Friedrich Durrenmatt to whom the film is dedicated.

Hyenas is a complex, humorous, pessimistic and chilling portrait of contemporary Africa that fulfills the duty of the film-maker as **Djibril Diop Mambety** sees it:

'. . . we as film-makers have the duty to be universal. We have just come to the end of the first century of cinema and really we have to win the second century. 'If I have any advice to give to African (and African diaspora) film-makers, I would say, above all do not try to please, if you want to be universal – and indeed if you want to be *heard*, still do not try too hard to please, but be true to your project.'[16]

In *Hyenas* an old woman returns to the village, Colobane, that she left when she was 17. Linguère Ramatou left in poverty because she was seduced and abandoned by Dramaan Drameh who chose to marry Khoudia Lo instead because, Linguère says, she had money. On her return to this run-down town in the Sahel she is fabulously rich, 'richer than the World Bank' in fact and is accompanied by an impressive entourage of three impassive and formidable black women, a uniformed Japanese woman, the former Chief Justice of Colobane and her own griot. She has made her fortune as a prostitute and as she herself was made a whore is determined to turn the whole world into a brothel. She offers the town a hundred thousand million dollars if they kill Dramaan Drameh as a punishment for deserting her.

Hyenas has none of the optimism of the other films discussed in this chapter: the ending is a far cry from the collective exhilaration of *Sarraounia* for example. It is an ambiguous film, its humour is dark and it treats its theme of human venality with laconic detachment. The film satirises the way the leaders of the town react hypocritically to events. Even before Ramatou arrives the mayor is preparing an ingratiatory welcoming speech that interprets Ramatou's early life in the most positive way and at the end of the film the townspeople are wearing judicial wigs before they do away with Dramaan Drameh.

The film develops its theme through a *mise-en-scène* which draws visual parallels between animals and humans. The opening shot of elephants lumbering across the landscape is matched by the group of men who trudge towards and into Dramaan Drameh's store. As they approach the store a shot of a monkey stretched out is matched by a shot of a customer languorously relaxing. The parallels are initially benign but gradually become more minatory as, increasingly, shots of vultures and hyenas become prevalent. These shots tend to be inserted in a very noticeable way and they illustrate how Mambety uses *mise-en-scène* and editing to create metaphors. In this way his style departs from conventional mainstream film-making in which each shot continues the narrative flow. Many of the images in *Hyenas* command the attention of the audience but leave it puzzling over their meaning.

Hyenas can also be interpreted as a commentary on the contemporary world order. An indication of a fierce response to the state of the world is a harrowing shot of a mother and child in footage of a famine that Dramaan Drameh sees on a television in a church. The television is a Sony and the implication of this scene is that the importation of advanced consumer goods can offer such disabling images but can supply no solutions for Africa. The answer offered by the film, in the song over the final credits, is that work is the only way to freedom. It is necessary to take responsibility for your own actions which neither the townspeople or the vindictive Ramatou are willing to do. Like the World Bank, Mambety implies, she can manipulate people and resources without reference to morality or fear of retribution.

 **FURTHER WORK**

Representations of Africa and Africans
Examine representations of Africa and Africans by examining two different films, one of which originates outside of Africa and one of which originates from within Africa. For example, compare and contrast *A World Apart* (Chris Menges, 1987, UK) with *Mapantsula*.

Compare and contrast two texts from different media that offer representations of Africa. For example:

Foster's Ice advertisement and *Yaaba*

A 1997 advertisement for Foster's Ice can be contrasted with *Yaaba*. The Foster's advertisement features an unspecified African location in which a young man speaks of his father who digs for toads to squeeze the moisture out of them. The advertisement is jocular: it mimics documentary style (the microphone dips into the top of the frame momentarily) and a displaced kangaroo pops up to surprise the father. The following contrasts can be made:

- *Yaaba* individualises: the advertisement stereotypes
- *Yaaba* is a view from the inside: the advertisement manipulates information from the outside
- *Yaaba* presents a stable society, adapted to its environment: the advertisement suggests there is no hope for development
- *Yaaba* suggests progress is possible and that positive links between the generations are possible: the advertisement suggests divisions between the generations
- *Yaaba* acknowledges there are competing explanations of Nopoko's illness and respects indigenous knowledge: the advertisement devalues the idea of traditional knowledge

Examples such as these establish that media texts make different representations of Africa available and therefore make it all the more important that there is a cinema by and for Africans.

FURTHER READING

Ashbury, Roy, Helsby, Wendy and O'Brien, Maureen, *Teaching African Cinema*, BFI, 1998.
Bakari, Imruh and Cham, Mbye, (eds), *African Experiences of Cinema*, BFI, 1996.
Diawara, Manthia, *African Cinema*, Indiana University Press, 1992.
Boughedir, Ferid, *African Cinema from A to Z*, OCIC, 1992.
Malkmus, Lizbeth and Armes, Roy, *Arab and African Filmmaking*, Zed Books, 1991.
Shiri, Keith, (ed.), *Africa at the Pictures*, National Film Theatre, 1993.
Ukadike, Nwachukwu Frank, *Black African Cinema*, University of California Press, 1994.

FURTHER VIEWING

Caméra Afrique (Ferid Boughedir, 1983), Connoisseur/Academy video
Caméra Arabe (Ferid Boughedir, 1987), Connoisseur/Academy video
Xala (Ousmane Sembène, Senegal, 1974), Connoisseur/Academy video
Halfaouine (Ferid Boughedir, Tunisia, 1990), Connoisseur/Academy video
Tilai (Idrissa Ouédraogo, Burkina Faso/Switzerland/France, 1990), Artificial Eye video
Denko (Mohamed Camra, Burkina Faso, 1992), Connoisseur/Academy video
Borom Sarret (Sembène Ousmane, Senegal, 1963), Connoisseur/Academy video
Certificat d'indigence (Moussa Bathily, Senegal, 1981), Connoisseur/Academy video

NOTES

1   Editorial in *Écrans d'Afrique*, Number 11, 1995.

2   *Index on Censorship* 6, 1995.

3   In conversation with James Leahy, *Monthly Film Bulletin*, January 1988.

4   At FESPACO 1997, quoted by Alexa Dalby in *Black Film Bulletin*, Spring 1997, Vol. 005 Issue 001, London.

5   Kidane Mengisteab, *Globalisation and Autocentricity in Africa's Development in the 21st Century*, Africa World Press Inc., 1996.

6   See Manthia Diawara, *African Cinema: Politics and Culture*, Indiana University Press, 1992.

7   Quoted in *African Experiences of Cinema*, edited by Imruh Bakari and Mbye B. Cham, BFI, 1996.

8   Report in the Ghanaian weekly, *The Mirror*, 15 March 1997.

9   Alexa Dalby, *Black Film Bulletin*, Spring 1997, Vol. 005 Issue 001, p13.

10 'African Cinema in the Tempest of Minor Festivals' in Bakari and Cham, *ibid*, p160.

11 *Black Film Bulletin*, Winter 1996, Vol. 3 Issue 4.

12 *Arab and African Film Making*, Zed Books Ltd, 1991

13 'Africa from Within: The Films of Gaston Kabore and Idrissa Ouédraogo as Anthropological Sources' in Bakari and Cham, *ibid*, p237.

14 *Black African Cinema*, University of California Press, 1994, p91

15 Jacqueline Maingard, 'New South African cinema: Mapantsula and Sarafina', *Screen*, Vol. 35, Number 3, Autumn 1994.

16 *Écrans d'Afrique*, Number 11, 1995, p12.

5

21 Practical Production: a guide for teachers and students

CHAPTER **21** # Practical Production: A Guide for Teachers and Students

A TEACHER'S INTRODUCTION TO PRACTICAL PRODUCTION

Production

Practical work

Practical work in A level media courses is often highly problematic. In many schools and colleges, technical resources are limited and no matter how hard teachers try to persuade students that low tech can be a vehicle for high calibre ideas, students still remain enamoured of high-tech glitz and superficial professionalism. It is not an intention here to preach the virtues of production work completed on an editing suite constructed out of an empty washing-up liquid bottle and the end of a toilet roll; learning about media technology is obviously a valuable part of the course. However, media products are only ever as good as the ideas behind them and perhaps greater reward should be given to creativity and innovation that doesn't quite work rather than to the pallid pastiche that does.

Individual work

Individual work is problematic for a number of reasons. Firstly, it is very difficult for teachers to motivate and monitor large numbers of individual productions. Secondly, individual productions often stretch technical resources to the limit and can mean that time is wasted while students wait to use equipment. The first problem can be addressed by providing one well-defined assignment which gives scope for individual creativity. Free choice assignments are an attractive concept but only work with highly knowledgeable and highly motivated students. Within assignments there should also be a succession of targets at intervals so that students feel motivated by small achievements. The problem of limited technical resources can be addressed by splitting classes and giving research tasks to some students while others are completing the practical assignment.

Group work

Group work is also problematic. Few production pieces are ever literally a group effort; often, some members of the group ride on the backs of others. This can be addressed initially by making sure that groups are small enough not to allow students to get lost within them. It can also be addressed by making sure that group members are allocated specific jobs within each assignment.

Summary

The best practical pieces are the culmination of study within a media topic; they enable students to experiment with, and justify, new ideas in the context of a particular genre and a particular medium or range of media. The worst practical pieces are inept pastiche. If students are going to learn from practical production then they should be encouraged to produce work which is creative and questioning experimentation not just pale imitation.

Evaluation

The evaluation is there for a purpose. All too often, students submit a self-congratulatory log and not a true rationale and critique of the problems involved in research and production. Ultimately, an evaluation should analyse the strengths and weaknesses of the finished artefact in the context of real media output; it should look at those aspects of the production that have succeeded and those that have failed and suggest where improvements could have been made. In discussing these aspects, an evaluation should have examined the production in terms of media theory and debates.

In early production exercises, it might help to frame a question for the evaluation which forces students to examine their artefact critically. For example an appropriate question for an advertising campaign which is repositioning a product at a new target consumer might be: 'What are the problems involved in creating an advertising campaign repositioning the product at this group? How successful do you think you have been in overcoming these problems in the light of your initial research and any repositioning campaign you have studied recently?'

Exemplar exercises

No apology is made for the fact that some of the exercises which follow are worked through in more depth than others. It was felt that some areas such as radio production were less familiar to students and teachers than perhaps print or video and so this area has been examined in some depth.

Some of the exercises which follow are exemplified with 'possible' student responses and some with 'actual' student responses; neither the former nor the latter are seen to be perfect examples but, ideally, they will give some idea of the responses possible.

PRODUCTION EXERCISES IN RADIO

Equipment needed

Gathering actuality

One of the following pieces of equipment will be required:

■ Portable domestic audio cassette recorder plus microphone

- Portable professional audio cassette recorder (eg Marantz) plus microphone
- Portable reel-to-reel tape recorder (eg Uher) plus microphone
- Portable digital audio tape (DAT) recorder plus microphone
- Portable mini-disc (MD) recorder plus microphone

and possibly
- Internet and sound card for gathering up-to-the minute news soundbites

Mixing

- Small mixing desk with at least one audio cassette player and one microphone channelled in and output to an audio cassette or reel-to-reel tape recorder

or
- Computer hardware and software capable of audio mixing with floppy disc drive and/or suitable audio player/recorder input/output plus microphone

Editing

One of the following pieces of equipment will be required:
- Audio cassette to audio cassette dubbing
- Reel-to-reel tape recorder with splicing block, china graph pencil, razor blades and editing tape
- Computer hardware and software capable of audio editing with floppy disc input/output and/or suitable audio player/recorder input/output

(**EXAMPLE EXERCISE 1**)—— **Radio Production Example (Individual)** ——

Production artefacts

- A **cue** and feature for Radio One's Newsbeat slot at 5.30 pm
- A cue and clip for Radio Four's News Bulletin at 6 pm

Cue

Usually an introduction to a clip, wrap, etc. read by the bulletin reader.

Introduction

The best practical work often explores the difference between similar content worked through in terms of two different media. In this radio exercise, however, content is explored in the same medium but in terms of different target audiences. An exercise such as this could well be the culmination of the study of a topic concerned with the selection and manufacture of the news; the exercise explores media manipulation and the underlying ideologies and brings up a variety of relevant questions not least those of news values, agendas and rhetoric.

This is a stimulating assignment as it mimics reality. Cuts in staff in most news agencies and organisations have made it necessary for reporters to supply variations of the same news items for a variety of outlets; some even turn the feature they have been working on for one outlet into a hard news story for another. This is a useful jumping off point for media studies students as it shows the opportunism associated with much of today's news gathering. The event becomes news because journalists/cameramen/etc. happen to be there, rather than the event being prime news in itself. A case of 'We've got a good picture so let's stick it on the front page.'

Possible research

◆ Who is the target audience for the Radio One feature?

◆ Who listens at this time of day?

◆ Are they likely to be involved in primary, secondary or tertiary consumption of radio output at this time of day?

◆ What mode of address are they accustomed to?

◆ How do they stand ideologically in terms of the issue being presented?

◆ Who is the target audience for the Radio Four clip?

◆ Will they be listening in the same way?

◆ How do they differ ideologically and in terms of mode of address from the Radio One listeners?

◆ What makes radio different from other media? What are the problems of radio and how can they be overcome?

◆ How are Radio One Newsbeat features constructed? Are there many segments? What do they consist of? Are there **vox pops**, interviews, **segues**, music, sound effects?

◆ Apart from the length, how does a clip for Radio Four news differ? How is a clip constructed? Are clips the only way news is presented in a Radio Four news bulletin?

◆ Who else can a student realistically interview to make a balanced feature for Radio One?

◆ What is a suitable question for a vox pop and where should it be conducted?

◆ Does the Radio One feature need other aspects of content such as music or intertextual references to make it more accessible for the target listener?

◆ Where can real news soundbites be obtained?

Vox pop

A vox populi (Latin for voice of the people) is a series of soundbites from the public in answer to one question on a particular issue.

Segue

This is a link spoken by the reporter between actuality.

Possible discovery

◆ The Radio One target listener is younger and more likely at this time to be doing something else as well as listening to the radio and is therefore a secondary or tertiary consumer. The Radio Four listener is often making a conscious decision to listen to the news and is therefore a primary consumer.

◆ Radio is an aural medium. 'Images' have to be created through the ear. People and places need to be aurally identified as no visual means of doing so can be employed. Words, sound and music are the tools used to create images; the essence of this medium is sound FXs (sound effects). For instance, when interviewing a train driver, there should be at least the sound of trains, a station or a station announcement in the background.

The natural urge is always to interview people where it is the quietest; this should be resisted at all costs.

◆ Radio One Newsbeat features are usually about three minutes in length. The feature is cued in by the bulletin reader in the studio. There are often several segments introduced and subsequently linked by segues from a single reporter (the links are often added back in the studio). The segments are made up of interviews (asking named people a number of questions) vox pops (asking a range of un-named people one question) and background or scene-setting ambient sound. Music is often used to add meaning quickly. It can be used behind the reporter in the links or sometimes it is added over actuality (beware – music added over interviews and vox pops can be intrusive and annoying.)

◆ Radio One features are always fast moving with short segments and in the lighter features there is often a deal of intertextual reference, ie clips from films, TV, etc. These obviously help build up meaning in an aural medium. The reporter usually speaks in the present tense as if the event is actually happening 'now'. The style of delivery gives the feeling that the young target listener is perhaps a secondary or even tertiary consumer whose attention must be 'grabbed' and then a great deal of work done to keep it.

◆ A Radio Four clip for news is much shorter, about 30 seconds, and consists of simply one sound bite from one interviewee with the cue spoken by the bulletin reader in the studio. The cue is usually longer and more formal than a Radio One cue; it is also written in the past tense which gives it less immediacy. Radio Four news targets an older listener who is more likely to be a primary consumer; consequently, the news has more information and little 'entertainment'.

◆ News is updated throughout the day on several web sites on the internet. Soundbites for news exercises can also be gleaned from this source.

(EXAMPLE ARTEFACT)—— *Radio One Feature* ————————————————

The news stimulus for this exemplar radio assignment is an actual announcement by Sir Paul Condon, the Metropolitan Police Commissioner, which claimed that most of London's street crime is committed by Black youth – a particularly contentious issue but one which contains any number of significant aspects for media students. This sort of feature also allows students to use material from an official source (eg a soundbite from the internet) and mix it with material they have gleaned themselves (eg a vox pop on the issue collected in school/college or locally).

The following feature is not a complete transcript but it should be detailed enough to give a good idea of the possible structure and content. It is a serious issue and therefore demands more respectful treatment than the usual entertainment based features at this time on Radio One. Nevertheless, this is a 'youth' issue and would certainly be a high news priority on this station.

Figure 21.1 Radio One: reaction to Sir Paul Condon's announcement

Cue:	Bulletin reader	Black community leaders are slamming the recent claim by Paul Condon that muggings in London are mostly committed by black youths. They are saying that the Police Chief's announcement will harm race relations. Fred Smith sends this report from the heart of London's black community.	Studio
Segue:	Reporter: Fred Smith	Community leaders here in South London are angry about this latest police claim. They accuse Paul Condon of trying to bring in new tough police 'stop and search' measures similar to the so-called 'sus' laws of the 1980s by the back door. But what do the ordinary people here in the community think? I asked them if London's Police Chief is right to be making statements such as these.	Either recorded in the studio or recorded on the street/at the press conference
Vox pop:	Various people at random on the street	'Yes, I do . . .' 'No, I don't . . .' (etc.)	Street
Segue:	Reporter: Fred Smith	The feeling here in South London seems to be that Paul Condon's remarks do not help . . . . . . but speaking earlier he was unrepentant.	Either recorded in the studio or recorded on the street/at the press conference
Interview:	Paul Condon	Answering these questions: Why have you made this statement now? Do you think this will harm relationships between the black community and the police in London? If your statement is correct why do you think it is the case?	Press conference
Segue:	Reporter: Fred Smith	Linking Condon interview with interview with community leader	Either recorded in the studio or recorded on the street/at the press conference
Interview:	Black community leader	Answering these questions: Why has Paul Condon decided to make this statement now? Do you think it has damaged race relations in London? What do you think is the real problem underlying this statement and what is the answer?	
Segue:	Reporter: Fred Smith	Rounds up and signs off	Either recorded in the studio or recorded on the street/at the press conference

(**EXAMPLE ARTEFACT**)— *Radio Four Clip* ————————————

From the above feature, there is an option of two interviews that could be clipped for the Radio Four news bulletin. We could clip Paul Condon's interview which might then be set up as follows.

Figure 21.2 A clip from Paul Condon's interview for Radio Four

| **Cue:** | Bulletin reader | Paul Condon has today defended his recent announcement that Black youths are to blame for 80% of the crime on the streets of the capital. At a press conference in London he said his statement was nothing but the truth. |
| **Clip:** | Paul Condon | I think . . . etc., etc. |

Alternatively, we could edit some of the community leader's interview for the news clip which might then be set up as follows.

Figure 21.3 Alternative clip from Paul Condon's interview for Radio Four

| **Cue:** | Bulletin reader | A black community has today condemned London's Police Commissioner for fuelling racist feelings by claiming that Black youths are responsible for much of the city's street crime. [Name of community leader] said the black community in London are right to feel angered by Paul Condon's announcement. |
| **Clip:** | Black community leader | We feel . . . etc., etc. |

Discussion points for the evaluation

The evaluation of assignments should refer back to the research undertaken at the beginning.

◆ Which clip would you choose to put on the Radio Four Bulletin? Choices such as this are being made by news editors in newsrooms every day of the week. What difference do these choices make to the way we view people and issues. Should news disseminators always present both sides of an argument or is there sometimes a case for just one point of view to be given? Is the Radio One feature more balanced? Do you think that, even in this, one view seems to be given more credence than the other? If so, how and why?

◆ Do the artefacts succeed in fitting in with the ideology of the institution they come from and the audience they are targeting? Would young people listen to the Radio One feature? How does the Radio Four clip fit in with the research undertaken?

◆ Do the artefacts fit the forms identified for each institution?

Production artefacts

The first requirement is a running order for a new half hour 'alternative sports' programme for 16 - to 25-year-olds on independent local radio. The running order should include all the items within the programme with timings and exemplar extracts (see below) should be asterisked.

The second requirement is for taped extracts (10 minutes maximum) from the new half hour 'alternative sports' programme for 16- to 25-year-olds on independent local radio. The extracts *must* include:

- An example of the style of studio presentation
- Two programme **idents**
- Two 30 second advertisements
- At least one three minute feature looking at an issue/personality within sport in general or within a particular sport
- A one to two minute report from a sporting event

  and could include any of the following:
- Quizzes, interviews, studio debates, vox pops, a trailer for another programme on the same station, sponsor's ident

Ident

In broadcasting, this refers to a jingle of a few seconds in length which identifies a station or programme.

Introduction

This exercise could well be the culmination of the study of a topic concerned with sport and the media. It could also link in with the study of a local media organisation such as a local independent radio station. Among other things, it will enable students to explore concepts and debates to do with genre, narrowcasting; gender, disability or race representation; alternative and mainstream; ideology, language and discourse.

It is a useful exercise as it requires students to conceive a whole programme although only parts of that programme need actually be produced. It is usually quite accessible to students as often they are involved in alternative sports themselves (eg skateboarding, stall ball, street hockey, wheelchair basketball etc.) and can easily glean the actuality. The boundaries of mainstream and alternative in this example don't have to be too rigid; the idea is to give students the notion that sport programmes don't have to mean football matches at Wembley and that there is news just waiting to be reported. Also it is important for the media student to realise that local news can be concerned with quite small events; particularly in the cases of some of the new radio franchises which are servicing fairly limited areas.

Possible research

- What day of the week and time of the day would suit the target listener?
- What demographic/psychographic group do they belong to?
- Are they likely to be primary, secondary or tertiary consumers of radio output at this time of day and with this particular subject?
- What mode of address are they accustomed to?
- What point of view might they take in terms of the issues being presented?
- Who is likely to buy advertising in or want to sponsor such a programme?

◆ What makes radio different from other media? What are the problems of radio and how can they be overcome?

◆ What is the construction of broadcast sports programmes in general and radio sports programmes in particular? Are there many segments? What do they consist of?

◆ How can this programme experiment with the genre and produce an alternative programme covering alternative sports?

Possible discovery

◆ This programme would have to be on once a week either in the early evening or quite late at night to catch this age group.

◆ This age group are usually more aspiring, unconventional and less inhibited.

◆ If it is in the early evening the listeners are likely to be dropping in and out of the programme and being primarily involved only with those items that interest them. The later slot would probably attract a more absorbed listener.

◆ This more absorbed listener would probably be looking for an aggressive posse-style mode of address with at least two if not more presenters depending on the time slot – late night radio tends to be more laid back and less aggressive. This target group like contentious presenters who might well question traditional norms and poke fun at the establishment. They do not like reverential treatment of issues.

◆ In terms of advertisements/sponsorship, this is the ideal programme for all the brand name sportswear manufacturers whose sportswear is a coveted item for this target group but the most likely advertisers would be local sports shops selling these brands. Isotonic drinks, adventure holidays and music would probably also be suitable. But, as this programme is looking at the alternative and individual, there is definitely room for less stereotypical advertising.

◆ Sport tends to be a visual event and therefore presenting sport in an interesting way on radio is not easy but it can be done. Attention must be paid to try and avoid too much speech in the presentation. Sound conjures up the image – even the smallest sound can create quite a vivid image. The sound of a roller blade on the pavement is pretty distinctive even without explanation, for instance.

◆ Sports programmes tend to be dedicated to one sport or to have segments devoted discretely to a sport. There is always clear signposting at the beginning of a sports programme to clarify which sports and events are to be covered. Sports programmes have traditionally looked at predominantly mainstream male sports and they have usually been presented by male presenters. Sports programmes have been among the slowest to revamp and change their style of presentation and it was only with the initiation of Channel Four and its new look sports programmes such as American Football that other broadcasters began to question their style of presentation.

◆ There is certainly room to move away from the formal one middle class male behind a desk image of sports presentation. The content will allow short items and a chance to bring in other texts such as music, film bites, etc.

(**EXAMPLE ARTEFACT**)— *No Contest Runnng Order* ——————

The following sample running order is for a programme entitled *No Contest* which would be broadcast at 7 pm on Friday nights.

Figure 21.4 The running order for *No Contest*

No Contest			
Item *denotes items to be included as taped extracts	**Description**	**Running time** in mins (') and seconds (")	**Elapsed time**
*Ident 1 *Intro	Station/Programme ident Presenters 1 & 2	20" 1'30"	20" 1'50"
Trailer	Trailer for what's coming up	40"	2'30"
Advert 1	Nike sportswear	30"	3'
*Advert 2	Sahara trekking holiday	30"	3'30"
Ident 2	Programme ident	10'	3'40"
Segue	Presenter 1	2'20"	6'
Sport on	Weekly run down of coming events	3'30"	9'30"
*Ident 3	Programme ident	10"	9'40"
Segue	Presenter 2	2'00"	11'40"
*Feature	Skateboarding	3'10"	14'50"
Segue	Presenter 1	1'30"	16'20"
Ident 4	Programme ident	10"	16'30"
*Advert 3	Government anti-smoking	30"	17'
Advert 4	Local sports shop	30"	17'30"
Segue	Presenter 1	1'	18'30"
Quiz	Phone in quiz Presenters 1 & 2	2'10"	20'40"
Segue	Presenter 2	30"	21'10"
Feature	Dangerous sports club	2'40"	23'50"
Ident 5	Programme ident	10"	24'
*Sport news	Presenter 1	2'	26'
*'Live' report	Wheelchair basketball	1'50"	27'50"
Outro	Presenters 1 & 2	2'	29'50"
Ident 6	Programme ident	10"	30'

(EXAMPLE ARTEFACT)—— *No Contest Taped Extracts* ————————

It is not advantageous here to give verbatim transcriptions of every item but some suggestions will be given in terms of content, style and format.

Example of presentation style – Introduction from presenters 1 and 2 (1' 30")

The aim is to have young presenters of both genders to give the idea that this is not going to be just another programme on male mainstream sports. The presenters should constantly be interrupting each other in an attempt to keep the programme lively and to give it a feeling of movement and pace. The music FX also adds to the feeling that the programme is young and fast moving while the cheering FX makes the listener feel that the programme is so good that it should be congratulated.

Figure 21.5 Example of presentation style with two presenters

Voice	Content	Sound FX
		FX of crowd cheering at a stadium breaks into music – fast moving fading down to . . .
Presenter 1: (female)	Don't go . . .	. . . music under
Presenter 2: (male)	. . . anywhere until you've heard from this week's *No Contest* . . .	music under
Presenter 1: (female)	. . . which brings you the sort of sport that other programmes cannot reach . . . etc., etc.	music under to FX of crowd cheering as presenter introduces the trailer for what's coming up

Example of programme ident – (10")

Idents have become an important part of broadcast media production. They are important in terms of broadcast flow as they are constantly reminding the audience of what they are consuming and why and even more importantly – in terms of station idents – that the audience are consuming one seamless production with a continuous narrative that must not be interrupted. The opening ident of a programme (ident 1) often places the programme within its station but the example here is purely a programme ident. Radio idents often benefit from intertextual references because they have to create meaning in such a short space of time and this meaning can be more easily carried in via another well-known text.

Figure 21.6 Example of a programme ident

Voice	Content	Sound FX
		Music extract from Gerry and The Pacemakers singing 'You'll Never Walk Alone' . . . 'Walk on . . . Walk on . . .' which is interrupted by an explosion . . .
Husky female:	No Contest	Bright jingle music

Example of feature – skateboarding feature (3' 10")

Features always seem daunting to the new radio student but a good hint here is not to record too much; usually, three or four questions to each interviewee will give more than enough actuality for a three minute feature. Students who come back with an hour's worth of recording on each interview have a huge editing job ahead of them. One component, not included in the following feature, but which always adds colour to radio is a vox pop; vox pops, like interviews, should be recorded as cleanly as possible to make them easier to edit.

Figure 21.7 Example of a feature

Voice	Content	Sound FX
		Opening sound of skateboard wheels on tarmac then music ('Wheels on Fire') fading down behind . . .
Reporter:	This week I've been looking at the renewed interest in that 70s pastime skateboarding . . . first of all, I talked to Fred Smith who runs a sports shop in Anytown and I asked him what the demand for skateboards had been like recently . . .	music under voice
Sports shop owner:	'Well, it's been so great I've nearly sold out . . .' etc., etc.	sound of busy shop
Reporter:	But many local councils have put restrictions on the use of skateboards in public areas so where can enthusiasts go to get some wheel burn. I found one group down at Anytown park and asked them if this was the only place they could go . . .	music under voice
Skateboarder:	'It is getting very difficult to find places but when you're really keen you can always find somewhere to go . . .' etc., etc.	sound of skateboards on tarmac and other ambient noise
Reporter:	Well it all looks easy enough to me so I think I'll give it a go . . . . . . perhaps not	sound of reporter getting on skateboard . . . skateboard moving off . . . scream . . . crash and wheels spinning, music ('Wheels on Fire') fading up . . . finishes on music.

Example of an advertisement – Sahara Trekking (30")

Radio advertising always seem to be stuck in a rut of the direct sell eg 'Buy your new windows and doors at See Throo, Double Glazing' and so students often have to be encouraged to try a short narrative piece. Again, the usefulness of intertextual references in advertising is evident.

Figure 21.8 Example of an advertisement

Voice	Content	Sound FX
		'Indiana Jones' music slowing to halt . . .
Female:	Brian, this isn't what I thought Africa would be like. It's really . . .	Sound of tea cups, tea pouring and being stirred
Male:	. . . boring	''
Female:	Perhaps we should have taken that package trip with Sahara Trekking	Tea cups chinking until the word Sahara when Indiana Jones music starts again
Male Voice-over	Contact your local travel agent for Sahara Trekking . . . With them, every trip is an adventure	Indiana Jones music fades up to crescendo

Example of 'live' report – wheelchair basketball (1'50")

It is quite important that students learn the difference between the prepackaged feature and the as-it-happens 'live' report. Obviously, for the purposes of student work, the 'live' report is also pre-recorded but the differentiation should be that this report remains unedited. This allows students to compare and contrast the construction of the feature with the construction of the 'live' report.

Figure 21.9 Example of a 'live' report

Voice	Content	Sound FX
Reporter:	The game has just finished and once again the favourites have won . . . and here is a breathless team captain to tell you what he thought of the game	Sound of people in a gymnasium throughout ↓
Winning team captain:	'Well . . . I'm certainly not sick as a parrot tonight but it was a tough game . . .' etc.	
Reporter:	Thanks [name of team captain] but let's talk to some of the supporters here tonight . . . what did they think of the game . . .	
Vox pop:	'I thought we played really well . . .' 'It was a real shame we didn't score early on . . .' etc.	
Reporter:	And how do the losers feel tonight?	

Figure 21.9 Example of a 'live' report – *continued*

Voice	Content	Sound FX
Losing team captain: Reporter:	'Sick as a paper parrot in a downpour but I'm sure we'll win next week . . .' etc. Well . . . that's all we've got time for . . . so it's back to you two in the studio.	

Discussion points for the evaluation

The evaluation of assignments should refer back to the research undertaken at the beginning.

- Do the artefacts succeed in fitting in with the ideology of the institution they come from and the audience they are targeting? Would young people listen to this programme at this time?

- How does this programme fit with the genre of broadcast sport programmes? What about the extract examples given? How do they fit in with their own individual genres?

- Is the presentation style apt or should it be more aggressive and anarchistic?

- Is the content innovative and does it present non-mainstream sports? Do you think this sort of programming is important? If so why?

PRODUCTION EXERCISES IN PRINT AND PHOTOGRAPHY

Equipment needed

Gathering actuality

- Spiral notebook and pen

and/or

- Dictaphone/audio cassette recorder

and

- Suitable photographic camera

or

- Digital camera which interfaces with DTP

Layout and printing (basics)

- Computer hardware and software capable of at least basic desk top publishing. In terms of software this could be as basic as a word processing package such as Word which can put text in columns which can then be cut and pasted onto a page with pictures. Or it could mean a designated DTP package such as PageMaker, PagePlus, Microsoft Publisher, or Quark Express

and

■ Black and white printer (inkjet or laser)

and

■ Basic black and white photocopier – useful for reducing/enlarging images/pages or for photocopying words onto images (using overhead transparencies)

Layout and printing (luxuries)

■ Black and white or colour image scanner with suitable software – if a scanner or digital camera are used then a photo manipulation package such as Photo Shop or Photo Styler can also be useful

and

■ A4/A3 Colour printer (inkjet or laser)

or

■ Colour photocopier so that colour/black and white text can be photocopied onto colour/black and white images

(EXAMPLE EXERCISE 1)—— **Print Production Example (Individual*)** ——

Production artefact
Extracts from the first edition of a new magazine targeting female teenagers which questions dominant ideas prevalent in current magazines targeting this age group.

■ Front cover

and

■ Written feature with photos

or

■ Photostory

and

■ One advert

Introduction
*If a group project is preferred then obviously a whole magazine can be produced.

This is a useful assignment to complement study of a magazine topic and it can be introduced early in an advanced media course because the students have had a great deal of exposure to these magazines and are already knowledgeable about content, style and form. It initiates debate about stereotypical gender and issue representation and requires a thoughtful approach by students who will have to reject or experiment with those stereotypes to produce something new and interesting.

The production of a photostory can be a useful way of approaching ideas about the construction of narrative and clarifying the difference between plot and theme.

Possible research

◆ What mainstream magazines exist for this group?

◆ What alternative publications are there for this target group?

◆ How easily can it be produced and published in the current market?

◆ What makes print different from other media?

◆ How are magazines for this target group constructed?

◆ What stereotypical images exist in terms of this target group?

◆ What issues/people are relevant to this group?

◆ Do adverts also have to cater for a stereotypical image of this age group? What needs, wants, aspirations would they have?

◆ How do these magazines address the readership? What sort of language is used and how does this effect meaning?

Possible discovery

◆ There are numerous magazines for this age group including *Just Seventeen*, *Sugar*, *Mizz*.

◆ There are no alternative magazines targeting female teenagers.

◆ Small scale production is easy on DTP but dissemination is more difficult with the large publishing houses dominating distribution.

◆ If they are not recorded, TV, radio and film are ephemeral media and consequently require the audience to gain immediate meaning from a text. Print is a permanent medium which is usually consumed at a time convenient to the reader; the consumption is usually primary and also readers can re-read a text if the meaning is unclear. This should allow the print medium more room for subtlety than other media.

◆ Teen magazines are bold and colourful with an emphasis on graphics and short items. There is a great deal of reader participation with letters from, and features about, readers. Competitions and quizzes are also popular.

◆ These magazines tend to represent females as thin and unblemished teenagers who are all looking for relationships and view themselves primarily in terms of their ability to catch their ideal boyfriend. The males are also unblemished and are viewed mainly in terms of their looks rather than any other attributes.

◆ The dominating issue in these magazines is (as stated above) relationships with the opposite sex. Many items focus on: how to find a boyfriend; how to look glamorous for a boyfriend; how to get over losing your boyfriend. Items on young soap/pop stars and drugs are also prevalent.

◆ Adverts tend to concentrate on selling a product by giving it cult status and the aspiring purchaser therefore buys into that cult. Conversely, the punishment for not buying the product is that you do not become part of that culture and you are alienated from the social group.

♦ Magazines such as these have a specific mode of address that is informal and uses a particular vocabulary. Pigeonholing expressions that underpin stereotypes such as 'boyfs', 'hunks' and 'chickstrels' are common.

(EXAMPLE ARTEFACT) — *Hers and Hers Magazine* —————————

This is one student's response to this brief. It is perhaps not perfect in that it would certainly be targeting the upper age group within the teen magazine market but it is a product that shows some experimentation with content even if, for the most part it conforms to the stereotype in terms of the technical conventions of the genre.

The following examples have been created using a 35mm camera, DTP package and colour photocopier. For the photostory, the photos plus relevant background colours were pasted onto A3 sheets with the speech bubbles. These A3 sheets were then reduced to A4 using the colour photocopier. This could easily be done in exactly the same way using black and white photocopier. The results are usually very effective.

Example of cover

Hers and Hers sets out clearly from the beginning that it is looking at the issue of female sexuality. The front cover has the two women in a suggestive pose but it is a picture which holds no implication that this should be a hidden relationship or that it is in any way an unnatural one. The student has used a 'script' typeface for the masthead which gives the magazine a feeling that it is informal and chatty. The front cover does fall down in that there are some crucial aspects missing including the issue number, date and price but there has been some real thought put into the iconography.

There is no doubt that the subhead 'A Weekly Magazine for Wiser Women' might create some debate, particularly among the male members of the class!

Example of photostory 'Sarah's Story'

This student has chosen to create a photostory rather than a written feature; it uses the stereotypical teen magazine format where the 'problem' photostory finishing up with 'help' line contact is a familiar item. Here, however, the content is unusual in terms of the teen magazine. This is not an easy subject for 'teen' treatment but the student has handled it with some delicacy and without bias.

The product is technically very sophisticated; the shots have been well thought out with a good use of the close up. The student has also tried to make the images flow on the page by slanting and cropping the photos to make them less uniform. The continuity of the whole magazine has been considered by the repeated use of the colours evident on the front cover. This red and black colour scheme gives the magazine a more sophisticated look than is the norm.

Example of an advertisement

The advertisement is well-targeted, simple yet effective. Obviously, because it is advertising a charity walk, it is getting away from the teen pressure of the

Figure 21.10 The front cover of *Hers and Hers*

social need sell eg 'If you don't buy this product, nobody will want to know you' (see Chapter 10).

Discussion points for the evaluation

The evaluation of assignments should refer back to the research undertaken at the beginning.

Figure 21.11 Teen photostory – *'Sarah's Story'*

Figure 21.11 (continued)

Figure 21.11 (continued)

- How does this production differ from the usual teen magazine output in terms of style, form, layout and content?

- Does the artefact succeed in fitting in with the ideology of the institution it comes from and the audience it is targeting?

- Would this artefact be more likely to be termed alternative rather than mainstream?

- How does each extract conform to the conventions of their individual genre?

- How easy is it to produce the artefact on the equipment available and how could it have been improved?

- What critical media debates/critical media theories have been examined in the production of this artefact?

(EXAMPLE EXERCISE **2**)── **Print Production Example** (Individual*) ──

Production artefact

- An original news story written for and with original photograph/s cropped for a quality daily/Sunday broadsheet

and

- The same original news story written for and with original photograph/s cropped for a popular daily/Sunday tabloid*

Introduction

*This exercise can easily be changed into a group exercise using a number of news stories or students can choose to compare the same news story in publications other than those indicated above.

Like the radio news exercise, this project allows students to examine the construction and manipulation of the news. It also is a good example of how news can be found anywhere and how images can have their meaning changed by cropping and by the anchorage. It is often more usual with this exercise to construct the same story for a local weekly newspaper and a national daily broadsheet newspaper as it is not always easy for students to find stories that are sensational enough to hit the tabloid headlines.

However, students should be made aware of how even a small local incident can be made into national news. In one response to this exercise, a student took a picture of some local roadworks that had been continuing for some time; the picture was cropped to frame a pedestrian picking their way through a warren of traffic cones and then written for the local paper under the headline: 'High Street Roadworks Cause Grief for Pedestrians'. The student had interviewed the pedestrian and phoned the local council for comment about the roadworks and included this with other facts to construct the news story. The same story supposedly written for the *Guardian* was given the headline: 'Country in Chaos: Will the government choose towns or traffic?' This time the picture was cropped to frame a derelict shop behind the roadworks and the story was written using interviews from local shop owners, the local council and a quote gleaned over the phone from a public transport lobby group.

Figure 21.12 An effective advertisement for a charity walk

Possible research

◆ What ideological differences/biases separate the chosen target newspapers?

◆ How are these presented in the discourse?

◆ Are there any stereotypical views and issues prevalent in the two newspapers?

◆ What set news agendas do the target newspapers have?

◆ What would be a suitable and accessible news story for both publications?

◆ How is the information collected for a news story?

◆ How is a news story constructed?

◆ How would the two stories differ in content and length?

◆ How are photographs used in the target publications and how will this affect the cropping, framing and caption of the photograph within each story?

◆ Would the story be in the same position within each newspaper?

◆ How would the story be laid out on the pages of each newspaper and how does this effect the meaning?

Possible discovery

◆ There doesn't have to be a great deal of difference between the ideological standpoints of the two newspapers but of course this depends on the newspapers chosen. However, the biggest difference will be between the obviousness of the ideological standpoint – in other words the overtness of the bias. In tabloids, bias is evident but in broadsheets bias is usually better disguised. There is no such thing as a newspaper without bias.

◆ The popular daily tabloids have a distinctive discourse with the reader which closes down any opportunity for disagreement with the point of view being presented. This is most evident within the emotive language that is used: this language is often peculiar to tabloid newspapers. The broadsheet discourse is less closed and hence open to a variety of readings.

◆ Most popular tabloids have stereotypical views about certain people such as Fergie or Paul Gascoigne as well as stereotyping certain issues such as youth crime and screen violence although these vary from tabloid to tabloid. Certain broadsheets will also have stereotypical views about issues but they are presented more covertly.

◆ The news priority in the popular tabloids tends to be entertainment and stemming from this is a fixation with elite persons in the entertainment world. Tabloid news' agendas also prioritise cultural and geographical proximity and so they are more likely to have The Spice Girls on the front page than President Clinton. Broadsheet news agendas tend to be broader and are likely to include foreign news but among broadsheets some papers are more likely to prioritise one issue over another.

◆ It is not so much a case of finding a suitable news story for both newspapers but finding an angle for each story that is relevant to both newspapers. News is not a natural phenomenon; it is manufactured and even the smallest event can be turned into front page news if it is given a suitable angle.

◆ News is usually collected from a number of sources. First of all there are primary sources such as the police or a person who has witnessed an event and then there are secondary sources such as other publications or other reference sources. All news stories should contain material from a primary source otherwise it cannot truly be news. Consequently interviews are of the utmost importance and these interviews should be conducted with a range of sources if a balanced view is to be presented. The budding journalist should always keep his/her eyes open as news opportunities are everywhere.

◆ A news story has a particular shape. The most important part is the first three paragraphs which should contain all the information to answer the five 'W's: Who? What? When? Where? Why? The intro (introductory) paragraph should not contain details only enough information to entice the reader to read on. After the first three paragraphs the material should be presented in a descending order of importance as the sub-editor will cut a story from the bottom up paragraph by paragraph.

◆ The story in the broadsheet will undoubtedly be longer than the story in the tabloid and the broadsheet is therefore more likely to present information from a wider variety of sources.

◆ In the tabloid, the photograph usually has more importance in presenting the angle of the story than the broadsheet and therefore great care will be taken to crop, frame and anchor the photograph to the story.

◆ It may be the news chosen would have more prominence in one paper than another. This will depend on the news values of the paper and the strength of the photograph. Juxtaposition is important; newspapers will often qualify one story by placing it next to another. For instance, the meaning gleaned from a story about underfunding in the NHS will be coloured by placing that story next to one about a hospital patient being left for hours on a trolley in a corridor.

◆ The layout of the story will depend on the target publication and the position within the paper but it will undoubtedly affect the way the story is read and, consequently, the meaning gained.

─────

(**EXAMPLE ARTEFACT**)── *News item written and laid out as if for the* _____
Guardian newspaper

The following story was constructed by a student who seized on an opportune news event – a one day strike by college lecturers! The student was swift to recognise how the item could be easily manipulated to suit the front pages of both the *Sun* and the *Guardian*. Fortunately, the student also obtained a variety of interviews and a good picture that had enough ambiguity to be cropped in a number of ways.

The full photograph was used in the proposed *Guardian* news story.

Headline
Education on the Picket Line

Caption
Freda Smith, 20 years a lecturer at Anytown College, is prevented from picketing by police who claimed she was a danger to traffic.

Story opening
The government's education policy came under attack once again yesterday when lecturers across the country took part in a one day strike against cuts in government funding. The lecturers from a number of unions are concerned that the new Further and Higher Education quangos are forcing a situation

Figure 21.13 Presentation of a photograph for the proposed news story in the *Guardian*

which will inevitably mean a lowering of standards combined with high levels of stress among teaching staff.

At Anytown College, lecturers were prevented from picketing vehicles entering the college because police claimed they were a danger to traffic. One lecturer, Freda Smith, said: 'I have been a lecturer and a union member for 20 years; I am appalled that we are not being allowed to show our disgust at the latest cuts in funding. We are fighting to keep a quality on the curriculum and these cuts will mean fewer lecturers working more hours and teaching bigger classes than ever which can't be any good for the students. I don't know who they are trying to fool.'

[The story then went on to balance this comment with a quote from Anytown College management. Of course, there should have been comment from a government source but this would have been a little difficult for the student to obtain.]

Juxtaposed headlines
'Nursing Shortage at Crisis Level
'Quangos on the Increase', says Report

(EXAMPLE ARTEFACT)— *News item written and laid out as if for the* _____
Sun newspaper

In this response the student has cropped the photo to cut off the face of the smiling van passenger; as no other faces are visible, the picture becomes a great deal more sinister. The student has also cut sections from the lecturer's quote and, in doing so, has significantly changed meaning.

Headline
Cops Stop Union Loonies

Caption
Union militants cause traffic chaos in picket free-for-all

Figure 21.14 Presentation of a photograph for the proposed news story in the *Sun*

Story opening
Loony left lecturers stopped schooling and traffic yesterday in a protest at cuts in their 13 week holidays.

Militant teachers, left raging by new government plans to slash wasted cash in schools, brought towns to a standstill yesterday when they put picket lines on the streets.

In Anytown, police were called in to prevent traffic chaos. A policeman said: 'The strikers were causing a nuisance to traffic and somebody could have been killed.'

Union ringleader, Freda Smith, 45, said: 'I have been … a union member for 20 years: I don't know who they are trying to fool.'

Juxtaposed headline
Head in Gymslip Shocker

Discussion points for the evaluation

◆ Does each artefact succeed in fitting in with the ideology of the institution it comes from and the audience it is targeting in terms of content, language and lay out?

◆ Have you seen/studied similar stories in the target publications?

◆ How easy/difficult was it to manipulate the story for each publication and is one version of the story more biased than the other?

◆ How easy is it to produce the artefact on the equipment available and how could it have been improved?

◆ What judgement do the juxtaposed headlines make on the two versions of the news item?

◆ What critical media debates/critical media theories have been examined in the production of this artefact?

PRODUCTION EXERCISES IN VIDEO

Equipment needed

Filming

■ Camcorder (VHS–C, VHS, S–VHS, Hi 8, Beta Cam)

Mixing, editing and titling

One of the following facilities will be required:

■ Editing in camera

■ Editing from camera to VCR or VCR to VCR

■ Anything from basic desk top editing and titling facilities to fully equipped editing suites

■ Computer hardware and software capable of non-linear video mixing and editing

(**EXAMPLE EXERCISE 1**)—— **Video Production Example (Group)** ————

Production artefact

■ A one and a half to two minute trailer for a new television programme/series or for a new feature film

Introduction

Treatment

A short outline of the film that would usually include the story, ideas about characters and location, etc.

Storyboard

This is a visualisation of the treatment but it would indicate how the characters are going to be filmed and would also include some dialogue, sound FXs, etc.

Preparatory work for this exercise includes producing a **treatment, story-board** and script for dialogue or voice-over.

The advantage of this exercise is that students are required to examine and produce an artefact that conforms with, or questions the codes and conventions of, two genres: the genre of the film and the genre of the trailer.

This is also a useful exercise for exploring narrative structure in that students need to construct the elements of a clear narrative for the film as a whole; then, from this narrative, the students must produce a trailer which presents key plot developments and introduces characters and in doing so attract a specified audience without revealing the whole story.

Students have to look at the way films are constructed and likewise the way trailers are constructed; especially, for example, in relation to editing and the use of the soundtrack.

Suggested research

◆ Why are trailers important for film distributors and TV programming?

◆ What kinds of trailers exist for film and television?

◆ Are there any essential differences between film trailers in terms of genre?

◆ Are there any essential differences between TV trailers in terms of genre?

◆ Are there any essential differences between film and TV trailers?

◆ How do these trailers target a specific audience?

◆ Do the trailers vary in terms of the number of shots used; the average shot length; the type of shot; the use of voice-over; the mode of address; the use of music and sound effects?

◆ Does the trailer have to match the actual genre of the programme/film?

◆ What generic conventions are being presented, modified or mixed?

◆ Does the trailer have to match the genre of the film/programme?

◆ Do different TV channels/film distributors have individual styles for trailers?

Discovery

◆ Trailers are adverts and must attract an audience to a TV/film text. Film trailers promote an individual text or sometimes a series whereas TV trailers have a wider range of aims. They are seeking to promote a specific text and perhaps also to maintain the allegiance of the audience to a particular series, channel or evening's viewing on that channel.

◆ There are trailers in and for specific genres but there are also different trailers for the same film or programme which target specific audiences.

◆ Some genres require action, fast-cutting and a display of special effects whereas others will put more stress on dialogue and others on creating questions that only seeing the film will answer.

◆ TV trailers will draw upon the attractions of the various genres for their audience. They will not be able to exploit the use of special effects in the same way that some film trailers can but they will be able to exploit personality; narrative developments in a series; the informative, challenging or experimental nature of the programme(s) or in a few cases the sheer weirdness of what is on offer.

◆ Distributors might produce a number of trailers, each of which targets a different group or they might pick out a number of areas within one trailer which target a number of groupings. For instance, the trailer for the film *Ghost* highlighted the romantic, the supernatural and thriller elements; thus, appealing to a wide spectrum of tastes. Film trailers try to convey an image of the narrative but many TV trailers are less concerned with this.

◆ Trailers are concerned with the compression of information although some stress content whereas others stress style. Action films tend to have fast cutting and a prominent soundtrack. There can sometimes be a more personal mode of address in TV trailers; they rarely use the resonant 'voice of god' declamatory tone.

◆ Many genres have become blurred; it may well be that some trailers are using elements of a number of genres or breaking generic stereotypes to surprise the audience.

◆ TV in particular has developed its own style of trailers which are in a different genre to the programme they are promoting. Some natural history programmes have been presented as if they were horror/sci fi and *EastEnders* has been promoted in the style of a thriller.

◆ TV channels tend to have different styles of trailer. In general, BBC and Channel 4 trailers tend to experiment more with the genre.

(EXAMPLE ARTEFACT)— *Highfield (a trailer for a new BBC costume* _____ *drama series)*

Highfield was the response to this exercise by a group of four students. This group chose to work within the conventions of the costume drama which entailed more stress on settings and costume than other likely responses to this exercise. By virtue of stressing the stereotypes, an element of parody was evident in the final product but this was a conscious decision on the students' part.

The trailer was filmed on VHS–C camcorders and edited in an editing suite. The soundtrack and voice-over were added after editing the images. The titles were word processed, filmed and edited in with the images.

One problem encountered during the post-production stage was the inaudibility of one section of dialogue which subsequently had to be over-dubbed. This is an all too frequent problem which is hard to solve without sophisticated equipment.

Discussion points for the evaluation

The evaluation of assignments should refer back to the research undertaken at the beginning.

◆ How does this production compare to the usual costume drama trailer in terms of style, form and content?

◆ Does the artefact succeed in fitting in with the ideology of the institution it comes from and the audience it is targeting?

◆ To what extent does the trailer effectively convey a narrative image?

◆ How easy is it to produce the artefact on the equipment available and how could it have been improved?

◆ What critical media debates/critical media theories have been examined in the production of this artefact?

(EXAMPLE EXERCISE 2)— **Video Production Example (Group)** _____

Production artefact

■ A one and a half to three minute excerpt from a new feature film

Introduction

Preparatory work for this exercise includes producing a treatment, storyboard and script for dialogue or voice-over. At this stage, it is also useful to consider how music can be used and what type of music might be appropriate.

1. slap

2. Slap: match on action

3. shocked reaction to the slap

4. happy house-maid

5. scandal

6. despair

Figure 21.15 Images from *Highfield*, a costume drama. Frames 1–6 are stills from the completed trailer. The first three illustrate an understanding of continuity editing.

This exercise works well when it springs from the study of a specific genre. It allows students to experiment with the conventions of a genre and test practically their understanding of how films are constructed to tell a story. This requires students to apply knowledge of *mise-en-scène*, camera work, sound and continuity editing in film.

Suggested research

◆ How are genres important for film makers, industry and audience?

◆ Does the genre exist in a range of media as well as film?

◆ What characters are typical of the genre?

◆ What settings, locations and historical periods are typical of the genre?

◆ What actors and actresses are associated with the genre and why?

◆ Are there any typical narratives and themes associated with this genre?

◆ How does this genre attract a specific audience?

◆ Does the genre have a particular visual style?

◆ Does the genre have a distinctive approach to the soundtrack?

◆ Has the genre changed over time and how open is the genre to experimentation?

◆ How important are individual film directors in this genre?

Possible discovery

◆ Film-makers, industry and audience benefit from the predictability of genres.

◆ Many genres started in literature and/or drama and some genres have been adopted by TV and radio as well as film. Some aspects of genres are more or less suited to the film medium.

◆ Typical elements are to be found in genres but novel elements and innovations keep genres alive.

◆ Most genres conform to the classical Hollywood narrative in terms of structure but different genres stress different themes.

◆ Some themes and narrative concerns within a genre will be more attractive to a specific audience despite the concern of the modern industry to attract the lucrative teen and twenty audience who are the most frequent cinema goers.

◆ Some genres place a particular emphasis on special effects whereas some use the potential of the big screen to full effect. Film noir, for instance, is renowned for its visual style.

◆ Genres can use soundtracks distinctively. In film noir there is the convention of the narrator whereas in action films sound effects contribute a great deal to the impact.

◆ All genres change over time as they incorporate new elements and respond to changes within society.

◆ Some genres are associated with individual film directors and particular actors; John Ford is synonymous with the western while Humphrey Bogart is synonymous with film noir, for example.

(EXAMPLE ARTEFACT)— *Spadework (the opening three minutes of a _____ film noir)*

Spadework was the response to this exercise by a group of four students. The group were given the opening of a short story called 'Spadework' featuring a private eye and they used this as a stimulus for their own film. In fact the group departed from the original story quite early in their preparation.

The excerpt was filmed on VHS–C camcorders and edited in an editing suite. The soundtrack and voice-over were added after editing the images.

Discussion points for the evaluation

The evaluation of assignments should refer back to the research undertaken at the beginning.

◆ How does this production compare to other films in the film noir genre in terms of style, form and narrative?

◆ Does the artefact succeed in fitting in with the ideology of the institution it comes from and the audience it is targeting?

◆ How easy is it to produce the artefact on the equipment available and how could it have been improved?

◆ What critical media debates/critical media theories have been examined in the production of this artefact?

1. The hero enters the bar . . .

2. he meets the femme fatale . . .

3. who watches him on his way . . .

4. to certain danger

Figure 21.16 Images from *Spadework*, a film noir. Frames 1–4 are stills from the completed excerpt.

PRODUCTION EXERCISES IN MIXED MEDIA

Equipment needed

As appropriate to the media (see pages 322, 323, 334, 335, 348, 349).

(EXAMPLE EXERCISE 1)—— **Mixed Media Production (Group)** ————

Production artefacts

A mixed media advertising campaign for a product which has been repositioned at a new target consumer and which should include the following:

- A display advert for a specified newspaper or magazine
- A 30" radio advertisement for a specified radio station
- A 30" TV advertisement for a specified station at a specified time

Introduction

This assignment complements a study of advertising and is often demanding enough to become the culmination of student practical production work. Obviously, mixed media exercises require students to have gained experience in a full range of media productions.

Repositioning campaigns tend to prove more successful than campaigns for products targeting the same old consumer segments because they require students to research the needs of, and the persuasive devices that target, the original consumer and the new consumer.

It consolidates debates about audience segmentation and consumer profiling and it allows students to experiment with the genre stereotypes concerned in both style and content.

Among others, products such as tea bags, pork pies, rain hats, wellington boots and Barry Manilow have successfully been repositioned at a 16 to 25 market; whereas personal stereos and Doc Martins have been targeted at a **silver-haired** market. Currently, in the event of the repackaging of Barry Manilow to target the teen and twenty 'dance' scene, life seems to be eerily imitating a student exercise.

Silver-haired

A marketing term which describes the over 60 market segment.

Suggested research

- ◆ What consumer is the chosen produce currently targeting and how is this group being persuaded to buy?

- ◆ What products are currently targeted at the group to whom the product is being repositioned and how do these products persuade this group to buy?

- ◆ Are there any stereotypical images that are commonly used when targeting particular groups and if so is it necessary to adhere to them or is there a case for challenging them?

- ◆ What are the strengths and weaknesses of the three media and how can these best be exploited?

- ◆ Is it best to have a campaign which has a unifying angle and if so how can the same angle be used in the three media?

Possible discovery

◆ It is necessary to see how the product is being sold to the original target group as there may be some merit in using part of the image already created; however, there might also be a case for completely rejecting that initial image.

◆ Many gender groups and ethnic groups are the subject of stereotypical advertising. Black people are rarely seen in anything but sport advertisements for instance. Old or fat people have also rarely been represented in advertising. However, it is also true that advertising needs stereotypes so that it can create meaning quickly. Nevertheless, advertising has power – people wouldn't bother to advertise if it didn't! It follows that it must be important that stereotypes are questioned or at least experimented with.

◆ TV and radio must create their meaning quickly as they are ephemeral media, whereas people can take their own time to look at a print advert. Video obviously allies sound and image, whereas radio only has sound to create meaning and print only has words and images. Radio adverts can be adventurous because they have low production costs – exotic locations can easily be suggested with sound effects. Conversely, a TV or magazine advertisement set in an exotic location can be very expensive to film/photograph.

◆ A campaign can be unified in a number of ways. One campaign can use the same personality to appear in a range of advertisements; Bob Hoskins in BT adverts for example. Other campaigns use a serial narrative such as the Gold Blend or OXO advertisements. The most important part of the campaign is the slogan or jingle which identifies the product; this will usually be seen in all the forms of advertising – 'Persil Washes Whiter' for instance.

(EXAMPLE ARTEFACT)— *Baddley's Pork Pie repositioning campaign* ———

This is a simple idea which proved to be an effective response to the brief. The student chose to reposition pork pies – which tend to have a particularly mainstream and middle-aged image – at 16 to 25s and came up with a campaign that had an exciting and youthful appeal. In this campaign, a range of young people are 'candidly' caught eating pork pies which combines the 'truthfulness' of the documentary style with the global village experience of the old Coca Cola advertisement.

Example of TV and magazine advertisement

Only the magazine advertisement is exemplified here because the student chose to use stills from the TV version and put them in a 'storyboard' format; the repetition between the two media is obviously a good persuasive and unifying device.

A wide variety of young people – all eating the pork pies – are represented on screen but, in the video, there is no dialogue just the background music of the band Supergrass performing 'We are young' with the product identified at the end. The magazine 'storyboard' swaps the Supergrass music for a vox pop with each frame supposedly having the comment of the person pictured.

Figure 21.17 The storyboard for Baddley's Pork Pics advertisement

The anchorage 'We'd like to teach the world to pork in perfect harmony!' refers back to the Coca Cola advertisement and therefore brings the power of that campaign with it while also having a risqué ambiguity which would appeal to the target group.

Example of radio advertisement

The radio continues the unity of the campaign by using a vox pop of a range of young people saying the words printed on the magazine 'storyboard' advertisement. The individuality of the voices would appeal to youngsters as 'individualists' but the message is quite open and at the same time the reading could be that you will only be one of the crowd if you eat Baddley's Pork Pies.

Figure 21.18 Baddley's Pork Pies' radio advertisement

Female:	Scrumptious	Fast music with a heavy
Female:	Tantalising	beat continuing through
Female:	Delicious	in the background
Female:	Gorgeous	until the end . . .
Female:	Exquisite	
Male:	Luscious	
Female	Phenomenal	
Male:	Crazy	
Female:	Fantastic	
Male:	Splendid	
Female:	All these people have been perfectly porked by Baddley's Pork Pies.	

Discussion points for the evaluation

The evaluation of assignments should refer back to the research undertaken at the beginning.

◆ How does this advertising campaign compare with other repositioning campaigns you have studied?

◆ Does the advertising campaign question ideological stereotypes accepted within the genre, the medium and the institution it is coming from?

◆ How does each extract conform to conventions of their individual genre?

◆ What persuasive devices were used within the campaign to target the new consumer?

◆ How easy is it to produce the artefact on the equipment available and how could it have been improved?

◆ What critical media debates/critical media theories have been examined in the production of this artefact?

(**EXAMPLE EXERCISE 2**) —— **Suggestions for alternative exercises** ____
in mixed media (Group)

◆ One news story targeting specific audiences presented in two different media.

This allows students to examine the treatment of the same material in different news institutions/channels in much the same way as the Radio Exercise 1 and Print Exercise 2.

- The production of a new magazine with a series of radio or TV advertisements to launch it.

  This allows students to promote a real product that they have formulated.

- A music video with accompanying video and CD cover.

  As stated above, this also allows students to promote a product they have actually formulated.

Glossary

Aberrant decoding   When the media text reader either mistakenly or willfully decodes the text in opposition to the preferred meaning.

Agenda setting   The way in which news organisations repeatedly select certain topics for dissemination.

Alternative   Media texts which challenge accepted ideas of form, style and content. They tend to be made outside mainstream institutions.

American dream   Refers to the belief that in America there is the opportunity for anyone, regardless of social background to be successful, financially or in public life.

Anchorage   Roland Barthes (1915–80) asserted that all images are open to interpretation and have many possible meanings. He called this phenomenon polysemy. If images are accompanied by a written text or sound, however, this makes the images less open to differing interpretations. He called this process anchorage.

Angle   Every story can be approached in a number of ways, for instance, a wedding report could be focussed on what the bride was wearing or where the couple were going on holiday.

Art cinema   Art cinema is geared to an international, educated audience. Films are exhibited generally in specialised cinemas. They are often financed by government subsidy and/or television involvement and sustained by film festivals, film critics and journals.

Audience reception theories   There are several notions concerning the way people receive the media. Passive notions of reception include: hypodermic, inoculation, two step flow theories. Active notions of reception include: uses and gratification theory and indirect active responses.

Broadsheet   A broadsheet is a full sized newspaper such as the *Guardian*. In Britain the term broadsheet also carries with it the idea that it is a quality newspaper.

Caption   Text describing the contents of a photo or cartoon in a newspaper or magazine.

Chiaroscuro   A combination of two Italian adjectives: *chiaro* meaning light and *scuro* meaning dark. It is used to describe high contrast lighting schemes in films.

Cinéma Vérité   Cinéma Vérité (cinema truth) was a documentary movement in France in the early 1960s. It aimed to go out and capture social realities by provoking a response from its interviewees.

Clip   A small piece of actuality. It could be a soundbite from a famous person or a vox pop, etc.

Conglomerates   Media organisations with vast global networks of interest.

Cropping   Selecting and clipping a photograph to leave only a specific part of the image.

Cue   Usually an introduction to a clip, wrap, etc. read by the bulletin reader.

Cultural competence   The French sociologist Pierre Bourdieu (1930–   ) initially described this concept suggesting that social class and gender carry with them different cultural competences and that these competences affect the ease of understanding and hence the enjoyment of different media and art forms.

Cut   The majority of shots are simply cut together directly. More unusual methods of joining shots include dissolves, fades and wipes which are sometimes used to indicate the end of a scene or to signal the start of a flashback sequence.

Dead donkey   This story usually ends a bulletin or is the filler at the bottom of a page. It is an insubstantial story, at best humorous at worst mawkish – often trading on the British love of animals – which is included purely to give the news a balanced composition. It is also the first item to be dropped should an important story break. Hence the saying 'drop the dead donkey'.

Diegetic   Diegetic sounds belong to the world of the film, television or radio programme and include, therefore, voices, sounds and any music that comes from a source within the setting, for example, from a radio or a juke box. It also includes a voice-over commentary from one of the protagonists.

Direct Cinema   Direct cinema was an approach to documentary filmmaking envisaged by Robert Drew, a *Time-Life* journalist, in the 1950s, that aimed to capture events as they happened without the intrusion of the film-makers.

Discourse   A discourse is the way that a media text will present an argument in such a way that other avenues of thought are closed down. For example, tabloid reports on so-called 'youth crime' require the audience to share their view that youth crime is a serious problem and this might be underpinned by emotive and judgmental words like 'yob' and 'hooligan'. Calling a 'joy-rider' a 'victim of society' opens up a discourse that many tabloids are unwilling to consider.

Drama documentary and documentary drama   Both draw on actual events and tend to use a visual style with an improvisatory feel. They will tend to use real locations and employ natural lighting and sound. Drama documentaries however tend to be reconstructions based on a single set of events whereas documentary dramas tend to put many different cases together to produce a single story.

Encoding/decoding   Any communication, and a mass media text is no exception, consists of a series of signs organised by certain rules or codes into a meaningful message. Codes can be visual or aural. In a newspaper, for instance, the type of language used and the way that the language is presented in a certain typeface within a certain layout on the page are all codes that form the message that is being conveyed.

Format   Refers to the way a programme or series is organised. For example, in one series each episode will be complete whereas in another there will be developments in the plot.

Gatekeeping   Is the way that key people within a news organisation select and reject stories or aspects of stories in the manufacture of their output.

Genre Refers to a category of media product that audiences can easily recognise because of the repetition over time of key elements, such as narrative, characters and setting. Examples of genre products include soaps, crime series, westerns and gangster films.

Hegemony The domination of ideas by powerful groups. These ideas have to be continually reasserted in the face of opposing ideas.

High key, low contrast lighting Refers to a style of lighting which allows a full range of tones to be seen in each shot. These scenes tend to be brightly lit, but a similar effect can be achieved with less overall light.

Hollywood studio system Refers to the way in which the five major and three minor Hollywood studios in the period approximately 1930–50 operated as factories, making films on an assembly line basis, as well as being involved in their distribution and exhibition.

Ident In broadcasting, this refers to a jingle of a few seconds in length which identifies a station or programme.

Ideology Ideology is the dominant set of beliefs and values in society that sustain power relations.

Information superhighway Refers to the communication of words, images, graphics and sounds using the technologies of fibre optics and digital compression. It also involves the concept of interactivity.

Infotainment These programmes mix the giving of information with light entertainment.

Intertextuality Refers to the way in which texts will sometimes draw upon other texts to create meaning.

Low-key lighting Refers to a system of lighting in which shadows are not eliminated by fill lighting, but used to add to the overall visual effect of the *mise-en-scène*.

Marx, Karl (1818–83) Marx established the idea that how a society produces its livelihood shapes everything else in society and is also the key factor in social change. He analysed capitalism as an economic system that produced two major social classes: the bourgeoisie who own the means of production and live off profits and the proletariat who sell their labour to survive. Eventually the working class would seek to overthrow capitalism as it became subject to greater economic crises and as they began to see through the ideas that served to justify the economic, social and political dominance of the bourgeoisie.

Media imperialism The possibility that the Western media strongly influence the culture of developing countries and inhibit the natural cultural growth within those countries.

Mise-en-scène This is a film studies term and literally means 'placed in the scene'. It includes all elements that are placed before the camera such as props, actors, costume, movement and the position of actors, etc.

Montage Montage (or editing) comes from the French word meaning to mount; it means the assembling of bits of film footage to form a whole.

Moral panic The mass media, in particular the tabloid press, play a key role in creating moral panics by responding to the concerns of public figures. The concern might be about the behaviour of certain individuals or groups or certain events which are perceived as threatening to social order. It is, however, the manner in which the situation is reported that blows its true significance out of all proportion.

MTV   MTV (Music Television) began as a 24-hour cable television channel on 1 August 1981, targeting an audience of 12 to 34-year-olds.

Narrative enigmas   Covert questions implicit within the narrative. For instance, part of the satisfaction that the audience gleans from soaps is how easily they can answer, or how accurately they can predict the answers to, these questions. An example of this might be the speculation whether Phil Mitchell will stay off the bottle in *EastEnders* or whether *Neighbours'* Darren Stark is really a hero or a villain.

Narrative   Another word for story.

Narrowcasting   Narrowcasting is the process of targeting programmes or channels at small interest-specific audiences.

News values   A set of criteria that determine the rejection, selection and prioritising of news.

Niche audience   TV stations such as BBC and Channel Four have historically targeted niche audiences with non-mainstream programming.

Non-diegetic   Refers to any elements that remain outside the world of the film, television or radio programme such as voice-overs, credits and mood-setting music that do not directly originate from the world of the product.

Objective and subjective   Most shots in mainstream cinema are objective. In a scene in which two characters are present, for example, the audience would be able to see both clearly. In a subjective shot of the same scene, however, the audience would see one of the characters from the point-of-view of the other.

Oligopoly   Refers to a market situation where a small number of firms have the power to control prices, etc. The position of an oligopolist is often protected because the price of entry to the industry is too high for newcomers.

Paparazzi   These are freelance photographers who are prepared to go to unscrupulous lengths to take candid shots of celebrities and royalty.

Polysemic   See Anchorage

Post-modern   The term post-modernism can be applied to all the arts. It refers to the way in which new artefacts can be constructed by making reference to existing ones. To be effective it relies on the audience possessing extensive knowledge of the original material the new artefact is based on. Quentin Tarantino's *Pulp Fiction* (1994), for example, is best appreciated by audiences who have seen a wide range of films.

Preferred reading/meaning   This term describes the way that a media message is specifically encoded so that the audience will make sense of it in a certain way.

Press Complaints Commission, The   The PCC is a body charged with policing the self-regulation of the press.

Primary definers   The primary definers are the initial source of information and interpretation of an event.

Propaganda   This is a term used pejoratively with reference to any film that consciously attempts to persuade an audience towards certain beliefs and values.

Property   In the film industry refers to anything that can be bought or optioned to form the basis or starting point for a film's narrative.

Protagonist   Refers to the central character of the film: the hero or heroine.

Public Service Broadcasting (PSB)   A non-commercial broadcasting institution that seeks to inform, educate and entertain.

Radio Authority, The   The Radio Authority has licensed and regulated commercial radio since January 1991 as it is one of three bodies which took over the work of the Independent Broadcasting Authority (IBA) after the changes brought about by the 1990 Broadcasting Act.

Screen time   The actual playing time of a film.

Segue   This is a link spoken by the reporter between actuality.

Semiology   The study of communication through signs and sign systems.

Silver haired   A marketing term which describes the over-60 market segment.

Social classification   Audience segmentation by social class is based on earning power. The six categories are A, B, C1, C2, D and E.

Social realism   There is a strong tradition of social realism in British TV drama and film. An influential movement was the British New Wave of the late 1950s and early 1960s which was in turn influenced by British theatre and novels. The tradition stresses a 'warts and all' revelation of working class life.

Soundbite   This is a short clip of opinion from a relevant 'expert' or politician. They are often only about 10 to 30 seconds in length and are enormously important because their pithiness or use of rhetoric gives them a great deal of impact and makes them useful to news broadcasters who are always short of time. Many politicians are now trained to speak in sentences which could become suitable soundbites.

Spin doctors   Spin doctoring was a term coined in the USA in the 1980s and it refers to someone whose job is to promote the positive image of a particular person, political party or business organisation within the media.

Steadicam   A damped suspension camera harness, worn by the operator. The device allows adjustments to be made to remove the jerkiness associated with hand-held filming. This can also give the impression that the camera is floating in mid-air. Its use was celebrated in *The Shining* (Stanley Kubrick, 1980).

Stereotype   Stereotyping involves prejudicial compartmentalising of people or issues within narrow definitions which do not allow for variation.

Storyboard   This is a visualisation of the treatment but it would indicate how the characters are going to be filmed and would also include some dialogue, sound FXs, etc.

Subgenres   Subgenres are subdivisions within a genre that become established through repetition. For instance, there are spaghetti westerns, Hammer horror films and science fiction space odysseys as well as crossgenres such as sci-fi spy thrillers or TV crime soaps.

Synergy   The idea of synergy in business terms is that by bringing together a number of linked activities under the same roof, each operation will make the others stronger and more profitable than any one could be alone.

Tabloid   A tabloid is a half sized newspaper which is particularly suited to a high degree of photographic representation. In Britain the term tabloid usually refers to down-market news publications but this should not necessarily be the case. *Le Monde* in France is a 'quality' tabloid.

Three point lighting   A term used to describe a system of lighting which uses three separate light sources for each shot involving central characters.

Treatment   A short outline of the film that would usually include the story, ideas about characters and location, etc.

Two-way   A discussion between the bulletin reader and a reporter on the spot.

Unrestricted narration   Narration in most films tends to be unrestricted rather than restricted. In other words the audience tend to know more than individual characters in a film.

Voice piece   An item from a reporter unpunctuated by actuality.

Vox pop   Literally translated from the Latin *vox populi* means 'voice of the people'. A vox pop is gained by asking one question on a news issue to members of the public who then offer an opinion. The anonymous answers are then edited into a fast moving sequence that can be included within a news bulletin or a news feature.

Women's movement   The women's movement is not a fixed set of ideas and institutions. It is composed of many different interpretations of feminism and different ways of achieving feminist goals.

Wrap   A news item that moves from the bulletin reader to the reporter to a clip of actuality and then back to the reporter.

Zoom lens   A shot employing a zoom lens is often confused with a tracking shot. Whereas a tracking shot involves physically moving the camera towards the subject, the camera in a zoom shot remains stationary. These two methods of getting closer to an object or character produce very different results on screen.

Bibliography

Aldgate, Anthony and Richards, Jeffrey, *Britain Can Take It: the British Cinema in the Second World War*, Basil Blackwell, 1986.

Ang, Ien, *Watching Dallas: Soap Opera and the Melodramatic Imagination*, Methuen, 1985.

Bakari, Imruh and Cham, Mbye, (eds), *Experiences of African Cinema*, BFI, 1996.

Balio, Tino, *The American Film Industry*, The University of Wisconsin Press, 1985.

Barker, Martin and Petley, Julian, (eds), *Ill Effects: The Media/Violence Debate*, Routledge, 1997.

Barr, Charles, *All Our Yesterdays: Ninety Years of British Cinema*, BFI, 1986.

Barthes, Roland, *Image, Music, Text*, Fontana Press, 1987.

Benjamin Ionie, *The Black Press in Britain*, Trentham Books, 1995.

Bennett, Tony and Bennett, Jane Woolacott, *Bond and Beyond: The Political Career of a Popular Hero*, MacMillan, 1987.

Bordwell, David and Thompson, Kristin, *Film Art: An Introduction (Fourth Edition)*, New York: McGraw Hill, Inc., 1993.

Bordwell, David, Staiger, Janet and Thompson, Kristin, *The Classical Hollywood Cinema: Film Style and Mode of Production to 1960*, Routledge, 1985.

Boughedir, Ferid, *African Cinema from A to Z*, OCIC, 1992.

Branston, Gill and Stafford, Roy, *The Media Student's Book*, Routledge, 1996.

Brierley, Sean, *The Advertising Handbook*, Routledge, 1995.

Briggs, Asa, *The Birth of Broadcasting, The History of Broadcasting the United Kingdom Volume I*, OUP, 1961.

Briggs, Asa, *The Golden Age of Wireless, The History of Broadcasting in the United Kingdom Volume II*, OUP, 1965.

Briggs, Asa, *The War of Words, The History of Broadcasting in the United Kingdom Volume III*, OUP, 1970.

Briggs, Asa, *Sound & Vision, The History of Broadcasting in the United Kingdom Volume IV*, OUP, 1979.

Buckingham, David, *Public Secrets: EastEnders and Its Audience*, BFI, 1987.

Burton, Graeme, *More Than Meets the Eye*, Edward Arnold, 1990.

Buscombe, Edward, (ed.), *The BFI Companion to the Western*, BFI, 1988.

Buscombe, Edward, *Stagecoach*, BFI, 1992.

Cameron, Ian and Pye, Douglas, *The Movie Book of the Western*, Studio Vista, 1996.

Cawelti, John, *The Six-Gun Mystique*, Bowling Green University Popular Press, 1971.

Chapman, Robert, *Selling the Sixties: the Pirates and Pop Music Radio*, Routledge, 1992.

Chell, David, (ed.), *Movie Makers at Work: Interviews by David Chell*, Redmond: Microsoft Press, 1987.

Cohen, Stanly and Young, Jock, (eds), *The Manufacture of News*, Constable, 1973.

Cook, Pam, *The Cinema Book*, BFI, 1985.

Cormack, Mike, *Ideology*, B. T. Batsford, 1992.

Corner, John, (ed.), *Popular Television in Britain: Studies in Cultural History*, BFI, 1991.

Corner, John, *The Art of Record: A Critical Introduction to Documentary*, Manchester University Press, 1996.

Crisell, Andrew, *Understanding Radio*, Methuen, 1986.

Crisell, Andrew, *Understanding Radio, Second Edition*, Routledge, 1994.

Crisell, Andrew, *An Introductory History of British Broadcasting*, Routledge, 1997.

Crowther, Bruce, *Film Noir: Reflections in a Dark Mirror*, Columbus Books, 1988.

Cumberbatch, Guy and Howitt, Dennis, *A Measure of Uncertainty: The Effects of the Mass Media*, John Libbey, 1989.

Curran, James and Seaton, Jean, *Power Without Responsibility* (4th edition), Routledge, 1991.

Curran, James and Seaton, Jean, *Power Without Responsibility: the Press and Broadcasting in Britain* (5th edition), Routledge, 1997.

Curran, James and Seaton, Jean, *Power Without Responsibility: the Press and Broadcasting in Britain* (2nd edition), Routledge, 1985.

Davies, Philip and Neve, Brian, (eds), *Cinema, Politics and Society in America*, Manchester University Press, 1981.

Diawara, Manthia, *African Cinema: Politics and Culture*, Indiana University Press, 1992.

Donnellan, Craig, (ed.), *Television and Censorship*, Independence, 1996.

Downmunt, Tony, (ed.), *Channels of Resistance: Global Television and Local Empowerment*, BFI, 1993.

Eco, Umberto, *The Role of the Reader: Explorations in the Semiotics of Texts*, Hutchinson, 1981.

Elley, Derek, (ed.), *Variety Movie Guide*, Hamlyn, 1994.

Ellis, John, *Visible Fictions*, Routledge, 1992.

Evans, Mark, *Soundtrack: The Music of the Movies*, Hopkinson and Blake, 1975.

Fenin, George and Everson, William, *The Western: from Silents to the Seventies*, Penguin Books Ltd, 1978.

Finler, Joel W., *The Hollywood Story*, Pyramid Books, 1989.

Fiske, John, *Television Culture*, Methuen, 1987.

Fowler, Roger, *Language in the News*, Routledge, 1991.

Frayling, Christopher, *Spaghetti Westerns: Cowboys and Europeans from Karl May to Sergio Leone*, Routledge & Kegan Paul, 1981.

French, Karl, (ed.), *Screen Violence*, Bloomsbury, 1996.

French, Philip, *Westerns*, Secker & Warburg/BFI, 1973.

Friedlander, Paul, *Rock and Roll: A Social History*, Westview Press, 1996.

Geddes, Keith, *Setmakers: A History of the Radio and Television Industry*, BREMA, 1991.

Geraghty, Christine, *Women and Soap Opera: A Study of Prime Time Soaps*, Polity, 1991.

Giannetti, Louis and Eyman, Scott, *Flashback: A Brief History of Film* (2nd edition), Prentice Hall, Inc., 1991.

Giannetti, Louis, *Understanding Movies* (6th edition), Englewood Cliffs: Prentice Hall, Inc., 1993.

Gledhill, Christine, *Stardom: Industry of Desire*, Routledge, 1991.

Goldman, William, *Adventures in the Screentrade*, Futura Publications, 1985.

Gomery, Douglas, *The Hollywood Studio System*, MacMillan/BFI, 1986.

Goodwin, Andrew and Whannel, Gary, (eds), *Understanding Television*, Routledge, 1990.

Gordon, Paul, and Rosenberg, David, *The Press and Black People in Britain*, The Runnymede Trust, 1989.

Grant, Barry, (ed.), *Film Genre Reader II*, University of Texas Press, 1995.

Grant, Barry, (ed.), *Film Genre Reader*, University of Texas Press, 1986.

Hall, Stuart *et al.*, *Culture, Media, Language*, Hutchinson, 1980.

Haralambos, Michael, (ed.), *Sociology: New Directions*, Causeway, 1985.

Hart, Norman, A., *The Practice of Advertising*, Heinemann, 1990.

Hartley, John, *Understanding News*, Routledge, 1982.

Hayward, Philip and Wollen, Tana, (eds), *Future Visions: New Technologies of the Screen*, BFI, 1993.

Hayward, Susan, *Key Concepts in Cinema Studies*, London: Routledge, 1996.

Hebdige, Dick, *Cut 'n' Mix*, Comedia, 1987.

Hewison, Robert, *In Anger: Culture in the Cold War 1945–1960*, Weidenfeld & Nicholson, 1981.

Hewison, Robert, *Too Much: Art and Society in the Sixties, 1960–1975*, Methuen, 1986.

Higson, Andrew, (ed.), *Dissolving Views: Key Writings on British Cinema*, Cassell, 1996.

Higson, Andrew, *Waving the Flag: Constructing a National Cinema in Britain*, Oxford University Press, 1995.

Hill, John, *Sex, Class and Realism: British Cinema 1956–1963*, BFI, 1986.

Hillier, Jim, *The New Hollywood*, Studio Vista, 1992.

Hirsch, Foster, *The Dark Side of the Screen: Film Noir*, Da Capo Press, 1986.

HMSO, *Broadcasting*, 1993.

Hodgson, F. W., *Modern Newspaper Practice*, Heinemann, 1989.

Izod, John, *Reading the Screen*, York Press, 1989.

Jefkins, Frank, *Advertising*, Made Simple Books, 1992.

Kawin Bruce, *How Movies Work*, Macmillan Publishing Company, 1987.

Kitses, Jim, *Horizons West*, Secker & Warburg/BFI, 1969.

Krutnik, Frank, *In a Lonely Street: Film Noir, Genre, Masculinity*, Routledge, 1991.

Kurosawa, Akira, *Something Like an Autobiography*, Vintage Books, 1983.

Leiss, William, Stephen Kline and Sut Jhally, *Social Communication in Advertising*, Routledge, 1990.

Lewis, Justin, *The Ideological Octopus*, Routledge, 1991.

Longhurst, Brian, *Popular Music and Society*, Polity Press, 1995.

MacCabe, Colin and Stewart, Olivia, (eds), *The BBC and Public Service Broadcasting*, Manchester University Press, 1986.

Macdonald, Kevin and Cousins, Mark, (eds), *Imagining Reality*, Faber & Faber, 1996.

Madge, Tim, *Beyond the BBC: Broadcasters in the Public in the 1980s*, Macmillan, 1989.

Malkmus, Lizbeth and Armes, Roy, *Arab and African Film Making*, Zed Books Ltd, 1991.

Marris, Paul and Thornham, Sue, (eds), *Media Studies: A Reader*, Edinburgh University Press, 1996.

Marwick, Arthur, *Class: Image and Reality in Britain, France and the USA since 1930*, Fontana/Collins, 1981.

Mast, Gerald, Cohen, Marshall and Braudy, Leo, *Film Theory and Criticism: Introductory Readings* (4th edition), Oxford University Press, 1992.

Masterman, Len, *Teaching the Media*, Comedia, 1985.

McQuail, Denis, (ed.), *Sociology of the Mass Media*, Penguin, 1972.

Mengisteab, Kidane, *Globalisation and Autocentricity in Africa's Development in the 21st Century*, Africa World Press Inc., 1996.

Miller, Mark Crispin, (ed.), *Seeing through Movies*, Pantheon Books, 1990.

Milne, Tom, (ed.), *The Time Out Film Guide*, Penguin, 1989.

Monaco, James, *How to Read a Film*, Oxford University Press, 1981.

Morley, David, *Family Television: Cultural Power and Domestic Leisure*, Comedia, 1986.

Morley, David, *Television, Audiences and Cultural Studies*, Routledge, 1992.

Morley, David, *The Nationwide Audience*, BFI, 1980.

Murphy, Robert, (ed.), *The British Cinema Book*, BFI, 1997.

Murphy, Robert, *Realism and Tinsel: Cinema and Society in Britain, 1939–1948*, Routledge, 1989.

Murphy, Robert, *Sixties British Cinema*, BFI, 1992.

Negus, Keith, *Producing Pop: Culture and Conflict in the Popular Music Industry*, Edward Arnold, 1992.

Nelmes, Jill, (ed.), *An Introduction to Film Studies*, Routledge, 1996.

Nichols, Bill, (ed.), *Movies and Methods Vol 1*, University of California Press, 1976.

Nichols, Bill, *Representing Reality*, Indiana University Press, 1991.

Nowell-Smith, Geoffrey, *The Oxford History of World Cinema*, Oxford University Press, 1996.

O'Malley, Tom, *Closedown? The BBC and Government Broadcasting Policy, 1979–1992*, Pluto Press, 1994.

O'Sullivan, Tim, Dutton, Brian and Rayner, Philip, *Studying the Media: an Introduction*, Edward Arnold, 1994.

Packard, Vance, *The Hidden Persuaders*, Penguin, 1957.

Palmer, Barton, R., *Hollywood's Dark Cinema: The American Film Noir*, Twayne Publishers, 1994.

Park, James, *British Cinema: The Lights that Failed*, B. T. Batsford Ltd, 1990.

Peak, Steve and Fisher, Paul, (eds), *The Media Guide 1997*, Fourth Estate, 1996.

Peak, Steve and Fisher, Paul, (eds), *The Media Guide 1998*, Fourth Estate, 1997.

Pennebaker, D. A., *Don't Look Back*, Ballantine Books, 1968.

Philo, Greg, *Seeing and Believing: The Influence of Television*, Routledge, 1990.

Price, Stuart, *Media Studies*, Pitman Publishing, 1993.

Price, Stuart, *The Complete A–Z Media and Communication Handbook*, Hodder & Stoughton, 1997.

Roddick, Nick, *A New Deal in Entertainment: Warner Bros in the 1930s*, BFI, 1983.

Scannell, Paddy and Cardiff, David, *A Social History of British Broadcasting Volume One 1922–1939*, Basil Blackwell, 1991.

Schatz, Thomas, *Hollywood Genres: Formulas, Filmmaking and the Studio System*, Random House, 1981.

Schatz, Thomas, *The Genius of the System*, Simon and Schuster, 1989.

Sendall, Bernard, *Independent Television in Britain: Volume I: Origin and Foundation 1946–62*, MacMillan, 1982.

Shadoian, Jack, *Dreams and Dead Ends*, MIT Press, 1977.

Shepherd, John, *Tin Pan Alley*, Routledge & Kegan Paul, 1982.

Shiri, Keith, (ed.), *Africa at the Pictures*, National Film Theatre, 1993.

Shuker, Roy, *Understanding Popular Music*, Routledge, 1994.

Silver, Alain and Ward, Elizabeth, (eds), *Film Noir an Encyclopaedic Reference Guide*, Bloomsbury, 1988.

Solomon, Stanley, J., *Beyond Formula: American Film Genres*, New York: Harcourt Brace Jovanovich Inc., 1976.

Street, Sarah, *British National Cinema*, Routledge, 1997.

Strinati, Dominic and Wagg, Stephen, (eds), *Come on Down? Popular Media Culture in Post-war Britain*, Routledge, 1992.

Sussex, Elizabeth, *Lindsay Anderson*, Studio Vista, 1969.

Taylor, John Russell, *Directors and Direction*, Eyre Methuen, 1975.

Thompson, John B., *Ideology and Modern Culture*, Polity, 1990.

Thumim, Janet, *Celluloid Sisters: Women and Popular Cinema*, St. Martin's Press, 1992.

Tristan Todorov, *The Poetics of Prose*, Blackwell, 1977.

Turner, Graeme, *Film as Social Practice* (2nd edition), Routledge, 1993.

Ukadike, Nwachukwu Frank, *Black African Cinema*, University of California Press, 1994.

Vahimagi, Tise, (compiler), *British Television: An Illustrated Guide*, Oxford University Press/BFI, 1994.

Walker, Alexander, *Hollywood, England: The British Industry in the Sixties*, Michael Joseph, 1974.

Wallis, Roger and Baran, Stanley, *The Known World of Broadcast News*, Routledge, 1990.

Warshow, Robert, 'The Gangster as Tragic Hero', in *The Immediate Experience*, New York, Atheneum Books, 1970.

Wasko, Janet, *Hollywood in the Information Age*, Polity Press, 1994.

Watson, James and Hill, Anne, *A Dictionary of Communication and Media Studies*, (Fourth edition), Edward Arnold, 1997.

Williams, Christopher, (ed.), *Realism and the Cinema*, Routledge & Kegan Paul/BFI, 1980.

Wilson, John, *Understanding Journalism*, Routledge, 1996.

Winston, Brian, *Technologies of Seeing: Photography, Cinematography and Television*, BFI, 1996.

Index